Never Drank
the Kool-Aid

Also by Touré

The Portable Promised Land
Soul City

{ *Essays* } # Never Drank the Kool-Aid

Touré

Picador

New York

www.picadorusa.com

Grateful acknowledgment is made to the following publications:

Rolling Stone: "The Family Man," "The Life of a Hunted Man," "DMX Drives Crazy, but He Loves You," "The Ivy League Counterfeiter," "Inherit the Wind," "The Mystery of Lauryn Hill," "A Woman Possessed," "The Next Queen of Soul," "Lauryn in Love," "D'Angelo Is Holding Your Hand," "Kurt Is My Copilot," "Jay-Z Has Got Guts," and "Do You Like My Jesus Piece?"; *The Village Voice*: "It Was a Wonderful World," "Best Rapper Alive," "Invincible Man," "Show Me the Money," "Love Your Niggas," and "Hiphop Familigia"; *The New Yorker*: "No Drinks in '96!," "Trainspotting," and "Night Moves"; *The New York Times*: "I'm Scared to Death, but I Gotta Live," "I Live in the Hiphop Nation," and "Are Gay Rappers Too Real for Hiphop?"; *Playboy*: "Hiphop's Biggest Kid Grows Up" and "Al Sharpton Has a Dream"; *Tennis* magazine: "The Greatest Tennis Player You've Never Heard Of" and "The Blackest Tennis Club in the World"; *Suede* magazine: "Ships Passing in the Night" and "Condoleezza Rice Is a House Negro"; *Icon Magazine*: "You Can Call Him Prince" and "Wynton Marsalis Wants to Kick Your Ass"; *XXL*: "The Toughest Record Exec Ever" (in slightly different form); *The Believer*: " 'Crack Is Responsible for Hiphop' "; *Vibe*: "The Five-Mic Personality, or Why I Hate Mary J. Blige"; *The Bastard on the Couch*: "An Invitation to Carnal Russian Roulette"; *The Best American Essays 1996*: "What's Inside You, Brother?"

Picador® is a U.S. registered trademark and is used by St. Martin's Press under license from Pan Books Limited.

For information on Picador Reading Group Guides,
as well as ordering, please contact Picador.
Phone: 646-307-5629
Fax: 212-253-9627
E-mail: readinggroupguides@picadorusa.com

Library of Congress Cataloging-in-Publication Data

Touré, 1971–
      Never drank the kool-aid : essays / Touré.—1st ed.
         p.   cm.
      ISBN 0-312-42578-3 (pbk.)
      EAN 978-0-312-42578-4 (pbk.)
         1. Popular culture—United States—Miscellanea.   2. Hip-hop—Miscellanea.   3. Celebrities—United States—Miscellanea.   4. United States—Intellectual life—Miscellanea.   5. United States—Social life and customs—1971—Miscellanea.   I. Title.

E169.12.T665   2006
306.0973'09045—dc22

                                                                            2005054631

10   9   8   7   6   5   4   3   2

Dedicated to my mom, who taught me how to write, and my dad, who taught me how to work hard, with a shout-out to the editors who put up with me through these pieces: Joe Levy, Fletcher Roberts, Anthony DeCurtis, Bob Christgau, Ann Powers, Bob Love, David Kuhn, Danyel Smith, Kevin Buckley, Joe Fielden, Vendela Vida, and Josh Kendall

Contents

Never Drank the Kool-Aid

Introduction

1. "Drinkin the Kool-Aid" is a great piece of modern slang that means buying into what someone else tells you. It springs from the story of the 1978 massacre at Jonestown, Guyana. The religious dictator and notorious cult leader Jim Jones initiated mass suicide, instructing his 900-plus followers to drink cyanide-laced punch. Many did; others were shot or injected. Jones shot himself in the head. After that the notion of drinking the punch or Kool-Aid became linked with being brainwashed or believing someone else's mind-set completely. A friend of mine began working for Puffy and one day called me, spouting Puff's philosophies. I said, "Sounds like you drank the Kool-Aid, nigga." We've called this collection *Never Drank the Kool-Aid* to suggest that I never bought into the philosophy of the rappers, singers, and celebrities I wrote about. I wasn't there to help extend their brands and the story they were selling. I was there to try to understand who they were beyond the image they want us to think they were.

2. You will probably notice that death bookends this collection. We begin with a *Village Voice* essay I wrote the day after Biggie's murder and end with an account of Jam Master Jay's funeral written for *The New Yorker* (unpublished till now). That's because death has been a major presence in the era I was writing about hiphop. In the early 80s, when I began my love affair with hiphop, no major figures had died. The deaths of Scott La Rock and Trouble T-Roy were terribly sad but didn't send shockwaves through the culture. The murders of Tupac, Biggie, and Jam Master Jay hit the Hiphop Nation like a neutron bomb, and the reverberations have been long and loud. Their names and images remain part of the hiphop zeitgeist to this day—you can't listen to hiphop radio or watch BET for long without hearing or seeing some reference to one of the three of them, and you certainly can't walk down 125th Street or any of the MLK Boulevards in this country without seeing some rendering of the dead triumvirate, often surrounded by Eazy-E, Aaliyah, Left Eye, and sometimes Big Pun. I always felt that hiphop would never be fully mature until we were rocked by tragic death just like jazz (Charlie Parker) and rock (Jimi Hendrix, John Lennon, Kurt Cobain) and R&B (Marvin Gaye). A human isn't fully mature until they've had to grapple with death, and neither is a culture. But even though the sadness remains, I sense no substantive change has come over hiphop as a result of those deaths, and I think it's just a matter of time before someone else joins the gang in Hiphop Heaven.

3. I've always felt that hiphop history does not begin in 1979 with "Rapper's Delight," but years earlier, when DJ Kool Herc began spinning parties in the Bronx. In August of 1970, at the urging of his sister Cindy, Herc started taking his sound system out to city parks and school yards. He staged mammoth noon-to-midnight block parties with his funk, soul, and reggae records and his Technics 1100A turntables, his supercharged Macintosh amp, and his gargantuan Shure speakers. There were a lot of DJs spinning block parties then, but only Herc would let a record build up to the climax (the break), and then, using two vinyl copies of the same record, mix the record with itself, restarting the climax over and over, prolonging the record's break until it was triple, quintuple, exponentially longer. While he did that, his man Coke La Rock would grab a mic and say little things, like he was chatting with his friends in the crowd. *Y'all feelin alright?!* Or, *B-boys, are you ready! B-girls, are you ready!* (B for break, for the kids who'd dance on the breaks.) Or, *To the beat, y'all!* Just little phrases, but that innovation eventually led to little rhymed phrases, which led to verses, which led to rappers.

Orthodox hiphoppers speak of a holy trinity of hiphop fathers: Herc, Afrika Bambaataa, and Grandmaster Flash. But, like moisture in the air before it rains, the conditions were ripe for hiphop before the holy trinity began spinning. Hiphop's prefathers or grandfathers are James Brown, Huey Newton, Muhammad Ali, Richard Pryor, Malcolm X, Bob Marley, Bruce Lee, certain celebrity drug dealers and pimps whose names won't be mentioned here, and Al Pacino's Scarface. From them, the boys of the hiphop generation derived a swagger, I mean a mental swagger, as well as massive self-confidence, a towering masculinity, a predilection for verbal rhythmic gymnastics, an imperative to play media games, a willingness, nay, an eagerness to take on all of America by yourself, and an unrepentantly pro-Black attitude. Ronald Reagan and crack were hiphop's 80s anti-fathers: both helped foster the intense poverty and the teenage drug-dealing millionaires as well as the urge to rebel against the system that appeared to be moving in for the kill, to finally crush Black America.

But a more potent anti-father has been my generation's widespread void of fathers in the home. We can never forget that the rampant fatherlessness of modern Black families has had an indelible impact on hiphop, causing much of the culture to grow up without positive male role models, forcing many of us to construct manhood on our own.

We built hiphop in the 70s with no thought of it ever growing larger than the parties in the park, so we took artistic chances. We built it faster in the 80s, when there was a pervasive sense that hiphop culture could possibly die if we didn't do everything we could to keep it pure. We felt the larger culture saw hiphop as a meaningless fad or a morally bankrupt subculture. Either way we felt under siege and we had to protect it by remaining artistically pure, also known as keeping it real.

That sense of being social outlaws electrified hiphop culture in the 80s. Those were the days when my relationship with hiphop grew firm. When I was eleven, twelve, thirteen years old I would walk out of my dad's office in Mattapan Square, go four stores down the street and into Skippy White's, a tiny music store owned by a kind white man with a long beard who was always there behind the counter. He knew my father and he greeted me by name and allowed me a very liberal return policy—he took back anything I didn't like—which meant I could buy tapes without fear of wasting money. I began buying hiphop tapes and soon had every hiphop tape he had in stock. In those days if you bought two or three hiphop tapes a month you had all the product there was. By the 90s, it was no longer a developing culture, and hiphop was far less rebellious politically and aesthetically. It's kind of like playing poker or backgammon or any gambling game: most people take chances and play courageously when there's not much on the line, but when the pots get high most people get scared. In the 80s, when there was relatively little money at stake, MCs rhymed dangerously, sampled ambitiously, and tried to innovate. But now that there's millions at stake, people are less willing to take artistic chances. The corporatization of hiphop made it clear to everyone that this culture wasn't going to die and that security sucked the danger right out of the music—both the aesthetic danger and the political danger. Back in the 70s, when it was parties in the park, in order to get on the mic you had to have community respect and be down with a tough crew. Now all you need to get in the studio is corporate sponsorship. That's why hiphop's soul is dying.

4. In the summer of 1992, when I was an intern at Rolling Stone, I thought most of the writing I saw about hiphop was facile and viewed rappers with a bit of condescension (except for The Village Voice, which back then covered hiphop better than anyone). I told myself that I would write about hiphop with the goal of expanding the complexity of the conversation about the culture. I wanted people who read my work to be able to talk with their friends about the artist or group on a deeper level. I set that goal for myself as an intern. (Incidentally, I was the worst intern RS ever had. I would delegate my little tasks to others—"She said you should Xerox this stuff"—and use the free time to talk to writers and editors about how to become a writer. Eventually I was fired, but the record review editor, Anthony DeCurtis, gave me an assignment and, well, I never left.)

5. I interview people as if I'm talking to a friend, being relaxed and folksy and familiar. I like to let the conversation take the shape that my subject wants it to take. I guide it here and there, but I'm al-

ways trying to make it a casual journey, and I'm always trying to sense what they want to talk about. I always listen closely and respond to what they say rather than just running down a list of questions and having a structured back and forth. Good interviewing isn't really about the questions you ask, it's about follow-up questions, it's about listening to ask the right follow-ups. Through active listening I often got people to tell me things I wouldn't have known to ask them. And I always assumed the people I interviewed were intelligent no matter what they presented onstage.

6. Among the best interviewees I've ever sat with are Jay-Z, Reverend Sharpton, Eminem, and Andre Harrell—articulate talkers who never shied from a question. Ghostface Killah gets an honorable mention because we only spoke once (for my MTV2 show *Spoke N' Heard*), but he was amazingly open, talking in-depth about struggling with undiagnosed diabetes and hearing voices while he and Raekwon were recording the classic album *Only Built 4 Cuban Linx*. When I started writing this paragraph, I was planning to give the title of Best Interviewee ever to ?uestlove from the Roots, who has been the most intellectual member of the Hiphop Nation for many years. But at the last moment I realized I had to give the Best Interviewee crown to Tupac. Every interview with him was an epic event. He was brilliant, he was theatrical, he was funny, he was out of his mind, was fearless about spouting his truth. He knew how to make words into Molotov cocktails.

7. I'd been trying to write a letter to Pac when he died. Actually, I'd been trying for years. It's not a short story. It begins in 1994 when I was covering his Manhattan sexual-assault trial for *The Village Voice*. One night during the trial's last week he was shot five times. The following day one of his tall, strapping defense lawyers whispered in the ear of certain reporters, suggesting the police might have set it up.

To me, suspecting the police made some sense, but only some. And when I wrote about the trial for the *Voice*, I said that suspecting the police made as little, and as much, sense as suspecting that Pac set himself up to be shot. I knew someone would be insane to have someone fire even small bullets at them, but in theory, and it was just a theory, it seemed plausible: Pac rolled away from the shooting physically unscathed, his reputation for bravery and boldness and badassness maximized. This gave us indisputable proof that he was indeed a modern phoenix, able to survive a rain of bullets. In just a moment, folks, Pac will leap a few tall buildings in a single bound. In the *Voice* I wrote that it's not probable he shot himself, but it's certainly conceivable that he orchestrated the event in order to magnify his myth.

Then, in his first jailhouse interview, published in *Vibe*, Pac said he'd read my piece and thought I'd said that he did have himself shot. He said when he read that, he cried.

I started then to write Pac a letter. Journalism is about truthtelling, but when you bring those instincts to the world of Black entertainment you step into a community that's not interested in or prepared for honesty. They don't want to hear the truth about their emperors' wardrobe. Honesty has earned Black music journalists verbal and physical lashings. If Pac had said he was going to kick my ass when he got out of jail, I might've laughed. Instead, he shocked me. He'd read the article and responded honestly and done something a real man is never supposed to do. And more, it was all over a mistake. I could explain what I'd meant and maybe make him understand and somehow wipe his tears, but I couldn't even put pen to paper because I no longer knew to whom I would write. In this generation music is attitude and gossip and anecdote and arrest and trial and headline and killing and death. An album is merely a stage for a personality. A good scandal is as important as a good record. Music is secondary in music. So much else is sold along with the lyrics and beats. A purchase in Sam Goody is as much a musical choice as a moral vote. The lives of our modern musical heroes are so public that their lives nudge their product out of the spotlight, as if they're asking you to buy a share of their bodies before the stock soars in death because, as Jimi Hendrix said, "Once you're dead, you're made for life."

Pac had turned his trial into a spectacle, a performance, an Event, and I had viewed it as part of his oeuvre. To me, his trials and ostensibly offstage—but actually perpetually onstage—life made up the most compelling, most brilliant part of Pac's oeuvre. And I had written about an icon—an abstract figure who symbolizes X, represents Y, and is the embodiment of Z. Someone who appears on stages and performs. But he cried. He responded as a human being with flesh and blood and soft spots and insecurities.

Throughout his Manhattan sexual-assault trial, Pac kept defending himself by saying, "I don't rape people—I'm a businessman. Don't get it twisted." I took him at his word and deconstructed his body and his life like they themselves were part of an art show. But art doesn't cry if it gets a bad review. I wish I could go back and write to him.

8. We arranged the book thematically (rather than chronologically). A few of the sections called for a little unpacking:

a. We begin with a section called "I'm Audi," borrowing the great but now dated West Coast slang for "I'm leaving." In 1996, when Biggie died, I was given two days to write a tribute to him for *The Village Voice.* I tried to capture the despair I felt over his death by saying I was leaving hiphop for good. People took it seriously but it was just an exaggeration meant to communicate my despair after watching both Tupac and Big be murdered within six months. But even as I wrote it I knew it was a posture meant to portray an emotion. I could never leave hiphop. It's more likely that hiphop will leave me.

b. "Sensitive Thugs" compiles stories about tough guys who showed me some emotion. I refused to let my stories simply further the image they were constructing. Whenever I profiled a tough guy I had to get his softer side into the portrait, to see them as people with complex emotions. So I asked 50 Cent whether he feels guilty about selling crack to his own people and I asked Eminem to talk about his family, the three kids who live with him and look to him as a father. And because Eminem talks so much about his hatred of his mother, I had to ask him, When you were a child who loved you? There had to be someone. He said there was an aunt and uncle, and their story broadened my understanding of him.

c. Icarus is, of course, the boy from Greek mythology who flew too close to the sun, melted his wings, and crashed back to earth. This section compiles stories about people who rose high and then fell dramatically.

d. "Almost Famous" consists of pieces that most closely mimic the movie *Almost Famous*, which was pitch perfect in portraying how it feels to follow a star on the road, chasing after them with a pen and pad, recording their fabulous and pathetic moments. The movie nailed the emotional connection that develops between subject and writer. Most of the time, they do want you to like them, and you do want them to like you because it makes the job easier, so brief mini-friendships sometimes sprout up. You can't travel with someone for days and interview them deeply and not forge some sort of relationship. It doesn't last but that doesn't mean there's not a connection. It's usually like a vacation friend, intense for that short period and then cooler once you get back home. These are the pieces where, when I got home I said to myself, "That was so *Almost Famous*."

e. "Get Involved" should show one way I developed in my philosophy of how to cover a story in the field. The first six or seven years of my career, I felt very strongly that the journalist should never be part of the story and when I was following a rapper or a band I would be a fly on the wall. But at some point I began to see that being more active could be good for the story. So, when the moment was right I'd say or do something to try to create a moment. These are the stories where I allowed myself to become part of the story and it made all the difference.

9. Some notes from behind the scenes:

a. The DMX story is the source of a small amount of regret. I think the piece is successful but it could've gone a little further. Before our interview DMX called his wifey and stayed on the phone with her for over an hour, laughing then arguing then laughing again. A real lovers conversation. They were unmarried but had been together for fifteen years and had two kids. But she was in the Bronx and he was, at that moment, in L.A. The next day at the mall he picked up some girl (granted, she threw herself at him) and the next morning she was in his hotel room in a robe. I left all that out of the story even though he didn't ask me to because I thought it could ruin his family. Months later, I heard that he picked up another girl in front of a reporter from *Spin* and I realized that if he's that indiscriminating about whom he commits adultery in front of, then why should I enable him by turning a blind eye?

b. It took months and months for *Vogue* to set up two days for me to interview and hang with Jennifer Capriati. Tennis players travel constantly, way more than rock stars, and she was hard to pin down, but we finally found two days in November when she'd be in Florida. I knew that if I missed that time I wouldn't have been able to get more.

I flew down to Florida, jumped into a rental car, and sped off to her place. I was going about seventy when one of the wheels slipped into a crooked sliver of concrete on the highway and the car spun out of control. It sliced to the right, the wheel no longer guiding the car, and the passenger's door banged into a concrete barrier, bounced off, and as I steered to no avail, banged into the other barrier. I don't remember how I got the car to stop but when I did people poured from their cars, surprised to see me standing. I walked away with nothing more than a fast-beating heart. After a short while a state trooper came to file a report. He asked what I was doing in town and I told him who I was going to interview. Her place was just two exits down the highway. I wasn't thinking of asking him to drive me but then he said, "I can't drive you there because it's out of ma jurisdiction, but if it was that Anna Kournikova . . ." Twenty minutes later I'd talked him into driving me over to Jen's. When I got there, she was doing sprints as her trainer watched. I wanted to get on her good side, and plus I had a tremendous amount of adrenaline to burn, so I ran the sprints with her. She was surprised that I was just as fast as her.

C. The story about Prince began quite poorly. I was one of about eight journalists selected to go to Paisley Park and have a thirty-minute interview with Prince, who was then going by just the symbol, meaning his name was unpronounceable. Each writer went in to speak with him and came out glowing as if they'd had an audience with Jesus. I was the last to go in and I sat at the head of a long table. We began talking but most of what he said was gibberish or nonsensical or about some other artist he was then promoting. I was very disappointed and knew I didn't have enough to write a story. I asked if I could supplement my interview with ten e-mail questions. His publicist okayed that and I sent ten questions. The last was, Will you play basketball with me?

I noticed that he ignored certain questions but answered that one, saying anytime. So I took him seriously. When the photographer went to Paisley to do the photo shoot I went with him and brought a basketball to minimize excuses. During the shoot I reminded him he said he'd play ball with me. He told an assistant to pull out a box of sneakers. He pulled out some Nike high-tops and we played one-on-one right inside Paisley Park all while he still wore his Black scoop-neck top and Black bell-bottom pants. He looked at home on the court, dribbling and moving and shooting like a player. For the rest of the story jump to page 248.

10. Writing about music for Rolling Stone and other mags has been a dream job and I hope my joy has shown through in the work. I always felt I was a cultural senator, asking the culture's leaders the questions that the community wanted asked. I've gotten to sit and talk with the greats—Biggie, Tupac, Jay-Z, Eminem, Nas,

KRS-One. And, greater than that for the boy who always loved seeing what he could get away with, I've had significant beef with Chuck D, the voluble Puff Daddy, and the notorious Suge Knight and lived to tell the tales.

A Methodology for Ranking MCs

A list of what should and should not be considered when ranking the greatest MCs of all time:

1. The MC Resume. How many albums has the MC released that the general hiphop community considers classics? How many times has the MC had the song of the moment, one that dominated culture from the clubs to the radio to your personal playlist? How many times has the MC dropped the unforgettable couplet that people repeated over and over, a couplet that shot into your mind like a dum-dum bullet, exploding within you as deeper levels of comprehension dawned upon you. How many years has he been a relevant MC? Has his music aged well? (Songs released on mix tapes are equally as valid as songs on commercially released albums. Every time you step to the mic counts.)

2. The MC Decathlon. An MC is primarily judged on what he does in four arenas: songs, stage performances, freestyles—a word that now encompasses both the old-school meaning (improvisational rhymes) and the new-school meaning (written rhymes that the audience hasn't heard before)—and battles. Battle rhymes are of a special breed, and though it's not possible to go an entire career without having beef, it's unlikely and not recommended. MCs get big points for winning big battles. If there were an MC decathlon, they'd have to make a song, pick a beat, then write a hook and verses and deliver them dopely; rock a crowd; kick a hot rhyme off the top of the dome; and battle somebody. A great MC must master all of these arenas.

3. The MC Microscope. When we get out the MC microscope, we look at voice (both literal and figurative), flow, lyrics, and the ability to pick beats. Does his voice alone transmit confidence to the listener? Is his voice original, compelling, powerful, seductive, tasty, or hypnotic? Has he innovated new facets of MCing? Can you dance to the bass line made by his flow? In his lyrics, does he coin original words or phrases; does he pick words we don't normally hear in hiphop; does he make words rhyme that don't really rhyme; does he have an interesting vocabulary; does he spit inventive metaphors, killer punch lines, clever slang, poetic wordplay, and double and triple entendres? Does he have original or interesting thoughts and stories to tell? Is he an interesting person, which does not mean has he been shot or shot someone? It means when he's on the mic, is he an interesting person to listen to? Does he have MC integrity, meaning, do you feel that he's telling the truth about himself and his world; is he representing himself honestly, or is he just playing a role, i.e., perpetrating? Does he have a point of view? Does the sum total of his oeuvre paint a world?

4. The Trash. What doesn't count? Sales are not a relevant variable. Sales do not matter. Also, being able to sing means nothing. MCs are only judged on rhyming. MCs also don't get points for shooting someone, getting shot, doing a movie, doing time, doing commercials, dealing drugs, having been a Blood or a Crip, owning their label, or anything else off-mic, including doing a great video. The artifice of the video world has nothing to do with being a great MC; however, doing a great concert and being able to rock a stage will matter as long as MC still stands for Master of Ceremonies or Move the Crowd. (Postmodern kids will argue that a video is another sort of stage, and it is, but it's really a commercial, and we don't count commercials.)

Ergo, my top five (all of whom have at least two classic albums, multiple songs of the moment, and tons of unforgettable couplets): #1 Rakim, #2 Jay-Z, #3 Biggie, #4 KRS-One, #5 Nas.

1. I'm Audi

It Was a Wonderful World

{ Biggie Smalls, *The Village Voice*, 1997 }

Dear Sakeem,

Because I love you, my sweet cousin, I did not give my hiphop CDs to you. Because I love myself I threw them out—*Paid in Full, Death Certificate, Strictly Business, Criminal Minded, Ready to Die*—they're all out there, classics and roaches, lying at the bottom of the old dented trash can on the corner. I've turned in my ghetto pass and burned up my hoodie, too. Stay and live in this Hiphop Nation if you want, but I won't. I can see now that murders and killings come with the beats and rhymes. And because those murders and killings are coming from the same hands that make the beats and rhymes, how is living in hiphop any different than living in the dysfunctional Black family writ large? Cousin, count me out. I'm gone.

If you're going to stay and love hiphop, know this: for a young Black man in America, loving yourself no longer necessitates loving hiphop. And, loving hiphop does not automatically mean loving yourself. The self-destruction has ended all that. It wasn't always this way. A few years ago, before Tupac was killed, before the East/West feud turned homicidal, before Eazy-E passed—back before I wrote this line: "I guess by now we should be used to Black heroes dying in public," the culture was still so young that people sometimes said, "You know, with the exception of Scott La Rock, no major hiphop icon has died. They're all still here." It was as though they were saying, You know, all my grandparents are still around. Back then the explosive joy of young Black men—us—riding rhythm for rhythm's sake and speaking our minds and making cash money was embedded in the beats, and it was all beautiful.

One summer toward the end of those days Big was the undisputed king of hiphop. You couldn't walk around Brooklyn without hearing his rhymes seeping from Jeeps, Walkmans, and thick brown lips. Oh my God them rhymes! No rapper was more like High John the Conquerer, the Black mythological hero who Zora Neale Hurston said "could beat the unbeatable. He was top-superior to the whole mess of sorrow. He could beat it all, and what made it so cool, finish it off with a laugh." That was that nigga Big and that's why you couldn't drag us off the floor when his records came on.

One night during that summer I go to Nell's. The place is packed. Everyone looks like they're getting dollars and gulping deep from the cup of life. Then the DJ spins into "Who Shot Ya" and you couldn't have told us we weren't in Utopia. As Big rhymes, "I can hear sweat trick-uh-lin down ya cheek/ Ya heartbeat sound like Sasquatch feet/ Thunderin'/ Shay-kin the concrete," a brother in the middle of the room starts doing pull-ups on a water pipe hanging from the ceiling. Then another does some pull-ups. Then a third, and as he strains through his fourth pull-up, the pipe breaks. Water rains down! The pull-up men rejoice, dancing in the downpour like kids in the stream of a fire hydrant. The rest of the crowd dances tenuously, unsure of their next move, until, a moment later, the DJ fades into "One More Chance." Then, though it's raining on the dance floor, everyone is moving with abandon, shaking and bouncing amidst the water and chaos, getting water all on their Tommy Hil and in their Moet and not giving a fuck. Over Big rhyming, "Lyrically, I'm supposed to represent/ I'm not only a client/ I'm the playa president," someone yells, "Rain, motherfucker! Rain!"

Toward the end of that year I interviewed Big. Even then things were changing. Tupac was in jail for sexual assault and Snoop was about to go on trial for murder. And Big, the man who'd been responsible for a summer's worth of joy, sat in the hallway of his building, gripping a gat, surrounded by six members of his crew, arrayed like Timberland-wearing Secret Service agents. Every time the building's front door opened up, someone looked down the three flights, to see who it was. Every time someone started coming up the stairs, Big stopped talking and called out, "Who's that?"

"Nigga could be coming to blow my head off," he said that afternoon in late 1994. "I'm not paranoid to the point where—" He paused. "Yes I am. I'm scared to death. I'm scared to death. Not all the time, but most of the time. Scared of getting my brains blown off. But if it happens it happens. That's why I never want to do nothing different. Like you would think a nigga that was scared to death would, as soon as he leave the Apollo, run in the limo and jet home, cuz he's scared to death, but," he said and started to smile, "I got to hang out with my niggas, I got to see what's going down, where the party's at. Nigga that's scared to death ain't supposed to be making no moves like that. But fuck it, I'm just ready. Can't live my life in no bubble."

Well, cousin, for me, all that's over. What do we gain staying in a family that's slowly dying by its own hand? From now on, when you come by you'll find me sitting up with my Louis Armstrong. And the next time you catch me walkin down DeKalb and you see my lips quietly flipping a rhyme, just know I ain't rhyming "Criminal Minded" or "Sucker MC's." When you get close you'll hear me singing, "I hear babies crying. I watch them grow. They'll learn much more, than I'll ever know. And I think to myself, what a wonderful world."

Your cousin,
Touré

P.S.: Send me a card when the first rapper dies of old age.

2. Sensitive Thugs

The Family Man

{ Eminem, *Rolling Stone*, 2004 }

Eminem has become a family man. During two long conversations over two days in Detroit in October, he constantly mentions the kids he's raising, as any proud father would: His daughter, Hailie Jade, will soon be nine, his niece Alaina is eight, and his half brother, Nate, is eighteen. In October, Marshall Mathers turned thirty-two. He grew up in Kansas City, Missouri, and Detroit without a father figure, but he has grown into a committed parent who goes to school plays and everything. He schedules most of his recording in Detroit and has put his movie career on hold so he can be home with the kids at night.

He has slowed down his drinking and his drug use since two 2000 gun charges that he feared would take him away from Hailie, but his ex, Kim Mathers, has slogged through her own legal morass. In June 2003 she was arrested for possession of cocaine, then failed to show up in court and for a short while hid from the police. Eminem says that explaining the situation to Hailie and Alaina "was one of the hardest things I ever had to go through." At the time of our first interview, Kim was in jail. At the time of our last interview, she had been released. "She's out right now," he said. "We're hoping that stays kosher."

Encore is Eminem's fifth solo album, and he remains one of the most skilled, compelling, audacious, obnoxious, and important MCs in hiphop. He thanks his mother for the troubled childhood that still fuels his anger in "Never Enough"; he tells Kim that he hates her in "Puke" and that he still loves her in "Crazy in Love"; and he declares his devotion to Hailie on "Mockingbird," which he calls his most emotional song ever. He also attacks President Bush for the Iraq War in "Mosh" and says, "Strap him with an AK. . . . Let him impress Daddy that way."

On *Encore*, Eminem refers to himself as "Rain Man" because, he says, he doesn't know how to do anything besides hiphop. He doesn't consider himself "a good talker" because his conversation is rarely as direct as his rhymes, but for two days when he sat for the *Rolling Stone* interview he was open and introspective. We started out in a dank little room at a photo studio and continued in the recording studio where he does most of his work. The first day he lounged on a small black couch, wearing Nike gear and Jordans and picking at white-chocolate-covered nuts. Ever the fifteen-year-old, he said, "What's up?" and then asked, "Would you like to eat my white nuts?" He laughed. "C'mon, put my white nuts in your mouth."

Who in your family loved you? Did any of the adults make you feel special?

My Aunt Edna, which would be my great-aunt Edna, and my Uncle Charles, my great-uncle Charles. This was in Missouri. They're from my dad's side. They took care of me a lot. My Uncle Charles passed in '92 or '93, and Aunt Edna passed away just six months ago. She was, like, eighty-six. They were older, but they did things with me; they let me stay the weekends there, took me to school, bought me things, let me stay and watch TV, let me cut the grass to get five dollars, took me to the mall. Between them and my Uncle Ronnie, they were my solidity.

Did they connect you with your dad?

They'd tell me he was a good guy: "We don't know what your mother's told you, but he was a good guy." But a lot of times he'd call, and I'd be there—maybe I'd be on the floor coloring or watching TV—and it wouldn't have been nothing for him to say, "Put him on the phone." He coulda talked to me, let me know something. 'Cause as far as father figures, I didn't have any in my life. My mother had a lot of boyfriends. Some of 'em I didn't like; some of 'em were cool. But a lot would come and go. My little brother's dad was probably the closest thing I had to a father figure. He was around off and on for about five years. He was the dude who'd play catch, take us bowling, just do stuff that dads would do.

When I saw you playing with Hailie back in February, you were so respectful. A lot of people talk down to little kids, but you talk to her like she's intelligent.

Thank you for seeing that. I just want her and my immediate family—my daughter, my niece, and my little brother—to have things I didn't have: love and material things. But I can't just buy them things. I have to be there. That's a cop-out if I just popped up once in a while, didn't have custody of my daughter and my niece.

Do you have full custody?

I have full custody of my niece and joint custody of Hailie. It's no secret what's been going on over the past year with my ex-wife. I wouldn't down-talk her, but with her bein on the run from the cops I really had no choice but to just step up to the plate. I was always there for Hailie, and my niece has been a part of my life ever since she was born. Me and Kim pretty much had her, she'd live with us wherever we was at.

And your little brother lives with you.

I've seen my little brother bounce around a lot from foster home to foster home. My little brother was taken away by the state when he was eight, nine.

You were how old?

I was twenty-three. But when he was taken away I always said if I ever get in a position to take him, I would take him. I tried to apply for full custody when I was twenty, but I didn't have the means. I couldn't support him. I watched him when he was in the foster home. He was so confused. I mean, I cried just goin to see him at the foster home. The day he was taken away I was the only one allowed to see him. They had come and got him out of school. He didn't know what the fuck was goin on. The same thing that had happened in my life was happening in his. I had a job and a car, and me and Kim, we bounced around from house to house, tryin to pay rent and make ends meet. And then Kim's niece was born, which is my niece now through marriage. Watched her bounce around from house to house—just watchin the cycle of dysfunction, it was like, "Man, if I get in position, I'm gonna stop all this shit." And I got in position and did.

So you have joint custody of Hailie, but she lives with you and spends most of her time with you and not with Kim.

I don't know if I'm inclined, or allowed, to say more than what is fact. In the last year, Kim has been in and out of jail and on house arrest, cut her tether off, had been on the run from the cops for quite a while. Tryin to explain that to my niece and my daughter was one of the hardest things I ever had to go through. You can never let a child feel like it's her fault for what's goin on. You just gotta let her know: "Mom has a problem, she's sick, and it's not because she doesn't love you. She loves you, but she's sick right now, and until she gets better, you've got Daddy. And I'm here."

What are your goals and principles as a dad? I'm sure there are boundaries.

Bein a dad is definitely living a double life. As far back as I can remember, even before Hailie was born, I was a firm believer in freedom of speech. I never wanted to compromise that, my artistic integrity, but once I hit them gates where I live, that's when I'm Dad. Takin the kids to school, pickin 'em up, teachin 'em rules. I'm not sayin I'm the perfect father, but the most important thing is to be there for my kids and raise them the right way.

What are your biggest rules as a parent?

Teach them right from wrong as best I can, try not to lose my temper, try to set guidelines and rules and boundaries. Never lay a hand on them. Let them know it's not right for a man to ever lay his hands on a female. Despite what people may think of me and what I say in my songs—you know, me and Kim have had our moments—I'm tryin to teach them and make them learn from my mistakes. It's almost like juggling—juggling the rap life and fatherhood.

Well, in the nexus of that juggling is Hailie, who's in some of your songs, like "My Dad's Gone Crazy," from "The Eminem Show." Does she get to hear the songs she's in?

Most of the time I'll make clean versions of the songs and play them in the car. When she made "My Dad's Gone Crazy," it's a crazy little story. If I feel like I'm working too much, I let the kids come up to the studio. I get this little guilt trip inside, so I would have Kim just bring her up and let her hang around the studio. So me and Dre were working together, and Hailie was running around the studio and she was like [*in Hailie's high voice*], "Somebody please help me! I think my dad's gone crazy!"

Instantly that locked in with a beat we'd made the day before. I went to my house, and I had her go in the booth and say it. When she opens up, she's just like her dad in a lot of aspects. I just told her what to say and she nailed it, the first take. It almost was scary, to where I had to slow it down. I don't know if I wanna put her on any more songs. I don't wanna make her any more famous. She can live a life. She didn't choose to have her father become a rap star. Nor my niece, nor my brother. So they're able to go outside and live a normal life, go to stores and do things normally that I can't do. Which is why, a lot of times, certain things I can't be there for.

What about school events?

School is different. In school, when they have plays, field trips, all that stuff, I don't miss them, even if I gotta deal with the craziness. And the teachers are really good about telling the kids, "When Hailie's dad comes in, he's Hailie's dad, Mr. Mathers." Last year I went and read to the class. Two books. It was reading month or something.

There's a Hailie love song on this album.

Yeah, a song called "Mockingbird," to Hailie and Alaina. When Mom was on the run they didn't understand it, and I'm not the greatest talker in the world, especially when I'm trying to explain to two little girls what's goin on with someone who's always been a part of their life and just disappeared. So that was my song to explain to them what was goin on, probably the most emotional song I ever wrote.

Michael Jackson called your mocking of him in the "Just Lose It" video "demeaning and insensitive." Are you picking on Mike?

I didn't do anything in the video that he hasn't said himself he does. With the little boys jumping on the bed and all that—they're just jumping on the bed. People can take what they wanna take, decipher it how they wanna decipher it. But it's not actually Michael Jackson, it's me playing Michael Jackson, studying the moves and doing the impressions. I don't have an opinion, really, neither here nor there, against Michael Jackson. When Thriller came out, you couldn't tell me nothin about Michael: Dude was the ultimate, dude is a legend. But the allegations that are thrown at him and the seriousness of the case—the guy's jumping on top of his van dancing?

And showing up to court late.

I showed up to that motherfucker an hour early every morning. I'm not playing with court. And now I think my fans should rally around me for making fun of myself.

Paris Hilton is in the "Just Lose It" video. She seems like the sort of person you'd normally be dissing, not doing a video with.

Well, when I was on MTV with La La it kinda slipped out. La La said, "How did you manage to get Paris?" I said, "Well, I love Paris. I love her almost as much as she loves herself." Then I was like, "Damn, that was fucked up." I try not to attack people who haven't attacked me first. As far as the image she portrays right now, as far as the way my girls look at her, do I want them to grow up to be like that? No. But for a video, for entertainment, that's a different thing. The song is about goin to the club and losin it, and you get so drunk you say the wrong thing. And we needed somebody to punch me, slap me, and pull my hair. Our first candidate was Jessica Alba. We couldn't get Jessica, and Paris happened to be in town.

There are two songs about Kim on "Encore." In "Puke," you hate her so much she makes you want to vomit. Then in "Crazy in Love," you're like, "I hate you, yet I can't live without you."

It's a love-hate relationship, and it will always be that. We're talking about a woman who's been a part of my life since I can remember. She was thirteen when I met her. I was fifteen.

What was it like the first time you saw her?

I met her the day she got out of the youth home. I was at a friend's house, and his sister was friends with her, but she hadn't seen Kim in a while 'cause she was in the youth home. And I'm standing on the table with my shirt off, on top of their coffee table with a Kangol on, mocking the words to LL Cool J's "I'm Bad." And I turn around and she's at the door. Her friend hands her a cigarette. She's thirteen, she's taller than me, and she didn't look that young. She easily coulda been mistaken for sixteen, seventeen. I said to my friend's sister, "Yo, who was that? She's kinda hot." And the saga began. Now there's the constant struggle of "will I ever meet somebody else that's gonna be real with me, as real as I can say she's been with me?"

You get deep into your feelings about President Bush and Iraq on "Mosh." Do you think the war in Iraq was a mistake?

He's been painted to be this hero, and he's got our troops over there dying for no reason. I haven't heard an explanation yet that I can understand. Explain to us why we have troops over there dying.

There is no good answer.

I think he started a mess. America is the best country there is, the best country to live in. But he's fuckin that up and could run our country into the ground. He jumped the gun, and he fucked up so bad he doesn't know what to do right now. He's in a tailspin, running around like a dog chasing its tail. And we got young people over there dyin, kids in their teens, early twenties, who should have futures ahead of them. And for what? It seems like a Vietnam 2. Bin Laden attacked us and we attacked Saddam. We ain't heard from Saddam for ten years, but we go attack Saddam. Explain why that is. Give us some answers.

Are you voting?

I'm supposed to hand my absentee ballot in today. I'm going for Kerry, man. I got a chance to watch one of the debates and a piece of another one. He was making Bush look stupid, but anybody can make Bush look stupid. I'm not 100 million percent on Kerry. I don't agree with everything he says, but I hope he's true to his word, especially about his plan to pull the troops out. I hope we can get Bush out of there, and I hope "Mosh" wasn't too little, too late. That can sway some of the voters or open people's minds and eyes up to see this dude. I don't wanna see my little brother get drafted. He just turned eighteen. I don't want to see him get drafted and lose his life. People think their votes don't count, but people need to get out and vote. Every motherfuckin vote counts.

There's a song on "Encore" called "Like Toy Soldiers" where you get into issues around the battles you've had recently. It made me think about how you're a battle rapper who came up in an era where battling was pure, and now it's like, "Damn, if I really go too hard, somebody might get shot."

Someone might die.

It's gotta be ill to not be able to just battle out like you want to. Battling has been such a great part of hiphop history.

It's sad. But I'm not gonna sit back and watch my people be hurt. It's like a Bush thing: You're just sending your troops off to war and you ain't in it. You're fuckin playing golf and you sent your soldiers over to get killed. As you get older, you start to think that if you're just beefin to be beefin or tryin to sell records, that's not the way to go. Because what usually ends up happening is somebody's entourage gets hurt. And it's not worth it. Battling always started out like a mind game: who could psych who out, who could look the scariest. Then it became people saying, "This is my life you're fucking with. This is everything I stand for, this is my career. If my career is gone tomorrow, then my life is gone tomorrow." That's how people end up losing lives.

Last year, The Source uncovered a tape that you made when you were sixteen where you said "nigger." What was that about?

This is what we used to do. I'd go in my man's basement and do goofy freestyles, and we'd call 'em sucker rhymes, and the whole point of the rap was to be as wack as possible and warm up before we actually did songs that we wrote. And that ended up just happening to be the topic that day. I just broke up with a Black girl, and the rest of the story I address on the album. I've got a song called "Yellow Brick Road," and it basically explains the whole story from beginning to end, how the tape derived.

How did The Source get it?

I don't know. The tapes kinda floated loosely. I never had control of them. It was something we just did and forgot about.

When it came out, were you pissed?

I was angry at myself. I couldn't believe that I said it. The tone that I'm using, you can almost tell that I'm joking, but the words are coming out of my mouth. If there was never no Eminem, it wouldn't be so shocking, but given who I am and what I stand for today, then what else could be Eminem's Achilles' heel?

When the shit came out I owned up to it. I apologized for it. But I can't keep apologizing for something I said when I was sixteen years old. If you wanna ask me about something I said during my career when I got signed as a rapper and knew that I was speaking to a lot of people, then we can talk about that. But until then, shit that I did as a fucking kid—I mean, we've all done stupid shit. Shit that you and your friends might have known was a joke, but had anybody else outside of that heard it, they might have taken it a different way.

In our generation the word "nigga" is used by Black and white kids as an expression of love, but even now you won't say it.

Yeah, it's just a word I don't feel comfortable with. It wouldn't sound right coming out of my mouth.

Do you see a similarity between "nigger" and "faggot"? Aren't they the same?

I've never really seen it that way. Growing up, the word faggot was thrown around. The two words were thrown around, they were always thrown around. But growing up, when you said faggot to somebody it didn't necessarily mean they were gay. It was in the sense of, "You fuckin dick."

But you don't see these two words doing the same thing?

I guess it depends on if you're using it in a derogatory way. Like, if you're using the word faggot like I just said, in the way of calling them a name, that's different than a racial slur to me. Some people may feel different. Some white kids feel comfortable throwing the word around all day. I don't. I'm not saying I've never said the word in my entire life. But now, I just don't say it in casual conversation. It doesn't feel right to come out of my mouth.

Does it bother you when a Black man says, "Eminem is my nigga?"

No. If a white kid came up to me and said it, I probably would look at him funny. And if given the time to sit down with him I'd say, "Look, just don't say the word. It's not meant to be used by us. 'Specially if you want something to do with hiphop."

You've sobered up some. Has that changed your music at all?

Nah. I feel like I still got the same passion for what I do. BD—Before Drugs—and AD—After Drugs.

You used to talk a lot about drugs, and you had a druggie manicness, and I wonder if you'll become more clear-eyed.

Well, I definitely feel more wide-eyed and more aware of my surroundings and what's going on. Going through them days and experimenting and mentioning different drugs, the way that I put it out there, like I got mushrooms and acid and weed, people automatically assumed

I was on drugs every time they saw me. Kids would come up to me like, "Yo, Shady, I know you got them 'shrooms!" And I'd be like, "Yo, I'm chillin." I mean, I went through my little phase, and I just realized it wasn't the thing for me. It wasn't the thing for me before fame, and there's no reason for it to be the thing for me now. Especially since I've reached a certain level of maturity that hopefully includes a happy medium of immaturity.

Let's talk about your process as a writer. How do you come up with hooks?

I think the beat should talk to you and tell you what the hook is. The hook for "Just Lose It" I probably wrote in about thirty seconds as soon as the beat came on. It was the last record we made for the album. We didn't feel like we had the single yet. That was a song that doesn't really mean anything. It's just what the beat was telling me to do. Beats run through my head—and rhymes and lyrics and wordplay and catch-phrases. When you're a rapper, rhymes are just gonna come at you. Those words are usually inside that beat, and you gotta find them.

Have you ever tried the Jay-Z method of not writing the rhymes out, just coming up with them in your head?

Yeah, I've done that. If you've ever seen my rhyme pads, my shit is all over the paper, because it's a lot of random thoughts. But a lot of times I'll be short a couple of bars, and I'll have a couple of lines wrote down and then I just go in the booth and try shit, and see what I'll say. I'll lose my space on the paper and just start blurting out, and it'll just come out. Music for me is an addiction. If I don't make music I feel like shit. If I don't spend enough time at home with my kids I feel like shit. Music is my outlet, my kids are my life, so there's a balance in my life right now that couldn't be better.

So you were a teenager when you first heard the Beastie Boys, and they allowed you to feel like, "Oh, I could be part of hiphop." 3rd Bass probably gave you more of that sense.

Yeah, but then along came the X-Clan. I loved the X-Clan's first album [*To the East, Blackwards*, 1990]. Brother J was an MC that I was afraid of lyrically. His delivery was so confident. But he also made me feel like an outcast. Callin us polar bears. Even as militant as Public Enemy were, they never made me feel like, "You're white, you cannot do this rap, this is our music." The X-Clan kinda made you feel like that, talking [on

"Grand Verbalizer, What Time Is It?"] about "How could polar bears swing on vines of the gorillas?" It was a slap in the face. It was like, you're loving and supporting the music, you're buying the artist and supporting the artist, you love it and live it and breathe it, then who's to say that you can't do it? If you're good at it and you wanna do it, then why are you allowed to buy the records but not allowed to do the music? That was the pro-Black era—and there was that sense of pride where it was like, if you weren't Black, you shouldn't listen to hiphop, you shouldn't touch the mic. And we used to wear the black and green.

You wore an Africa medallion?

Me and a couple of my other white friends. And we would go to the mall.

Whoa.

I remember I had the Flavor Flav clock. The clock was so big and ridiculous, it was the perfect Flavor Flav clock. It was fuckin huge. And me and my boy are in matching Nike suits and our hair in high-top fades, and we went to the mall and got laughed at so bad. And kinda got rushed out the mall. I remember this dude jumpin in front of my boy's face and bein like, "Yeah, boyyyeee! What you know about hiphop, white boyyyeee?!"

You must've had drama with the Africa medallion.

I'd be tryin to explain to my Black friends who didn't really feel like I should be wearin it, like, "Look, I love this culture, I'm down with this." But you're a kid, so you're not really sure of anything, you haven't really experienced life yet, so you don't really know how to explain yourself to the fullest. You're tryin to find your own identity and you're stuck in that whole thing of who am I as a person? Walkin through the suburbs and I'm getting called the N-word, and walkin through Detroit I'm getting jumped for being white. And goin through that identity crisis of, "Am I really not meant to touch the mic? Is this really not meant for me?"

And all this is inside you as you're coming up as a white rapper trying to enter this Black culture.

Even growing up as a kid, being the new kid in school and getting bullied, getting jumped. Kids are fucked up, kids are mean to other kids.

School is a tough thing to go through. Anybody will tell you that. I didn't really learn how to fight back till seventeen, eighteen. I reached my peak around nineteen, where people would call me and say, "Yo, I got beef with such and such—can you come help me out?" They knew I'd fight. I had a friend named Goofy Gary. He'd call me and say, "Yo, I just got jumped up at Burger King." And I'd say, "All right, Proof, we gotta go fight for Goofy Gary. Let's get in the car. C'mon." Then I found myself being the aggressor, which was a little strange from the few years prior to that being the loner kid who didn't fuck with nobody, wasn't lookin for trouble.

When was the last time you got into a physical confrontation with anyone?

It's been a while. There's been a couple little push-and-shove incidents but nothing really recently. Nothing since catchin them gun cases and standing before that judge. That changed me a lot. I realized that this dude controls my life, and he can take me away from my little girl. It slowed me the fuck down.

Used to be Eminem was in the police blotter from time to time, but since that case you've made a conscious change.

Yeah. When I got off probation I remember sayin to myself, "I'm never fuckin up again. I'm-a learn to turn the other cheek." I took on boxing just to get the stress out. Plus I chilled out a lot as far as the drinking and the drugs and all that stuff. Just chillin out on that made me see things a lot clearer and learn to rationalize a lot more. Sobering up, becoming an adult and trying to just become a businessman. Not sayin that I don't still got it in me. Not sayin I'm not still down for mine. But things changed.

What I want to do is make records, get respect, have fun, enjoy life and see my daughter grow up. I don't feel like I portray myself as a gangster; I feel like I portray myself as somebody who won't be bullied or punked. If I feel like I'm being attacked and somebody comes at me sideways with something I didn't start, then that's a different story. But I just try to do what I do, get respect, and that's it. If I can make people laugh and spark some controversy, good. It is entertainment.

Sparking controversy is key to you being who you are.

It kinda is. It's part of the whole mystique and the freedom of speech.

I see a lot of similarities between you and Madonna in the first phase of her career, because you both work with the idea that "if I make some people hate me, then that will make those who like me love me that much more intensely."

Yeah, definitely. You can't cater to every fan. Everyone's not gonna love you. Imagine how many people are on the planet. How can everybody love you?

But if some people hate you . . .

It's gonna make people who love you, love you more. I remember when 8 Mile came out and suddenly I was the good guy, and I was being appreciated for what I do. That was a little strange to me. I was like, "Oh, shit, I got old people comin up to me sayin they love my music and I got them into hiphop."

Do you want to do more movies?

I kind of want to finish my music thing first. There was a point in time with *8 Mile*, doin the soundtrack, the score to the movie and *The Eminem Show* that I felt like I was really neglecting life at home. I'm busy, and I stay busy, but I want to remain in control of things where I can stay in the city and go home at night to my kids. I'm a father before anything else, and anybody who knows me knows that that's the most important thing to me, that I can be close to my kids and be there.

Where's your relationship with Kim now?

Neutral at best.

Romantic side is over?

Yeah, that seems to be pretty much out the window, but we've still gotta show each other that mutual respect. I can't walk around the house tryin to mess with Hailie's head, saying, "Your mom's wrong." I used to get caught up with that with my mother, as far as saying bad things about any boyfriend she had that I liked. I don't wanna get them caught up in "Your mom's wrong," and then Hailie goes to see her mother, who says, "Your dad's an asshole." We don't do that. It's about raising these kids. She's out now. And hopefully she can get her life back in order. Before anything, it's gotta be for these kids. She knows it, I know it.

The Life of a Hunted Man

{ 50 Cent, *Rolling Stone*, 2003 }

It's well past three a.m. and 50 Cent's six bodyguards are outside in the hotel's hallway, lazily leaning against the wall or completely asleep, but 50's still pulsing with energy, keeping a roomful of friends in stitches, animatedly telling stories and holding court for hours. There's a thin wifebeater covering his six-foot chiseled torso and a Yankees hat balanced at an abrupt angle atop the white do-rag on his head. His dark navy bulletproof vest is over there, on the floor.

When he gets around to stories about his six-year-old son Marquis, who appears in the "Wanksta" video, his son's mother, Shaniqua, pulls the boy's picture out of her wallet. She calls him a hiphop baby. "One time he was watching TV with another little kid," 50 told them, "and a person got shot and died. He said to the other kid, 'That's weak. My daddy got shot a lot of times. He didn't die.'" The whole room laughed and 50 jumped up and melodramatically ran out of the room. "I had to tell him that was a special situation," he said when he came back. "You're not supposed to get hit that many times and get away!"

Twenty-seven-year-old 50 Cent, government name Curtis Jackson, nickname Boo-Boo, is the most exciting new MC and the coolest new villain in hiphop since the emergence of Eminem. Two point one million people ran out and bought his gory, brilliant debut album, *Get Rich or Die Tryin*, in its first three weeks in stores. He's already beginning to work on a Hollywood film about his life and to write another album, which he expects to release this year. Part of his success is because he's an MC who makes you feel what he means—no one in hiphop projects the mien of the scary bully crack dealer on records like 50 Cent. Another part is his life story—he actually was a widely feared crack dealer. "I think kids like me like the fuckin bad guy in a film," 50 says. "People love the bad guy. I watch movies all the time and root for the bad guy and turn it off before it ends because the bad guy dies. It's cinematic law the bad guy has to die. But sometimes the bad guy gets a record deal and becomes a superstar like 50."

In the corner of his hotel room 50 sits like a jaguar in repose, exuding supreme self-confidence from his physically imposing physique and seeming deeply secure in his own skin even though there are several people hunting him this very minute. Some have suggested that it's other rappers who want him dead, but his enemies are far more vicious and have far less to live for than rappers. Hatred from his old competitors in the crack world has multiplied because of his fame. "This ain't no rap war," 50 said. "This have nothin to do with no rappers. The gangsters don't like that I do whatever the fuck I wanna do. I'm movin around, I'm all over the country, I'm makin money, I'm a motherfuckin star. That bothers a nigga. The people that dislike me, who envy me for my situation, have nothin to lose. I'm from the bottom. They're uneasy about still bein on the bottom."

50 gets through his days in bulletproof trucks, walking with four to six bodyguards just inches away, ushering him briskly through streets and doors, but his body language and demeanor show him unmoved by the threat on his life. He never refuses to stop for an autograph or photo request, even when it exposes him to danger. He seems extremely confident he won't be killed and repeatedly says it truly doesn't bother him that people are actively trying to end his life. "It don't matter to me," he said. "That shit is not important when you got finances. Do I look uneasy to you?"

He won't say where he lives, but he will say, "It's a gun state. That means you could bear firearms in the house. They [the guys trying to kill him] could stop by."

Is he worried about his grandparents, who still live in Queens in the house where he grew up? He says his reputation is enough to protect them. "They [his would-be killers] know how I am. Anything go on around there, they need to move everything they love. They mammy, they pappy, they kids, all that shit. That'd start some real nasty shit. And they don't wanna go through that."

50 said his most familiar emotion was anger. "Somethin happen that another person might start crying about, I get mad," he said. "Some people know how to express themselves emotionally and cry and do all that other shit. Me, emotionally, I'm probably like thirteen." Eminem said, "If he says he's gonna pop you, you think he might. There's that little chemical imbalance that I think he has in his brain that you wonder, Will he or won't he. You hope he won't. He's a good guy. Just don't get on his bad side." But 50's friends called him extremely pensive and strategic and at some point he learned to control his emotions and use his street toughness only when necessary. In a heartbeat he can switch from the charm of a soft-spoken choirboy to a teeth-clenched ice-grill that would make you throw your wallet at him in fear, and he's clear when and where to employ each one. "I know I gotta be able to separate in order to progress," he said. "I'm not one way, not one track. For a person that has my kinda background they think I should be screw-faced all the time. That's cuz the fake rappers came and painted that picture for them. But a nigga got a sense of humor."

Curtis Jackson was born July 6, 1976, on the south side of Jamaica, Queens, then a rugged, drug-infested strip. A man who lived a few blocks away said, "That was the main arena for all the up-and-coming crack dealers. That was their playground. That's where they got their stripes. A lot of niggas dumped bodies on that side of town."

Young Curtis never knew his father and doesn't want to. "Let's give him a warning in this article," he said. "Don't you even dare crawl your ass out this way. I don't wanna know the nigga." His mother, Sabrina Jackson, was only fifteen years old when he was born and wasn't around very long. She dealt cocaine. "My moms was hard," 50 said. "She's real worse than me. She wasn't really feminine like that. My moms was tough-tough, like man-tough." Curtis spent most of his time with his grandparents because his mom was out working, but she compensated with presents. "She used to substitute finances for time," he said. "Every time I seen her it was somethin new for me. Christmas every day. She put jewelry on me early." At age seven he was one of the few kids in the neighborhood with a motorbike.

But when Curtis was eight someone went home with Sabrina, presumably someone she knew, put something in her drink that left her unconscious, closed the windows, turned on the gas, and left her for dead. She was found a few days later. "Had to be something to do with the drugs," 50 said. "Her body was all fucked up." She was twenty-two.

He moved in with his grandparents, who tried to steer him away from the street, but he was Sabrina's boy and thus able to hang out with the older guys in the neighborhood. When he was twelve they gave him some cocaine to sell. "If you tell me you hungry should I give you a fish, or a pole and teach you how to eat for yourself?" he said. "They knew nobody was there for me so they gave me a little three and a half grams and said, Here, start hustling. The other kids my age wouldn't even know what to do if you gave 'em a scale and bakin soda and a pot to cook it up. But they conditioned my head that I'm supposed to work for me. When I'm twelve." Of course, at twelve he could only hustle between three and six in the afternoon when his grandmother thought he was in the after-school program. "I did things in the street, then I was able to adjust and leave that at my doorstep. Once I get in the house I'm my grandmother's baby. But once I'm outside I do whatever I gotta do to get by."

One day when he showed up for ninth grade at Andrew Jackson High School, the metal detectors uncovered something strange in his sneakers. It was crack. He said he accidentally brought the sneakers he used to stash his product. He was arrested and given juvenile probation. He transferred to another school, but he'd never cared. "I was fashion show in high school. After the first time I got in trouble I'd pop in when I had something nice to wear and shit." He stopped going altogether somewhere around tenth or eleventh grade. (He got his GED in prison a few years later.) By this time he was a budding boxer and a rising street icon, a ghetto celeb known and feared throughout Queens, in control of a crack house and the main drug-selling strip around the way. "I had the longest capsules on the strip," he said. At eighteen he was making $5,000 a day selling crack and heroin. He bought himself a white Land

Cruiser and then a white Mercedes-Benz 400 SE. "He's always been known for doing something crazy and wild," said Sha Money XL, a longtime friend and the president of G-Unit Records. "He's always been that kid that's been in the mix with somebody that you would fear. People around Queens be like, I know Boo, he was crazy in school. He used to come to school with mad money and guns."

50 used a lot of intimidation and strategy to maintain his hold on the strip. For example, he employed thieves from Brooklyn whom he'd met in prison to rob the hustlers around the way who weren't in his crew. He'd let the stickup kids keep whatever cash and jewelry they got as long as they gave him all the drugs. Then he gave the stolen drugs to his customers when they bought his crack as a buy-one, get-one-free deal. This devalued his competitor's product and forced them to carry guns, which meant they had to scatter when the cops came. "So they had to come and leave, come and leave," he said. "Consistency is the key to all success. If you can consistently sell crack without the cops comin you gonna be successful. If you consistently put out quality material in your mix tape it'll build anticipation for your album."

50's not proud of having sold drugs, but he feels no guilt about it, either. "Guilt?" he said, a little annoyed. "Hell no. Guilt for how? How would I eat if I didn't do that? Try tellin a kid that's twelve years old if you do good in school for eight more years you can have a car. And let a kid's curiosity lead him through his neighborhood and find somebody who got it in six months on that strip. It don't seem like one of the options, it seem like the only option. I provide for myself by any means. I don't care about how anybody feels about it. Cuz when I'm doin it I really don't have intentions to hurt nobody. I'm not a thrill seeker. I don't expect everybody to understand. But there's people that's from where I'm from that understand."

In the summer of '94 50 was arrested twice within three weeks and ended up doing seven months in a youth shock-incarceration camp. He knew he was headed for death or jail. "It was comin," he said. "Long as you stay there you don't beat the odds."

For years he'd been going to friends' basements and rhyming to instrumentals for fun. Now he thought it was time to get away from the drug game and try hiphop. He knew nothing about constructing songs, but he told himself he would succeed. "Once I focus on something it gotta work for me," he said. "I won't turn off from it. I convince myself it's gonna work and then no one can convince me that it's not."

In 1996 a friend introduced him to the late, legendary Jam Master Jay, who was then organizing his label, JMJ Records. 50 talked his way into becoming an artist and Jay taught him how to structure a song. "Jay knew 50 was that shit," Sha Money said. "He was treating 50 like a big-budget artist." Jay produced 50's first album, but it was never released.

In 1999 he moved on to Columbia Records, where he recorded another album, *Power of a Dollar*, including the underground classic "How to Rob," in which he described mugging a slew of rap and R&B stars and laid out who 50 Cent was: the fearless and funny thug who's just a minute off the street. In truth, 50 was never into mugging. "Robbery isn't a big thing for me," he said. "The only time I would ever even think of tryin to take some money from a person is if I'm rock bottom. I hustle. That's my thing." But on the record something in his voice makes you certain he could and would empty the pockets of anyone he chose. The song exploded on the hiphop underground and on the radio. 50 had always admired how KRS-One had roared into hiphop behind a diss record ("South Bronx"). Now he'd done the same.

One night in a club 50 said what's up to a man he knew who'd happened to have stolen Ja Rule's chain. Ja saw 50 talking to the man and felt disrespected. Thus began a feud. "Wanksta" and a slew of records dissing Ja and Irv Gotti followed. (50's relentless in his attack on the whole Murder Inc. family. "Ashanti's sideburns are thick as hell," he said. "Think I can't see that?") But things got physical one day in Atlanta. Ja and 50 were staying in the same hotel and when 50 saw Ja he pulled him to the side to talk. "He was lookin real stupid," 50 said. "He had one of them little bats they give you at the baseball games for your kids. He had the ill-tough look on his face." Their talk didn't last long. "I let him go on for about a minute or two and then I just punched him in his eye," he said. "I heard enough of that shit."

There were eight people with Ja but, 50 says, they were reluctant to fight. "His crew jumped off just so it wouldn't be said they let him get beat up," 50 said. "But they didn't really want none with me. No-body got hurt. If you got eight people with you against one person I'm supposed to get peeled off the street. Paramedics supposed to come get me. Instead, I walk out of that situation with his jewelry." In the excite-ment Ja's chain broke and fell to the ground. "I picked it up and walked off with it. It was real movieish. I got mad later cuz I was like, man, I shoulda really whupped his ass. But it was all good. They gave me a watch to get the chain back." Later, in a scuffle with Ja and his crew at the Hit Factory, 50 was stabbed, though not seriously. He remains unre-pentant. Recently he was told that Chris Gotti, Irv's brother, had been shot in the leg. He said, "That fool probably shot hisself. I woulda shot him right in his head. Write that."

But while the Ja Rule beef merely got people talking about 50, he gained respect when Jay-Z responded to being dissed in "How to Rob," by saying, "I'm about a dollar/ what the fuck is 50 Cent?" on "It's Hot (Some Like It Hot)" from *Vol. 3 . . . Life and Times of S. Carter.*

"When he responded I was complimented," 50 said. "He wouldn't say nothing back to somebody he didn't think was hot. I never went to radio until after he said that about me. I don't know if my career would be where it's at if he didn't respond."

He was poised to be a star. In weeks he would shoot a video with Beyoncé and in a few months his album would be released. But there was at least one contract on his life, some say three. "Where I'm from the price of life is cheap," he said. "For $5,000 you could kill somebody. You could pick a shooter. You could have a few different choices. Might do it for less than that if they like you." On May 24, 2000, death came for a visit and his life changed forever.

He was at his grandmother's house, on his way to the tattoo par-lor and then to the studio. It was about twenty past eleven in the morn-ing. He got in a friend's car, then was asked to go back in to get some jewelry. When he came back outside and slid into the car another car pulled up beside his. Someone crawled out of the back and came up on 50's left side with a gun cocked. "Sneaky motherfucker, man. He did it right. He just didn't finish. He like Allen Iverson shakin a nigga, go to the basket, and miss." The man hit him with nine shots at close range.

Shots hit him in the hand ("shell hit my thumb and came out my pinky"), the hip ("that one hurt-hurt"), the calf, the chest, and one to the face that went through his left cheek and into his mouth. "Once I got hit, there was nothin else going on. Just a bunch of shots. You don't actually feel each one hit you. The adrenaline is pumping. You movin and tryin to get out of the way. I was bouncing around the backseat. We pulled off. We got a block or so. We had to pull over to get rid of the tote [gun]. Threw it in the sewer, then we got to the hospital. But I was up and still talking the whole time." At the hospital he figured out who shot him.

He spent thirteen days in the hospital, then straggled out on a walker. Six weeks later he began walking on his own. And that which had failed to kill 50 made him exponentially stronger. Now life was more precious to him, so he began working on his body with endless push-ups, pull-ups, and sit-ups that turned him from kinda fat to a chiseled jail body. And he eliminated friends who failed to share his continued fearlessness. "After that a lot of people showed me they're cowards," he said. "Cuz of our altercation with people that we grew up looking up to, they were afraid of the whole thing. You know your reputation is the cornerstone of power. They were intimidated by previous things. I'm not impressed by that. So what you killed people in the 80s. Kill somebody now." A short while later the shooter was murdered. 50 denied responsibility.

But more importantly for an MC, now there was a large squarish hole through the left side of his lower jaw and a piece of bullet left in his tongue. He'd lost a bottom tooth and a U-shaped chunk of his gums, but his lazy tongue and the hole in his jaw gave him a slur like no one in hiphop. "There's a different sound now when I talk, cuz of the air around the tooth," 50 said. "I'm more slurry now. Gettin shot just totally fixed my instrument."

"It's fucked up that it happened," Eminem said, "but it almost was like a blessing in disguise. It made his delivery more pit bullish. He talks with a sound that's almost like somebody's jaw wired. It brought a certain slur to it that's catchy. People love it. He's definitely out there. And that's me sayin that."

The story of the shooting of 50 Cent spread throughout hiphop and made him seem mythical, perhaps even unkillable. "Kids wanna see a guy that got shot that many times and lived," Eminem said. "There's a whole mystique about him, but at the same time, the same kids that are goin to the shows are a little bit intimidated by him. Maybe not all, but most."

But as soon as Columbia heard that 50 had been shot they dropped him. Record-business people say, Nobody wants to buy a problem, and a man with people trying to kill him was a big problem. "I wasn't sure if the industry was ever gonna embrace me again," he said. In January of 2001 he began spending every day at Sha Money XL's studio making songs for the underground mix-CD world. He released four albums of material within months, flooding the market as no MC ever had. "I thought, this dude got shot, got back up, and is still poppin shit?" said Eminem, who was then riding around L.A. listening to 50's mix CDs. "He came back stronger than ever. That made me stop."

Everyone in hiphop was talking about the unsigned 50 Cent. There was a bidding war, though there was also extraordinary trepidation. 50 said, "They looked across the table and they saw me and they said, Whoa, I'm not sure I wanna get involved with this guy." Meanwhile, in Los Angeles, Eminem decided he had to sign him and flew 50 out to L.A. for a meeting. "When everyone else was afraid to work with me for reasons outside of music, he looked straight past that," 50 said. "He was so excited. I wanted real bad to roll with him, but I didn't have an opportunity to tell him because he jumped off first, telling me how excited he was."

"One of the things that excited me about Tupac," Eminem said, "was even if he was rhymin the simplest words in the world you felt like he meant it and it came from his heart. That's the thing with 50. That same aura. That's been missing since we lost Pac and Biggie. The authenticity, the realness behind it."

Eminem urged Dr. Dre to come along on a deal and they offered a $1.7-million advance for a joint venture between Eminem's Shady Records and Dr. Dre's Aftermath Records. 50 signed with them even though some labels offered a few hundred thousand more than Shady/Aftermath. Chris Lighty said, "I don't know of any other companies that could really deal with the drama, embrace it, and speed-bump over it. It's hectic. It shakes the core of your company if you don't handle it correctly. And 50 thinks it's funny cuz he's always had the drama."

Back in the hotel room, it's around four a.m. and 50's still telling stories, first about when Foxy Brown came to visit him in the hospital, then about an old friend with such bad luck he got arrested almost every time he left home. It's almost time to leave, so he slips on his bulletproof vest and begins pulling the Velcro straps tight. He could die tonight, but he knows he made the right move. "Niggas out there sellin drugs is after what I got from rappin," he says. "When you walk into a club and the bouncer stop doin whatever the fuck they doin to let you in and say everybody else wait. He special. That's the same shit they do when you start killin niggas in your hood. This is what we been after the whole time. Just the wrong route."

Everyone turns when Shaniqua holds up a tailor-made kiddie-size dark navy bulletproof vest that Marquis will wear onstage this summer at his father's shows. There's something cute and funny about it, but no one laughs.

DMX Drives Crazy, but He Loves You

{ DMX, *Rolling Stone*, 2000 }

We're behind the wheel of a black Cadillac Escalade, cruising down Sunset Boulevard in Beverly Hills, where they drive like it's Sunday afternoon every day, all day. They move along at a careful pace, never cut each other off, come to a full stop for pedestrians, and—no matter what, even if someone does cut someone off—they never, ever honk. But the black Escalade of our story is being driven, no, commandeered, by Earl Simmons, 29, of Yonkers, New York, alias DMX. DMX doesn't drive like they do in Beverly Hills. DMX drives like he's mad. Hell-bent. Fearless.

His left hand is tight on the wheel, knuckles turned toward him; his right is busy with a Newport and a plastic cup of Remy Red; his feet are unaware of any shade of gray—he's hard on the gas, then hard on the brakes, mashing one pedal or the other, jerking the mammoth Caddy forward, sweeping into traffic, swiping in front of the smaller cars, bobbing and weaving past the palm trees, the Mondrian hotel, the Beverly Center, the U-Wash Doggie, the Cash Cow Cafe.

Late one Monday night, he screeched to a halt in the middle of an empty intersection and thought out loud, "Where the hotel at?" A bodyguard said, "It's back there, behind us," and X sent the truck into a full-speed 180 that felt, for a long three seconds, like we were sliding over the road, not gripping it at all but hovering just a bit above it, on the precipice of being completely out of control as we leaned hard to the right and my stomach churned with fear and I was certain, as I was each time we pulled off, that this time, on this street, he was really going too fast and was now going to have the smashup I knew was imminent every single time we started moving.

"I wish I had my license," he said once the car straightened out and we were zooming toward the hotel. "Yeah," a bodyguard said. "I wish you had it, too." I sat silently wondering whether X meant "I wish I had my license in my pocket" or "in my legal possession." (As it turned out, it was the latter. A few weeks later, DMX spent the night in jail after an arrest outside Buffalo for driving with a suspended license and possessing a small amount of marijuana.) Then, embracing and mocking the cliché that his life can sometimes resemble, he said, "You know how famous rappers do."

This roller coaster was made a touch more surreal by the sound of Stephanie Mills—"Tell me, whatcha gonna do with my lovin'?"—on the stereo full blast. "This is all I fuck with beside my shit," he said later, meaning disco-y R&B classics. In his black traveling CD case there are four hiphop albums, three of them from him or his camp, along with Donna Summer's greatest hits; a few Earth, Wind and Fire collections; The Best of Candi Staton; Chic Live at the Budokan; Teena Marie; Shalamar; Chaka; Cameo; Contraband: The Best of Men at Work; Evelyn "Champagne" King; and The Best of Regina Belle, signed by her: "To DMX, You are a most beautiful spirit. Stay positive and sweet. Love R." DMX grew up with this music in his childhood home. "When it was music playin, it was cuz people were over. It was usually durin the holidays, and they were havin a good time. I had to look out my room down the hall, but I could see people dancin and hear the music. That's why I like these songs. It was, like, the only time I was happy as a kid."

DMX is among the hardest-working men in modern showbiz. Less than two years ago, he was known only to hard-core rap fans; today, MTV reports he has the highest Q rating of anyone on the network. He has released a remarkable three albums in that time: It's Dark and Hell Is Hot in 1998 (which sold 3.7 million copies), Flesh of My Flesh . . . Blood of My Blood (2.8 million) in December '98 and . . . And Then There Was X (1.9 million so far), which came out the day after Christmas 1999 and debuted at number one. He also made time to shoot a pair of films. He starred in the visually stunning though narratively chaotic *Belly* and he plays a small part in the new action vehicle *Romeo Must Die*, costarring Aaliyah, Jet Li, Delroy Lindo, and Isaiah Washington.

His onscreen and on-mic personas are very similar—he gives you a man you know is tough at a glance, who's gritty and growling whether he's whipping your ass or philosophizing about the constant struggle that is life. He is sonic testosterone, a man's man who'd rather ride with his niggas than anything else. He is a direct descendant of Tupac, giving you the adrenaline-addled masculinity with occasional thought-provoking sentiments, though without the political framework or the public drama in his offstage life.

He raps in the roughest and grimiest voice in hiphop, the sound of gravel hitting the grave. His records speak of death constantly, crime casually, and moral consequences occasionally. His music—the best of it from producer Swizz Beatz—is skeletal, drawing on the brittle sounds of dance-hall reggae, the pulse of old-school hiphop, and ominous keyboard swells that resemble horror-movie scores. His success has turned his label, Ruff Ryders, into a brand name, spinning off a hit album from his posse (*Ryde or Die Vol. x*, 2 million sold) and another from the self-described "pit bull in a skirt" Eve (1.3 million sold). His oversize, invulnerable persona has made him a rock star to white teenagers, but he has become one without compromise and remains realer than real to the hiphop faithful. He is someone you'd want to share a blunt with, someone you'd want on your side in a war, someone you'd feel comfortable having with you as you walked through hell.

But that's DMX, the famous rapper. His life is often little different than high-school summer vacation with money. Wake up late, hang with friends, experiment with substances, go to the mall, stay up talking till all hours, play little pranks, do it again the next day. But instead of sleeping on someone's couch and driving Mom's Volvo station wagon, you're bling-bling.

On Tuesday around noon, DMX awoke in Beverly Hills' L'Ermitage hotel, in an $800-a-night room decorated in soothing browns and beiges, with a forty-inch television set, a DVD player, a stereo, and a box of nine exquisite chocolates on the living-room table. It was approaching seventy degrees and the balcony windows were open, floor-to-ceiling drapes billowing out toward the palm trees across the street as Luther Vandross boomed a cheery song about love—"I just don't wanna stop! Nevertoomuch, nevertoomuch, nevertoomuch, nevertoomuch!" On the table, beside the chocolates, sat a crispy, two-inch-high stack of hundreds held tight by a rubber band; a tiny Motorola cell phone ("Forty-seven calls missed," the screen said); a half-smoked, tightly rolled blunt; a thick Breitling watch with a blue face; a nearly empty jar of pickles next to a salt shaker; and an empty container of sardines. X was on the couch, on the phone, slouching back, with half a hand in his pants like Al Bundy, rocking a sun-yellow long-sleeved Gap top, dark denim jeans, and crisp, loose-laced Tims in that classic beige, with a diamond-flooded Ruff Ryder R dangling halfway down his chest on a platinum chain. His lashes are surprisingly long, his teeth blindingly white, his face softer and rounder than when "Get at Me Dog" ruled the streets. He really does look a lot like Seattle SuperSonics point guard Gary Payton.

"I just wanted to call you and say I love you, Boo-boo," he said, opening one of today's five or six conversations with his love of thirteen years, wife Tashera, whom he incessantly calls Boo-boo. They have two sons together, seven-year-old Xavier and eight-month-old Tacoma. "I miss your stankin ass, too, Boo-boo." Unlike DMX, Earl Simmons, regular person, is an extremely nice guy.

Slowly the crew assembled in X's room, a crew not unlike those orbiting so many rappers. There's the tough-minded, oft-annoyed road manager, Kenneth Butler, whom everyone calls by his last name or the first syllable of his last name. There's two large, bald, Black bodyguards—Ben Manner and Mark Smith of Premier Guardian, both of them retired NYPD. They meander behind or bookend X whenever he's in public, or laugh and philosophize with him in private. "You can't just say, 'All right, hold me down and I'm payin you,'" X said. "You gotta dig a nigga somewhat. They have to be able to put up with your bullshit, and you have to be able to put up with theirs. You gotta be compatible. Cuz it's not just a job. It's an adventure."

And then there's Nockie. Every crew has a Nockie. Ostensibly he's a barber but his true role is court jester. He'll tell you so. He's X's man from the old 'hood and a natural comedian—a Harlem-born hustler who keeps his baseball hat cocked at an offbeat angle, holds his pinkie up when drinking, and is always spitting jokes. "I'm known for the happiness," Nockie said. "Cuz it gets rough, namean? And every day is a good day to me, as long as I'm breathing. So I'm the court jester. I keep a smile on everybody face."

Around two p.m., some of them jumped into X's Escalade and the rest into a silver Range Rover 4.6 HSE, which quickly lost sight of the Escalade. They ran into the Fox Hills Mall (X strolled into K-B Toys and phoned his son: "Dawg!" X said, "I'm in K-B Toys!" "You are?!" "You want somethin'?" Long pause. "I know I want something," his son said. "I just don't know what it is!"). They zipped back to downtown L.A. and into a Rite Aid. Suzzanne Douglas, the mom from *The Parent Hood* (that Robert Townsend show), was there and X bought a camera to take a picture with her; they ended up exchanging numbers. Then it was on to a restaurant, Roscoe's, where they saw Tyra Ferrell, who played Morris Chestnut's mom in *Boyz N the Hood*, and ate big, thin waffles; fried chicken wings; smothered potatoes; and a pitcher of sunrise (lemonade and OJ). X left the hot-sauce bottle nearly empty.

Through it all, he was unendingly friendly to strangers of all races. Unlike the rapper who harks, "I'm not a nice person!" on "What's My Name," he was gregarious, speaking to doormen, waitresses, random passersby, yelling, "Wassup!" or "God loves you!" or "LAPD!" or whatever occurred to him, eager to speak to everyone and make them smile. "They think I'm a dawg," he said as we crossed La Cienega Boulevard, "but I'm a gentle giant."

Late Tuesday night, on the way back from watching *The Sixth Sense* with friends and a stop at a karaoke bar on Sunset Boulevard, he was driving down Santa Monica Boulevard and saw a flock of twentyish white men and women in suits and classy dresses lounging on a corner, seeming to have nowhere to go. He stopped the Escalade in front of them, rolled down the passenger window, and in mock seriousness, yelled out, "Yo! Is this the heroin spot?" They laughed, in on the joke, and a blond boy in a gray suit grinned drolly and said, "No."

"Damn!" X yelled, banging the wheel in mock frustration. He smiled and peeled off.

But the fun was undercut with a slice of apprehension. DMX's crew hadn't changed its itinerary since reading death threats from L.A. rapper Kurupt in the hiphop magazine XXL—"now [DMX] got [his] Cali pass revoked [he] can't come out to the West." The thought lingered in the crew's collective mind, like the sense in a horror flick that the killer might be in the vicinity. Kurupt, who came to fame with Snoop Dogg's Dogg Pound, was engaged to Foxy Brown until he came to believe that DMX had slept with Foxy (both deny it) and began threatening both their lives. A short time ago, the entire situation was ratcheted up a notch when one of Kurupt's security guards was shot and killed outside a Los Angeles recording studio. "Me and my partner are always peeled," bodyguard Ben Manner said. "We're very concerned. On a scale of 0 to 10, it's a 9.8. Cuz if a nigga get his drink on, then he wanna prove that shit."

DMX refused to be afraid and refused to bad-mouth the artist. "I feel for Kurupt," he said heartfully. "I feel for him, knowin how tight me and my peoples is. That's why I say I sympathize—no, I feel for Kurupt and his loss. I'm sorry for his loss, cuz I know what that loss would feel like to me."

An hour later, it was just past ten and X was back at L'Ermitage, in his seventh-floor suite. *The Best of Sade* played in the background—he sang along with one of his favorites: "Jezebel wasn't born with a silver spoon in her mouth!" A friend did his nails, clipping, filing, digging into his cuticles, and applying a clear polish meant for men, a twenty-minute process. And he talked. Like Anthony Hopkins's Hannibal Lecter, he's too complex for direct interviewing. His mind is too restless, the moats in his memory too wide. Questions often receive pat, clichéd answers. The only way to interview him is to turn on the mic and leave him free to talk, to let him tell his story his way, in his pace and time. I put the tape recorder down in front of him around ten-thirty p.m. He finished just after two. Stories, rage, mock poetry, stream of consciousness, long silences. It became like therapy. He spoke about sex ("My first sexual encounter was with a relative from down South. Not really a relative, but a relative's wife. I was twelve.") and doing dumb stuff ("I used to take my mother's mascara, the eyelash shit, and put it on my lip like I had a mustache.") and his children ("Xavier has my personality, 100 percent. When I wake up, I'm not the nicest person, and I get mad to the point where I gotta break somethin. He's like that."). And then, around midnight, he turned to his childhood.

DMX spent the years between fourteen and twenty-one as a thief, constantly in and out of jail. "I robbed niggas," he said. "I'm not ashamed of that. That's my shit. Robbery. I'm not a hustler. I've tried it. That's not me. I'd rather do the stickup shit. But what got me over was, I had a rep in Yonkers. Niggas knew DMX would get ya. And I'd be straight-up robbin niggas no mask or nothin. Half of my weapon was my face. I'd just walk up to niggas and be like, 'Yo, lemme get that.' I wasn't the biggest nigga in the world. I couldn't beat everybody, but dawg, my rep superseded me."

Jail didn't scare him, because he had been constantly institutionalized from ages seven to fourteen in homes for troubled boys in upstate New York. The trouble had begun long before he turned seven. He lived in Yonkers, in the projects, with his mother and five sisters, where a series of humiliations and misreads by everyone around him turned him into a rage-filled recluse who exploded one day and launched his course through the various penal systems.

"I didn't have much of a childhood," he said grimly. "It was always dark in our house, and depressing. That's what I remember."

He said his childhood was miserable. He was often confined to his room for small misdeeds and punished more severely for larger transgressions. Sometimes, he says, he'd be woken up in the middle of the night and wasn't even sure what he was being punished for. "You know how scary that shit is, dawg?" His relationship with his mother did not survive his childhood. They haven't spoken in years, and she refuses to talk about him.

He went to kindergarten wearing hand-me-downs from other boys in the school and was shamed by them. " 'Yo, you got on my old shit, man! You poor, man. Your mother on welfare.' And it's all true!" He became an antisocial little boy who would fight anyone who bothered him as if battling for his life. "I didn't fight right. Head butt a nigga, grab a nigga nuts and pull 'em out—I'd fuckin bite you, I'd dig in your nose all the way up. . . . I didn't give a fuck, yo. I was fightin from real anger—fuck you, you nice-dressin motherfucker. So what you keep a haircut!"

Though he was smart, he struggled to find his way in the classroom: "I'd finish my work fast and get bored. Or be frustrated with the shit she'd be askin. And I wasn't afraid of teachers. I'd tell 'em to shut up. They called me Crazy Earl. I didn't give a fuck." This was first grade. One day during that long first-grade year, he traded words with a classmate. "So I jumped up, grabbed my number-two pencil, and stabbed him right in his fuckin face." He turned gnarled and enraged as he told the story. "Then a teacher put her hands on me. In breakin the fight up, she kinda threw me down. . . . Charged her . . . I'm wildin, now. . . . Throwin desks aside . . . They cleared all the kids out, called the principal and the gym teacher, and they wrestled me to the ground and sat on me for, like, ten minutes, until I calmed down." The impression of him as a problem kid was cemented. "They thought I was a bad kid, pain in the ass. I was actually a very bright child who was easily bored and frustrated. They wanted to treat me like every other kid in the class. Can't do that to me. I wasn't every other kid in the class, man. I thought a lot more than every other kid in the class. . . . Wasn't no bad fuckin kid, man." At the end of the school year he was shipped upstate, to his first institution. "Bitch [his mother] just dropped me off like I was a fuckin piece a shit," he said, frothing with anger. As he said this, it seemed uncertain whether he would leap up and throw a chair across the room or burst into tears. "Fuckin bitch. My sisters didn't get treated like that. But all of 'em have different fathers, so I think she just don't like niggas."

He paused. His eyes glazed over with hatred, and a hot rage seemed to bubble beneath his surface. "So many times, I thought about killin that bitch. But I would always think of how I would feel if she was gone, and I knew I wouldn't like it. No matter what she did, I knew I still loved her. I love her, though. I love her, but I can't stand that bitch. That's a fucked-up kinda love."

At this point, hiphop is like a minor league for Hollywood, a sort of off Broadway for the film industry. MCs create a persona and introduce it to the subworld of the Hiphop Nation, then refine that look and image in the minifilms that are videos. In time, the big leagues call and say, "Hey, Mister Snoop Dogg—or Busta, or Latifah, or Cube, or Tupac—let's make a movie!" DMX, one of the newer members of the club, got the call on a Wednesday evening, when Hollywood megaproducer Joel Silver sent a black, chauffeured Chevy Suburban to L'Ermitage.

Silver greeted X in his office, a bungalow on the lot of Warner Bros. that was decorated with framed posters from his nearly forty movies—48 Hrs., Commando, Richie Rich, Conspiracy Theory, the first two Die Hards, all four of the Lethal Weapons, and The Matrix—as well as a larger-than-life statue of the monster from Predator and a Joel Silver pinball machine with a caricature of the producer on it. Silver had a protruding belly, a thick beard, and the dominant manner of a rich, powerful man.

But tonight, Silver was a bit supplicant, fawning over X. Silver produced Romeo Must Die, in which X plays a nightclub owner–gangster, and he is itching to do more with DMX. Within two minutes of X's sitting on Silver's gorgeous leather couch, Silver was playing him the Romeo trailer, first the international version and then the American. "In a world of vicious rivalries and violent betrayals, only one thing is certain," the announcer said dramatically. "Romeo must die." Then Silver was doing backflips to get X involved in the movie's marketing: "I'll get a jet, and I'll fly ya anywhere I have to. Your presence is so incredibly effective. I need your presence. You give the film so much credibility. Staggering credibility with the hiphop people we so desperately want. We screened it for kids, and I thought they were gonna kill us when you got killed. I just wish you were in the film even more!" He was doing a sort-of forceful pleading, talking in a tone that melded begging and demanding. X was silent during the entire meeting in part because Silver dominated the conversation, standing throughout, gesturing demonstratively—but it was completely unclear, if X had shown resistance, whether Silver would have begun to gruffly demand, banging his hands on the table, or gone down on his knees and begged.

"I wanna do another movie with you," Silver said. "Not a shitty movie, but something big. What do you think of this guy Steven Seagal? Would you wanna work with him? That could be a big urban hit. He'll be a cop who got fucked up somehow, and you're a guy in the street"— he was making it up as he went along—"and somehow you'll get together. This is called a 'blind commitment.' You guys agree to a picture, then we make up a script. I love having you in the movie. I think your stuff is so real, and you're just coming from the heart and everything." Though it was never said, it seemed that X's long and intense prison experience had much to do with delivering him here tonight, molding him into the urbanly grizzled, heroic, and sympathetic figure he is. It plays to the American fascination with the Incarcerated Negro and puts X in a club with Rubin "Hurricane" Carter, Malcolm X, and Tupac.

They stood and walked across the lot, to a music studio where they could touch up a few voice-overs. Silver walked beside X and then put an arm over his shoulder, like a brother. "We're gonna do a lot of things together," the multimillionaire movie producer told the famous rapper, the shadow of the Warner Bros. water tower draping over them. "I promise."

On Thursday it was eighty degrees. In X's L'Ermitage room, the curtains were blowing out the balcony window as if trying to escape, and Michael Jackson's Off the Wall was on loud. X was bent over a little table-clothed table, on which sat scrambled eggs, potatoes, juice, and some fruit. His eyes were shut tight, and his lips moved quickly as he silently mouthed a half-minute prayer. It was yet another day in the life of a famous rapper, another high-school-summer-vacation-with-money sort of day. There would be a stop at the recording studio, maybe a photo shoot, maybe a meeting with Oliver Stone, probably a trip back to Roscoe's. But all that was later. There is a time, in a famous rapper's life, for work, and a time for summer vacation. Right now, it's almost one o'clock. It's time for breakfast.

I'm Scared to Death, but I Gotta Live

{ Biggie Smalls, *The New York Times*, 1994 }

Standing on the corner of 125th Street and Eighth Avenue in Harlem at three a.m. one recent Sunday, the six-foot-three, 280-pound rapper Biggie Smalls appeared not so much large than literally larger than life. Moments before, he had finished the third of three sold-out concerts at the Apollo Theater and, wearing the same caramel-brown leather army suit and beige Kangol cap he had worn onstage, he then slipped out the back door of the theater. At the corner, he relaxed in the middle of a circle of friends, but soon heard, just below the general din of late-night Harlem, his own voice booming back at him. The majority of cars cruising through or stopped at the intersection were tuned to the same radio station, and so, as Biggie surveyed the scene he found himself inadvertently saluted by his own song, "Big Poppa."

Such a moment isn't an unlikely occurrence in Harlem, or any place dense with hiphop fans. With a gold debut single, "Juicy," and album, *Ready to Die*, Biggie, who is known professionally as the Notorious B.I.G., and to his mother as Chris Wallace, is right now, among hiphop aficionados, the most popular rapper. In a medium where newness is a constant demand, 1994 has been an especially portentous year. Despite releases from veterans like Dr. Dre and Snoop Doggy Dogg, Public Enemy and Arrested Development, nearly all of the most acclaimed albums of the year have come from new artists like Queensbridge native Nas, Staten Island–born Method Man, and Long Island–grown Keith Murray. In that group Biggie is not the best vocalist but stands out because of the emotional honesty of his lyrics. Biggie rhymes about his crime-filled past, but he also discusses how much pressure and anxiety he felt back then: he was so stressed out that he sometimes considered suicide and concludes *Die* with "Suicidal Thoughts," where he calls a friend, confessing that he wants to put a gun to his head, "And to squeeze/Until the bed's/Completely red/I'm glad I'm dead." At the end of the song he shoots himself.

The evening after the Apollo show, Biggie sat in the third-floor hallway of the apartment building in the Bedford-Stuyvesant section of Brooklyn where he was raised and still lives with his mother, Voletta Wallace, and detailed his past career: "I used to sell crack. My customers were ringing my bell and come up on the steps and smoke right here. They knew where I lived, they knew my moms."

He says he began dealing around the age of twelve, working the area on Fulton Street between St. James Place and Washington Avenue while his mother was busy teaching preschoolers during the day and attending school at night. (By her account, she remained ignorant of her only child's drug dealing until recently. "I found out about my son and his little antics through his music and through magazines," she said. "I read this thing and said, 'Huh?' I never knew.")

A high school dropout, Biggie was arrested for selling crack in North Carolina at age seventeen. He was locked up for nine months before being bailed out (the case is still pending). Biggie says he never openly courted a career in hiphop, but that a tape that he recorded for fun found its way into the hands of a young, ambitious A&R executive at Uptown Entertainment named Sean "Puffy" Combs. "His flow was ill," Combs said, "so I called him in, had a meeting with him. We just hit it off. He was real. I was real. It was on."

Combs played Biggie's tape for Uptown president Andre Harrell, who was also impressed. "He had a voice that just sounded like it was heavy and it was funky and rhythmic," Harrell said. "And it had a lot of personality. Like a light-on-his-feet kinda big brother."

Biggie's voice is not all that distinguished him. Biggie writes detailed, visual lyrics and delivers them with the crisp, clean annunciation one might expect from the son of a school teacher: "Every time I say a word wrong she correct me," Biggie said of his mother. "Like if I say a word in a wrong tense, or something, she'll scream on me. I'll be like, 'I ain't got nothing.'" He imitated his mother's voice: "'I don't have anything.' She always do that. Now you don't really catch me saying, 'I ain't got nothing.' I'll be like, 'I don't have anything.' And I really will mean it from the heart."

Shortly before the completion of *Die*, Combs and Harrell had a falling-out that led to Combs leaving to start his own company called Bad Boy Entertainment. ("It was time for him to spread his wings," Harrell said.) Biggie followed Combs to Bad Boy and was one of the company's first releases.

Now, with more than a half million records sold, Biggie has put drug dealing behind him, but retains the dealer's constant fear. He explained matter-of-factly that he expects to be murdered in the hallway of his own building—even though, on that day, help was as close as the pair of black nine-millimeter Rugers that sat between his matresses. "I'm not paranoid to the point where," he said, then paused. "Yes I am. I'm scared to death. Not all the time, but most of the time. Scared of getting my brains blown off."

His fear is hardly unjustified. Last month alone, two rappers—Ol Dirty Bastard from Wu-Tang Clan and Tupac Shakur—were shot in what police described as robbery attempts. Still, Biggie doesn't let fear dominate him, as the Apollo performance aftermath attests. "I got to see what's going down, where the party's at. I can't live my life in no bubble."

Though most rappers exaggerate about their lives before becoming performers, some are actually former drug dealers. Few have ever been as open in detailing their criminal past as Biggie, and none have ever been as clear about the depth of emotional pain they felt at the time. "He doesn't want anyone to see that he's not as tough as he thinks he is," said Ms. Wallace. "He cries inside. He bleeds inside. But he doesn't want anyone to see the vulnerable side of him." A Jehovah's Witness, she has not listened to much of her son's album. If she does she'll discover that he does indeed reveal his internal tears.

"In street life you're not allowed to show if you care about something," said Combs. "You gotta keep that straight face. The flip side of that is his album. He's giving up all his vulnerability. He's letting you know how he has felt about his mother. He's letting you know how he cried. How he has thought about killing hisself."

Indeed, *Die* is marked by pathos unusual not only in hiphop, but in pop music. Despite its immorality, Biggie's drug-dealer past could have tremendous hero value with the young Black audience he craves. The dealer has disposable income in neighborhoods where most are visibly poor and thwarts the most visible arm of the oppressive larger society, the police, on a daily basis. Though most dealers wind up dead or in jail, those ends contibute to their martyrdom.

But the value of martyrdom is a lot easier to appreciate when you are not dead. So the dealer spends considerable time and energy watching out for his enemies: the other dealers who want his turf, the stickup men who want his money, and the parents, including, often, his own, who want him to stop dealing. What makes Biggie's rapping distinct is that he rhymes about both the excitement and constant anxiety endemic to the drug dealer, making *Die* a more balanced and honest portrait of a drug dealer's life than hiphop has ever seen. "He's trying to enlighten people to the way your mind thinks when you're broke when you young growing up and not feeling like nobody cares about you," Combs said.

On "Everyday Struggle," for example, Biggie rhymes: "I know how it feel to wake up . . . Pocket broke as hell/Another rock to sell/People look at you like you's the user/Selling drugs to all the losers . . . But they don't know about your stress-filled day/Baby on the way/Mad bills to pay/ That's why you drink Tanqueray/So you can reminisce/And wish/You wasn't living so devilish."

Exposing the self-loathing and self-doubt he felt while dealing, Biggie sacrifices much of the heroic potential of his position, but forges a complex, revelatory piece of art. In another song, "Respect," he is clear about his drug-world ambitions and what derailed him: "Put the drugs on the shelf/Nah, I couldn't see it/*Scarface, King of New York*/I wanna be it . . . Until I got incarcerated/Kinda scary . . . Not able to move behind the grate steel gate/Time to contemplate/Damn, where did I fail?/All the money I stacked was all the money for bail."

Part of why Biggie isn't afraid to sacrifice the hero value of the dealer is because he knows that there's an audience of people who aren't listening for some thrill, but who are in the same anxiety-filled position he was in not long ago. "I wanna hit that spot in niggers that be like, 'Damn, that be happenin, man,' " Biggie said. "That's the part of nigger's head that I wanna hit. Them stressed out niggers that be like, 'Yo this nigger be hittin it right on the nose, man.' That's what I'm tryin to do."

Apparently, he's succeeding. The album has sold well enough that in January Ms. Wallace will move from the apartment where she's lived for twenty-five years into a house in Park Slope. But despite newfound economic independence and the mortal fear he feels while sitting in his own Bed-Stuy home, Biggie himself is reluctant to move.

"I could never see myself moving in the suburbs," he said. "It ain't gonna be right and the lyrics gonna be soundin nasty. I know it. There won't be nothin to rap about except the birds."

The Toughest Record Exec Ever

{ Dick Griffey, *XXL*, 1995 }

One evening not long ago, Dick Griffey, the fifty-nine-year-old chairman of Solar Records, and Marion "Suge" Knight, the twenty-nine-year-old CEO of Death Row Records, had a meeting. Griffey and Knight are certainly legitimate businessmen, but their sit-down had all the trappings of an underworld assemblage. It was conducted hours after midnight in the weight room of Knight's offices, which are in a remote section of Tarzana, California, which is north of Los Angeles, and not exactly near the beaten path itself. More, both of the principals were linebacker-size multimillionaires with fearsome reputations. "Suge to me is a real gangster," someone familiar with his criminal record said. "He has a very heavy violent side and if I were giving any advice, just don't cross him and expect to get away with it easily. He's a dangerous guy." "Everything Suge ever thought about doin I've done," Griffey said the afternoon before the meeting in the parking lot of the Solar Tower, the Hollywood building he owns. He spoke deliberately and from deep in his chest, something like Wilfred Brimley with soul. "Ten times. He know who to bring that to. I come from the same streets." And finally, Griffey and Knight were locked in a dispute. At issue was a hundred million dollars or so.

Griffey arrived at Tarzana's Death Row studios in a white baseball cap, silk multicolored short-sleeve shirt, and loose-fitting jeans, with his ever-present reading glasses dangling from around his neck. He has enough pairs of reading glasses that they almost always match his outfit.

He was patted down by one of a pair of armed security guards in a darkened reception area, and then escorted back to Knight's private office through a long, thin, ominously quiet hallway. At six feet two inches and a solid two hundred pounds, Griffey outsized both security guards, and as the balding, dark-skinned executive found his way through the corridor, walking a bit hunched over, stepping hard and pigeon-toed, he moved like a battered ex-running back. He was finally left to idle in a kitchen-cum-waiting room that was improbably, no absurdly, decorated: while sitting tight for the man behind Dr. Dre, Tupac Shakur, and Snoop Doggy Dogg, Griffey peered at framed posters of Marilyn Monroe, James Dean, Lucille Ball, and Elvis Presley.

After a few moments Knight burst from his office, sporting a blue denim shirt and pants and a gold and diamond watch, ring, neck chain, and stud earring. He did not appear gaudy, though he did seem to have on enough jewelry to, say, pawn for a new Lexus. Knight panned the room and when his eyes landed on Griffey, he smiled slowly and widely. They bear-hugged sweetly. Knight then gave Griffey a tour of his office, pointing out his immaculately clean bloodred carpet, couch, and love seats, his tank of piranha and goldfish, and the back room where he keeps a bed. He seemed like so many young men escorting their fathers around their first apartments, beaming simply about having something of their own. "I'm impressed, son," Griffey said, then asked how often the carpet was cleaned. Before he could answer, Griffey said, "You know, at Kenny's house"—he meant Philadelphia International Records chairman of the board and legendary hitmaker Kenny Gamble—"they got the white carpet. I said, 'Damn, that must get dirty real fast.' He said he didn't know, cuz they got it cleaned every day!" Together, they laughed deeply.

The meeting was meant in part to help repair a once-tight relationship. The two were introduced in 1990 and almost immediately Griffey became a sort of father to Knight. That evening in Knight's office, when Griffey stepped out to hear some music, Knight settled deep into a love seat, lit a nearly finished cigar, and a bit mischievously, said, "I used to do shit just to fuck with Dick so he'd come up on the third floor [where Knight had an office]." After Knight started coming to Solar regularly, he traded in his Corvette for a canary-yellow two-seat convertible Mercedes, the vehicle Griffey drove. And whenever he beat Griffey to the office, he grabbed Griffey's parking spot. "I knew if I parked my shit in his shit Dick'd come and talk to me. If he come talk to me I know we fittin to go downstairs to the Italian restaurant about three blocks down from Solar. That's his little restaurant. So, we had one of the best relationships you could think of." Eventually, Griffey assigned Knight the parking spot adjacent to his. "Dick didn't have an older son," Knight said. "I think that was his way of sayin, 'You family.'"

After more than two years of free office space, free parking, and free lunch, the pair had a falling-out and stopped speaking. Griffey turned his attention from making records to distributing them while Knight led Death Row to gross over one hundred million dollars in four years, placing it among the most successful labels in the industry. However, Griffey now claims to be entitled to a significant percentage of Death Row and to have a signed agreement to back him up. In January of 1996, he readied a $125 million breach-of-partnership suit against Knight, and the pair began speaking again.

"Dick is like an older brother," Knight said that night in his office. "Every person, even brothers, disagree. Even when they grow up they fight over toys. That happens. But if it's love it only last a second and shit stronger and better."

"I like Suge," Griffey said, zipping back to his office after the meeting. "I love Suge, as a matter of fact. This is just a family dispute. He owes me money based upon what we agreed. It's a family dispute. Big brother have to go after little brother to get his righteous piece of the pie."

The kind words, like the smiles and hugs, mask the feelings of a man grappling for a solution to a most complex battle with a most beloved son. A man who has built his life around paternal relationships in order to forward communal economic empowerment only to find that goal challenged by the success of one of his most successful sons. To Griffey, it is beyond trying. "It makes me wanna cry."

That night I had a private meeting with Suge. He and I sat alone on facing bloodred love seats for almost an hour in his large office, the door closed, talking about his old days with Griffey. He was articulate and funny and put me at ease. I was nervous to ask him about the lawsuit Griffey had filed against him, but as my list of questions dwindled and my confidence grew, I felt I could. So, I did.

"I don't know what you talkin bout," he said playfully.

He'd been so affable and cooperative that I'd forgotten where I was and who I was sitting with. "Aw, come on, man," I said, pressing Suge. "You know what I'm talkin about. What's up with that lawsuit?"

His teeth clenched slightly. For a moment he just stared at me. In a cold, steely voice he said, "Turn off that tape recorder."

I did.

"Man . . ." he said disdainfully, "a nigga wan come up in here talkin bout lawsuits . . ."

I picked up my tape recorder and began to stand.

"Where you goin?" he said forcefully.

I told him I was going outside. He said no, I wasn't. I was sitting right there. I did.

He got up and opened the door and called to someone. He stood in the doorway, facing me, his arm draped across the void. His office was a cell with a single, horizontal, chiseled bar. A young muscled street soldier with a bandana over his head came running up to him.

"You see that nigga there?" Suge said to him. "This nigga wan come up in here talkin bout lawsuits. . . ."

The street soldier looked Suge in the eye and began striding right at me. I thought, If I walk out of here with only bruises, nothing broken, I'll be alright. But before he could complete two steps Suge touched him and he stopped. They spoke quietly, laughing and taunting for another half minute, maybe deciding exactly what they should do with me. I tried to imagine what the pain of a punch to the ribs or a boot stomp to the lower back might feel like so that when it happened I'd be mentally prepared. The soldier disappeared. Suge closed the door and walked back over to me. I couldn't keep my hands from shaking.

He stood near me and said, "Come 'ere." Warily, I stood up. He put his left arm over my shoulders and tugged at me to come with him. I held back, he dug his fingers into my shoulder muscle and half dragged me across the room. We inched into the corner, toward the piranha tank, the top of my head level with his shoulders,

We stopped in front of the tank. With one hand he turned me to face him, he turned me so easily I felt like a doll in his hands, and looked me in the eye. "If you ever fuck with me . . ."

My heart was bouncing around its bony little cage like a crashing skiier.

"Yes, yes, sir . . ."

"If you ever come up in here askin bout some lawsuit . . ."

"Yes, no, sir . . ."

Then he released me and I walked toward the door to leave. He told me to sit down on the bloodred love seat. I did. He sat across from me. I thought, At least I still have a good interview on tape. He said, "Rewind the tape." As it surged backward I sat silent and motionless, trying to keep him from noticing my shaking. "You done burnt your bridge with Death Row," he said. "Someday you gone need us, to do a innaview or summin. But you done burnt your bridge."

The tape clacked to a stop and he told me to press Record. Then, he proceeded to give me another interview, saying the same things he'd said the first time in the same order, repeating everything he'd covered during our original conversation of almost an hour. It was an impressive display of total recall of every detail of a talk that, for him, was largely mundane. Without any prompting or pausing he went on and on, retelling all the old stories about Griffey and explaining the genesis of Death Row, until he reached that part in our conversation about the lawsuit. Then he stopped.

I thanked him, got up, and walked out of his office, still shaking.

"He's like the prodigal minority father," a former Solar employee opined about Griffey. "Doesn't exactly tell you love and hugs and kisses all the time, but you always know that he's there." Griffey's personal style—often gruff, usually tough, always smart and dead serious— could equally fit John Shaft the private detective played by Richard Roundtree in the Blaxploitation classic *Shaft*, and many Black fathers of his generation. But fatherwise, Griffey shares more with the classic

Black evangelical preacher. Like Daddy Grace and Father Divine, Griffey leads his congregation—the community of employees and artists who have surrounded him through the eighteen years since Solar Records was founded—with a combination of paternalistic charisma, seemingly heaven-sent vision, and a well-delivered slice of practical teaching, all while quietly doing good by his own pocket.

Beyond the most rarefied pantheon of record executives—which includes John Hammond (who discovered Billie Holiday, Bessie Smith, Bob Dylan, and Bruce Springsteen), Ahmet Ertegun and Jerry Wexler (Aretha Franklin, Ray Charles, John Coltrane, Led Zeppelin), and Berry Gordy (Michael Jackson, Stevie Wonder, Diana Ross, Marvin Gaye)—there may be no record man, white or Black, who could not envy Griffey's record for locating talent. Griffey unearthed both L.A. & Babyface and Jimmy Jam & Terry Lewis, far and away the top two teams of R&B songwriter-producers of the past decade. Subtract them and it's very possible there would be no Boyz II Men, no Janet Jackson, no TLC, no Toni Braxton, and no *Waiting to Exhale* soundtrack in its present form. Griffey is also responsible for Leon Sylvers, a top R&B producer in the early 80s; Reggie Calloway, a top R&B producer in the mid 80s; and the Solar galaxy of stars from the 80s including the Whispers, Shalamar (from which the singer Jody Watley emerged), Lakeside, Midnight Star, and the Deele. He educated Suge Knight as well, and without him America would almost surely have less Tupac Shakur, less Dr. Dre, and conceivably, no Snoop Doggy Dogg.

Griffey has not compiled this record by simply aligning himself with obviously talented people: thanks to what he called "a gift from God," he consistently recognized more talent in people than even they saw in themselves. "Most of the major producers Dick found he saw early on," said Babyface. "Picked the talent before they turned into the talent. Before they actually got it right." The most compelling example is Babyface (born Kenny Edmonds, he and L.A. split up in 1990), undoubtedly the greatest R&B songwriter-producer of the past decade, the Steven Spielberg of the community. At three separate points in Babyface's early career, Griffey urged and paid for him to sing lead, produce music, and record a solo album, at times when the shy Babyface consid-

ered himself unable to complete those tasks. Most of Griffey's great dis-
coveries tell similar stories. "He put dreams in your head," a former employee said. "Impossible dreams in your head."

Meanwhile, he pulled from your wallet. In the 80s Griffey became
a multimillionaire, owning racehorses and a five-story office building in
Hollywood, zipping around the country with the Reverend Jesse Jackson
as the national finance committee chairman for Jackson's '84 presidential
campaign, and developing an African diamond, oil, and gold-mining
company called ADPIC (African Development Public Investment Corporation). At the same time he maintained contracts with his artists that
were, according to a high-ranking source very familiar with them, "un-
conscionable." The source added, "A lot of the artists loved him because
he gave a shot to groups and producers that had no shot otherwise. What
happened later on was a big letdown in that as they got more successful
they realized they weren't gonna make it with him because they realized
he was still gonna jerk around with the royalties."

Considered in the context of his industry, however, Griffey's
record becomes more reputable. "He had unfair contracts, but so do
most record companies," said L.A. attorney Don Engel, who has represented Griffey and represented artists against him. "It's a business that
encourages it. I have yet to have an audit of a record company, and I
conduct them regularly, I've never had one that didn't show a substantial underpayment. All the major record companies. On an absolute
scale, he's a bad guy. But he's in a business where the other companies
are not doing much better if they're doing better at all."

And also like the evangelists and a host of twentieth-century Black
preachers, Griffey has a boldly Black nationalist goal for his ministry. Believing that Black culture is a resource as natural and potentially profitable for Blacks as oil is for Arabs, he has handpicked and trained a
squadron of producers, artists, and behind-the-mics folk—like the
people who would become the manager for the million-selling singing
group En Vogue, the top Black concert promoter working today, and the
Hollywood producer behind the films *New Jack City* and *A Thin Line Between
Love and Hate*—in hopes that, armed with knowledge of their industry,
they would snatch economic control of Black culture for Black people.

"We always gettin some crumbs off the table," Griffey said. "But we need to get the whole pie. And then we pass out the slices. See, you look around at this industry and our culture is responsible for a lot of stuff. When I say 'our culture' that means us and those that copy us. Whether it's Miles Davis or Kenny G, our culture. Bob Marley or Snow. Hammer or Vanilla Ice. Mariah Carey or Whitney. You name it, it's us and people who borrow from us and you see it being exported all over the world. You go to Japan and you see little kids runnin around with baggy pants and their caps on the side of their heads. But we don't own nothing. We're still sharecroppin. And what I'm tryin to do is keep us from sharecroppin."

The evening after Griffey's visit with Knight, hours after Solar staffers punched out, a crew of seven twentyish Black men—their heads bald or cornrowed, their thick chests in dark warm-up suits or khaki shirts—sauntered into Solar's offices. The young men—who Griffey will later call, in their presence, "a roomful of killers," (to which they will laugh approvingly)—were Crips and Bloods as well as friends of Griffey's: he also referred to them as his "children" and a few of them called him "Pops." Griffey has long been friendly with young Black L.A. gang-bangers, helping them try to grow out of the gang life and, if possible, join the record business. That night they sat with Griffey in his office, well-mannered and reverent, hanging on his every word as he lectured them in an impromptu class. You could say it was the night session at what many call the University of Griffey.

Professor Griffey leapt from behind his desk and snatched up a large framed photograph of himself standing between Reverend Jackson and Samora Machel, the late president of Mozambique. He pointed to Machel. "This is the man here who started the revolution against the Portuguese to free Mozambique and Angola," he said passionately, nearly preaching. "He was takin the Portuguese—takin the crackers—out in the bush and cuttin their heads off and sendin 'em back sayin, 'We got to have our freedom!!' The bottom line is: we can do some shit, but we gotta have some discipline. They had to have discipline."

The class was quiet and impressed. After a pregnant silence, one piped up. "How you pronounce his name?"

"Sah-more-ah Michelle."

"Sah-more-ah Michelle," they repeated to themselves as if in a language class. "Samora Machel."

Griffey ambled back behind his desk and pointed to a white cordless telephone. "See this phone right here? When I made my deal with Sony in 1989 [for the company to distribute Solar], I got a call on this phone right here. It was a conference call from Andre Harrell [the president of Motown] and Russell Simmons [the president and founder of Def Jam]. 'Dick Griffey!! You is the baddest motherfucker we ever seen in the history of the bizness!!' "

They laughed.

"Man, I was just a smart Black man out here doin the same thing y'alls doin in the streets—survivin!"

One particularly large, cornrowed man named Wes Crockett turned toward the others. Big Wes, as he's called, was among the very first to join the Bloods, a fifteen-year employee of Griffey, and Knight's older brother. "That's how he used to do Suge," Big Wes said. "And he listened."

When Griffey was four years old his parents divorced and his natural father, by and large, exited his life. He grew up in the projects of Nashville, Tennessee, traveled to Los Angeles with the navy, worked as a male nurse and a jazz drummer, played semipro football in a league that has since folded, and became a successful club owner, a very successful concert promoter, and the talent coordinator for the long-running TV show *Soul Train*. In 1975, he convinced *Soul Train* host and mastermind Don Cornelius that the clout and exposure of the show would make for a can't-miss label, and they founded Soul Train Records. Three hitless years later Cornelius dropped out and Griffey rechristened the label Solar for Sound of Los Angeles Records.

The man who has been like a father to Griffey for the last four decades is John T. McClain, Sr. When they met in the 1960s, McClain owned L.A.'s baddest jazz club, The It Club, where a who's who of jazz supernovas played. McClain was also one of the city's biggest drug dealers. Some say he was "the Black Godfather." His clientele consisted largely of stars, which apparently led him into some interesting situations with some interesting people. McClain "introduced Ava Gardner to Negroes," was present at Bugsy's Siegel's home the night he was murdered, and had Peter Lawford testify as a character witness for him at his trial. Nevertheless, he was convicted ("for narcotics," McClain said) and sat in prison for nine years where the magnetically charismatic McClain, "was treated like a king," he recalled proudly. "The warden loved me. The police loved me. Did anything I want." Now, he's largely a ghetto philanthropist. "He's known for takin care of all the youngsters in the hood," said Griffey, who called McClain "filthy rich." "You got somethin to be financed, go see Mr. McClain." It's said the actor Denzel Washington wants to put his life story on-screen. McClain isn't interested.

From McClain Griffey got money—"We couldn't put together a business plan and go to Wells Fargo and get no money," Griffey said—as well as lessons in conduct. "I learned from him to be an honorable person," Griffey said. "I learned from him to pay my bills. I learned from him to keep my word. I learned from him you didn't need no contract to keep my word. I learned from him to be respectful." Asked why he helped Griffey, McClain said simply, "I just liked him."

One sunny afternoon Griffey went to visit McClain at his Beverly Hills apartment. As usual, McClain's door was unlocked, so without knocking, Griffey tiptoed in. "Pops?" he called out. A short moment later the wire-thin seventy-four-year-old eased into view, his dark skin slightly wrinkled, his gray hair combed neatly back, wearing a double-breasted navy blazer, gray slacks, and a large sapphire pinky ring. He radiated gentlemanly elegance.

Griffey hugged McClain delicately, as if the elder man would crumble into ash if squeezed too firmly. They stepped into McClain's dimly lit living room filled with incredibly plush furniture and sank down. Just then, a tear began finding its way down Griffey's cheek.

The day before, immediately following the Samora Machel lecture, Griffey led his Crip and Blood friends down to the Solar Tower's basement parking lot. They were about to head over to a local Spanish restaurant where, Griffey promised, they served, "chicken so tender it falls off the bone." As men moved toward their cars, the two largest among them, one a Crip, one a Blood, began arguing. Then, one pulled up his sweatshirt, showing the handgun tucked into his sweatpants, and threatened to use it. Chaos was a hair-trigger away. Some lined up behind their ally, others leapt to their cellulars. "Niggas is trippin!!" one yelled into his phone. "Get down here with all the homies!!" Griffey stood between the two, a hand on each chest, keeping them apart. Over and again adrenaline would subside, the battle nearly done, but one or the other would say something or recall something said or recall that there was an audience around him, and Griffey alone—less his arms than their respect for him—would keep them separate. Finally, he managed to convince one and thus the other to go home. But he was reminded how little it took for his young friends to shift gears. Despondent, he went to the Spanish restaurant alone.

"They're killing each other, Pops," Griffey told McClain, a handful of tears now slipping slowly down his face.

"Yes, that's right," McClain rasped. He crossed his thin legs at the knee and both legs pointed straight down.

Griffey suddenly dropped to kneel on the floor and placed a hand on McClain's knee. "All they want is an opportunity, man," he said, his voice breaking. "And they don't know how to do nothin."

"They won't let ya tell 'em."

"They will!" he said with steely conviction. "I'm gettin 'em to listen!"

"That's a miracle in itself."

Griffey laughed. His eyes began to dry. "Them kids, when they was comin up, they ain't never had nobody do nothin for 'em. So they down there doin what they do. They would rather sell records, or sell diamonds, or sell clothes, or sell whatever. See, you have to work with 'em a certain way. You let them go and do—just like you do with me—and if you see them makin a mistake, you call 'em and you tell 'em." He paused.

"Pops," Griffey continued, "before you go, and we all gon go."

"We all gon go."

"We all got to go. I just want you to help me save these niggas lives out there that's killin each other, before you go. We gon work on doin that."

"Yes."

"I got the Bloods . . . I got Suge . . ."

"He's completely crazy."

"No." Griffey put his hand up. "No. He ain't completely crazy."

"He ain't?"

"No, Pops. He respects you. He respects me. He just don't know no better."

"He should learn something from you, too."

"He needs to hear our story. He needs to know how we worked together. And then he'll work with me the way you worked with me."

"Yes."

After an hour of talking, McClain tired. Griffey took him outside for a short walk and then McClain went up to bed.

When Griffey schools his flock about the music business, he has two central principles. One is that the foundation of the music business is the song. "Take Babyface, great producer," he said one rainy afternoon while guiding his black Lincoln Town Car down the freeway, "and Whitney Houston, great singer, and a mediocre song, and a great marketing effort. You'll have a well-performed, well-produced, well-marketed piece of shit. But if you start with a great song you'll usually end up with a success. You can go to any Baptist church any Sunday and find some folks up there in the choir that could outsing anybody you hear on the radio. This ain't the singing business. This is the songs business."

His other favorite principle is that power in the music business flows from owning the master tapes that you, or your artists, create. Griffey compared owning masters to "a license to print money."

The import of owning masters is stressed in what may be Griffey's best teaching aid: an hour-long videotaped lecture called "From Slave Ship to Ownership." In the tape, Griffey is seated in his office, wearing a Hawaiian-print short-sleeve shirt, speaking to an off-camera interviewer in language that occasionally sounds Farrakhan-esque. "We picked cotton," Griffey says, "and at the end of the day we turned that over to the master who would then market and distribute it for us and we'd get back a royalty. In other words we'd get back enough to get a little shack and a horse and buggy. They called that sharecropping. Well, today, we pick talent. Whether it's Michael or Sunny Ade or Janet or Snoop or Dre or the Whispers. And in the end it comes down to something we call a master. Then we turn that master over to the master who markets and distributes it for us so now some of us can get a royalty. So we can get a bigger house and a Mercedes, but the name of the game is still the same. We still sharecropping. We still creating assets for other people."

In a recent article, Knight said, "[My] first goal [as CEO of Death Row] was to own our masters. Without your master tapes you ain't got shit, period." "I read that," Griffey said, "and I remember smilin.'"

Ownership of Death Row's masters, it seems, is among the things that have come between Knight and Griffey. In an agreement signed January 7, 1991, back when Griffey was tutoring Knight on a daily basis, Griffey promised to advise Knight in his "career in the entertainment business in general" for three years in return for "an irrevocable 25 percent interest in [Knight's] gross publishing income." The following week Knight returned to Griffey's office with the D.O.C. (born Tracy Curry) and Dr. Dre (Andre Young), respectively, one of the greatest lyric writers and probably the greatest music producer in the history of hiphop. The three played Griffey music that he didn't particularly care for, but clearly saw the value of. "I told Suge," Griffey said, "if these cats can go out and make these kind of records, not only can I show him how to get paid, I can show him how to own his own company. And it was at that point I put Death Row together."

The next week the four signed an agreement to create a music-publishing and record company of which Griffey would own 50 percent and Dre and D.O.C. would own 50 percent. Knight was not offered a share because he was merely managing Dre and D.O.C., but per Knight's request, after it was signed, Griffey said, he excused the lawyers and Knight, and he asked Dre and D.O.C. to give Knight a piece of the company. They agreed: Griffey would keep 42.5 percent, as would Dre and D.O.C., and Knight would take 15 percent. The written agreement does not reflect this new arrangement.

Knight, Dre, D.O.C., and Calvin Broadus, better known as Snoop

Doggy Dogg, went into the studio on the third floor of Griffey's Solar Tower and recorded The Chronic, the 1992 album that would sell over three million copies and put them on MTV ubiquitously and in Mercedes permanently.

But before the album's release, the distribution arrangement Griffey had set up with Sony was dashed for virulent lyrics, and at the urging of John McClain, Griffey introduced Knight to top executives at Interscope, where McClain's son, John, Jr., was an executive. Griffey then traveled to San Diego on business. He returned a few days later, but it would be years before Knight would again return his beeps.

"One of them [at Interscope], I don't know who did it, one of them convinced Suge that Griff was tryin to fuck him over," said Wes Crockett, Knight's older brother and, recently, D.O.C.'s manager. "So they [Knight et. al] made a deal behind his [Griffey's] back with Interscope. Even though Griff had brought them to Interscope. Even though Griff had paperwork [signed agreements] on everybody: D.O.C., Dre, Suge, the whole thing. They still went behind his back and made a deal and sold out his portion." Like Knight, Griffey begged off specific questions about the interlude because of the pending litigation. But Griffey acidly offered an explanation for why Knight would leave him after their years together: "Our slavery mentality that tells us white folks' ice is colder."

Reluctantly, Griffey allowed Interscope to distribute The Chronic, and was paid between three and four hundred thousand dollars for the rights. But Griffey was never paid for his share of Death Row and has never seen a dividend. A source close to the situation said that in recent settlement talks, Knight offered Griffey, "two million dollars and other stuff." Griffey turned him down. "It makes me sick," Griffey said. "I am in a fight with Suge over crumbs, while the white boys is makin all the money off of what we created. MCA just bought half the company for two hundred million dollars and me and Suge, my little brother that I brought into the business, that didn't know nothin, now me and him got to fight over crumbs. So there we go again. Sharecroppin and buildin assets for other people."

3. Big Willies

Best Rapper Alive

{ Puff Daddy, *The Village Voice*, 1997 }

Uncle Herbie was a rapper. Six foot three with long, gangly limbs and a voice so deep and smooth Barry White would've stopped in his tracks, Herbie spent nights at Pegasus, the nightclub he owned, and days at the racetrack. His name stayed on Mom and Dad's lips. *Herbie says he's earned $1 million in his life. . . . Herbie had another fight with his new girlfriend. . . . Herbie's declaring bankruptcy. . . .*

One day Herbie and my father, his younger brother, went out on the porch and played chess. The game, number five hundred-something in the decades-old rivalry, was fought to the death. I, just tall enough to see the board, stood by, watching their little war. I don't remember who won, just that while Dad seemed to be moving pieces, somehow the way Herbie's pawns and bishops and knights were flowing told on him, his passion, his sexuality, his way of elegantly powering through life like a classy bull.

Uncle Herbie was a rapper. So what he never saw the inside of a recording studio, never held a microphone. For some, the medium is their life. The constraints of traditional technique are thrown out because they're dealing with something larger. Their art tools are cultural heat, a willingness to live onstage, a ferocious ability to self-mythologize, and a way of making art that is somehow a window onto their life. Their life is the medium.

Sean Combs is a rapper. Not much of an MC—his flow is often slow and choppy, his voice low in texture, his rhymes often uninspired. But Sean is an American Star, and he plays the role with such gusto it's pointless to talk about him in strict musical terms. The man approaches life as a dramatic art form and lives more epically than anyone in hiphop still breathing. The album is John Blaze (read: dope) because of its three-dimensionality, the way it is not simply music, but statements from and on a specific life so that it all tells on Sean, his willingness to put himself on the world's stage, warts and all. Love him or hate him, Puff brings to the table a star power no amount of MC expertise can match. Shit, at this moment he's the best rapper alive. More after this commercial break.

To the Mad Writer (little brother of the Mad Rapper and the Mad Producer):
     Can't be a sun without planets. Can't be a star without fans. Can't be a pimp without ho's. And certainly can't be a player without player-haters. So, from me to you, thanks for hating.
Sincerely,
T.

What is an MC? Someone who makes art with rhymes. Who impresses hiphop experts and is rewarded with the term, much as one is knighted.
     What is a rapper? Maybe an MC, maybe not. If a great rapper, a star. He has presence, style, charisma, flava. He entertains, no, captivates with rhymes as well as his body, his face, his life.
     An MC is a poet.
     A rapper is a performance artist.
     An MC—Rakim, Guru, Kane, Q-Tip—needs a tasty voice, liquid flow, and something to say.
     A rapper—Snoop, Tupac, Big, Chuck D, KRS—needs a life that is perpetual theater.
     An MC gets onstage and drops dope rhymes.
     A rapper never gets offstage.
     Indeed, all the world's successful people are either MCs or rappers. Anyone who succeeds mainly through raw ability is an MC. Those who make the show be their lives and their lives be the show—they are rappers.

Ol Dirty is a rapper. The Gza an MC.
     Dennis Rodman is a rapper. Scottie Pippen an MC.

Tyson, rapper. Holyfield, MC.
Mary J., rapper. Whitney, MC.
Jean-Michel Basquiat, rapper. Romare Bearden, MC.
Clarence Thomas, rapper. Thurgood Marshall, MC.
Pryor, rapper. Murphy, MC.
Zora Neale Hurston, rapper. Toni Morrison, MC.
Satchmo, Bird, Miles, Billie, rappers.
Duke, Ornette, Ella, Sonny, MCs.
Magic, rapper. Bird, MC.
Michael, rapper. Janet, MC.

Ask yourself: If my life were a movie, would it be exciting? The key word there is not exciting. It's movie. We're not talking film—intelligent, introspective, expertly crafted. I mean movie—populist, over-the-top, and electrifying, chock-full with gunplay and trials and ILM special effects and classic dialogue and long, sweaty sexual escapades. You judge a film on how artful it is. You judge a movie on how much fun it is—whether it entertains. Is your life a movie? You may be living a movie if you've hidden in the Amtrak bathroom three times a week so you could get from Howard University in D.C. to intern at Uptown in Manhattan, begged your way to an Uptown A&R job at twenty-one, performed mouth-to-mouth on the stairs at CCNY as nine people died around you, survived the subsequent public outcry, architected the cultural skyscraper named Mary J. Blige, spat on a coworker at Uptown, seduced a writer into doing a lengthy *Vibe* profile on you while you were still an employee, gotten fired from Uptown by your father figure with the line "There can be only one lion in the jungle," survived to create a major entertainment company on the back of a drug dealer turned genius rapper and virtuoso MC, become a multimillionaire before twenty-five, gotten punched in the face by Grand Puba, produced Mary J.'s perfect *My Life*, told Andre "You're over! Harlem is mine!," done interviews and said "I'm on God's dick," gotten dissed in front of the entire *Source* Awards audience by Suge Knight and survived, knocked Michael Jackson out of the No. 1 slot with "One More Chance," seen Suge's homeboy murdered in Atlanta, gotten accused of setting it up, survived, been present the night Tupac was shot (in Manhattan), gotten accused of setting that up, survived, called Minister Farrakhan's son in an attempt to squash the escalating beef with Suge, heard of a photograph to be put in the Source of Suge with your son on his knee and his arm around your son's mother, put Allen Iverson and Stephon Marbury on your team at the Rucker tournament, been rumored to have tried to slit your wrist (or actually slit your wrist?), mysteriously split with Mary J., helped make one of the greatest hiphop albums ever, Big's Life After Death, seen a naked photo of yourself on the Internet, said on a record, "Young, Black, and famous/With money hangin out the anus," stood just feet away as Biggie was perforated by bullets, survived, appeared on the cover of Rolling Stone wearing Versace just days after his murder with the cover line "the New King of Hiphop". . . .

And the memoiristic No Way Out only extends the movie. Before you even crack open the jewel box the album tells: the mere fact of it proves Sean's arrogance—originally the debut was called Puff Daddy's Greatest Hits—his narcissism, his business acumen. The songs are something else. It's not as difficult as Sly Stone's There's a Riot Goin On, but it's not as listener-friendly as Life After Death. The work of a man who doesn't need the money but can't help making it, a man of insurmountable resilience faced with an unbearable loss, No Way Out is filled with brilliant, exhilarating party records—smashes—like "Victory," "It's All About the Benjamins," and "Been Around the World," and personal, poignant, anticommercial moments like "Pain," "If I Die Tonight," and the prelude to "I'll Be Missing You" ("I can't wait 'til that day I see your face again," he says softly to Big), on which you wouldn't be surprised if his voice cracked like Michael Jackson's on "She's Out of My Life."

As Marvin Gaye's Here, My Dear is an album for his ex-wife and second for those who've had a heart-breaking fallout, No Way Out is first for Big, and afterwards for anyone who's lost someone. The message to Big is exactly what the first two songs—"Victory," a classic Big joint, and "Been Around the World," featuring Mase—and the last two songs—"I'll Be Missing You" and "Can't Nobody Hold Me Down"—suggest: We're still thinking of you and We're going on like you would've wanted. The aesthetic holes, the album's weaknesses, speak of where Big might've gone, of what might've been.

I know it's cool, at least in New York, to hate Puff Daddy. But I can't be that cool. Sean may not be extending the limits of hiphop music with his flow, but he is extending the limit of hiphop generation celebrity by living every day like it's his last. Herbie's last day followed a severe liver problem, a hospital stay, a wedding, a family fight. Then he was gone. That day, a long, indigo Saturday, I sat in my room trying to imagine all the missed opportunities, all the squandered days, all the moments that would never come.

Does the sun shine forever?

Sean, live your life.

Hiphop's Biggest Kid Grows Up

{ Russell Simmons, *Playboy*, 2005 }

Let me tell you two stories about Russell Simmons. I first met him in 1994 at Time Café in downtown Manhattan. I was there to interview him for a magazine story. We spoke for twenty minutes and then his partner in crime Brett Ratner, then a little hiphop video director, now a Hollywood director, showed up smiling like the boy who's successfully stolen cookies from the kitchen. After a few minutes Russell left the table without a word—back then he lived in a gigantic apartment above Time Café—and didn't return for thirty minutes. When he came back we finished the interview. Funny thing is, he'd showered. Later I found out that Simmons had gone up to his place and had sex with a sumptuous model whom Ratner had just finished with, then washed up and came back. But I wasn't surprised: back then for Russell Simmons loose sex with a hot model in the middle of the afternoon was an average day.

But over the last ten years Simmons has grown into a completely different being and that's what the second story is about. Earlier this year, we were doing an interview for this story in his beefy SUV, being driven down Seventh Avenue by his longtime driver and friend from back in the days in Queens, Kenny Lee. The cab in front of us stopped abruptly and Kenny slammed on the brakes to avoid a collision. Lee, jaw clenched with road rage, pulled up beside the cab and was just about to curse the driver out, but before he could say anything Simmons, as serene as Buddha said, "He's doing the best he can." Simmons's patience calmed Lee and he leaned back in the truck and said to the cabbie,

"You're a nice guy." It was an impressive display of love thy neighbor even in spite of thy neighbor's shitty driving. "I try to see what's good," Simmons said. "Spit out the bones. Let that shit go. Just try to plant good seeds. Promote good karma. You're better off just fuckin with God. Everything else is bullshit."

In the sentence, "You're better off just fuckin with God," you see at once how much Russell has changed over the last ten years and how much he has not. Nowadays he speaks of God and spirituality as much as a proselytizing evangelical, while a decade ago he was a world-class hedonist who had lots of women and did lots of drugs. And he's talking about *fuckin with* God, his classic all-but-politically-incorrect blustering style.

Russell Simmons is forty-five and over the last ten years he has grown and changed as much as any person I've ever seen. Where he once was frenetic, hypersexual, and immensely self-centered, he's become patient, spiritual, forgiving, and, sometimes, calm. "He was a guy who could never be alone," says Nelson George, a longtime friend and the author of Simmons's autobiography *Life and Def*. "One of the reasons he had so many women was because he didn't wanna go home alone. He always had a posse around him and there was always a lot of shit goin on. That's not true anymore. Now he can sit by himself in a room. He used to be all action, adventure. What's happenin next, where we goin next, where the bitches at, where the drugs at, where the party at? That guy is gone. Replaced by a guy who can sit by himself and think. Who can actually reflect. Who enjoys the idea of calmness. Who values it."

Simmons has always been a relentlessly on-message salesman (he would make a dream candidate). Once upon a time he would talk nonstop about Kurtis Blow, back when he was his manager. Then he was nonstop about his artists at Def Jam, like Public Enemy, LL Cool J, and the Beastie Boys. Then all he talked about was Phat Farm, his clothing line. Then his films, like *Nutty Professor* and *The Funeral*. Now it's religion, yoga, his philanthropies, his work with the Hip-Hop Summit Action Network. All of that springs from the same place: he's been spiritually awakened by passing forty and becoming a father, and now he's driven to give back, to be a public servant.

And yet, while he's changed immensely, he remains very much the same. Simmons has always been something of a boy-king. He smiles like a naif, dresses down, says he doesn't read, plays dumb, begs you to underestimate his intelligence and even, perhaps, his power. His ex-girlfriend Michelle Griffin says, "He totally plays dumb. He's like Jessica Simpson. People think she's a dumb blonde and she's like, OK, I'll take the dumb blonde. Russell will be like, I'll play the dumb nigger. But he gets in there and it's like, joke on them."

His empire is built largely on his charm. "Russell is the second most charming person I've ever met," says Nelson George, who ranks Quincy Jones number one. "Russell's always comfortable in many different spaces. Back in the day you might go with him to dinner someplace downtown, then a hard-core hiphop spot, and then an elite party where Madonna might be and rich white people, and then a gay party, and he was able to move in all those spaces. One minute he's talking to some rapper about his girlfriends and the next he's talking to the head of a corporation about his wife and kids and how they'll hang out in the Hamptons this summer. And he was able to keep flowing through all these spaces. And that's always amazed me. But one of his keys to this whole thing is the intangible, that personal ability to connect with people, and he's really, really good at it. That ability to make people laugh, to feel comfortable, to be drawn to him. That's made everything possible." Bill Adler, who worked at Def Jam in its early years, said that back in the early 80s, before Russell was rich and famous, "he had carte blanche everywhere in the city all because of his charm."

Russell is someone who loves to dominate the moment with shocking jokes that seem to challenge the social convention, saying things that are potentially uncouth or playfully rude—like telling someone's mother a dirty joke or calling a prominent white businessman "nigga" in a crowd—and yet he has a certain funny way of saying it and smiling with innocent twinkling eyes that gets everyone laughing with him. With women he has the same power. "He managed somehow to say things to women that other guys could not say," a friend says. "Like, come in the bathroom and suck my dick. And girls would do it. This is even before he was a millionaire per se. He always had a charming way about him and he was very good at picking out the girl who was willing to go for it. He always had a really remarkable capacity for getting girls to do things that other guys couldn't."

Russell just gets people. His success in the bedroom comes from the same place as his success in the boardroom: he understands people and knows how to win them over to his side. "Most of the pussy people get is because some girl wants a hug," he said. Reverend Run, Russell's younger brother by seven years, says, "I find that people don't care about what you have, they care about if you care. People love Russell because they know he cared. And your net worth is determined by your network. So he networks very well."

Several friends called him the virtuoso of the phone and noted that his ability to stay on the pulse of things without reading came from being amazingly social and sponging information from people. "He does not waste a moment being around people he could learn from," says Glenn Friedman, a photographer and an old friend. "He does not waste a second. He soaks it all up." Gary Harris, a record executive and another old friend says, "He's this great social chameleon who can tap into other people's perspectives and begin to, through osmosis, learn what their get-down is. His whole thing is transference of information. That's the secret to his success. Listening to what you're talking about, disseminating what has value to him, chucking what has no value to him, and then lasering in whatever his objective is and making it all work for him."

He's also an incredibly passionate and persistent salesman. "If he saw a movie guy he'd pitch a movie," Ratner says. "If he saw a record guy they'd start talking about promotion. If he ran into a radio-station guy he'd say, let's start the first hiphop satellite network. He's always throwin ideas out. He's the best salesman. He's a showman. He's P. T. Barnum. He's a guy who's just constantly selling."

He manages people with a benevolent hand, hiring people he thinks are smarter than him, giving them power, listening to all around him, inspiring loyalty. And he gets others involved in his mission by getting their ideas involved with his. "One of the things I learned from Russell," says Danny Simmons, his older brother by four years, "you don't lose anything by including people. You just make what you're do-ing stronger. You don't try to exclude people. Include as many people as you possibly can, because then it becomes something more significant. If I took anything away from Russell, it's not to be selfish with shit. Like ideas. When you give other people credit it makes you bigger. You don't need all the credit for your damn self."

Wendy Credle, a lawyer who's worked for Russell, says, "You wanna see him win, you wanna help him win, because he's a nice guy. He's lovable, he's fun, and what he says makes sense so you support it. It's good business and I like you. And Russell wants to hear your opin-ion. It's not all about him. He always wants to stay in touch rather than thinking he's above it all. And that makes your employees feel impor-tant."

As he showed me around his office he referred to several of his top people as "my boss." Later he said, "As a person who runs a com-pany you become a servant of everyone in the office. Your job is to di-rect their talent. As a leader you're a servant whose job is to give direction. No is not a good answer. Let's work on it, let's figure it out. Most of the people who work for me stay because I think using people's ideas is very important and using their talent and giving people auton-omy and giving people room but direction and trying to help them get their ideas across."

He seems to always be at work, every second of the day, but that's because he loves his work passionately. "I believe that he finds his work to be play," Adler says. "Including the roughest negotiations. I remem-ber one day at Def Jam he was screaming at somebody and while he was genuinely hot, he was also playing. I went in to his office to see who he was yelling at and he caught my eye and in the middle of a rant he turned this huge thousand-watt smile on me. And I got the idea that he was just putting it on. He likes the deal. He loves negotiating. He loves the action."

He's the boy-king who takes a real sense of play into everything he does, rumbling into new businesses based on instinct alone, taking big risks because he loves the action as opposed to, say, Puffy, who comes across much more calculating and arrogant. "There's an undercurrent anger in Puff that boils over," says someone who knows both men well. "He's just not charming. Puffy is naked ambition without the charm. Russell is charming. And charm buys him a lot of leeway." Where both Russell and Puff have built empires based around personality, taste, lifestyle, and icon, only Russell has a way of maintaining his humility while plastering his name all over the country, because Russell's movement doesn't seem to be about his ego. "I think it's about the job more than about him," Danny Simmons says. "I think he sees himself as a tool. I don't think it's about his personal satisfaction and ego, I think that he realizes he's a brand and he sees himself as a brand. He's selling Russell Simmons, but it doesn't necessarily make him any better than anybody else."

Let me do two more stories about Russell. The first isn't really a story, it's more of an anecdote. "When Russell came home from the clubs," Reverend Run says, recalling his youth as the little brother, "I went and cooked breakfast for him. I remember him coming in in the morning with Kurtis Blow, laying on the couch downstairs. I'd be just getting up and they'd be just getting in and I didn't wanna really wake them up, but I would make a lot of noise cuz I was excited to see dudes older than me laying around. And I'd cook up as much bacon and eggs as I could so they'd smell it, then I'd wake 'em up. I'd say, 'Wake up, Russell, look what I got!' And he'd say 'Wow. Unbelievable. Thanks Joey.'"

The other story is from Danny Simmons, Russell's older brother, who remembered that at the beginning, when he was a party promoter in Queens, Russell had everyone in the family lending him money. One day when he had no one else to turn to, he asked Danny for two thousand dollars so he could rent a hall to throw a party in Hollis, Queens. Danny gave Russell money from his college fund and Russell had a profitable party. But then Danny got wind that some group was planning to rob Russell after the party and, being larger and tougher, Danny had to run down to the club to secure Russell's money. When they got home Danny asked for his two thousand dollars back, after all he'd saved Russell twice now. But Russell refused. I gotta reinvest this, Russell said. They went back and forth, the anger escalating, until a fight broke out.

"We had a huge fight, very physical, in my parents' house," Danny says. "Up and down the stairs we battled. But Russell was pretty good in karate. He had on cowboy boots and he kicked me in my ear, split my ear open. I had to go to the hospital and get my ear stitched up." Danny never got the money back.

Once upon a time, the man was nicknamed Caligula. He was a sexually decandent, world-class hedonist who had lots of ménages à trois and not a few orgies. In the 90s he dated a bisexual woman who opened his horizons and for years he was obsessed with bisexual women. His posse was a traveling bacchanal. "The funny thing about Russell as a sexual being is he was a rainmaker," a friend says. "There was such an atmosphere of carnality around him at that time that if you just hung around long enough and were cool, you would end up getting some pussy." And, of course, Simmons was getting all kinds of pussy. "I can't tell you how many girls said, Russell, you will never get this," according to Glenn Friedman. "And sure enough, he would call me the next day sayin, Why wouldn't she give it to me? Of course she did."

In the 90s Simmons spent lots of time chasing models and once seriously considered starting a model-management agency with Ratner. It was to be called, of course, Rush Model Management. "Every time we went out we went up to models and were like, you guys gotta join our agency!" Ratner said. "You wanna be down with us! We'll put you in music videos and if you have a voice you could be an artist. It's not just an agency, it's a full-service model agency! We didn't have contracts, but girls would say, I'll sign with you!" But it went nowhere.

One day, backstage at a show during Fashion Week in New York, he met a sixteen-year-old model named Kimora Lee. He began sending her tons of flowers, his normal wooing method. "He sent me a jungle, a tree, a safari," Kimora said. "They could barely get it up to my apartment. It took several people to get it up to my sixth-floor walk-up. They were the most beautiful things I'd ever seen and I called Tyra [Banks] and said, 'Girl, you can't imagine how beautiful they are,' and she said, 'Actually, I can. He sent them to me about a month ago.'"

They were married in 1998 and have two kids, Ming Lee, who's almost five, and Aoki Lee, who's two. Both Russell and Kimora say they want to adopt. "We're thinking about renting some kids," Russell says. Kimora sees them adopting at least three, possibly more. Russell says, "I think we should."

Sometimes the two seem to be a publicity mismatch. Russell is the charismatic, down-to-earth kid in school who gets along with absolutely everyone (can you ever remember Russell having an enemy?) while Kimora is more, shall we say, controversial. Sometimes this is because she comes on a bit strong. Asked why he chose to marry her, Kimora sort of gloated, as if she'd won a tournament.

"Well, if you looked at all the women in Russell's life and looked at what they were doing today, I think that would maybe answer itself." Russell doesn't exactly help the situation by saying off-color things about his wife in public. For example, he's a strict vegan (he says, "Everything I eat is nonanimal, nothing to do with no egg, dairy, fish, none of that shit,") but she's not, and though he's completely accepting of her choices, he'll still say to people, "My wife will eat an elephant's armpit."

But Russell loves her because she challenges him, because she's outspoken, because she's controversial. "He's had some really ill artists," says Nelson George. "He loves them the most. He loves the artists who cause trouble. He loves them. And he really enjoys the notoriety of his wife. She's ill and people talk about her and that's so consistent with the artists he's loved the most."

And he respects her because she's a good businesswoman. "Somehow people think I paid for her shit," he says. "I don't buy her shit. I did buy her one of those cars, but I would never buy her shit like that. I don't buy her shit. Ever. Really. I don't buy her anything. She just made twenty million dollars the other day."

She's building a Russell-esque empire based around her image and lifestyle. She has Baby Phat, a syndicated TV show called *Life and Style*, a line of cosmetics, a fragrance, and a book coming, as well as a line called Hello, Kitty by Kimora Lee Simmons. "They've never cobranded in their life," she says with pride. She went on to pat herself on the back. "I was a young woman when I met this wealthy, charismatic, famous guy," she says. "Most women that get married to rich, famous men, they don't work. I know there are some that do, but most women sit on their ass. I was not a dancer before I met him, I was not a waitress looking for a turnaround in my life. He did not buy me my first Herve Leger or Manolo Blahnik or nothing. I was a model! That's a whole other category of girls, I know. But I'm one of the ones with a brain. And now I'm a working mother with 155 jobs." Both insist that Kimora's businesses are not secretly run by Russell, but one suspects he must be the ghost in the machine: her empire looks just like his, selling a lifestyle as promoted by a specific individual who is cobranded throughout various mediums from clothes to phones to Hello, Kitty.

She also reminds him of his mother. "Yeah, Kimora's like my mother," he says. "Just like her. Independent, doesn't take any shit from anyone." And that's why Russell will take shit from her.

Gary Harris told me a story that seems to perfectly capture Russell and Kimora's relationship. Russell was waiting to board a helicopter that would take him to meet one of his partners in Phat Farm. Kimora, par for a diva, was late. Russell said, "She always does this." He was upset. Harris said, "So what you gonna do?" Russell replied, "Nothin."

In '96, when Russell got serious about Kimora, he was living in Los Angeles and devoting most of his attention to his film-producing career. His time in L.A. is critical in the grand scheme of his life—he committed to Kimora and yoga—but he did not have fun. He produced a few bad movies but despite his best efforts he failed to become a major player in Hollywood and also never cottoned to the slow pace of L.A. "Being able to go to yoga on time every day was not appealing to me," he says. "That's what Hollywood allows you. There was no such thing as work. Everybody has to see each other in the face to have a meeting and it was very difficult to take that lifestyle. Everybody went to lunch at a certain time. The secretary would be like, why do you think they're in? It's one o'clock. I prefer people goin to work every day."

But when he moved back to New York in '97 he continued doing yoga on a daily basis. He'd begun going for the girls and the social aspect, but quickly became hooked on the spirituality. At first he said to himself, "If I keep doin this shit I'ma lose all my money." But the opposite happened. "Because I was able to let go just for a minute, I was able to make a little more," he said, "Letting go is the key. Not being fearful and not being hung up on results. I'm not concerned with making money at all and I'm making more money than I've ever made in my life."

Indeed, yoga has helped him become a much better businessman. "I think it's enhanced his moneymaking ability," says Nelson George, who also does yoga. "It's calmed him down, given him more clarity, more focus. His sense of perspective is clearer about what he should be doing. At one point he and Brett were serious about starting a modeling agency. You guys are trying to make a business of meeting girls? That kind of stupid stuff he doesn't say anymore. That doesn't take up his mental time anymore."

But what's interesting about Russell's faith is that even in spirituality he's willing to listen to everyone's ideas and tries to include everyone in his tent. Ten years ago he was friends with Suge Knight and Martha Stewart. Now he's close with Muslim ministers, including Minister Louis Farrakhan; Christian ministers, including his brother; Jewish rabbis; and yogis. He prefers to see the similarity of the faiths and has a deep and equal respect for all of them. "All the books are the same," he says. "There are some observances that are different, but I think they're all the same. They're all exactly the same." He won't commit to any particular camp. "I believe in Christ consciousness," he says. "To be like Abraham, Muhammad, Lord Buddha, and all those things are one. The yogis call it sumati or a state of yoga. A total union with God. The Christians call it heaven on earth. Buddhists call it nirvana. I forget what the Muslims call it when you're in complete union and the yogis say . . ." and on and on, a pan-religious sermon that values complete focus on the Almighty. "When you call Run's house you know what he says?" Russell asks. "Praise the Lord. Keep your mind on God at all times!"

Spirituality led Russell to reconsider his values and lose interest in his wealth. "My house is thirty thousand square feet," he said of his place in Saddle River, New Jersey. "My movie theater is modeled after the Chinese Mann Theater. Indoor pool, meditation room is crazy. But it don't make no difference: I can only sit in one seat at a time. It doesn't

matter how many movie theaters you got, you can only sit your ass in
one seat. It's fun to make it and all that, but it's got nothing to do with
happiness. The more things you get the more unhappy you are. I got
thirteen billionaire friends. If I got thirteen billionaire friends I got ten
unhappy ones. Cuz they wanna keep getting money, they wanna keep
that one second of rush. But the rush is no good no more. You can get a
new Bentley, but I have more fun in my Volkswagen Bug." And those
feelings propelled him into giving back.

"When I met Russell he didn't know who the president was," says Brett
Ratner. "That might be a slight exaggeration, but he definitely didn't
know who the vice president was. He didn't know the difference between a congressman and a senator, he was just hiphop." But now he's a
political player who can get New York Senators Hillary Clinton and
Chuck Schumer on the phone, who's had meetings with Senators John
McCain and Joe Lieberman, who's thrown fund-raisers for Andrew
Cuomo and Jesse Jackson, Jr. In 2000 he hosted a panel at the Democ-
ractic National Convention about defining hiphop activism. He once
protested New York Mayor Mike Bloomberg's education budget cuts by
leading a march of thousands across the Brooklyn Bridge. His Hip-Hop
Summit Action Network barnstormed the country during the 2004
presidential campaign, registering thousands of urban voters in swing
states.

Russell's central political goal now is forcing a change in the
Rockefeller drug laws that minimize the amount of discretion judges
have in sentencing in drug cases. Sentencing is based on the weight of
drugs in your possession rather than the role you played in the operation, meaning judges find themselves with little choice but to give long
sentences even to nonviolent felons. "First time nonviolent drug offend-
ers are going to jail for twenty years," he says, incredulous, "and 95 percent of the people in jail because of this law are Black and brown. And
what's funny about that is whites and Blacks use and sell drugs at the
same rate. I know because I was high my whole life! I know who I got
high with. Just as many white people as Black people. But now that I'm
sober I see the absurdity of this law. I know that after thirty years that

law is gonna be changed." His politics aren't based around race but around class and he sees himself a crusader for the poor. And in this way, his political mission is related to his Def Jam mission of a generation ago. "Russell has built an empire on the taste of the working class," Gary Harris said. "Now he's attempting to address the problems of the working class, like the Rockefeller drug laws."

Russell's power as a political activist draws from his money, his fame and/or media savvy, and his reverence within the hiphop community. But as both Howard Dean and John Kerry saw in the 2004 election, it's difficult to depend on young voters. One day a year back Russell led a demonstration in front of city hall against Bloomberg's education budget cuts that included Jay-Z, Chuck D, Puffy, LL Cool J, Foxy Brown, and DJ Big Kap on the turntables. The celebs came up and spoke a little politics and the DJ kept it funky. Five thousand high-school kids were squeezed together, cheering along. It felt more like a small scale hiphop concert than a political rally, with rappers rhyming a little and then saying a little about education. They'd be followed by a little music, then a politician or an activist and then another rapper. But it's not always easy to mix hiphop and politics.

When Russell took the mic at the rally thousands of students quieted to hear him. He had on a baby-blue shirt that read "Education First." "What we are here today for is the most important thing in your life," he began. "Last year the mayor cut millions out the budget. Many of you don't have desks, you take Xeroxes home instead of textbooks. You have a very poor quality of education. You have to work twice as hard to be as good. We are not gonna let this go away! This isn't a party! This is about your future! This is . . . ." He was in the middle of his sentence when Jay-Z came into view on the crowded stage for the first time all day. The screaming and neck craning ended Russell's moment. Jay wasn't supposed to take the mic just then, but the crowd's reaction demanded it. He stepped to the front of the stage and Russell smiled wide as he gave Jay the mic. "No billion-dollar cut," he said. "Make some noise." And with that he walked off the stage. Russell took the mic back and said, "What do we want!" It was clear they were supposed to say, "No budget cuts!" but instead the kids said, "We want Jay-Z!"

But Russell will persevere because he believes in his mission and, some say, that the murders of Tupac and Biggie have changed him. "He feels he should've taken more of a leadership role in the Tupac, Biggie thing," Nelson George says. "He feels he should've intervened more. But the reason he didn't is that he didn't understand or feel comfortable with being that kind of big figure and had that much clout. Now he accepts that. That's the big difference. He's grown into accepting his role as a leader." Bill Adler agreed that the two deaths had impacted Russell deeply. "In the wake of the death of Tupac and Biggie he thought the artists ought to be standing up, ought to have some moral authority in the Hiphop Nation. Someone had to stand up and speak in terms of right and wrong. He believes it was time for someone to stand up and say this stuff is wrong, we must be more peaceful. And nobody else did it. So he self-consciously stepped into a leadership vacuum."

How far does his desire to lead go? In many ways Russell Simmons is an attractive candidate for mayor of New York. Every voter knows him, the business community respects him, he's rich, charismatic, good on TV, knows how to stay on message, loves to talk to people, and has values. He's also got a long past filled with women and cocaine, but then so did President Bush. But friends say no, there isn't a selfish motive behind his political work, he's not the Black Bloomberg. "I think he wants to be a kind of power broker," Nelson George says, "but I don't think that he'll be running for mayor one day. For a minute I thought he was feeling himself, but now I don't think he'll be running for mayor. I think he wants to have an impact. I think he feels he has had an impact on the culture but it's incomplete and there's more stuff that he could do and he's in a unique position to do it."

In his political movement as in everything else, Russell sees himself as a servant of everyone else, doing simply what needs to be done without ego. "Of course I wanna help people," he says, "but these various political moves are not really political, they're social moves. They're political moves that have to be made for social purposes. God's work you do until you lay in the box."

The Power of Radio

{ Andre Harrell, unpublished, 1996 }

The omnipotence of MTV makes it easy to overlook the impact pop radio can have on people's lives. Take Andre Harrell. For almost ten years Harrell ran Uptown Entertainment, a premier R&B label, but last week he ended a delicate eight-week negotiation that left him the CEO of Motown Records. One evening, just days before he closed the deal, Harrell sat in the beige-tinted living room of his Upper West Side apartment wearing a gray sweatshirt that read "Motown USA." Harrell is known for his calm composure and this night to a casual observer he would've appeared serene, but underneath the sweatshirt was not the serenity that characterizes Harrell, but a deep nervousness. Thirty-five years after he was born in a housing project in the South Bronx, Harrell was about to leap from running a company he'd founded with thirty-nine employees to commanding 150 in a company he called "the treasure of the music business." All because of radio.

"I always wanted to build Uptown into a multimedia, full-service, iconic entertainment company," Harrell began. "And I couldn't seem to get the level of support I needed to make my Black stars—Mary J. Blige, Heavy D., Jodeci—into Black superstars on a pop-star level."

Harrell said that the key to leaping from star to superstar was the support of pop radio—the 220-plus Top 40 radio stations across America. And the way to influence pop radio, ergo one difference between having real power in the record business and not, is controlling "a pop staff"—a group of people whose job is getting pop stations to play a label's singles.

In January, Harrell wrote a fifteen-page letter to Al Teller, the chairman of MCA Music, Uptown's parent company, asking for a pop staff. Teller refused. Harrell released two albums that went platinum and went back to Teller. This time Teller agreed to grow Uptown, but still wouldn't give Harrell a pop staff. Then, in early July it was announced that Doug Morris, the former chairman of Warner Music, had formed Rising Tide Entertainment as a joint venture with MCA. Rising Tide's focus, The New York Times reported, would be on mainstream Black pop music. "Doug Morris's deal was the straw that broke the camel's back between me and MCA," Harrell said.

Harrell got PolyGram to offer MCA fifty million dollars for its 50 percent share of Uptown. The offer was declined. Finally, Harrell asked to be let out of his executive contract. Teller agreed on one condition: the only company he could talk to was Motown. "He felt, because of the cultural significance of Motown it would look good for MCA," Harrell said.

In late July Harrell flew to London on the Concorde and met with Alain Levy, the chairman of PolyGram, Motown's parent company. The morning of the meeting Harrell told himself, " 'Motown needs Black glamour. I'ma give it to 'em.' So I put on a black suit, white shirt, with a white handkerchief and gold frame glasses. And I said, 'Every time they see me I'm gonna look fabulous and in the best of taste—what Motown represented to me.' "

Harrell told Levy exactly what he wanted: "The power to push the button and make people all over the world jump and sell my records." Levy gave him what MCA wouldn't. "Two days later," Harrell said, "I got offered forty million dollars over five years with twenty-five million dollars in the first year. And a phantom equity of 20 percent in Motown and 25 percent in the publishing company. It's one of the biggest executive packages . . ." he said then stopped and doubled his volume and his cadence: "It's the biggest executive package for a Black man in the history of the game! It's one of the biggest executive packages, period!"

That wasn't all ego talking. Though far behind one of his idols, Clive Davis of Arista, who is believed to have a package worth seventy million dollars over five years, Harrell will be paid on a level with Sony chairman Tommy Mottola, whose annual base salary is estimated at eight million dollars. Among those Harrell will be outdistancing, men reportedly pulling down only four to six million dollars per annum, is MCA chairman Al Teller.

"Evidently," Harrell said coolly, "I was not bullshitting at that meeting."

Al Sharpton Has a Dream

{ *Playboy*, 1997 }

The Reverend Alfred Charles Sharpton Jr. adjusted his chalk-striped, double-breasted suit and ran a thin comb through his shoulder-length, slowly graying mane. It was a Friday evening and the minister, activist, and candidate for mayor of New York City was in his Harlem headquarters, a sprawling building called the Hall of Justice. Hundreds of New Yorkers were waiting to hear him speak in an auditorium down the hall. It was going to be a long night, and Sharpton had only a moment to make his point. But he wasn't going to rush.

He swaggered across the room, past a framed portrait of Dr. Martin Luther King Jr., and, with beaming pride, swept up a photograph from a table. It showed Sharpton leaning over to speak into the Reverend Jesse Jackson's ear as both men sat on a stage. Sharpton pointed to a second photograph, of a young Jackson sporting a large Afro and leaning over into Dr. King's ear moments before the legendary "I have been to the mountaintop" speech on the final evening of King's life. It was a present from Jackson on Sharpton's recent 42nd birthday. The photo was signed in gold ink: "Al, the struggle has continuity. Keep hope alive, Jesse Jackson."

And that was Sharpton's point: He is taking over from Jackson as America's preeminent Black spokesman and leader. His challenge to New York City Mayor Rudolph Giuliani in September's Democratic primary guarantees a continuing media spotlight. Sharpton, of course, has long been in the New York spotlight. He became a celebrity activist in the mid-80s but was often dismissed as a shrill self-promoter: Once weighing in at over three hundred pounds, he was clownishly fat to boot. Sharpton seemed like a combination of Malcolm X and William "Refrigerator" Perry. But in the past several years Sharpton has shed some of his incendiary style, along with more than one hundred pounds. As he seeks a national audience from his New York pulpit he has already demonstrated, in New York state senatorial primaries in 1992 and 1994, that he can win votes.

"I'm thirteen years younger than Jesse. He was thirteen years younger than King. So in many ways it's like a continuation," Sharpton said. "Once a woman said to me, 'I grew up watching Malcolm and King. The only activism my kids know is you. And I hope you don't let 'em down.' She's right. What white America won't deal with is that in my generation, I am the Jesse Jackson."

Sharpton again smoothed the comb through his hair and followed his longtime chief of staff, Carl Redding, a former pro football player, out into the buzzing crowd. Sharpton strutted, melding a bull's brutishness with a rooster's righteousness. Just by walking Sharpton seemed to embody the character of New York: larger than life, outspoken, ethnic, epic. You could also see the Black street style that makes him a pariah to many whites: "I'm a street nigger," Sharpton said, "I come out of the projects. We hung on the corners and we wore slick hair and we listened to James Brown and we whistled at the girls. That's who I am. But I'm also a candidate. So I'm making street niggers politically acceptable."

Sharpton does not campaign with speeches, he campaigns with preaching. He began preaching to crowds when he was four years old and has never stopped. Sharpton at a podium can sound the way some gutbucket soul music feels. His oratorical style weaves cadence, repetition, rhythm and tremendous passion with audience participation. One is apt to hear him exclaim, "Black folk have a bad habit."

"Well!" someone will call out.

"We love our dead leaders!"

"Yasss!"

"And kill our living leaders!"

"Tell it!"

"Soon as one of our leaders die, we hang up pictures all over the place. We change the street name up after them. But while they among us, we don't do nothing but criticize them. We are like vultures, we hang out at the cemetery."

"Come on, Rev!"

Tonight, up on the stage, he greeted his wife Kathy, a former backup singer for James Brown. Together, they stood at the podium and sang in gritty, soulful voices, "I believe I can fly!" from R. Kelly's song of the same name. It is Sharpton's unofficial campaign theme song. "I believe I can touch the sky!" they went on, as some in the crowd joined in. "Spread my wings and fly away! I think about it every night and day!"

Later, at home, they seemed like typical middle-class parents. Wife Kathy retired recently from the Army reserves, and Sharpton has a steady income (approximately $60,000 a year) from preaching and speechmaking. His average college campus fee is $3000. James Brown helps bankroll the family, in part by paying for the private educations of daughters Dominique and Ashley, 11 and 10. Kathy fixed dinner that night while the two girls watched Nickelodeon in their room with the sound blaring. Sharpton flipped through the day's mail: some bills, an autograph request, two pleas for help from people who said they were victims of discrimination, and a death threat. He paused to listen to the cacophony from his daughters' room.

"My kids are experiencing the decline of the trend that I grew up watching," he said a bit solemnly, referring to the election of Black mayors in cities throughout the country. "In running for mayor," Sharpton said, "what I'm trying to do is hold a torch that America—of the Newt Gingrich to Giuliani era—has tried to put the flame out of. I must run for mayor, if for no other reason than because the kids behind me will aspire."

Sharpton remains a racial Rorschach test. Despite his mellowing, many whites continue to see him as Joan Didion, in her 1992 essay "Sentimental Journeys," put it: "clearly disqualified from casting as the Good Negro, the credit to the race. It was left, then, to cast Sharpton, and for Sharpton to cast himself, as the Outrageous Nigger." Despite Sharpton's attempts to appear more statesmanlike, many Blacks continue to agree with boxing promoter Don King, who said, "Joan was on the money, 'cause he is an outrageous nigger. And I think that's good. We need more outrageous niggers. We got a lot of niggers that's sleeping, sleeping through a revolution. Sharpton is an outrageous nigger for good, fighting for his community."

Sharpton said he was uncomfortable with the label, though he prefers it to "Good Negro." He defined himself this way: "It's not a question of me sitting in a room saying, let me cast myself as this. I'm the natural result of a generation and of growing up around the 'outrageous niggers' of that generation. If one were to look past the sound bite and look at my mentors and my development, I couldn't have been anything else."

One day in 1958, three-year-old Al Sharpton came home from church, lined up his sister's dolls and preached to them. After a few months with the Raggedy Anns and Andys he was given a chance to preach to a few hundred real people at the family's church, the Washington Temple Church of God in Christ. Sharpton, at the age of four, preached from the Gospel of John (14:1): "Let not your heart be troubled: Ye believe in God, believe also in me." He was nervous at first, but soon felt right at home.

By the time he was nine he was known in Black holiness circles as Wonderboy. He lived with his parents, Al Sr. and Ada, twelve-year-old sister, Cheryl, and seventeen-year-old half-sister, Tina, his mother's daughter from a previous marriage, in a middle-class neighborhood in Queens. One day in 1963 the family learned that Tina was pregnant with Al Sr.'s child. The family cracked forever. Tina moved out and gave birth to a boy named Kenneth. Sharpton fled with his mother and sister from their ten-room house to a five-room apartment in the projects in Brooklyn. Al Jr. began a lifelong search for a replacement for the father whom he has never forgiven.

Preaching continued to be Sharpton's life. "He was a child prodigy," said Jesse Jackson. "His interest in athletics and children's games, even dating, was limited." Sharpton was ordained at the age of ten, and began preaching in at least one church every Sunday, a ministry he has continued his entire life. His home church's elders took him on a Caribbean tour when he was ten (where, in Jamaica, he took it upon himself to meet the widow of Marcus Garvey) and arranged for him to tour with gospel singer Mahalia Jackson, to preach before her concerts. In the pulpit Sharpton developed and refined the oratorical and personal style that remains the root of the adulation and the scorn he draws. These days he visits close to eighty churches a year.

One day when he was eleven, Sharpton was browsing in a bookstore and came across a ninety-nine-cent paperback about a Black preacher and congressman from Harlem, the Reverend Adam Clayton Powell, Jr. For a spell in the 60s, the dashing Powell was one of the most famous Black leaders in America. Joe Klein described him in *The New Republic* as "the first modern rogue civil rights leader, the progenitor of the badass school of Black leadership." In 1967 Powell was expelled from Congress for a slew of offenses, including the misappropriation of government funds. (Two years later, however, the Supreme Court ruled that Powell had been unfairly excluded from Congress.) Today, a prominent boulevard in Harlem is named after him.

"This was amazing to me," Sharpton said. "Here's this guy fightin for Black people, pastorin this church, congressman, do-or-die attitude, whites couldn't tell him nothin. I mean, I really started admiring this guy." One Sunday in the mid-60s Reverend Sharpton walked into Harlem's Abyssinian Baptist Church in search of his idol. He walked out thinking he had seen God. He and Powell became fast friends.

"Any time he came to town I attached myself to his entourage," Sharpton said. "He gave me a sense of a Black man havin power, but havin arrogance with it. I was in his office one day and the secretary answered the phone and said, 'Congressman Powell, it's President Johnson on the phone.' Adam said, 'OK.' And she said, 'What'll I tell him?' He said, 'Tell him you'll give me the message.' "

One day in 1969 Powell appeared on *The David Frost Show* and took young Sharpton along. "The second question of the show," Sharpton recalls, "David Frost said, 'You've been described as a womanizer, a tax cheat, an agitator, a Black racist. How would you, Adam Powell, describe yourself?' And Powell, without even thinking about it, said, 'I'm the only man in America, Black or white, who doesn't give a damn.' I never

forgot that don't-give-a-damn attitude. I mean, in the heat of controversy, I'd always think about Adam saying, 'I don't give a damn.' "

Also in 1969, fourteen-year-old Sharpton joined the New York
branch of Operation Breadbasket, a Chicago-based civil rights organization that had grown out of Dr. King's Southern Christian Leadership
Conference. He learned about protesting and community activism and
quickly became Breadbasket's national youth director. He participated in
a successful all-night sit-in at the Manhattan corporate offices of A&P,
the supermarket chain, protesting unfair hiring practices. One day
Breadbasket's national director, the Reverend Jesse Jackson, came to
town. "In them days Jesse never wore a suit and tie," Sharpton recalls.
"He had a big 'fro, a Martin Luther King medallion, a dashiki, the whole
bit. So the first night I met Jesse I immediately saw him as the charismatic, flamboyant type, like Adam was. And I immediately became like a
protégé to him."

Powell died in 1972, and the next year Sharpton went backstage at
a concert in Newark, New Jersey, and met James Brown. In his autobiography, *Go and Tell Pharaoh*, Sharpton said, "I thought that when I'd seen
Adam Clayton Powell I'd seen God, but after I saw James Brown, I *knew*
I'd seen God."

Sharpton soon started working for Brown as a promoter and
learned about connecting with the masses. "James taught me to not be
afraid to keep your natural, African-based style," Sharpton said. "James
doesn't water down soul, or water down his Black-based personality.
James was one of the first superstars who made it off grassroots Black
people because James is the ultimate Black street guy."

One sign of that identity is Brown's straightened hair. Ironically, in
the 50s, when Brown's career started, conking was an assimilationist attempt to imitate white people's hair. But over the decades it became an
emphatically Black gesture. Sharpton noted that straightening his natu-
rally kinky hair to achieve an authentically Black style "is a paradox." He
vows he will never change it, in honor of Brown.

While working with Brown, Sharpton met Don King. In 1974 King
was trying to convince Zairean president Mobutu Sese Seko to host the

Muhammad Ali–George Foreman heavyweight title fight, called "the Rumble in the Jungle." Mobutu told King he would host the fight if James Brown performed. "So I meet Don," Sharpton recalled, "and he's got that hair and he's quoting Socrates and Plato and saying"—Sharpton cuts to a flawless imitation of King's loopy, circus showman's voice—"'Ya know, Reverend, I just got out the joint four years ago and I'm rehabilitated.' I said, 'What'd you go to jail for?' 'Murder!' I'm like, Whoa!"

Through the late 70s and early 80s Sharpton and King supported each other in various ways. King donated money to Sharpton's National Youth Movement, a grassroots community-action group he founded in 1971. NYM had a broad agenda that included protesting police brutality and boardroom discrimination. King also provided access to boxers and celebrities for NYM events. Sharpton, in turn, helped convince Black athletes such as James "Bonecrusher" Smith and Mike Tyson that they should employ a Black promoter, namely King. In 1984 Sharpton helped King secure the rights to promote the Jackson Family Victory Tour, then traveled with the tour helping the Jacksons with community relations in each city. Sharpton said Don King taught him "to believe in your ideas, to try to do something nobody ever did and to go for the dramatic moment to project your story."

It was also in the early 80s that Sharpton found himself in a conversation with a man who turned out to be an FBI informer, and who taped the meeting. According to Sharpton, "The government, posing as a boxing promoter, called a meeting and then turned the meeting from talking about boxing to talking about drugs. On the tape I clearly said I wasn't into that." Sharpton described the encounter as "a failed entrapment attempt by the government. Obviously, or they would have indicted me."

Nevertheless, Sharpton soon began collaborating with the FBI. "When they came after me to turn on Don King I wouldn't do it. I told 'em, 'Let's go after some drug dealers.'" For several years he was an informer, dealing with organized crime and drug investigations. But, according to New York Post columnist Jack Newfield's book Only in America: The Life and Crimes of Don King, Sharpton did inform on King, providing the FBI with tapes of conversations. Sharpton denies this.

While Sharpton was working for the FBI, New York's racial climate turned searingly hot. First, in September 1983, a Black teen named Michael Stewart lapsed into a coma while in the custody of transit police and later died. Then, in October 1984, sixty-six-year-old Eleanor Bumpurs, a three-hundred-pound emotionally disturbed Black woman, was shot twice and killed by police who had come to evict her from her apartment because she was late with her rent. The six police officers, who were equipped with the usual weapons and bulletproof vests, maintained that Bumpurs menaced them with a ten-inch kitchen knife. In December 1985, Bernhard Goetz shot four Black teens on the subway. The void in Black leadership in New York was obvious. "In many ways," said a source close to Sharpton, "the fact that we didn't have somebody out there stirring things up was what allowed somebody like Al Sharpton to rise. I think that had Jesse and others not continued in that vein, an Al Sharpton would probably never have happened."

In the early hours of December 20, 1986, Sharpton got a phone call that told of another outrage that had happened just hours earlier. Three Black men had walked into a pizzeria in a predominantly white New York neighborhood called Howard Beach to call for help after their car had broken down. They soon found themselves face-to-face with a group of white men screaming, "Niggers, you don't belong here!" The three Black men tried to run away. One escaped. One was caught and beaten. Michael Griffith, twenty-three, ran onto a highway, where he was struck and killed by a car.

Mayor Ed Koch told a press conference that afternoon that Griffith and his friends were "chased like animals through the streets." Koch compared the incident to "the kind of lynching party that took place in the Deep South." Nevertheless, no single Black leader arose to denounce the crime—until a few days after the Koch press conference. Then Sharpton went to the Howard Beach pizzeria and roared, "We did not have our children so they could be target practice for some white mobs that can't behave themselves!" He led a tense march of hundreds of Blacks (and a handful of whites) through the streets of Howard Beach. The crowd chanted "This is not Johannesburg" while hundreds of locals screamed racist slurs. Hundreds of police officers kept the peace while every television news show in town recorded the noisy, dangerous scene. On television Sharpton was outsize, brash and dramatic, even by New York standards. He combined the flamboyant arrogance of Adam Clayton Powell and the street sense of James Brown with the hustler's theatricality of Don King. Later, Sharpton paid homage to Dr. Martin Luther King, Jr. "Dr. King," Sharpton said, "embarrassed America in breaking down segregation. People around the world saw kids with water hoses on them. Well, we did the same thing. When they saw on TV people in Howard Beach standing there with watermelons, calling us niggers, they couldn't say it wasn't racism. All of the scholarly speeches in the world couldn't have done that. Two seconds on the news does that."

Sharpton became, for better and worse, a star. Then he got into trouble.

In late November 1987 in Wappingers Falls, New York, a small Hudson Valley town eighty miles north of Manhattan, a fifteen-year-old Black girl named Tawana Brawley, who'd been missing for four days, was found, alive, in a plastic garbage bag. Her body was smeared with feces and someone had scrawled "nigger" and "KKK" on her body. She said she had been abducted and raped by a group of six white men, one of whom had worn a police badge. The police did not confirm her story and soon expressed skepticism.

Sharpton went to work, organizing marches and orchestrating Brawley's campaign for justice. He moved with special fury because, he said later in his autobiography, the case reminded him of "what happened between my father and my sister. The harder they attacked Tawana, the more I saw a vulnerable Black woman, like my mother, who no one would fight for. At some point it stopped being Tawana and started being me defending my mother and all the Black women no one would fight for. I was not going to run away from her like my father had run away from my mother, like so many other Black men had run away."

Ten months later a grand jury concluded that Brawley's horrifying story was fabricated.

Not long before this embarrassment, *Newsday* had exposed Sharpton's secret work for the FBI. For many New Yorkers, his credibility was

gone forever: "I just can't forgive a guy," says critic and columnist Stanley Crouch, speaking of the Brawley episode, "who was a part of the
hoax that had that kind of a divisive effect on New York for that long. At
some point along the way he must have known that it was a fraud."

For Ted Kennedy there is Chappaquiddick. For Jesse Jackson there is
"Hymietown." For Al Sharpton there is his FBI work and Tawana Brawley.

During the late 80s and early 90s, a series of hate crimes rocked the
New York area and Sharpton marched and made headlines through
them all. He won respect from some, animosity from many, and attention from all. A 1990 *Washington Post* editorial asked "why we in the news
business give such prominence to professional provocateurs like Reverend Al. We distort the larger picture by training our blinding spotlight
on an assortment of kooks, crazies, and crackpots whose mission is to
divide and polarize."

On January 12, 1991, as Sharpton prepared to lead a march in a
Brooklyn neighborhood, Bensonhurst, where a Black man named
Yusuf Hawkins had been killed, a white man named Michael Riccardi
stabbed Sharpton in the chest, just missing his heart. Sharpton was
rushed to a hospital where, he wrote in his autobiography, he realized "that your life can go, can be taken from you, just like that. I realized that if my life was so fragile, so contingent, then I had to be
more serious about what I was doing and saying, I had to be more careful about the message I was leaving people with. I realized I was a Christian activist, out of the tradition of Adam Clayton Powell, Martin Luther
King, and Jesse Jackson—a minister."

When he regained consciousness he asked to speak with Reverend
Jackson. The two had known each other for more than twenty years but
had not spoken for some time. Nevertheless, Jackson was at the hospital
the next morning. "Jesse and I always have this relationship," Sharpton
said, "where we love each other, but you know how men don't say that.
He said, 'Well, I had to come 'cause Jackie [Jackson's wife] was crying
and bothering me all night.' I said, 'Yeah, well, Kathy wanted me to call
you.' It was that kind of thing. Then he prayed with me. I told him I
wanted to do more with electoral politics and he said, 'Well, I've always

been available to you since you were fourteen.' You know, that whole father thing."

Sharpton recovered completely and not long afterward he flew
with Jackson to Las Vegas, where they spent five days taking in the Mike
Tyson–Donovan "Razor" Ruddock fight and organizing a surprise birthday party for Jackson's wife. In Las Vegas, Sharpton said, they "reglued
and got really, really tight." Ever since, the two men have spoken almost
every day, usually at six in the morning.

His brush with death and rekindled friendship with Jackson
seemed to mellow Sharpton. He became less shrill and more statesmanlike and, by 1992, people took notice. He put together his first political
effort and finished a respectable third in the Democratic senatorial primary, getting 15 percent of the vote. Then-governor Mario Cuomo
called him the primary's "classiest" candidate and "the real winner."
Two years later Sharpton ran in another senate primary and received 26
percent of the vote.

Along the way, Sharpton devoted more of his time to battling corporate racism. In 1996, thanks to Sharpton's lobbying, a New York television station hired its first Black woman news director. Sharpton and
Jackson were counseling six Black Texaco employees who had filed a
discrimination lawsuit when a tape was made public of company executives flinging racial epithets. (The suit was quickly settled.) And during
the summer of 1996, Sharpton called former mayor Ed Koch and said,
"I just want you to know that I've decided I am taking the road of Jesse
Jackson, not Minister Farrakhan." Koch said it was "a very significant
statement. I believed him and I still do."

Even Don King forgives the preacher. Not long ago the two men,
who see each other regularly, met in a New York hotel room and a visi-
tor asked King about the FBI episode. "When they feel threatened by
your presence they use these type of devices to cause divisiveness and to
snatch whatever credibility one may have from them. This is a semantic
game, one of the most sophisticated games in the world." King's eyes
grew wide and his voice gained in volume and bombast. "This is mas-
terful, diabolical, deductive thinking. Shifting gears so the discussion
leaves the person who's in dire straits, or the issue that has to be con-

fronted, into personal calumniation. It's what they call in psychology 'transferring.' Rather than confront the issue they throw up a subterfuge. This is a game that's played all the time in my country." He paused, then said, "You got to be able to understand. We all make mistakes."

But does Don King trust Al Sharpton? Let King make it perfectly clear again: "I believe in America, and I want to help America," King said. "I think America is bigger than me trustin or not trustin Sharpton. I think that's irrelevant and immaterial. The goal we are both trying to seek is a better America. I don't even get into whether I trust or don't trust. I don't trust myself. So how am I gonna get mad if they tell me I don't trust Sharpton? It's probably true."

These days Jesse Jackson is one of the most outspoken advocates of Sharpton's candidacy. The two men speak of each other, in public and private, in father-and-son terms. Sharpton introduced Jackson at a recent campaign stop in Harlem and said that if "everything in society told you you wasn't somebody, it was important for somebody to affirm you, that you were somebody." The crowd cheered. Jackson, Sharpton said, "did that for me in my early teens. And is still doing it for me in my early forties."

Jackson took the podium to a standing ovation. "Al Sharpton is a freedom fighter," he preached in his trademark rhythm, his voice low and calm and heavy with his characteristic Southern accent. "I've known Al since he was a teenager. His heroes were freedom fighters. Pulpiteering, protesting, defying the power structure is all he ever wanted to do." The crowd was silent, their attention rapt. "As a child Al wanted to be a protesting preacher of power. A freedom fighter," Jackson continued, gathering volume and steam. "What makes Al different? He's a full-time freedom fighter. This is all he does! Wakes up every morning and listen to the radio. Who got in trouble last night? Who got abused last night? Who got shot last night? Full-time freedom fighter. This is all he does!" He leaned back from the microphone and became more conversational. "Those who did not have those struggling washing machines cannot appreciate. There was a thing in the washing ma-

chine that went up and down, called the agitator." He placed his fists in
front of him and began pumping them aggressively. "And it shook the
dirt out of things. And agitators shake the dirt out of things. Shake the
injustice out of things and shake up oppressors!" He began to yell. "Al
Sharpton is an agitator!"

"Teach!" someone in the crowd yelled back.

"What does he do? Al disturbs the comfortable and comforts the
disturbed!" Jackson paused dramatically, then added in a crisp, hushed
voice, "Dr. King wouldn't argue."

Sharpton will spend a lot of his campaign time in New York pul-
pits. Are New York voters ready for Black preaching? "In the Black
church," said Michael Eric Dyson, a professor of communication studies
at the University of North Carolina in Chapel Hill, and an ordained Baptist minister, "how you say it is just as important as what you say. Now,
people take that to mean, even if you ain't saying nothing just make it
sound pretty. No, what it means is that style is an agent of substance, not
a substitute for substance. Style becomes the vehicle through which
substance is born."

Will Sharpton have enough substance to attract whites and suffi-
cient style to satisfy Blacks? Can he make his case on issues such as
housing, education, and police conduct without becoming an Outrageous Nigger or a Good Negro?

Jackson's influence may make the difference. "Jesse always tries to
encourage me to be more than somebody reacting," Sharpton said later.
"Jesse's thing is, you're not speaking to tomorrow's paper, you're speaking to history. Being young and hardheaded, sometimes I just shoot
back. A guy like me learned, growing up, how to survive off natural instinct. Sometimes you gotta learn how to discipline your instinct. And
that's always been the struggle with me and Jesse. You know the old
story of the two bulls on the hill? One run down the hill and screw a
cow. The other walk down and screw 'em all. You just learn how to deal
with things differently."

Sharpton was right at home at the Brown Memorial Baptist
Church in Brooklyn early one Sunday morning not long ago. He wore
an ankle-length white robe with brick-red trim. Sharpton began his ser-

mon slowly, with a benign weariness. "We meet this mornin knowing the challenges on us are as pervasive as they've ever been."

A baby began crying, then screaming. "We live in a time where Black women will starve four-year-old children!" Sharpton boomed.

"Aw Lord," the congregation answered.

"And we sittin up talkin about we don't know what to do. We're in the church, but we're not bringing the church into the community."

"That's right!"

"God didn't save you for a personal thrill," he said.

The congregation fell silent. Sharpton seemed angry. The baby screamed.

"You supposed to come here and get the fuel to go out into the world and make a difference. Church is like a fillin station. You supposed to get your gas here so you can go and run somewhere. You don't go to the gas station and sit with a full tank and just keep runnin your motor."

He flew through the story of Samson and Delilah, mentioned a Mike Tyson fight and jabbed at Giuliani. Soon, he cruised into the home stretch singing God's praises, the organist coming right behind him, filling the spaces in his rhythm while the congregation clapped and shouted.

"And God has all the strength you need!" he said, singing "God" and "need," as the organ played lightly behind him.

"He can look into the darkness and say, 'Let there be light,' " he sang in his gritty, raw baritone, sang as much as James Brown can be said to sing.

"Some people, when they get in trouble," he sang, and the organ answered, in a sloppy, staccato burst of sound: *Buuh-lah-oww!*

"They look for some hotshot lawyer."

And the organ answered twice, *Buuh-lah-oww! Buuh-lah-oww!*

"But my Black brother I saaay."

Buuh-lah-oww!

"I know where my strength comes from!"

Buuh-lah-oww! Buuh-lah-oww!

"I have———"

Buuh-lah-oww!

"Not come from City Hall."

Buuh-lah-oww! Buuh-lah-oww!

"I have——"

Buuh-lah-oww!

"Not come from the White House!"

Buuh-lah-oww! Buuh-lah-oww!

"I have——"

Buuh-lah-oww!

"Come from the Lord!"

Buuh-lah-oww! Buuh-lah-oww!

"Yes!" And the drummer came in behind the organ and they gained altitude, and Sharpton's eyes were large and bright and he rocked up and down from heel to toe with the rhythm, as if he might just leap on up and touch the ceiling in another moment. He had taken flight, he had transcended English and was pulling the congregation right up with him, floating not on words but on the strength of the preaching form itself. The people applauded and screamed and smiled and hollered and flew alongside him until finally, after nearly an hour of preaching, with the congregation breathless, Reverend Sharpton stepped down from the pulpit. He hugged Brown Memorial's pastor, Reverend Samuel Austin, and disappeared into the backrooms of the church. The congregation began slowly sitting back down. With the organ playing sweetly behind him, Reverend Austin stepped up and leaned into the microphone. "God bless you, Reverend," Austin said. "Didn't he preach?"

Ships Passing in the Night

{ Barack Obama and Colin Powell,
Suede magazine, 2004 }

They're like two ships passing in the night, or, better, two elite mountain climbers at the midpoint of Mount President: General Colin Powell and Star Politician Barack Obama. The General never officially entered the race for president, but he got higher up Mount President than any Black man ever has in 1995, when the nation's respect for him was so toweringly high it appeared the Oval Office was his to lose. The Star Politician has begun his career higher than any Black man ever has. But I'm still afraid—I've always been afraid—that when there's finally a Black president I'm going to hate him. But we'll get to that.

The General was the star of the first Iraq war who found the will of the country blowing him up Mount President, perhaps faster than he was ready to go. There was a long moment in 1995, during the book tour for his autobiography *My American Journey*, when the country seemed to beg him to run. But he declined to join the race, saying he lacked a fire in the belly, a statement that was somehow, both clear and cryptic. In 2000 he joined the Bush administration as secretary of state and was easily its most popular and charismatic cabinet member, more popular than even the president himself. But he was marginalized during Bush's first-term war planning to the point of public embarrassment and then went to the United Nations and told stories about Iraq so scary that Stephen King might be jealous. But when no weapons were found in

Iraq, the General's image suffered again. In late 2001 his approval numbers were in the mid to high 80s, but after a steady decline, in late 2004 they were in the mid 60s. He resigned just after the 2004 election.

There is no chance for the General to become president now. He's a well-loved, well-respected General in a country still at war, who won't have to convince anyone he'll be tough in the War on Terror. But he's also prochoice, proaffirmative action, and not a true conservative in a party and a country that's trending more and more conservative. In 2008 he'll be seventy-one years old, he'll have been out of politics for a few years, and should he find a fire in his belly that Tums can't put out, he'd have to do battle with not one but two eight-hundred-pound GOP gorillas: former New York mayor Rudy Giuliani and Arizona senator John McCain. And there's a third potential gorilla lurking in the mist, considering a run: Florida governor Jeb Bush. A decade ago the White House was his to lose, but now he faces a tougher climb.

Barack Obama exploded into Star Politician in mid 2004 as he waltzed from the Illinois state senate, where he'd spent four terms, into the U.S. Senate. He stepped onto the national public stage and the word "presidential" seemed to fit immediately. He's a tall Midwesterner with a relaxed charm who isn't stiff or wonkish like politicians usually are. And let's be honest, it's helpful that he's very light-skinned, a high-yellow brother. Many of the most successful Black elected politicians of the last twenty years are high yellow: New York mayor David Dinkins, Virginia governor L. Douglas Wilder, Atlanta mayor Maynard Jackson, Tennessee congressman Harold Ford. Of course, being high yellow is far from a requirement for electoral success; many brown and dark-skinned Blacks have won important elections (Illinois senator Carol Mosley Braun, Chicago mayor Harold Washington, Dallas mayor Ron Kirk, California congresswoman Maxine Waters). But the disproportionate success of lighter-skinned Blacks seems to build upon long-held, rarely discussed stereotypes around color, the expectation in both races that lighter-skinned Blacks are more intelligent and pensive and are more like whites. High yellow still means something in this country, still has status, and the rapid success of the Star Politician reaffirms that.

But more important than color (rather than race) is character, and

Obama, like Powell, is never so aggressively Black as to make whites scared. The two are Black men who can charm and disarm whites, who don't wear their Blackness on their sleeve, who are post-Black smooth as opposed to the pro-Black pride, diction, and manner of men like Jesse Jackson and Al Sharpton. Their pro-Black bluster, deeply rooted in the mores of the 60s, recalls that difficult era and reminds us of the continuing battle to reach racial equality. The Star Politician and the General are Blacks who make whites feel that progress has been made, that academia and the military are avenues to success for everyone, that racism is ending and equality is here. Where Jesse and Al appear still angry about slavery, segregation, the four little girls in Birmingham, and everything else that's happened to Blacks throughout American history, Colin and Barack have a cool that suggests they're looking ahead to a brighter future. Where Jesse and Al seem to be on the public stage as Black America's representatives, Obama and Powell appear to want to represent everyone. They are the sort of Black men you see so rarely on the public stage: both liked and respected by both Blacks and whites.

But the Star Politician has massive hurdles to overcome to reach the White House. He did cocaine and smoked weed as a teenager. He's already admitted it and written about it in his autobiography, *Dreams from My Father*, but in a presidential contest that'll surely come back up. He's pro-choice and pro–gun control and that would hurt him in the red states. The Democrats should be very wary of nominating yet another intellectual from Harvard (Obama went to Law School; Al Gore was an undergrad; John Kerry went to Yale but outside of New England no one sees a difference). And since the 1930s, only one sitting senator has won the presidency and that was John F. Kennedy, perhaps the most gifted politician of his generation. The presidency is most often won by governors—Dubya, Clinton, Reagan, and Carter were all sitting governors. The advantage they have is that they're executives who live amongst their constituents and aren't infected by Washington. More important, being governor allows you to run for the presidency as an outsider, an agent of change, a posture a senator cannot take.

In 2008 Obama will be forty-five years young with a long way to go to reach the White House. His celebrity emanates strictly from his persona, not his ideas. What sort of legislation moves him most? Many successful national politicians are known for some legislative achievement or crusade, as if it were their big hit record. Hillary Clinton is linked to health care, Al Gore was all about the environment, John McCain's signature is campaign finance reform, President Bush is all about terror, excuse me, the war on terror. We don't yet know what cause Obama will look to make his own, and his choice will reveal much about him. In the Illinois state senate he pushed to have all capital-crime interrogations videotaped, to reform campaign finance laws, and to create healthcare initiatives for poor families. In order to move from a good-looking politician to a substantial one, he'll need to find some sort of legislation to make his name with, and that's hard to do as a freshman senator in an institution that puts great value on seniority.

If Obama finds a fire in his belly in the next few years, in '08 he'll have to compete for the nomination with Hillary, the Democratic eight-hundred-pound gorilla, as well as former North Carolina senator John Edwards, Indiana senator Evan Bayh, and other tough challengers who lack the extra hurdle of being Black.

One day we will elect a Black president. But I fear, nay, expect that it will not be the glorious moment we want it to be. Convincing millions of white Americans (especially red-state white Americans) to vote for a Black candidate will require he or she convince voters they will not give special privileges, benefits, or attention to Black people. If that social contract is not made clear—if white Americans suspect they're voting for a Black president, instead of a president—the candidate won't stand a chance. Anyone who can make that social contract with white America will have Black America deeply conflicted, the way we are about Clarence Thomas and Condoleezza Rice, proud of their achievements, but cringing about their politics, their clunky personas, the lame way they inhabit the public stage. We are undermoved (as in, not completely unmoved, but moved less than we would've liked) by them. Colin always had a sense of cool about him, and Barack seems to have that same sort of post-Black cool. But the Black man who slides into the White House will not have Black America dancing in the streets. He'll have us undermoved.

4. Icaruses

Invincible Man

{ Tupac, *The Village Voice*, 1995 }

This [trial] is all about my image, this has nothing to do
with me . . . I'm selling records. This is what I do for a
living: I'm selling records. Don't get it twisted. This is not
my real life.

—Tupac, Monday evening

Riding across the Brooklyn Bridge around nine thirty on Thursday
morning, the day the verdict in Tupac Shakur's sodomy trial is delivered,
a day after he was shot five times, feels like riding into the front lines of
a war zone. Waiting just across the approaching shore are warring gen-
erals and soldiers—lawyers and reporters who battle to shape and/or
report an event that could stretch on interminably or end at a moment's
notice—at least one man who is injured and, at the moment, MIA—
Tupac—and the gnawing probability, call it tension, that soon, maybe
before the day is over, there will be a casualty to report. Tupac's.

"No matter what happens," Tupac proclaims to a beehive full of
reporters Tuesday afternoon outside the courtroom, "innocent or guilty,
my life is ruined." But after what happens Thursday evening—for those
sequestered on some other case: not guilty of two counts of sodomy,
one count of attempted sodomy, and three counts of criminal possession of a weapon, guilty of three counts of sexual abuse that could net
him between two and a third and seven years in jail—his life is far from
over. See Tupac as part of the Whitney Museum's Black Male exhibit and
the events of last week as scenes in a live performance-art exhibit. This is
an act that questions the place of rebellion for its own selfish and/or
self-destructive sake, debates the value of outlaw subculture, and gauges
the universe of distance between the militantly politicized generation

that gave birth to the militantly commercial one that has taken its place. And it stars a master performance artist whose canvas is his body and whose stage is the world.

There is a massive distance between Tupac's fame and the amount of substantive professional work he has completed. Despite being an actor with tremendous presence, with the exception of a costarring role in *Juice*, he has never acted in a good movie. Despite being, along with Snoop, one of the two most famous rappers in the world, he is merely an average vocalist and lyricist, even by West Coast standards, and has yet to record one aesthetically important song. But the performance art—the Black Panther bloodline; the flurry of arrests in L.A., Atlanta, East Lansing, and Manhattan; the escape from five of those six arrests with only a minuscule fourteen days in jail; the fact that while everyone else talks about it, Tupac is *the only known rapper who has actually shot a police officer*; the walking away from being shot five times with no permanent damage, and walking away from the hospital the next day and the rolling into court for a brief but dramatic wheelchair-bound courtroom appearance—it's been dangerously compelling and ecstatically brilliant. It's kept his lackluster professional work artistically interesting and commercially viable, just as the films and albums have given him the money, attention, and legitimacy necessary to carry it off. And it's threatening to subsume the rest of the Whitney exhibit.

From the front row, that is, in person, the act steps to another level. Tupac is an animated conversationalist who gestures for the back row, makes lots of audience eye contact while delivering his sometimes funny, usually passionate, and always provocative lines. On Tuesday evening he speaks about the court proceeding and his perception of its Kafkaesque nature, then pauses and slays the assembled crowd, adding, "I don't wanna see the Tupac Bronco chase on the freeway." The overall effect is neatly seductive: it makes you want not only to listen to him and to like him, but to believe him. And a convincing performance is the goal of every actor. "I'm not saying I'm a thug cuz I wanna rob you and rape people and things," he says Tuesday afternoon. "I'm a businessman! You know I'm a businessman because you find me at my places of business!"

So when he rolls into court just after ten on Thursday morning, it's just another scene, and it's played out with just enough passive-aggressive behavior toward the press that our star remains not only squarely in the middle of the stage, but also maintains the illusion that we were actually not onstage. Tupac is wheeled in surrounded by six Fruit of Islam bodyguards who slice through the deluge of cameras and microphones with elbows and shoves. Keeping the press from their charge seems to be the FOI's explicit purpose, but after parking in front of the court building's Lafayette Street entrance, the entourage marches around to the building's Center Street side—adding fifty or so yards and four to five minutes to their journey. And opening the door for the wheelchair-bound, NY Yankees–ski hat–wearing images that dominate the news of the near future. "I'm a businessman."

When a performer is perpetually onstage it's hard to know, or worse, believe them, when they do step off. Or, rather, if. For over an hour leading up to about eleven thirty, Tupac sits in his wheelchair outside courtroom 677 waiting for Judge Daniel Fitzgerald to take the bench. He is surrounded by his FOI bodyguards, his mother, and a handful of friends, including actresses Jada Pinkett and Jasmine Guy (Mickey Rourke arrives a few hours later). While he sits, he takes off his Yankees hat to reveal what appears to be heavy bandages covering the upper two-thirds of his head. But later, he removes that revealing it to be only a white skully: his actual bandages appear significantly less dramatic. They aren't quite as thick, and cover his forehead but only circle the top of his head, leaving unwrapped an area of approximately two to three inches in diameter. When the jury walks in for a read-back around one p.m., the Yankees hat is off and he's wearing the skully, and elicits looks of compassion and curiosity from numerous jurors.

At about two p.m. it becomes known that Tupac isn't returning from lunch break—because, his lawyer tells the court, he felt numbness in his leg—and his official whereabouts go unrevealed for the rest of the day. My worry that he will turn up dead never returns. It's more than simply knowing that Tupac is now probably strapped and surrounded by bodyguards wherever he is that keeps the thought at bay. More than not hearing any ominous music in the background. It's simply my feeling that this scene won't feature a second shooting sequence.

Tupac's brief, wheelchair-bound courtroom appearance is read by many reporters and hangers-on as a rather transparent attempt to manipulate the jury, and leads to skepticism about what really motivated the shooting that landed him in that chair. The incident's timing—during the jury deliberation in a high-pressure trial—makes it nearly impossible to believe the police conclusion that it was a random robbery. "What thug would shoot Tupac?" one reporter asks. "Tupac is a thug hero."

While it's debatable whether a good thug would shoot his idol, it's still hard to believe that the police had a hand in the shooting, as Tupac's attorney, Michael Warren, hints. Though it would be in character with Black Panther history, it's hard to accept simply because of Tupac's minimal political significance with respect to the power structure in America. The afternoon following the shooting a thin, Black, middle-aged passerby stops long enough to tell a group of reporters that authorities know Tupac is someone capable of getting the Black Panthers started again and they need to shut him down before that happens. But for anyone to ascribe him that much power is horribly ignorant of one key fact: though Tupac is, in some ways, a spiritual descendant of the Panthers, he has no political framework for his dissension and anarchy. He may be an urban superhero, but it's quite a leap to go from getting people to sing "I Get Around" to having them quit jobs to run free breakfast programs, and giving up fly Fort Greene apartments to live underground, and forgetting afternoons spent watching *Menace II Society* yet again (while lamenting that the film could've been even better with Tupac as O-Dawg) in order to attend rallies to applaud the pronouncements of Comrade Tupac.

"The way this country is successful," the Minister of Outlawness told a crowd Tuesday afternoon outside the courtroom, "is if we have one set of rules and everybody follows them. If anybody gets outside of that set of rules and they're in the public view like I am, it's like detrimental to everybody following the rules. What they think is that I represent lawlessness and the outlaw mentality and I represent that thug mentality from the street. So they feel like if they can punish me, that it'll punish people that are like as brave as I am, who don't speak out against things like me." But Tupac's character is far from Huey Newton the revolutionary leader and political organizer, and a lot closer to Huey Newton the chauvinist pig and self-destructive rebel. He is Huey with the misogyny, the sex appeal, and the guns, without the ten-point plan.

Indeed, Tupac's argument that the point of the trial and shooting were to stop someone who speaks out against things is mocked by the presence of his lawyer, Michael Warren. A tall, grand-looking, light brown–skinned Black man with close-cropped hair who appears to be in his fifties, Warren keeps an office in Clinton Hill, Brooklyn, and lists on his card, under his Christian name, his Muslim name—Tarif Khalil Salim. Warren used to be a member of SNCC and has known Tupac's mother and surrogate father for fifteen years, dating back to his days in the Black Liberation Army. Now, full of Black gladiator cool, Warren swaggers through the halls of court buildings with the grace of say, a slightly battered but still elegant athlete and makes a living defending the likes of Sheik Omar Abdel Rahmen, the blind cleric convicted of plotting to bomb the World Trade Center. Taking Warren out would be a far smaller news story, but a far greater loss to whatever remaining Black liberation movement there is.

Warren's competition, assistant district attorney Melissa Mourges, is, by comparison, a frail, mousy white woman who wears glasses and speaks tentatively and haltingly. If there is a villain in this scene, she is it, but unlike, say, Marcia Clark circa the O.J. pretrial hearings, she doesn't seem to relish her role, but appears to feel powerless to do anything about it. During a slow moment on Thursday afternoon, around three thirty, she and her second chair find themselves in a conversation with a few reporters, one of whom jokes that soon on Court TV there will be a credit reading "Prosecutor's wardrobe by Armani." After slight laughter she self-deprecatingly jokes that her credit would be "Jacklyn Smith by Kmart."

As for the shooting and subsequent whodunit, it makes as much sense (albeit conflicted) that Tupac himself orchestrated the incident. Why? Possibly to cause a mistrial, or evoke jury sympathy, or to boost his position as a feared political figure, relentlessly attacked by the conniving, hapless Man in the courts and the streets. But really, in the context of live performance art, it doesn't matter who shot Tupac or why, and the lack of clarity and attendant controversy only add to his myth and heighten the dramatic impact of the most enigmatic and climatic part of the show.

At four forty-five, while Tupac is offstage tending to leg numbness, the jury buzzes. They have something to say. It will be almost two hours before it's revealed what it is they have to say after over two hours of deliberation. During those two hours reporters debate as to what the buzz was about—a verdict, another read-back testimony, another law to be explained, possibly a hung jury (before lunch they buzzed to say they were deadlocked on some counts). During those hours reporters also debate the legitimacy of Tupac's numbness claim. We soon discover there is a far more important numbness.

Not only had Tupac's bandaged and wheelchair-bound courtroom appearance seemed to elicit faces of concern and compassion from numerous jurors, but on Wednesday attorney Warren observed that on the day after the shooting, when the jury entered the courtroom and for the first time in weeks, Tupac was not in his seat, no one seemed surprised. He was right. As the jurors sat down no one seemed taken aback by Tupac's absence. Warren, and Tupac's codefendant Charles Fuller's attorney, Robert Ellis, asserted numerous times that the jury was aware of Tupac's ongoing performance. "No sequestering is fail-safe," said Warren on Thursday afternoon; "jurors get information in the strangest ways." "From a practical standpoint," added Ellis after the verdict was delivered, "one could assume that the jurors probably already knew what had occurred since everybody in the world knew what occurred."

But Thursday evening, about six thirty, juror Richard Devitt emerged and said that the twelve had been completely ignorant of Tuesday night's shooting. "We knew nothing," he told reporters. "We were totally shielded from all information. TVs were taken out of our rooms, radios were taken out of our rooms, we were moved to a hotel that was much farther away and in a very remote place. No phone calls were ever permitted at any time."

Devitt also said despite the much-discussed looks of compassion, the jury had not been affected by the wheelchair-bound appearance. "The judge instructed us to make no speculations whatsoever and we honestly didn't. We were much too involved with trying to figure out the details of the evidence that we had."

Among those details, Devitt said, was nothing beyond the facts of the case. "The whole tact of trying to attack the woman's character was totally archaic and unnecessary and everybody immediately disregarded it," he said. "We just threw that all out." "But," a reporter asked, "do you think it was important to know as a jury that all these things had happened that led up before this event?" "The business at Nell's and all that stuff?" Devitt responded. "No. We all agreed that that was utterly irrelevant. And we immediately threw that all out." And suddenly it was clear that while Tupac had been putting on the performance of his life, the most important audience of the moment hadn't been paying attention at all.

Sexual abuse is officially defined by the prosecutor's office as sexual contact with an intimate body part by forcible compulsion. In this case that was kneading and separating the buttocks. It carries a term of two and a third to seven years in prison, but, the prosecutor's office said, could be merely a probationary offense. The prospect of Tupac escaping time in jail for yet another crime is a significant postscript to the history of the Panthers. One that signals maybe we have begun to see the level of freedom Arthur Ashe spoke of when he said we wouldn't be free until we were able to be mediocre and still succeed.

Still, Tupac could do over two years in prison for this conviction, taking him off his official stages, but certainly not ending the run of his inspired act. Think of it as merely a setting change. When you're perpetually onstage, you never get off. The stage simply comes with you. Even if death happened to Tupac's body, he wouldn't really die because the audience would keep watching like you do at the end of a really great film when the credits start rolling. The hero/villain's been blown away and all the other characters have gone home, but you stay, hoping, maybe, there's one more shot, one more bit of greatness to savor.

After last week's command performance, we probably won't take our eyes off the Tupac show for a long time, but Tupac himself may be ending the act. About six hours before he was shot he said, "I don't wanna just say, 'I'ma stop smoking, stop drinking, just be regular.' That's one of the impossible dreams, but I'm definitely looking for some enlightenment from somewhere. Wherever I see that there's the light that's where I'm headin. I'm looking for the light. But I'ma change for sure, cuz this is not it. This is not it. This is really not it."

To be continued . . .

The Ivy League
Counterfeiter

{ Cliff Evans, *Rolling Stone*, 2000 }

In the summer of 1995, Cliff Evans was broke. He'd just finished Columbia University and owed thousands on student loans. He had run up
debt on a number of credit cards, and his rent was two months late.
He'd started a small recording studio in Manhattan, but the few artists
cutting records there weren't able to pay, and the venture was driving
him deeper into the red. Evans had grown up on the streets of Chicago,
and through academic prowess he earned a scholarship to Milton Academy, the prestigious Massachusetts prep school, and admission to Columbia, New York City's Ivy League university. Surely his educational
achievements promised a meaningful and well-paying job, and his experience in the two academic establishments had shown him where the
right path could lead. But Evans was not a patient man. And he could
not stand to be broke.

One evening, in the spring of 1996, he went down into the Columbia School of Journalism's print shop with a friend, Edward
"Teddy" Olulenu, who worked there. Evans walked over to a Kodak
color copier, put a dollar bill facedown on the glass and pressed the
Print button. To his astonishment, "the shit came back perfect."

Evans is telling his story while sitting on the stoop of his house on
a quiet block in Inglewood, a neighborhood on Chicago's notorious
South Side. On one side of the street is a girl in a white graduation
gown, walking home. Directly across from her, two men emerge from a

brief trip into an alley, one of them hurriedly pocketing something, the other adding a few bills to a thick stack of cash.

Evans says that when that photocopied dollar bill came out of the machine, something inside him clicked. He was no stranger to hustling, to making money the shady way. He had sold a little weed at Milton and been tutored in the ways of the streets by his older brother Joe Solomon, a convicted bank robber. When Evans was broke, the academy in him went silent and the hustler spoke up. "One thing that Milton Academy taught me," Evans says, "was to calculate, to plan. You know, the five-paragraph essay: Outline everything you're gonna do. And when I got frustrated, I forgot that. I didn't think clear."

Evans sips a little Remy, then says, "As soon as I saw that first bill, in my head I was like, 'Let's go!'" His voice is filled with a breathless-ness betraying the rush of those heady first days. "'Go get the paper. Let's line this up. Let's do this. Let's do that. I know some people. If this works, I got ideas.'"

Evans has short hair, a lean, muscled frame and a tattoo of his fi-ancée's name on his arm, along with two Chinese characters. He walks on his toes and doesn't immediately come off as a tough guy, but after a few minutes you sense not to test him.

Evans says that first night down in the basement-level print shop, he and Olulenu stayed for hours, making $10,000 in counterfeit money. Evans, Olulenu, and some friends split up the usable money and went in separate directions to pass it. They paid for five-dollar cab rides with phony twenties and collected the change, then split their take evenly. Each share was more than $2,000. "I just planned initially to make $6,000, pay the little rent I had due, catch up on a couple of bills, and pay back my loans," Evans says. "But when I made half of what I needed to make the first night, I was like, 'Yo, I'm fittin to do this.'"

Evans gathered currency made before 1990: Pre-'90 bills lack a security thread—the bar running down the left side that can be seen when money is held up to the light. They discovered that the money came out best with the copier's color dial at what Evans calls "Magic Johnson-Larry Bird," or "32–33." Once they had a few hundred copies of bills, they spent hours cutting them apart with X-Acto knives. Then they crumpled the bills and put them in a clothes dryer with some coffee beans for twenty minutes. "We figured that when they get hot, it would rub off a little bit, so we hoped it'd give the bills a dingy color," Evans says. "We tried it, and it worked."

A pair of counterfeiters in their twenties interviewed for this article have a source in upper Manhattan who makes hundreds by bleaching dollar bills and printing over the blanks. "It would feel right, and you could do all of these [anticounterfeiting] techniques, like draw on it with a marker or hold it up to the light, and it would pass whatever test," says one of the duo. (The marker is the infamous brown pen the government introduced a few years back. If you draw with one on the white space of a counterfeit bill, the mark turns brown.) Sometimes the bills would be too white, so the twentysomethings would dip a brush in coffee and run it over the bills to make them look older. Or they'd iron the bills, or step on them, or poke them with tiny pins to give them a certain old-money texture.

When he saw his money coming out right, Evans says, "I put my full efforts into it. Stopped working, stopped doing everything. I became a 100 percent full-time dedicated hustler. All my life I'd seen 'em. I knew what to do. I said, 'I gotta be serious. Ain't no tellin what could happen. I gotta get guns, I gotta get everything. Someone could run up in my house and try to kill me.' I got a couple of pieces and put together a crew of go-getters who was down for me, who I knew I could count on."

The United States Secret Service, a branch of the Treasury Department, was created in 1865 to stop counterfeiting. At that time, U.S. currency was made by individual state banks, and one to two thirds of all American cash was counterfeit. Marc Connolly, a special agent with the Secret Service for thirteen years, says $500 billion worth of U.S. bills and coins is now in circulation worldwide. In 1999, about $139 million in counterfeit money was reported here and abroad, or less than three hundredths of one percent of the total money supply.

Some counterfeiters say those estimates are wishful thinking. The twentysomething duo estimate that as much as five percent of American currency is illicit. "This is a huge industry," one counterfeiter says. "It's motherfuckers that live for this shit. They pay their mortgages, car notes, everything with the shit, 'cause they're so good with it. After drugs and prostitution, this is America's biggest criminal enterprise."

Along with Teddy Olulenu, a Columbia student who was, Evans says, "your prototypical buppie: khakis, Hilfiger knit shirt, oxford collar, drove a BMW," Evans's counterfeiting team included Keith Blackwell, "Black's a Harlem street kid with a background similar to mine," Evans says. "Went to a good school in Westchester [New York] that had a lacrosse team."

Evans and his crew started out passing bills on short cab rides. Evans himself would ride from near the top of Manhattan to near the bottom—from 116th and Broadway down to Canal Street—changing cabs every twenty blocks. He would do this four times a day, and after seven or eight hours he'd have more than $700. "I didn't take it that serious at first," he says. "I'm not committing a crime. I'm tricking them."

Sometimes, to break the counterfeit bills, they would buy a hat, a movie from Blockbuster, a bottle from a liquor store, a necessity from Rite Aid, a drink in a bar, always something small so the change would be large. They'd go in groups so that the same face would not appear on in-store cameras, and they might wear Band-Aids on some of their fingers so no prints would get on the funny money. They would go to stores in different areas of New York and New Jersey, never going to the same location twice. They'd avoid cashiers who dealt with money enough to develop a sense for the look and feel of it: jewelers, bank tellers, subway token clerks.

Evans says that he and Blackwell were on the street making sales, while Olulenu spent his time down in the Columbia print shop creating the money, and a fleet of minions was cutting the bills apart, working eight-hour shifts at fifteen dollars an hour. The organization quickly blossomed. "One of my guys came to me with the idea [of selling to drug dealers]," Evans says. "I knew one guy who sold coke. I hit him off for one of his buys, and he told a couple of his partners. Next thing you know, every couple of weeks someone was comin. I charged one dude $50,000 for $100,000. You know how much it cost me to make that

$100,000? About $120. I said to myself, 'I'm makin some decent money here now. Great.' But I'm also like, 'OK, a whole can of hell could've just opened up, too.' "

Evans's mother, Dr. Maxine Evans, lives in the house where she raised the boy who she, like many others in Chicago, still calls Pooh. She calls her neighborhood middle-middle class but admits you need only go a few blocks in almost any direction to find drugs and gangs. "You got a lot of good sittin right in the middle of a lot of bad," she says.

The house has a large flower bed, a driveway for Maxine's white cloth-top two-door Mercedes 450 SL with a license plate that reads POOHS MA and, downstairs, a beauty salon called Tiffany. Maxine, who has a doctorate in cosmetology, has been doing hair for forty years. Her clients have included Gladys Knight and the Staple Singers. "I did so many people's hair, everybody knew me," says Maxine, a feisty woman who made her son pay a dollar for a can of Coca-Cola whenever he came to visit. "In 1969 I paid $45,000 to furnish a beauty salon," she says, sitting on a leather couch in her spacious living room, wearing green shorts, blue socks, and white sneakers. "Some people don't spend that now. It was the salon, I was doin fifteen, twenty people's hair every day, and I had five, six operators, and they were doin that many; so everybody knew Pooh. He was the beauty-shop baby."

Cliff is also the son of Nelson Evans, a retired Chicago policeman. "Everybody in Chicago knows your mother or your father," Maxine says. "There's nowhere he could go that he could do anything and somebody wouldn't see him. Had you been here," she says, turning to her son, clearly still bitter about his crimes, "you wouldn't have been involved with anything like that. We know the good, the bad, and the ugly. You couldn't have gotten away with all this in Chicago."

Maxine says that her son was smart as a child, a dreamer with a desire to be accepted by the wrong people. "I always worried about him," she says. " 'Cause one minute he's like, 'Aw, man, I know the Bloods and the Crips, and I'm straight.' And the next minute he's reading Truman Capote. They don't know if he gonna be the gangbanger or the professor or what."

As Evans neared his teens, his life began to come apart. His brother Joe was locked away for the first time in Cliff's life. His parents were fighting, on their way to a divorce. He was a latchkey kid with time to run the streets.

But Evans had always done well in school, and through A Better Chance, a program that helps inner-city kids get into elite private schools, he was able to escape Chicago for Milton. "I left home and went to boarding school at the age of twelve," Evans says. "My brother had taught me how to make it out here. And I couldn't see myself workin at the post office for the rest of my life. I wanted to leave a mark. So I took off, and I said I wasn't goin back till I came to a point where I needed to be."

At Milton, Evans was popular with boys, girls, and faculty. At first he struggled in class and had to repeat the ninth grade, but later he excelled. He earned a reputation as a ladies' man and starred on the football field as a running back. Living alongside rich kids, he became eager to enjoy the luxuries his classmates took for granted.

"Milton made him want too much too soon," his mother says. "It made him impatient. He felt like he should have everything they have. He seen these little rich kids with they money and doin rich things, and he felt like he's supposed to do 'em instantly."

"These kids were living in a dream world," says Ali Danois, who grew up in Brooklyn's rough Bedford-Stuyvesant neighborhood and became a close friend of Evans's at Milton. "I couldn't understand how they didn't realize how good they had it. You come home and be talkin about, 'I got a chance to go to Harvard or Princeton,' and these brothers are talkin about going to Rikers Island and Dannemora."

But if Evans and Danois noticed how bleak futures were in the ghetto and how bright the futures of their classmates seemed, why were they still awed by the street? "When you grow up in situations like me and Cliff," Danois said, "there is a lot of respect for brothers like [drug lords] Alpo and Nicky Barnes, those major hustler-player cats. 'Cause they made it. They made it against society's laws. They were the kings of their own domain."

After graduating from Milton in 1991, Evans moved on to Columbia. He joined the freshman football team as a running back and was being groomed for the varsity, but he injured his knee, fell out with the coach and quit athletics. He began spending most of his time in Harlem, Brooklyn, Queens, and the Bronx, accumulating friends on the streets.

"I had homeys everywhere," Evans said. "That's just who I vibed with. Having one or two connects on the street led to a bunch of others. With almost anybody I wanted to know, I had somebody who legitimized me and said, 'OK, this motherfucker's a standup guy.' They knew I was someone who could be trusted. Just knowin people casually led to other things."

Evans ran his counterfeiting operation with fierce determination. "My life revolved around this," he says. "You have no idea the work I put in doin this. When I was havin fun, I was handlin business at the same time. It was on my mind all the time. That's what stopped them from bein able to lock me up for a long time: not allowin anything to go unmonitored. I committed myself to it, and I went to the extreme. You can't get up in that game and tiptoe around in it."

He was constantly under stress, worried about being arrested, robbed, or murdered. He memorized the serial numbers he used on his money in the thought that he would have a leg up if he ever got busted. He maintained what he calls "access to guns," but says he never used them. He managed his stress by making certain that in every situation he was in control. "If it wasn't on my terms, I wasn't dealin with it," he says. "Meet me where I tell you to meet me, when I tell you to meet me."

But the worries didn't keep Evans from enjoying himself. "As fast as I got money, I spent it. I got scummy with broads, rented limos for weekends, drove around gettin hammered, shopping sprees—you know, the typical things people do when they got that type of dough. It wasn't nothin for me to go to a bar and spend $1,500 on people I didn't even know. Gave a lot of money to friends. The money had gotten so crazy it had no value. It was spendin paper. We make this stuff now. I couldn't buy a big-ass mansion, but I was a fly guy. Clothes, money in my pocket, smokin the best weed, goin in the club every night." He became what he had dreamed of: "I was that ghetto-fabulous cat."

One day, an associate was arrested for an unrelated crime with fake money on him. Evans held his breath until the man was released without the police noticing that the bills in his pocket were homemade. One night, Evans and his crew got drunk, stumbled out of a club and got robbed. A man dug in Evans' pocket, pulled out $5,000 and ran off—but the real money was in the other pocket. Another day, Evans pulled a stack of twenties from the pocket where he kept the legal tender and found three bills that had come full circle, products of his own Bank of Harlem. "Who knows how, but somehow, some way, that money got back to my pocket," he says with a laugh. "That's when I knew we'd blown up."

In 1996, Evans went to his five-year reunion at Milton. "Everybody's like, 'So, Cliff, what are you doin'?'" he says. "And I'm tellin 'em about the recording studio. Meanwhile, I'm thinkin, 'Oh, I'm doin illicit motherfuckin things. Bein around them kids, I totally had to revert. And I kinda missed the sanctuary of Milton, the shelteredness. It wasn't really stressful there. It was a simpler life, and seein it again, the kids running around trees, the perfect little hamlet, it had me bugged out that I came from that to where I was, that nothing at Milton had really changed and I had changed so much."

When Evans got back to New York, the malaise deepened. "It became like *Brewster's Millions*," he says. "I had to spend money in order to get money. And I found out one thing: It's hard as hell to spend money. You might say, 'Never could I get tired of spending money.' But you get tired of goin to stores. And you gotta find different stores, 'cause I can't hit the same spots, so now I gotta go further into Queens, into Jersey. I used to take trips to different cities just to spend the money—Atlanta, Chicago, D.C., Virginia."

Evans began to dream of a big score, something that would allow him to retire. "My goal," he says, "was to get with a hustler in some other country. Just nuke 'em with, like, a million dollars and I'm done. Come back to America and just be sittin on the money, chillin. Mexico is the country I really wanted to do it in. That would've been the final hurrah."

In May 1996, the Secret Service was contacted by a Park Avenue bar complaining that someone had passed bogus twenty-dollar bills there. Investigators analyzed the ink and quality of printing of the counterfeits, and were able to determine that a sophisticated, very expensive copy machine was used. Presuming the counterfeiters were local, investigators contacted the copier manufacturers, who were able to narrow the possibilities down to a small number of machines in the New York area. The copier that Olulenu and Evans had used was one of them.

Just before Thanksgiving that year, Evans says his partner Keith Blackwell sold money to a man who promptly deposited it into an ATM. Within hours, agents arrested Blackwell.

Blackwell was on the street making sales because Evans trusted him not to rat. But in the custody of the Secret Service, Blackwell confessed. With agents listening in, he phoned Olulenu and led him to say self-incriminating things. By week's end, Secret Service agents had picked up Olulenu and were moving toward Evans.

Evans was living in a new, barely furnished two-bedroom place on 140th Street and St. Nicholas Avenue in Harlem, a place he called the Chop Zone "because that's where all the money got chopped up." He was sitting in a back room, smoking a blunt, very high. He had a deal to do that day—he was going to sell $20,000 of his dollars for $6,000 of the government's, and even though he already had about $80,000 in fake money there, stacked on the living-room table, in the kitchen cabinets and in a clothes chest, Evans was waiting for Olulenu to make a delivery of more counterfeit cash.

When Olulenu arrived, he told Evans he didn't want to be involved in counterfeiting any longer. Evans was immediately suspicious. For ten minutes he talked to Olulenu, scoping him out, noticing that he was stuttering and not making eye contact. Finally, Evans said, "What, you got a wire on or somethin'?" At that moment his door was blown off its hinges by a battering ram, and men poured into the apartment.

"I thought I was gettin robbed," Evans says. "I thought I was fittin to get murdered." He ran at them, hoping to grab a gun or somehow stop the onslaught. "I rushed 'em," he said. "I thought that was my only chance of living." But there were at least fifteen Secret Service agents coming at him. He was smacked on the forehead by a shotgun. "I hit the ground, and they stood on my neck and started screamin, 'Where the motherfuckin guns! Can we search the place?' I said, 'I don't give a fuck.' I knew I was goin to jail. The question was how long."

With the overwhelming evidence against him, Evans pleaded guilty to two counts of counterfeiting and one count of conspiracy on September 22nd, 1997. Evans was released on bond after his mother put up her house as collateral, and he awaited his sentence without fear. He received a fifteen-month sentence along with three years of supervised release. Neither Blackwell nor Olulenu served jail time. "Jail would be hard for most people," he says, "but Milton was harder for me than jail was." At Milton he had struggled to complete five hours of homework a night and to learn to live in an all-white world. "I had some background in how to survive jail from just seein guys I know and hearin the stories," he says.

In March 1998, Evans began his sentence at a federal prison camp in Pennsylvania. "I'm not gonna go nowhere near to say that imprisonment rehabilitated me," he says. "But it allowed me to basically get some rest and think and get my shit together."

Upon his release, Evans considered moving back to New York. "If I'd gone back to New York, I'd still be doin the same things. So I came here to Chicago. And I never had a relapse."

After a few months on the street, with a little hustling in the old-fashioned sense of the word, Evans landed a job at a Chicago telecommunications firm that specializes in cable television. He found a company willing to look beyond his past. "The guy who was hiring me told me, 'Look, don't even stress that [conviction],' " Evans says. " 'If you can do the job, then we want you.' " After a few months, Evans was promoted to department supervisor, in charge of a crew that upgrades cable systems. He looks to have his own subcontracting firm within a year or two.

"Everything I'm reading forecasts that the next wave of multimillionaires is going to come out of the telecommunications industry," he says. "Not necessarily that I'm gonna become a multimillionaire over cable, but it makes more sense to immerse myself in that growth industry. I'm not makin a lot of money now. But I will."

Evans is also managing some singers and MCs, and saving toward starting a record label. He is getting married and hopes to start a family soon. He recently took his brother Joe's oldest son into his home, to live with Evans and his fiancée until Joe is released in the fall of 2002. Evans is also looking forward to his tenth Milton Academy reunion next spring.

"I tried the slick way," Evans says. "Worked but didn't really work. 'Cause it was the wrong way. I work like a dog now. I'm up every morning at five and I don't get in the house from work until eight at night. I reinvest all my money. I'm puttin all my efforts into positive things, and it's gonna blow. It has to blow. I know too much for it not to. I went to school with Kennedy kids. I went to jail. I've seen it all. There's nothing that I can't do."

The Greatest Tennis Player You've Never Heard Of

{ Al Parker, Jr., *Tennis* magazine, 2001 }

Middleton Albert Parker II is thirty-two years old and an investment banker at JPMorgan H&Q in Atlanta who absolutely loves golf and will not play tennis. But once upon a time he was pretty good at our game. In 1981, during his second year in the twelve-and-unders, he won the singles and doubles at all four national tournaments. A double grand slam. He is the only person in the history of American junior tennis to do that. People said he was the future of American tennis, the successor to McEnroe and Connors. As he grew older the talk grew louder. Despite competition from what may be the greatest generation of American juniors of all time, including kids named Pete Sampras, Andre Agassi, Jim Courier, Michael Chang, Malivai Washington, David Wheaton, Todd Martin, Chris Garner, Stephen Enochs, Jonathan Stark, and Jeff Tarango, this kid from Claxton, Georgia, was ranked number one in all four age divisions. He is the only person in the history of American junior tennis to do that. Of course he was going to be a great pro. In 1987, his last year in the eighteens, he won his twenty-fifth national title and set the record for cumulative national titles that stands today. His bedroom at his parent's home is filled with more than one hundred pieces of championship hardware in every form tournament directors have ever conceived—plates, trophies, bowls, cups, medals, rings, watches, and the tiny balls the USTA awards at nationals. Among the twenty-five gold balls for winning, there are thirteen silver balls for finishing second. Al Parker, Jr., is unquestionably the greatest junior player of all time.

After four years at the University of Georgia, and being voted an All-American four times, Parker ventured on to the pro tour. Boys he'd spanked a few years earlier were winning grand slams. He'd arrived to join them. And I was rooting for him.

I don't usually root for Goliaths, but I'd watched Parker, the tall blond who always won, grow from a cherub with a delicate Prince Valiant haircut to a lanky stud with the long scruffy mane of a disaffected rock star. The same way we come to feel a deep familiarity with the long-term famous, to believe that certain movie stars and hometown athletes are our people, I'd come to feel he was a friend. As well, Parker was the ultimate representative of the junior tennis circuit. For him to win at the professional level would mean that the junior circuit worked as a training ground, that all of us who had, like him, driven and flown across state lines to play tournaments at age twelve and thirteen had at least been on the right track. I didn't know much about him and I'd never seen him play, but I wanted him to win.

But he never showed up on television. I scoured the box scores of tournaments like a lawyer poring over fine print, but I never saw him listed. The gorilla had somehow hid behind the pole. My man Al Parker had just disappeared.

One day I checked the Internet and found he'd played on the tour a short time and never cracked 250. What? Did he have a game built only for the juniors and couldn't make it translate to the pros? Was he pushed too hard by his parents as a kid and couldn't take it when he got older? I wanted to know what life was like at the absolute top, to be the guy who was always seeded first and almost always won. But more than that, I had to find out what happened in the pros. How is it that the can't-miss kid missed?

By luck I found someone who knew Parker. He was in Atlanta, they told me. But, they said, he didn't play anymore. I couldn't imagine what life without tennis was like for someone to whom the game had been so kind. I had to know what'd happened to my friend. It turns out that Al Parker's life, with and without, tennis, was not at all what I'd imagined and the reasons why he quit were complicated.

The history of sport is littered with tales of meteoric prodigies who flamed out before proving themselves on the highest level and landed in a virtual gutter. This is, and is not, one of those stories. You see, Al Parker, Jr., never became the best player in the world, but he did become the happiest ex-player in the world.

Claxton, Georgia, is a town of 2,500 that's forty minutes west of Savannah by car. There's a giant water tower there with the words "The Fruitcake Capital of the World" printed on it. In 1945 a man named Albert Parker bought a local fruitcake business for ten thousand dollars. Unlike most fruitcake, the Claxton Fruitcake Company's product was extremely high in fruit and nut content and in the 50s Parker and his children, including one Mid Parker, began building the business into a multimillion-dollar operation. Today the company moves six million pounds of fruitcake a year. "We used to sell a lot more cake," Mid said with a touch of bitterness. "Then Johnny Carson started tellin fruitcake jokes. That really hurt our business."

Parker grew up with his eye on a blonde four years his junior named Sally Edwards. "When I was in the seventh grade," Sally said, "my mother would come home and she would say I saw that Mid Parker downtown today. As usual he made me stop and roll down my window and he said, 'Miss Ginny, when are you gonna let me go out with Sally?' Well, I said the same thing I always say. 'Never, you wild Indian! You're too fast for my daughter!'" Miss Ginny liked Mid—Claxton is so small everyone knows everyone well—she just thought him too old for her daughter then. When Sally reached the ninth grade Miss Ginny finally let him take her out. He was a football and baseball star. She was class valedictorian. They were married in 1964. Their first child, Al, was born three days before Christmas in 1968.

During a family trip to Hilton Head, South Carolina, Sally put six-year-old Al into a child's tennis clinic so she and Mid could have time for some laugh-and-swing mixed doubles with friends. The pro told her he'd never seen a child so gifted. Sally decided to get him lessons, but waited two years. "A child only gets to be a child once," she said. "I had a feeling that once it ever started it would be nonstop."

Mid and Sally remember young Al as a serious and extremely disciplined child—"he was more disciplined than we were," Sally said. He was a perfectionist and a neatnik who made his bed as soon as he was tall enough to reach it. He overstudied for his tests, overprepared his school projects, and got A's in every single class he ever took. When he began playing tennis he became obsessed with hitting every ball perfectly and supplemented his lessons by hitting against a wall outside his home every day for hours. "He could stand there and never miss a dang shot," Mid said. "He got to where he could hit that thing one thousand times without missing."

Because the fruitcake business operates largely between September and December, Mid had plenty of time the rest of the year to drive Al to lessons in Savannah. When Al began entering local tournaments he was big for his age, extremely steady from the baseline, and more mentally mature than his peers. "I was able to focus better and stay in the match a little bit better than the other kids," he said, reclining in the living room of his cozy home in the suburbs of Atlanta on a warm Saturday afternoon. He was wearing shorts and Birkenstocks. "I don't know why I had that ability." He also hated to lose. "I don't care if it's tennis, croquet, or whatever," Sally said, "he will get after you with 200 percent of his being and make you think you cannot win." At nine he won club tournaments, at ten he won Georgia state tournaments, and at eleven he won a twelve-and-under national in Houston. After that, the board outside the Claxton town church said: "Al's Humility Makes the Boy a Double Winner."

Parker's second year in the twelve-and-unders he won his legendary double grand slam and the singles title at the Orange Bowl. "I had some bad days, but not so bad that I lost," he said. "I don't know how to explain it. There's some luck in there, some fate in there, and some good work on my part. It all just came together." (Chris Garner is also a reason for the double grand slam. Garner, Al's partner in the doubles at the National Hard Court Championships in San Diego, recalled a semifinal against David Wheaton and Malivai Washington in which he and Parker were down match point. "One of those guys hit a drop volley to Al and Al didn't run for it," Garner said. "I ran it down, put it back, and one of those guys missed an easy shot. They choked. We wound up winning 9–7 in the third. And I always gave him crap that he would've never had his double grand slam if I didn't run for that ball.")

It's incomprehensible that this kid won sixty-three consecutive matches under high pressure in national and international competition. In one tournament, before match point in a third-set tiebreaker in front of a giant crowd, Sally overheard a man say, "If I were that kid I know that there would be no way that I could even draw the racket back. I'd be so scared."

Everyone prefers winning, but Parker won so much it became what he now sees was a curse. "Once I started having the big success I was expected to win and if I didn't win then I'd not succeeded and that was when it became more of a job and a pursuit of a goal as opposed to loving the sport." The pressure grew immense and though he liked competing enough to continue winning, his love of the game began to seep away. It would never stop. "This unbelievable double grand slam," Sally said, "catapulted him into junior stardom and put tremendous pressure on him from that day forward, because where do you go from there but down?" There was a crush of press (he was named Tennis Magazine's Junior Player of the Year); an appearance on the TV show To Tell the Truth; letters from colleges, agents, and Georgia senators; and impossible expectations. Few could see the potential long-term effects. "I had a tennis-mother friend," Sally said, "who told me, you know, I honestly think that one of the worst things that can happen to a kid in junior tennis is to be unbeatable in the twelves because he's always the one the pressure's gonna be on. And, you know, the pressure of the pressure on him was immense on us. That's still your baby out there that's been thrown to the wolves and it's such a naked sport. Have you ever thought about that? Tennis is such a naked sport. I mean, you're out there on your own. And for him it went on for so long. It felt like it took him away from being a child. It felt like he had a man's job from age twelve." But stopping was impossible. "It was too far gone," Sally said. "He didn't wanna stop. We never pushed Al. We would never have insisted he go on."

One day someone mentioned that the record for national junior titles won was twenty-four by Scott Davis. Parker already had nine. "Once I realized there was a shot, that was something I was focused on," he said. "The only reason I kept playin juniors was to try to break that record."

In the fourteen-and-unders he won six more titles with a baseline game that was changing but not by his own accord. "I didn't really have weaknesses," he said. "My backhand was a pretty good weapon when I was younger but people tried to stay away from that, hitting to my forehand, and as I got older my forehand became more of the weapon." In two or three years he would add a crushing serve, but his edge was truly mental. "I seemed to get up more for the bigger matches and my game would be the same as if I was playing in practice, as opposed to some kids who get lost in the moment and lose the focus. I don't know how you get that except experience over time, but I think I had a little bit from the start. Maybe I was just born with something."

By then he had such presence and such a reputation that he won a lot of matches before he even walked on the court. "He was a larger-than-life figure," Jim Courier said. "When you were gonna play Al you just booked your flight. Okay, it's off to the next tournament now. It's over."

He also began winning sportsmanship awards, which he'd continue to do throughout college. "He gave points back if he wasn't 100 percent sure of a call," said Murphy Jensen, a fellow junior. "Such a sweet dude. He was extremely serious about being fair and about class and doin the right thing." Andre Agassi once told a reporter, "Al was always a polite kid. He was never as obnoxious as myself. He is a good guy and was never really conceited."

When he won his celebration was minimal. "He always wanted to win real bad," Mid said, "but when he won he looked like he was embarrassed." Sally said, "People would always come to me with the question, Is Al upset about anything? Is he not happy that he won? Because he was very subdued. But it wasn't in him ever to gloat." Al said, "The biggest thing for me was to never rub it in anybody's face."

Gery Groslimond, his coach throughout the juniors, said, "He might be the most normal national champion of all time. He never acted like a prima donna. He was very humble, very gentlemanly, treated everyone with respect. That made it difficult to beat him. Everyone liked the kid. He wasn't a jerk who you wanted to beat. He let his racket do the talking. He reminded me a lot of Rod Laver in terms of character. Laver would hit a winner and he wouldn't go crazy like Connors. He would say, Isn't that what I'm supposed to do?"

Mid and Sally did everything they could to make the tournament circuit fun for Al. They bought a big van and drove to tournaments in the South, bringing his younger sister, Ginny, and sometimes Sally's mother. Mid's father was a little mystified by the whole situation. He once told Mid, "I don't understand why in the world y'all fly all over the country, San Diego one week, Michigan the next week, and I see in the paper where he beats the same boys every week. Why don't y'all get together in a place in the middle there, play about ten times and get it over with?"

After matches the Parkers' van was the place to be. "That family was just so loving," Murphy Jensen said. "What I love about their character is not only when they were kickin everyone's butt they were great, cuz it's easy to be super friendly when you're winning, but when guys started getting their wins over him, they were just as great a tennis family."

Sally said, "We loved all the kids. They called Mid the pied piper because everyone wanted to get in Mid's van and go get hamburgers." Some of those kids eating hamburgers would grow up to be legends, giving Mid and Sally a front-row seat for history. "I always knew Agassi was special," Mid said. "His hand-eye coordination was phenomenal even as a little kid. Courier was a bulldog. Chang surprised me. Now when they changed Sampras from a two-handed backhand to a one-handed backhand I said, 'That's the dumbest thing I've ever in my life seen. The kid's got the best backhand in the world! They're destroyin his tennis career!' "

But Parker's love for the game continued draining out of him. "It wasn't as much fun as it was in the early stage," he said. "I didn't hate it. I just don't think I had that unabashed love for the game anymore. My enjoyment came from trying to prove that I could still do it with all the pressure on me, not from hitting the ball." He could no longer practice by drilling. "For me to practice I needed to play matches," he said. "Very rarely would I—and it probably hurt me—be okay with losing practice sets cuz I was working on a one-handed backhand slice." Though he kept getting better, his development slowed.

At fifteen he shot up six inches to six-foot-three in a handful of months and lost his coordination. He served entire matches underhand. And there were more mental problems. "I definitely felt like I was tired mentally," he said. "It had been intense since I was twelve and over time that takes a toll. Potentially some of my success early on, I think, was a curse." His first year in the sixteens he was ranked fifth in the nation. The next year he won just a single title, but because no one had a great year, he finished number one. Going into the eighteens he had only sixteen national titles. Scott Davis's record seemed out of reach. But in his first year he went on a tear and won eight titles, tying the record. His last year in the eighteens he traveled with the Junior Davis Cup team to pro tournaments and broke into the top 200, but in pursuit of the record he played the National Indoor Championships in Dallas. In the semis of the singles he lost to Courier, but he and Jensen won the doubles. "We won reasonably handily," Parker said, "but I remember continuing to bear down until that last point. There wasn't a lot of laughin and smilin going on." After the final match he felt a tremendous release. "I felt such a sense of relief that for the rest of that year I'd have a little less pressure, because in the pros I got to be the underdog and do to people what they had been doin to me for years." He played just one more junior tournament after that, the Championships at Kalamazoo, and only because the winner received a wild card into the U.S. Open. He lost in the semis to Michael Chang.

You could barely dream of having a junior career as successful as Parker's, but the reality was far from fun and now, at eighteen, it had come time to pay the bill. Years of slowed development was the result of a decreased love of the game and that was a result of the pressure of always being the hunted one. If years at the top are difficult for an adult, imagine the impact on a child. Perhaps that's why most of those who are giants in the juniors don't make it in the pros, and most who make it big in the pros don't have spectacular careers in the juniors. Parker said, "They [Agassi, Sampras, Chang, and Courier] didn't have the real early success in the juniors that may have led them to, well, I don't wanna say I burned out, but I definitely felt like I was tired by the time I was sixteen, seventeen. Tired mentally. And some of that translates to physical. I was tired before I got to the part where I was gonna be makin money playing. I mean, who has had tremendous junior success and gone on to be a top player in the world?"

Parker was slowly trending downward, away from the top players, but at eighteen there was a fork in the road: should he move on to college or the tour? At that point it was still uncommon for Americans to skip college completely. McEnroe and Connors had spent a year or two and when Agassi jumped people like Stan Smith and Arthur Ashe were public about their dismay. But Bollettieri and others were urging their top players to jump to the pros, Aaron Krickstein and Jimmy Arias had proven it could be done, and Agassi was quickly successful on the tour. Parker couldn't see that his tennis future hinged on his decision, but of that great generation, only those who skipped college—Agassi, Sampras, Courier, Chang—would become top pros. Some who went for a year or two—Mal Washington, David Wheaton, Todd Martin—would have strong careers on the tour. Most who spent three or four years in college would not. Many people told Parker he should skip college but he didn't consider it. "I was pretty focused on doin college and doin it at Georgia," he said. "I didn't look at college as something that would hold me back from successful tennis. I looked at it as another step up in the competition. It was a chance to go get great-quality coaching from one of the top programs in the country and to also provide myself with the other options education would afford me if tennis didn't work out." Even with a ranking in the top 200 and a past that seemed to promise a glorious pro career, he still had it in mind that he might not succeed as a pro. "I've never really looked at myself as invincible," he said. "I was always bearing down in the event that something wouldn't work out. I don't know if that's an insecurity problem or what, but I've never knew that things would work out."

He declared a finance major and earned a 4.0. "He would stay up so late I used to cuss him out," said Dan Magill, his coach freshman year. "I said you gon lose a match for Georgia for you stayin up all night studyin." He also joined a fraternity and had a rich social life. "Girls loved the guy," Jim Childs said. "We would trail Al around town. Let him be the lead guy, we would be his wingmen." He continued, of course, to be unbelievably meticulous. "In college your apartment's supposed to be a wreck," said friend and fellow player Wade McQuire, "but in his room everything would be perfect. You go into his closet, everything was perfectly lined up. You open his desk drawer and the tacks would all be in order."

He won his first two collegiate tournaments. But in his third, the SEC Indoors at the University of Alabama, when he stretched for his semifinal match he felt a strange tweak in his back. As the match went on it turned into serious pain. He lost in three sets.

Back at Georgia the orthopedists discovered he had spondylolisthesis, a condition that causes discs in the lower spine to push on one another and cause tremendous pain. In Parker's case, one of his discs was cracked.

Parker thinks that if he'd been on the tour, focused simply on tennis and taking care of his body, that maybe the condition wouldn't have hit him then. "Maybe in college I was spread too thin," he said, "tryin to do schoolwork and social life and tennis all at the same time. Who knows if that would've happened if I was playin on the tour instead of Georgia. I had enough doctors look at it, and I assume what they're saying is right, but it just seems weird to me that all of a sudden my freshman year in college it's gonna decide to hit me after having played eighteen years. But I was still able to perform at a high level even with the back problems."

His last three years at Georgia, Parker won two big tournaments and got straight A's. "That 4.0 was of the utmost importance to him," said Manuel Diaz, Georgia's head coach during Parker's last three years. His junior year, the NCAA named him the Academic All-American of the year for all spring sports. His senior year he graduated summa cum laude and was named the Academic All-American for all sports. Meanwhile, out on the tour, the boys he used to beat were leaving him behind. "Al had a blast in college and was the big man on campus," Courier said, "but while he was havin fun we were breakin through."

In the summer of 1991 Parker hit the pro tour. His back was aggravated by long flights to places like Kuala Lumpor, Jakarta, and Dubai. He won four satellite tournaments but in Challenger and ATP events he usually lost in the first or second round, often to players of lesser ability. "It's hard to play after flying twenty hours in coach." Then the rotator cuff in his serving shoulder tore, then he suffered stress fractures in his foot, and shin splints, and a torn stomach muscle. "I was just continuously injured," he said. "It was incredibly frustrating. It felt like I was goin backwards."

His body was falling apart as if every part of him was screaming no mas, as if the curse of early success was exacting its final revenge. You have to wonder what part his mind played in all that, if the injuries weren't psychologically induced, if he wasn't collapsing under the stress of ten years of what his own mother had called a man's job, ten years of burning the candle from all sides. "Al got a lot of attention from day one," Jim Childs said. "Look at Todd Martin. He operated behind the scenes until college and then he burst onto the scene. Todd got to work on his tennis game and be a guy until he was eighteen or nineteen, whereas Al was out in the public eye from a very young age."

Parker might've kept trying to break through, but he's a very social creature and the tour is an extremely lonely experience. His enjoyment level, dropping steadily since the double grand slam, was reaching zero. There'd been a community in the juniors, with all the players he saw at every tournament and their parents and siblings. At Georgia he had his teammates and coaches. In the pros he had no one. The reasons why he wanted to win escaped him. "I don't know that my desire was fully there," he said. "I don't know if I ever really wanted it bad enough on the tour. In the juniors and college I wanted to win bad. I was into the competition. And I was into it for reasons other than just internally wanting to win. In the juniors I was playing for these records and goals. In college you're playing for your team and for the school and there's five thousand people watching. I loved playin in college. I loved the college team environment and having more on the line than individual accomplishments. Once I got to the pros and it was all about me and it was all about the job, I didn't enjoy it at all. One day I was in Bangladesh, no, it was Bangalore [India], and the poverty, man, it's one of those places where either you're really wealthy or really poor. You got three people watching and nobody cares and this guy's serve hits a rock on the court and rockets out of the stadium and I'm saying to myself, what am I doin here?" He was miserable and he knew he could do something else with his life.

One blistering hot day in Texas, with Mid in the crowd, Al lost to a lesser player.

He walked off and said, "Dad, this is not working out. I think I'm gonna quit."

Mid told him, "Buddy, I concur with ya 100 percent."

"We all breathed a collective sigh of relief," Sally said.

He'd quit the tour after just two and a half years. He now faced one of the biggest challenges of his life. Many players find it hard to adjust to life without the thrill of competition, life as a civilian. His parents feared he would feel he'd been a failure and would lose the self-confidence he'd gained in tennis. Parker was almost twenty-five years old with no headway on a career, three years behind his peers in the workforce. And he had no idea what to do with his life.

He called John Ross, a friend who'd played on the tour and now worked in investment banking. In a series of conversations Ross suggested Parker think about investment banking, a career that would satiate his need for intensity and competition. "You work such inhuman hours," Parker said, "and you pack so much experience into a couple of years. Two years as an analyst is almost like working four years since you rarely sleep and that would help me make up lost time spent on the tour."

Parker moved quickly. Within a few months he got engaged to his college sweetheart, Christy Falcon (they married in 1994), and he applied to only one business school: Harvard. Like most business schools, HBS favors applicants with at least two years of experience in the business world, so Parker wrote that his time on the pro tour should be looked at as running a business. "It's not traditional business, but it's a business career in its own right," he said. "You're self-employed in an entrepreneurial-type venture and you're managing your own schedule, you're arranging your own travel, you're coordinating expenses, budgeting, sponsorships, and equipment. I knew it was a stretch, but I figured I'd give it a shot anyway."

"He thought he could talk Harvard into thinking that a couple of years on the tennis tour was conducting a business," Sally said, giggling. "I'm sorry, it's just kind of comical. In a way, he did have a point. It is a business, you are trying to earn money, but it's not corporate experience."

Parker was turned down, but Ross helped him get a job as a financial analyst at his own firm, Bowles, Halliwell, Connor, and Company, in Charlotte, North Carolina, a firm helmed by then White House chief of staff Erskine Bowles. After two years he was accepted to HBS. After graduating in 1998 he returned to Atlanta. The next year, a week before Halloween, his wife gave birth to Middleton Albert Parker III.

By all accounts Parker moved away from tennis with grace. "He never seemed to be the least bit depressed," Sally said. "Now, I've heard him say it's kinda hard to watch these guys out there doin so great and he wonders why didn't it work out for him, but he doesn't brood about it. He's busy with what he's doin now. And I'm so thankful that all of this did not take a negative toll on him because I think it could've destroyed somebody. I really do think it had that potential."

Gery Groslimond said, "There's a lot of guys who were number one in the world and they're not really nice people or they're empty people. He's well-rounded. He's very happy today and I don't know if a lot of players who are number one in the world can say that after their playing days are over. Or even while they're number one."

Parker said he has no regrets. "Certainly I think about what it might've been like if I was a top player in the world, but I've moved on from it. It does not bother me. I don't ever look back at my tennis career with any sort of bad feelings because I couldn't be happier with what I'm doing today. I enjoy my career, I enjoy my family, I enjoy the fact that I'm not still out there trying to grind through injury problems on the tour. I love my life and I'm incredibly happy and happy for those guys."

Those guys, said Parker's Junior Davis Cup coach Greg Patton, became who they are in part because of Parker. "The stars all gotta be right for a generation like that to happen," Patton said. "If Al hadn't been there I don't think they would've been that good. He was the rabbit the greyhounds were chasing, the standard for great tennis in that generation. I think Sampras, Agassi, Courier—they all owe something to Al." In the scheme of life, it doesn't matter that the greyhounds overtook him, because Parker made something of his life. The game's great gift to him—unimaginable early success—became a curse, but the measure of character is not the peaks you reach, it's the valleys from which you escape. The boy who was strong enough to get to the mountaintop was an even stronger man when he was thrown from it and that has made all the difference. "I wouldn't say his life is incomplete because he didn't make it on the tour," Courier said. "I shudder to think that you throw all your eggs of happiness in the basket of tennis."

Nowadays he can't serve two games without tremendous pain, he doesn't watch tennis on television because he'd rather play with his son or hit the links, and he almost never discusses his past. "Occasionally I'll have a meeting with a client who'll recognize my name or something and everyone else from my firm will be like, you used to play tennis?"

His son, Middleton, almost two, is already showing a little athletic ability. Will he play tennis? "I don't have a feeling either way," Parker said. "I think it would be hard for him to play tennis and to try to live up to some of what I've done. Then again, by the time he's playing hardly anybody will remember what I did."

Inherit the Wind

{ Dale Earnhardt, Jr., *Rolling Stone*, 2001 }

Dale Earnhardt, Sr., was a man of few words, gruff and slow to trust. Before he was killed on the track at the Daytona 500 in February, he was considered one of the best race-car drivers who ever lived. Quite a bit has been said about Dale Sr. by many people. Tributes by the dozen have sprouted up, with Earnhardt's Number 3 set in roses in the infield at tracks around the country and trios of doves released before races. This is the first time his twenty-six-year-old son, Dale Jr., a rising NASCAR star, has talked at length about his feelings toward his father since his death.

Dale Sr. had a reckless dirt-track style marked by banging and bumping his way to the front, as well as an almost supernatural ability to find the air ahead of him. He was as successful as Jordan, as powerful as Shaq, and as controversial as Rodman. He won the Rookie of the Year title in 1979, the season championship the next year, six more during the next thirteen years, and seventy-six races in total. He painted his Number 3 Chevy black and became known as the Man in Black, Big E, the Intimidator, Ironhead, and fans loved or hated him—a drama that helped infuse the sport with a new level of passion. He became one of its biggest draws and helped shepherd NASCAR into its modern, multimillion-dollar, network-television era as he parlayed his own image into a multimillion-dollar enterprise. At his death, Dale Earnhardt Inc., a 250-person company, owned an auto dealership, five planes, one helicopter, thousands of acres of real estate, a seat on the New York Stock Exchange, four chicken houses under contract to Perdue and home to some 36,000 chickens, and a single-A minor-league baseball team in North Carolina called the Kannapolis Intimidators.

Dale Earnhardt, Jr., didn't see his father a lot while this empire was being built. "When I was a little kid, there was not a lot of hangin out and becomin buddies," he says. As Junior grew up, there were personality clashes. Where Senior was driven and serious, Junior was a slacker. Senior awoke with the sun; Junior slept till noon. Senior loved country music and deer hunting; Junior preferred PlayStation, the Internet, hiphop, and rock and roll. Senior criticized him often and worried openly about Junior's future: "When I was eighteen, he said, 'Junior, what I worry about is if I leave the world today, will you make it on your own? I know Kelley [his older sister] would make it, because she's workin already, but I don't know about you.'"

In 2000, when Junior began racing in the Winston Cup circuit alongside his father, their relationship changed. "Immediately, when I started driving race cars, that's when we started to relate as adults," he says. In the seventh race of the season, the DirecTV 500 at the Texas Motor Speedway in Fort Worth, Junior took his first Winston Cup victory. After the race, Senior ran to his son's car. "He didn't say he loved me often, but he said it as soon as he got to the car in Texas. 'Good job, I love you. Get the fuck out this car.' Our relationship was primo from then on out. We talked like equals almost. We had conversations that were a whole lot fuckin cooler."

Junior won two more races last year, and as the world took note of the hot young driver, he became a man in his father's eyes. "He felt content with what I was doin with my life," Junior says. "'OK, you've gotten to a point where you can take care of yourself. I'm done tryin to direct you, and now I'm just going to be here for you.'"

On February 18th, father and son were at the Daytona 500, the first and grandest stock-car race of the year. Before the race they went to the drivers' meeting where all drivers convene to hear special instructions and a group prayer. The Earnhardts sat together in the front row, as they often did. There is great symbolism in where each driver sits in the meeting, and though Junior's sophomore status should've put him toward the back, Senior often saved a seat for him in the front—a way of saying that Junior would soon be one of the leading drivers. After the meeting, Senior threw his arm over Junior's shoulders, and they walked out together. "He said the typical kinda stuff that he would say," Junior says of that final conversation. "That I had a car that was capable of winning if I just stayed out of trouble. 'Be careful.' Things like that. Gave me a hug."

During races, Senior would occasionally give Junior little hand signals, telling him to watch out or complimenting him on a nice maneuver. With only twenty-six laps to go in this Daytona 500, there was a nineteen-car pileup that sent driver Tony Stewart flying in the air. The cars that survived the crash—including those of both Junior and Senior—stopped on the track while a crew cleared away pieces of car. During the red flag, Senior silently praised Junior for avoiding the melee. "He pulled beside me and was like, 'Good job makin it out of there,'" Junior says. "That was the last bit of communication me and him had."

Once the racing began again, Junior's car was fast and loose, and he led the pack for five laps until he was passed by Michael Waltrip, a veteran driver in his first race for Senior's team. As the race wound down, Junior was second, just feet behind Waltrip, while Senior was third, a few car lengths back, just ahead of a crowd. Senior was battling to hold onto his position, swerving a bit to block cars from passing him, a typical racing maneuver. Many have surmised that Senior was blocking less for himself and more to protect Waltrip and Junior, but Junior doesn't believe that. "He woulda blocked anybody from his position no matter what position he woulda been in," he says.

On the final lap, a car tapped Senior's bumper. Number 3 rocketed up the track and went head on into the wall. Junior saw the whole thing in his rearview mirror. "I'm goin through the corner, and as soon as I look in the mirror," he says, "I kinda see his car shoot up the racetrack, and I was like, 'Shit! Fuckin had a wreck. Damn! We were gonna have the top three. Now we're not.'" He had no idea he'd just seen his father die.

When he pulled around the track, Earnhardt saw his father's car and all the smoke. "It just looked like a movie scene," he says. "Like somebody was over there with a smoke machine. It looked really dramatized. Just looked odd to me." He thought about jumping out of his car then but didn't want to draw too much attention to the scene, so he pulled onto the pit road and asked what had happened to his father. No one knew. He made a beeline for the medical center. "There were a lot of TV and radio that were ready to interview me, but I just didn't wanna do that," he says. "I wanted to go see Dad." At the medical center he got in a car with Teresa Earnhardt, Dale Sr.'s wife, and went to the hospital, still knowing nothing. "I was pretty nervous," he says. "I was really nervous. I did not like the fact of not knowing. That was the worst part. Still—" He pauses and is silent for a while, the words hard to say. "Him dying hadn't crossed my mind at that time. I just thought it was maybe a little more serious than his past injuries had been."

Senior broke both his collarbones in 1979, his sternum in '96, and various ribs in other crashes. There were also countless other injuries that he kept to himself for his personal doctor to fix. But no matter how bad the crash looked, Ol' Ironhead always jumped out of his car and waved to his fans, creating an aura of invincibility. Senior became known for being unbreakable in spirit and body. It's not so much that racing fans like to see horrific crashes—they like to see drivers walk away from horrific crashes. At that, no one was better than Earnhardt.

But this time he'd gone head on into the wall, and, Junior believes, his seat belt broke upon impact. "The only thing that could explain the injuries is he broke his seat belt," Junior says. "He broke a lot of ribs on the left side of his body from impact with the steering wheel. How did he get there? How did he fly into the steering wheel if he's strapped in?"

There was some controversy over the cause of Earnhardt's death and whether the seat belt was broken by the force of impact or cut by EMTs trying to save him. Bill Simpson, the president and CEO of the company that made the seat belt, has demanded that NASCAR publicly absolve him of responsibility for Earnhardt's death. Junior feels certain of the cause of his father's death, but he's also not looking to place blame. "This was a new belt that was in my dad's car," he says. "It should not have broken. All the belts that they tested withstood, like, five times more force than my father's body put on the belt, and it makes you wonder whether we're doing something wrong when we mount the belts."

At the hospital, Junior looked into the operating room just once—"I didn't get in there real close or anything; I just kinda peeked around the corner of the door and saw a table full of doctors, and they're all elbows and assholes"—then went to a waiting room. For forty-five minutes he sat with his Uncle Danny. "All kinds of stuff's runnin through your head," Junior says. "Like, you don't know how serious it is, you don't know whether someone's gonna come say, 'Well, he's in stable condition,' or 'He's in critical condition,' or 'He's paralyzed'—you don't know what they're gonna tell ya. Then they come in there, and the lady said they did the best they could. That was her words exactly. You felt like . . ." He's quiet for a moment. " 'This is not happenin.' " He stops again and is silent for a long time. His demeanor is calm, and though it seems that the words are already chosen, getting them out is hard. "You're just like . . ." He stops. "Fuckin blown away."

When they told him his father was gone, there was a burst of tears. "I was hysterical. I just fuckin exploded." He was given the opportunity to see his father one last time but couldn't do it. "I wanna remember what he looked like when he had life in him," he says. "There'll always be that side of me that says I wish I woulda looked at him one last time. I'd do anything to see his face, and that woulda been the chance, but it's not the same if he's not alive, man."

Soon, a lot of friends arrived, and Teresa was surrounded by people she loved. Junior made sure she was taken care of, and then he bolted from the hospital. "I just, like, wanted a cigarette real bad," he says. His voice is even, but intense. "Just wanted to smoke one after the other." After he left the hospital he did not cry. "I couldn't cry because . . ." He pauses for a while, thinking. "I just wouldn't for some reason."

Earnhardt jumped on a private jet and flew home to North Carolina, trying to corral his thoughts. "I was like, 'All right, let's try to sit down and try to make some kinda sense.' This was so much bigger than me losin my father. I had to keep that in mind. And that kinda made it easier at times to, like, deal with it. He meant so much to all these fans, all these other people. It was like, 'Man, a lot of people kinda feel my pain,' ya know? And it's not my pain, it's everybody's pain. And it made ya feel really good that your dad meant so much to so many people. He was just fuckin cool, ya know what I mean? He's just like . . ." He stops to search for the words . . . "hero material all the way."

Later during that jet ride home, he thought, "I'm never drivin another race car again. Fuck this sport!"

Earnhardt's front door stays open, and friends often drop by without calling. When he got home from Daytona that day, a lot of his friends were already there. Then a few of his ex-girlfriends and his mother showed up. They all went down to the bar he built in his basement and drank beers, told stories about the old man, stayed up till four in the morning, and did the same thing the next day. "I didn't cry much at all," Junior says. "I just hung around friends and talked about him."

He is soothed by the fact that he was beginning to build a really good relationship with his father. But he's also hurt by the fact that he was just beginning to build that relationship. "It makes it easier overall that I had a good relationship with the man," he says. "He knows how I feel about him down to the core. We had some good times together, and we were in the Winston Cup series together, so I can sleep at night. But it hurts." A giant garage recently went up behind Junior's house to store the bus he uses each race weekend. Senior and Junior were constructing it together, sharing all the decisions, and now that the garage is finished, the accomplishment is bittersweet. "We were buildin that together, and I can't escape the thought that he'll never get to see it. If I win another race, he won't be able to see it. If I get married, he won't know my wife, and he won't know my kids."

Junior has found some solace talking with people who have also lost their fathers, but, really, nothing can make this time easier. "It changes your life," he says. "It is nothing that you want to happen but it will better you as a person. It will force you to decide what side of the tracks you're gonna walk on. When you lose somebody you depend on, you've gotta make some serious fuckin decisions, and that's one of the few fortunate things that comes from such a tragedy as that. You roll up in a hole and be a little bitch, or you get up and you become really strong."

Earnhardt's decision to quit racing didn't last long. "After a day I was like, 'I just can't wait to get to the racetrack,'" he recalls. "And then another day goes by, and I'm like, 'Man, it's gonna be different without my dad at the racetrack. Without Dad, where do I fit in? Who am I? Ooh, this'll be interesting.' And you go to the track and you're like, 'This is where I belong.'" (The other drivers have let him know where he belongs in a subtle way at the drivers' meetings. "Now Dale Jarrett or Rusty Wallace or somebody like that sits in [Senior's] seat, and I gotta sit in Row Six. And I sit back there because that's my position." He's not concerned. "When I whip everybody's ass on the track, I'll whip everybody's ass in the seating order, too. That's very minute, but it speaks volumes.")

He threw himself right back into racing, getting on the track the week after his father's death. At first he struggled, doing better than twenty-third only once in his next five races. But in the following five weeks, he finished eighth or better all but once. Just days before this interview, at the Napa Auto Parts 500 in Fontana, California, on what would've been his father's fiftieth birthday, he finished third, his best result since Daytona. After that race he announced, "I ran well today. Think I'ma go home and do like the rappers and pour one out for Daddy."

Earnhardt has exhibited many of the classic responses to death. According to those around him, he has grown up seemingly overnight. "When you're a kid and your dad would go away on business, on his way out he'd always tell you, 'OK, dude, you're the man of the house,'" says Steve Crisp, Junior's former manager. "On a much larger scale, that's kind of the case. Right now, people within the company and within the sport are lookin to him to step up. And he's done it."

Now he's racing for himself, and he's taking on more responsibility in his life. "I really grew up and began dealing with people more on a professional level instead of hoppin and skippin through life like it's a field of roses," Earnhardt says. "I really became a lot more assertive. I was always afraid to ask for what I wanted, because I thought people would consider me conceited and a brat, but it's made me be more demanding not in a bossy, asshole way but to be pretty honest about how I feel, so people will know what to expect."

But his emotions are difficult to control. He's still expecting his father to walk through the door, he notices people who look like him ("That's not too fun"), and his day can be made or ruined by a comment or story about him. "He's like a yo-yo," his bus driver, Shane Mueller, says. "He does really good until a fan that means well hands him a picture of his dad, and that sets him back three days."

He's also immersed himself in making highly detailed miniature radio-controlled cars, some of them models of his own race car, piecing together one a week, the kind of consuming busywork people often take on after a death. He tried to maintain a relationship with a gorgeous brunette, a young woman every bit as breathtaking as a race-car driver's girlfriend in a Hollywood movie would be, but it's hard to let anyone get close now. ("There'll be a black Number 3 cloud hanging over him for a long time," she says.)

There are all sorts of mementos of his dad in his life, like Senior's black-and-white Goodwrench hat, plucked from the gearshift of the wrecked car, which sits ceremoniously in Junior's truck. "Some people would be scared of that," he says, "but it gives me strength." At his home there's lots of photos of him and Dad. On the fridge there's Junior, just a little runt, sitting beside Dad, whose shirt is off, his chest thick with manly hair. On the wall there's he and Dad sitting side by side in their racing suits at the track. "I never had pictures of my dad in the house," he says. "It never crossed my mind. But pictures of me and my father are really kick-ass now. You see those, and it'll be a jolt of energy."

But not all tributes are welcome. "He gets in the car," Earnhardt's publicist, Jade Gurss, says, "straps in, and then the announcer gets on and says, 'In honor of the man who won more races here than anyone else . . .' and you can see his face and his body language change. He's totally taken out of his aggressive mind-set. I feel so horrible for him."

Earnhardt is not a fan of these memorials. "Rusty [Wallace] won that race this past weekend [the Napa Auto Parts 500]," Earnhardt says. "His immediate reaction was to make some sort of tribute. In a moment that is his, he gave it to my dad. That's awesome. That's honorable. But just to be fuckin throwin doves in the air for the hell of it is kind of ridiculous to me. It's more of a production than anything else. Paintin the 3 in the infield. It's all you can stand to fuckin look at it. I'm not sayin it for just me, I'm sayin it for you or for anyone. Before long you're gonna be like, 'I'm sick of it.' The fuckin guy was awesome, but this is tearin it apart."

In racing-crazy North Carolina, Earnhardt memorials are inescapable. On the way to the airport, Junior came up behind a pickup truck. In the back window the driver had put a homemade decal with Earnhardt's Number 3, a pair of wings, and a halo. "That shit is retarded, man," he says.

More upsetting was the *Orlando Sentinel* suing for access to Dale Sr.'s autopsy photos. "That really pissed me off," Earnhardt says. His voice turns loud and defiant. "I'm pissed off about that. All these people can say, 'Oh, we gotta have it for safety reasons, and I can't believe the Earnhardt family would be so stingy and ridiculous about it and not allow us to improve on safety standards—and what are they hiding?' Man, I don't want nobody to see a damn picture of my daddy on a damn metal table! That's just not how I want people to remember him. It just comes down to, 'I don't want you to see it. That's all it is. I'm not hiding nothing. That's my dad! You can't look!' "

Anyone who watched his father die in his rearview mirror might consider quitting racing. If Senior's new seat belt could break, why not Junior's? How could he feel safe in the car again? He says that he's not worth much away from the track, then adds, "The odds are in my favor that my seat belt won't break. Because that's one seat belt that's broke in the last fifty-one years. We don't have a belt breakin every year. And that's all ya got when ya get in that car, to think, 'Well, it's not happenin all the time.' "

But the real answer is that some people need to risk their lives to feel their lives are worth living. The proximity of death does not scare them; it gets them up in the morning. Even after his father's death, Earnhardt can—he needs—to go to the track every week and risk his life. "I don't wanna die," he says. "But I like the fact that it's dangerous. It's treacherous. The possibility of hittin the wall is exciting. That's some of the draw for me. I'm ballsy enough to do it. When I'm in the car, I feel macho, like I can bench-press 350 pounds." Though his father is the fourth driver to die on the track in the last nine months, Earnhardt is not looking to NASCAR to make the sport safer. "What are you gonna change? What? There's not a huge amount of options and improvements to make it a safer sport." He has begun attending religious services at the track—"I believed in God, but I really didn't put a lot of effort behind it. Now I go to church on a regular basis." But he says he will not wear a HANS (Head And Neck Support) device that stabilizes a driver's head and neck in the event of a crash; many say one would've saved his father's life. "I won't be wearin one anytime soon," Earnhardt says. "If I go into a wall with an impact that's detrimental to my health, do I want my neck to be broke and for it to be done and over with, or do I want it to be half-ass broke and be like a fuckin vegetable the rest of my life?"

Yet his dad's death brings home the fact that his life could end any Sunday. "Death is closer than it was," he says. "If I'm sittin on a plane, death is sitting closer than it was before. It's a couple of rows back now."

The Mystery of Lauryn Hill

{ *Rolling Stone, 2003* }

{ *Da Capo Best Music Writing 2004* }

In 1998, when Lauryn Hill was recording her debut solo album, she was on a mission. "She was aiming for big hits so she could outshine the Fugees and outshine Wyclef," says someone familiar with the sessions. Her 1996 album with the Fugees, The Score, had sold more than seventeen million copies and made her rich and famous, but something was missing. After The Score, many perceived Wyclef Jean as the group's musical genius. Hill began plotting an album of her own that would change that. "Her solo career wasn't based on 'I wanna do an album,'" says Roots drummer Ahmir Thompson. "It was based on not being Wyclef's side girl."

Twelve million people bought The Miseducation of Lauryn Hill, and Hill was established as one of the great female MCs, a quadruple threat: a rapper as well as a world-class singer, songwriter, and producer. She was critically acclaimed and extremely rich. In 1998 and '99, sources say, Hill grossed forty million dollars from royalties, advances, touring, merchandising, and other revenues, and pocketed about twenty-five million dollars of that. When Hill was thirteen years old, she already knew she would grow up to become an entertainer. In '98, Hill became an international superstar.

Hollywood beckoned her onto the A list. Sources say she was offered a role in Charlie's Angels, but she turned the part down, and Lucy Liu took the job. Hill met with Matt Damon about being in *The Bourne Identity*, with Brad Pitt about a part in *The Mexican*, and with the Wachowski brothers about a role in the last two films in the *Matrix* trilogy. She turned down lots of work. "Lauryn wasn't trying to do anything," says Pras Michel of the Fugees, almost lamenting. But she did begin developing a biography of Bob Marley in which she was to play his wife, Rita; started producing a romantic-comedy film set in the world of soul food called *Sauce*, in which she was to star; and accepted a prize part in the adaptation of Toni Morrison's *Beloved* but had to drop out because she got pregnant. The doors were open for Hill to create a multimedia entertainment empire of the sort that J. Lo, Janet, and Madonna have built. Hill could have been J. Lo with political substance. Someone who once worked with Hill says with regret, "She woulda been bigger than J. Lo." Instead, she disappeared.

"I think Lauryn grew to despise who Lauryn Hill was," a friend says. "Not that she despised herself as a human being, but she despised the manufactured international-superstar magazine cover girl who wasn't able to go out of the house looking a little tattered on a given day. Because Lauryn is such a perfectionist, she always sought to give the fans what they wanted, so a simple run to the grocery store had to have the right heels and jeans. Artists are a lot more calculating than the public sometimes knows. It don't happen by accident that the jeans fall the right way, the hat is cocked to the side just so. All of that stuff is thought about, and Lauryn put a lot of pressure on herself after all that success. And then one day she said, 'Fuck it.'"

In 2000, Hill became close with Brother Anthony, a shadowy spiritual adviser, then abruptly fired her management team and the people around her. In 2001, she recorded her *MTV Unplugged 2.0*. Few bought the album, but many talked about how she could be heard on the record breaking down in tears and saying, "I'm crazy and deranged. . . . I'm emotionally unstable," and repeatedly rejecting celebrity and the illusions that make it possible. "I used to get dressed for y'all; I don't do that anymore," she said on the album. "I used to be a performer, and I really don't consider myself a performer anymore. . . . I had created this public persona, this public illusion, and it held me hostage. I couldn't be a real person, because you're too afraid of what your public will say. At that point, I had to do some dying."

Her honesty was both touching and confusing. She was rejecting so much of what she'd spent years being. The only thing that was clear was that she was suffering. "Artists do fall apart," a record executive says. "The most commonly held falsity in the game is that they have it all together. They fall apart. Look at Mariah, Whitney, Michael, all the great ones. They all have a moment where you go, 'Are they really all there?' And I think Lauryn chose to expose that to the world."

Until recently, the twenty-eight-year-old Hill lived in a high-end hotel in Miami with Rohan Marley, the man she called her husband, and her four children. Her fourth child was born this past summer. Sources say that not long ago, Hill moved out of the hotel and that her relationship with Marley may be over.

She now insists on being called Ms. Hill, not Lauryn, and is working on a new album, albeit very slowly. "I heard from a friend that she don't really wanna do music right now," Pras says. "I heard from another friend that she wants to do a Fugees album."

So what caused the Lauryn Hill of *Miseducation*, viewed as regal and brilliant, to morph into the Lauryn Hill of *Unplugged*, seen as possibly unstable, and then into someone willfully absent from the public? Confidential conversations with more than twenty friends and industry figures and a lengthy interview with Pras have clarified much of what has happened during the five years since her zenith. "I don't think she's crazy," Pras says. "People tend to say that when they don't understand what someone's going through. Walk in her shoes, and see what would you do."

Hill was born in 1975 and raised in middle-class South Orange, New Jersey. By her teens, she was determined to have a career in entertainment. At thirteen, she sang on *Showtime at the Apollo*. The audience was rough on her, and after the show she cried. In 1998, her mother, Valerie Hill, told *Rolling Stone* about her post-Apollo talk with her young daughter. "I said . . . now, if every time they don't scream and holler you're gonna cry, then perhaps this isn't for you," Valerie recalled. "And she looked at me like I had taken leave of my senses. To her, the mere suggestion that this wasn't for her was crazy." At seventeen, Lauryn had a role on the daytime soap *As the World Turns*; two years later she appeared in *Sister Act 2: Back in the Habit* and had a small role in Steven Soderbergh's *King of the Hill*. Meanwhile, she was also spending nights working on music with friends Wyclef Jean and Pras Michel. She was eighteen when the band's 1994 debut, *Blunted on Reality*, flopped, but two years later, with *The Score*, the Fugees' cover of "Killing Me Softly" made her a star. She was sex-symbol beautiful, and her music and public persona seemed politically savvy and spiritually aware.

After the explosion of *The Score*, Jean began recording a solo album. Hill and Pras supported him emotionally and creatively. But when Hill started writing her own songs, Jean showed no interest. Pras says, "I remember when Pepsi wanted her for a commercial, and they were like, 'All we want is you. We don't need the other two cats.' She said, 'Without them I'm not doing it.' There's a lot of things she didn't do because of the group. Then when she goes to work on her [music] and she doesn't have the support, that can have an effect mentally. She felt—this is based on conversations we had—she felt there was no support on that angle. When you feel the ones you stuck your neck out for ain't doin the same for you, it brings a certain animosity and bitterness."

Once, the three Fugees were close friends, but now Pras has little good to say about Jean. "He's the cancer of the [Fugees]," Pras says. "He's the cancer. You can quote me. He's the reason why it got wrecked to begin with, he's the reason why it's not fixed." Is he the reason for Hill's troubles? "Maybe, indirectly, she's where she's at because of him," Pras says. "Maybe. But not directly." Jean politely declined to be interviewed. "I'm somewhere else in my head," he says on the phone from his studio. "Certain things I don't talk about. I'm in another zone." He pauses. "I wish it didn't go down the way it went."

Hill responded to an e-mail request for an interview. "I am not available for free interviews at this time," she wrote. "The only interviews I will consider are those that amply compensate me for my time, energy, and story." It was signed "Ms. Hill." She asks for money, friends say, because she feels she's been exploited by the media and the record industry. When *Oneworld* magazine contacted her about a cover story, she demanded ten thousand dollars.

People close to the Fugees say there has always been competition between Jean and Hill. "Not competing for something in particular," says one. "It's more competing just who's better, who's greater." Hill's solo music was intended to settle the matter. When Jean finally came around and offered his production assistance on the record, she no longer wanted it. "She said [to Jean], 'I'm thinking about working with this producer and that producer,'" a friend says. "He said, 'Oh, no—I'm producing your whole album.' She chewed on that for a minute and then said, 'Nah, I got my own vision.' That's when who Lauryn really is started to take form."

At the same time, Hill's love life began to get really complicated. For years she'd been clandestinely dating Jean. Their relationship started long before he married his current wife and continued afterward. But Pras says, "I think he was kinda, like, playing with her emotions."

But in the summer of '96, when the Fugees were on the Smoking Grooves Tour, she met Rohan Marley, who was on the tour with his brother Ziggy, both sons of Bob Marley. At first Hill was uninterested in Rohan—a former University of Miami football player—because she was still seeing Jean. "Honestly, she didn't even want the relationship," says a friend. "Everyone was pushing her towards [Marley] to get her out of the other thing. They pushed her towards him, like, 'Why don't you give him a chance, come on, go out on a date. Just do it,' not knowing that this man had all this other baggage and drama in his life."

Pras singled out Hill's first pregnancy as a turning point for the group. "When she got pregnant, definitely things started goin on," he says. "Things got crazy." While Hill's stomach grew, the Fugee camp wondered whether the baby was Marley's or Jean's. Says a friend, "The conversation between everyone on the low was no one knew until that baby came out." The day Hill went into labor, Jean told a source he was flying to her side to see his new child. "People don't know how calculating she can be," a friend says. "Lauryn used Ro to pull herself out of the relationship with Clef, and she happened to get pregnant. She hoped that baby was Wyclef's, because it would've forced his hand. But it wasn't." Hill named her first child Zion Marley.

For years, Hill claimed that she was married to Rohan Marley, but at some point after Zion was born, Hill got another surprise: Someone told her Marley already had a wife. On March 18th, 1993, when he was a sophomore at the University of Miami, Marley married an eighteen-year-old woman from New Jersey in a ceremony in Miami. "The reason [Hill and Marley] aren't married is because Ro is already married," says a friend. Sources say Marley has two children from the marriage.

Hill decided to ignore it. "I think she was kinda like, 'Put it in the closet and don't even pay attention to it,' " says a friend. *Rolling Stone* could find no record of the dissolution of Marley's marriage, and even now it's unclear whether Hill and Marley were ever married in a conventional sense. "She has her own rules about life," another friend says. "According to her, she's married. Marriage to her is not a piece of paper, and it's not part of some civilization—civil-lies-ation. If you say to her, 'You're not married,' she'll say, 'What, do I have to get a government official to tell me I'm married?' "

It was critical that on *Miseducation*, Hill was credited as the sole auteur. "That was why she had to be seen as doing it all herself," says someone familiar with the sessions. "To show, 'I'm better than [Wyclef]. He's getting credit as the genius in the group. I'm the genius in the group.' "

But when musicians collaborate in the studio, it's often difficult to establish exactly who has written what. "It gets real gray in the studio," one artist says. At the time, people close to her suggested Hill needed documentation that would define everyone's role, but she was against the idea. "Lauryn said, 'We all love each other,' " a friend says. " 'This ain't about documents. This is blessed.' "

The album was released crediting Hill with having produced, written, and arranged all the music except one track, and Hill was established as a self-contained musical genius. Then she was sued by four men who had worked on the record who alleged that she had claimed full credit for music that they'd been at least partly responsible for. Her label, Columbia, urged her to settle, but she wanted to fight. "She felt settling would've been an admission of guilt," says a friend. "She was very concerned about credit. It's what eluded her from the past success [with the Fugees]. She didn't wanna be just a pretty face and a pretty voice. She wanted people to know she knows what she's doing." But she had to go into depositions and discuss making her art with lawyers. "That fucked with her," another friend says.

Eventually, Hill settled the suit. A source says the four producers were paid five million dollars. It wasn't nearly as painful financially as it was emotionally. A friend says, "That was the beginning of a chain effect that would turn everything a little crazy." She was far from the first recording artist to have a crisis of faith and career, but few have had such a crisis so publicly.

She was a working mother of two, who, according to many, was unhappy in her relationship. She felt pressure to look like a model every time she left the house. She had several members of her family working for her or being supported by her. "To have your whole family depend on you for their well-being, that can be a lot of pressure," says Ahmir Thompson. "I said, 'If I was in that situation, I would snap.'" And she felt betrayed by the musicians she'd thought of as family and thus was increasingly mistrustful of people in general. Friends say she wanted to get out but didn't know how. "It was tough for her to admit all that to someone," a friend says. "So I think she spoke to God, and maybe it wasn't God, but somebody showed up." Another friend says, "A person came in, and they divided and conquered. They destroyed this whole thing." Around this time, Hill met a religious figure named Brother Anthony, a tall Black man in his forties. Within three months she was going to Bible study with him two or three times a week. A friend says Brother Anthony taught Hill that "she should be whoever she wants to be, because she doesn't owe her fans anything. God didn't create us to be beholden unto people and entertain them. God holds us to be the people that we want to be."

The two became inseparable, and Hill began starting many of her sentences with the words, "Brother Anthony says . . ." Shortly after recording *Unplugged*, Hill told MTV Online, "I met someone who has an understanding of the Bible like no one else I ever met in my life. I just sat at [his] feet and ingested pure Scripture for about a year." But Hill's friends found Brother Anthony bizarre. "His whole demeanor was real possessive, aggressive, and crooked to me," a friend says. "You know how people are slick? He's a quick talker."

No one was certain what church he was from or what religion he belonged to. "I don't think he had a religion," a friend says. "I think he was more like, 'My interpretation of the Bible is the only interpretation of the Bible. I'm the only one on earth that knows the truth.'"

"Brother Anthony was definitely on some other shit," Pras says. "I had a tape of [his teachings]. That shit is ill. Fucked me up. I can't really explain it. It was some weird shit, man. It was some real cult shit. When I heard the tape, I couldn't believe that this dude was really serious. He was sayin, 'Give up all your money.' I don't know if that meant 'Give it to me' or whatever, but on the tape he said, 'Money doesn't mean any-thing.'"

Many believe Brother Anthony drove a wedge between Hill and the rest of the world. "It was like she was being brainwashed by this man," a friend says, "believing everything he was saying and tellin her what to do." Another friend says, "I think he's just looking at a cash cow."

She recorded her MTV Unplugged 2.0 in July 2001 while she was pregnant with her third child, Joshua. In a rehearsal the day before, Hill ripped up her throat but refused to reschedule, and on the record her voice is raspy and ragged. She accompanied herself on guitar, the lone instru-ment on the album, which was courageous given that she hadn't been studying very long. But a veteran industry executive says, "Anyone with ears can hear there are only three chords being played on every song. I saw it with a roomful of professionals, and someone said, 'I feel like jumpin out a window.'"

"A lesser artist, it would've never been released," an industry in-sider says. "A lesser artist would've been shot and thrown out the win-dow." Unplugged sold just 470,000 records, a failure. Another industry insider says, "I'm sure Columbia lost money on it." In the past few years, Hill has been in Miami, where she's working on a new album. She's determined to get full credit this time. "A lot of different people have been called down there and had strange experiences," says an industry figure. Sources say the musicians are required to sign a waiver giving Hill sole writing credit for the tracks they work on. The sessions have gone slowly. A few people spoke of her flying in a gang of top-flight musicians, putting them up in a nice hotel, and paying for their time. But for more than a week they sat around each day, expecting to play, then getting a call saying, "We'll start tomorrow." Eventually they all left without ever getting into the studio. While no one is clear what stage of completion the tracks are in, those who've heard the music describe it as thrilling. "What she's doing and where she's going with it, ain't nobody even touching her," says an industry insider. "Nobody's even thinking that way. In the sad state of music we're in, I feel deprived knowing that she's got some real flavor that she's holding back."

"She gonna sit down and record until she feels happy," a friend says. "Whoever can't wait, she don't care." Some sources say she's spent more than two and a half million dollars, and Columbia has cut off her recording budget. The label denies this and maintains that Hill's new album will be out next year.

"Plenty of artists spend two million dollars," says an industry insider, "but she had to fly all these people around and she had to build a studio in her Miami apartment, because she couldn't drive half a mile to the studio. Columbia bent over backwards for her, in pure self-interest, and I think they still believe in her, but you can't abuse the system like that. You can't do that."

Several of Hill's friends and associates are clearly worried about her. "She's Dr. Jekyll and Mr. Hyde," one says. "But not, like, two faces but, like, eight faces of that. You don't know who you're gonna get from one hour to the next. Not just one day to the next but one hour." Others recall Hill talking entirely in Bible-speak, "quoting Scripture, fanatically religious," one friend says. She sometimes answers business questions by saying things like, "We'll see what God has in store." A few tell a story in which Hill asked people to work with her on the new album, but when they asked how much they would be paid, she said, "Do it for God," meaning, do it for free, and God will reward you.

"I feel like she's lost," a friend says. "Something's not right. I just feel like she's sad and lonely and alone. I think she wants to cry out for help, but she has too much pride."

Others disagree. "Really, it's about restructuring her life and her lifestyle," an associate says. "I think maybe for a long time she thought she knew what she wanted. But, in reality, she didn't. She's gonna come through it, but she doesn't think anything's wrong with her. She used [Brother Anthony] to get rid of stuff in her life that she didn't wanna struggle with. She used him to her advantage, then she went too far, and she doesn't know how to come back. It'll be a process. It'll be a couple of years."

"She wants to do another album," a friend says. "Deep down, Lauryn is still Lauryn. She always wanted to be famous, she always wanted to sing, she always wanted to hear the applause. That's what she grew up to do. So to now not want it, that's not believable. She wants it the way Brother Anthony thinks it should be. His opinion is the only opinion that matters to her."

Many still have faith in her. "Sometimes people gotta find themselves, man," Pras says. "I don't believe that's crazy. People go through certain things, they gotta fight certain demons, and she's entitled to do that. Because her life isn't to please people. At the end of the day, Lauryn is not happy with herself. She's not gonna do some disc because she gotta make money for Sony. It just so happens that she's done something that captured a moment in people's lives. They want more of that, but she's not ready to give that."

5. Almost Famous

A Woman Possessed

F rom the moment Beyoncé lands in London she's treated like a princess. A British Airways agent meets her at the lip of the plane and whisks her and her four-person crew down an almost hidden set of stairs and into a waiting British Airways car. The rest of the passengers making connections are shuffling through the long corridors of Heathrow in order to trudge between terminals on a bus, but the twenty-two-year-old from Houston, who says she's really a New Yorker now, is zipping through Heathrow's back streets, trying to figure out whether her final destination—Cannes, France—is pronounced *can* or *kahn*. She wears no necklaces and no rings, but she's still dressed very girly in big chunky earrings, a pink off-the-shoulder cashmere sweater with a sort of bow in the front, a brown fur-lined wrap, fuzzy pink boots, jeans, and a hot-pink baseball hat with embroidered sparklies on the front adding up to a primitive cat and on the back more sparklies spelling out Beyoncé. It's something a teenage girl probably made. Her shoulders and neck flow gracefully out from under her sweater, recalling old French sculptures that romanticized the curves of the female form. She has golden skin, three small birthmarks on her face, perfect teeth, and a dancer's posture that makes her seem much taller than five-foot-seven. And her tight jeans reveal her to be a healthy girl, someone the brothers would call thick, with a booming system in the back.

The last six months have seen a sort of Beyoncé explosion, where she went from the most popular singer in a hot group, Destiny's Child, to a ubiquitous solo megastar whose *Dangerously in Love* has sold more than two million copies, earned her five Grammy nominations, and spawned two of the biggest and most infectious songs of the year, "Crazy in Love" and "Baby Boy." Beyoncé has become a crossover sex symbol like Halle Berry, a Black girl who's not so overwhelmingly nubian that white people don't appreciate her beauty. She's the new Janet Jackson, the tastefully sexy Black sex symbol who's giving you R&B–flavored pop hits and signature dances as well as well-concepted videos, tours, and some movies, too. 2004 will see still more Beyoncé ubiquity as she gives us a tour with Alicia Keys and Missy, a new Destiny's Child album, and a tour with Destiny's Child. But offstage, the girl is careful to maintain a distance between the person who's famous and the person shaped long before fame. "I don't want to get addicted to fame," she says. "Then when I'm no longer famous I don't know what to do and I just seem desperate and lose my mind. I refuse to get addicted to fame and I know now the importance of going on vacation and having another life because one day everything comes to an end." Beyoncé comes from money and has that finishing-school polish, but she's the beautiful girl in school who's disarmingly down to earth.

When she lands in Nice, France, she's met by an agent who takes her through a special, empty line at Passport Control. But nowadays even princesses sometimes hit potholes. While she's standing at the baggage carousel, tired, hungry, and clearly running on empty after a long pair of flights from New Jersey, someone from British Airways runs up and says there's two bags missing. Beyoncé mumbles that the missing bags are surely hers. She's annoyed. Anyone would be. She could throw a tantrum or even just make one little nasty comment and no one would blame her. But Beyoncé's not that kinda girl. "You wanna think she's a bitch because she's so fine," says her choreographer Frank Gatson. "But I've never seen someone so sweet. It trips me out. Knowing she wants to go off on somebody because somebody's pissed her off, she catches herself because she knows that humility is important. I think it's her upbringing in church." She just rolls her eyes and grins. It's a fake smile, but it's polite, even professional. She lives like a princess, but doesn't have airs.

Every princess must have a prince and for now Beyoncé's is the recently retired MC Jay-Z, who's more than a decade older than her. "I know dude a long time," an insider said of Jay-Z. "I've never seen him sprung like this. He cares about her, gives her great advice, he wants his woman to look right. They adore each other." Jay and Beyoncé both refuse to discuss the relationship. "I don't say I'm single," she says. "I don't deny anyone. I just don't talk about it. People are like, Why does she say that they're just friends? I don't say that. I just don't talk about it. I see a lot of the actresses that have had successful relationships and I see that a lot of people don't talk about it. I just wanna protect my private life."

But even though she won't talk about the relationship she's open to discussing what sort of girlfriend she is. "In relationships I think a lot like a guy," she says. "If I do something wrong I don't get emotional. I think about it and I change it and I fix it. And I've always been very logical, maybe because I'm a Virgo, I don't know." Still, she can find herself overcome by emotion sometimes. "When I do anything I do it," she says. "If I fall in love I'm there."

And even though she absolutely won't talk about the relationship, she will talk about him. She's very free with saying "we," the way people in couples replace the singular "I" in their vocabulary with the plural "we." Asked where she was during the New York City blackout of 2003, she replies, "We were at the 40/40 Club." There was a generator at the club, so the party never stopped. "At four a.m. we took a plane to Italy," she says. "We got to Rome and they had a blackout there. The first one in years." She still had a good time. "I went to the Vatican and I almost cried. I was just in awe."

She said that "Crazy in Love" was rhymeless until the night before she had to turn the album in. "I asked Jay would he rap on the song," she says, "and he came to the studio at two a.m. and in like, what, ten minutes, he listened to the track, came up with a rap, and didn't write it down. It's miraculous to watch [his creative process], it really is." Jay was there for her through much of the recording of *Dangerously in Love*. "He helped a lot with a lot of the songs," she says. The night she recorded "Baby Boy," she had the chorus but just didn't like the verses until Jay stepped up and told her exactly how to rewrite them. "I'm amazed how much he knows about how much," she says. "He can write a song for a woman, he can write a song for anybody, and he has all of these details that he knows about and it's like, How did you know that? How did you think of that? It's amazing to me."

She says she'd like to have children one day. "If it was a perfect world I would have two boys and a girl," she says. "I love little boys and girls are so much drama." But how could she maintain superstar ubiquity and be a mom? "One day I wanna have a family and be a mother and occasionally put out albums or do like Anita Baker and perform occasionally. I love that. That's so hot to me. Sade's career [releasing one album every four years]? That's ridiculously hot to me."

Now, you needn't be friends with Jay and Beyoncé to know where they are on a daily basis (and, soon, whether or not they're pregnant) because the gossip press all but stalks them, constantly snapping photos that Beyoncé is often unaware are being taken. "It's very strange," she says of having the papparazzi constantly following her. "I can spot a camera. I see the little glare from miles away. So then, I'll be like OK, it's no one around. But they're everywhere. I think paparazzi take regular cameras so you think they're fans. It doesn't bother me but I don't like it. It's just they always catch you at the craziest point. The whole trip they get me jumping off of a boat."

She was referring to a recent picture that, once again, she didn't know was being taken, which showed Beyoncé leaping into the ocean from the second story of a boat as Jay and friends watched. The boat was very high. "Yeah, it was," she says. "It was. I don't know what's wrong with me. And I looked at the picture and said, 'That's really dumb.' I do it every year. I think that's my let go, start over, this is a vacation and I'ma be free. That's my jump. It's a ritual. I have to jump off of something so I can let go of everything that happened before the last vacation and start over. It's like bein baptized."

Before Beyoncé was baptized her father, Matthew Knowles, was an executive at Xerox in medical sales, selling multimillion-dollar pieces of equipment and making six figures. "I was blessed to be the number-one sales rep in the medical division of Xerox for years," he says. Matthew is Beyoncé's manager, the one who negotiated everything from her initial record deals with Elektra and Columbia to her recent endorsement deals with L'Oreal and Tommy Hilfiger, and executive produced all of her albums. He's pleasant though self-serious, but with an easy laugh. There's nothing like massive public success to make a man feel good about himself. You talk about laughing all the way to the bank, Mr. Knowles laughs like a man who just got back from the bank.

His wife, Tina Knowles, has light skin, long wavy hair with blond streaks, and green eyes. Matthew says, "Beyoncé's still not as beautiful as her mama." Where Beyoncé is underaccessorized, Tina visited Beyoncé in New York wearing a giant diamond ring on each hand, a diamond tennis bracelet and diamond watch on her left wrist, and what looked like another diamond watch on her right wrist. She owns one of the top beauty salons in Houston, called Headliners, where Beyoncé says she grew up. "She got a lot of influence from my clients," Mrs. Knowles says. "We catered to the professional woman so we had judges and attorneys and I really credit that to her having that drive and ambition. She had a lot of great women around her who inspired her to work hard and do great things."

The Knowleses made good money long before Beyoncé came along and lived in a large house in Houston with all the accoutrements of the upper middle class. "We lived in a house the same size as we do now and in a neighborhood as nice as I do now," Beyoncé says. There is probably no Black music megastar of the past twenty years who grew up as rich as Beyoncé with the exception of Michael and Janet Jackson. You can see the finishing-school poise and polish on her. Still, just because the Knowleses had money didn't mean they never had money problems.

In 1981, while Tina Knowles was pregnant with her first child, she realized that her family name was dying. Tina is the youngest of seven, but only one of her brothers had had a son. "I said, 'Oh God we'll run out of Beyoncés,' " Mrs. Knowles said. So she gave her daughter her maiden name. Grandpa Beyoncé, a creole who lived in New Orleans and spoke French, was unimpressed. "My family was not happy," Mrs. Knowles said. "My Dad said, 'She's gonna be really mad at you because that's a last name.' And I'm like, It's not a last name to anybody but you guys."

Beyoncé was a shy, quiet kid. When she was seven and in the first grade at St. Mary's, a Catholic school in Houston, a dance teacher, Miss Darlette Johnson, pushed her to join the school talent show. "I was terrified and I didn't wanna do it and she's like, C'mon baby, get out there," Beyoncé says. "I remember walking out and I was scared but when the music started I don't know what happened. I just . . . *changed*." Both of her parents were in the audience. Tina recalls, "We both said, 'Who is that?' "

That was Sasha. It was many years before Beyoncé's stage persona got her name, but from that first time onstage it was clear that when the shy, humble girl got onstage she became someone new. "I don't have a split personality," Beyoncé says, "but I'm really very country and would rather have no shoes on and have my hair in a bun and no makeup. And when I perform this confidence and this sexiness and this whatever it is that I'm completely not just happens. And you feel it and you just start wildin and doin stuff that don't even make sense, like the spirit takes over. That magic, that's what I love. If you see me on TV I'm not a humble, shy person, but it's a transformation into that. It's a job. In real life I'm not like that."

Her choreographer, Frank Gatson, said that when she gets onstage she gets the Holy Ghost. "She's fearless," Gatson says. "When I worked with Usher, I wanted to think Usher was that, but Usher has fear sometimes. Kelly and Michelle don't have the nerve that she has. She has no fear. I think when you get out there you have to give it to the audience with no inhibition. You gotta let the spirit take you. Something powerful takes her over and in that time onstage she's gone. On *VH1 Divas* she threw her $250,000 earrings and later she said she didn't know why she threw them. That's losing yourself. I've been in shows where people booed Beyoncé. And she'd be right in their face dancin, lettin 'em have it like it was nothing. Most people would panic in that, you'd see them buckle down. But Beyoncé has learned to dismiss fear."

Actually, Beyoncé knew how to dismiss it when she was in the first grade. At the end of her performance she got a standing ovation and won the show. "I was like, oh Lord, this is amazing," Beyoncé says. "So I knew I wanted to do that, I knew I wanted to be a singer. I think before that I knew I wanted to be a singer, but I'd never been on a stage before that." Matthew began taking her to local talent shows where she won thirty-five times in a row. Soon a group was formed, which made it all the more fun. "I was nine the first time we performed," Beyoncé says. "It was at a day care. We didn't even know the name of the group cuz I remember we were backstage, well, not backstage but in this little room on the side," she laughs, "and we were tryin to write down names and logos. There were kids out there cryin while we performed, but I realized how much I loved bein in a group. Because I was always so nervous and to have those girls with me before the stage, during the stage, and after the stage and we could talk about it, it was even more exciting for me." The groups became the entirety of her social life. "All her friends basically her entire life have been her group members, whoever they were at the time," says Angela Beyonce, her cousin and assistant.

When Beyoncé was ten the group, now called GirlzTime, earned a place on *Star Search*. It would be a turning point, but not one they were expecting. They lost. As his daughter sobbed backstage, Matthew vowed to leave his job and manage them full-time. "Him leaving his corporate job was very scary for me," Tina said. "I don't know many people who would give up a job makin the kinda money he made. I thought he had gone a little nuts. I was like, What are we gonna do? I had a large salon and it was generating good money, but we were accustomed to two incomes. All of a sudden we have to totally alter our lifestyle. But he's just like that about whatever he does. He's just really passionate."

Matthew took a class at Houston Community College on the business of music, but found his corporate background gave him most of the training he needed. "Quite frankly, when I came into this I was more qualified than 75 percent of the managers out there, who have no business background and don't know how to move inside of a corporation. Coming from corporate America, I understand how to navigate through those political issues at the record label that have nothing to do with music." He agreed that selling is pretty much the same no matter the product, that the mechanics of selling high-level medical supplies is ultimately the same as selling Beyoncé to America. "When you're a good salesperson then you're a good salesperson," he says. He's been called a stage dad many times and bristles at that because, he says, he simply used his expertise to help his child achieve her dream, just as any parent would. "It never mattered to me if my kids did music," he said. "If Beyoncé came to me and said, Dad, I wanna be a doctor, just my personality, I would find a way of buying a hospital."

Matthew created his own artist-development program, which Beyoncé suspects was modeled after the Motown system. "I'm sure he got it out of reading Berry Gordy," she says. In the summers Matthew led a sort of R&B boot camp where Beyoncé and whoever else was in the group at that point would start their mornings by jogging while singing to build up the ability to sing and dance at the same time. They had team-building exercises, choreography lessons, vocal coaching, media training, and walking lessons from a model. And they watched lots of video of the great performers—Michael, Janet, Whitney Houston, Tina Turner, Madonna. "We'd study those tapes like football teams study their competitors tapes," Matthew says. Tina was pressed into styling and then designing their clothes.

When Beyoncé was thirteen the group, now called Destiny's Child, signed a deal with Elektra Records, achieving their dream. But it was the beginning of a streak of bad luck that tested the Knowles family more than anything they've ever had to deal with. Things quickly went sour at Elektra and the group got dropped. "Then we got hit with some tax problems and everything kinda came crashing down," Mrs. Knowles says. "We had to sell our house for way less than we could've gotten if we'd had time to sell it right. It was very emotional because my kids grew up in that house and they were not happy at all. They didn't know it was because Matthew gave up his job for them. You really don't explain it. You just say, listen, we gotta scale down." They bought another house but after the sale when Matthew went in he found the previous tenant dead in the bathroom, a suicide. Then Matthew and Tina's relationship began to fall apart. "At that point we were just not getting along good at all," Mrs. Knowles says. "I felt like Matthew was obsessed and should go get a job. So we separated for maybe about six months. The lowest point was when I moved out. I moved into an apartment, which my kids had never lived in in their lives. That was really difficult for them. We were just miserable without each other because we'd been together forever." They'd married in 1980. "He was always like, I'm gonna make this happen," she says. "I just thought that something had to wake him up."

Even after his wife and children moved out and his family was collapsing, Matthew kept working his contacts at Columbia, trying to get a deal there, still chasing the dream. "Well," he recalls, "I had this vision and when it doesn't happen right away and your friends are saying, What is wrong with this guy, and that's bringing on some personal issues, that's pretty difficult. Your husband is focused on music rather than his job and the bills are there. We had a lot of success so we had a pretty hefty lifestyle. There was a point when Tina thought I maybe should reconsider this dream and I didn't wanna give up on it."

Beyoncé, about fourteen then, didn't really understand what was going on until several years later, but she said the group had become the center of the family and it wasn't succeeding and she could feel pressure building on her. "The group is where we get everything," she says, "so if the group doesn't happen then my life is over and I felt like it was my fault. Until I realized that my mother owns a hair salon, one of the best ones in Houston, and my father made great money and still has many degrees and is gonna go out and do many things. They didn't give up everything because that was our only hope to get us out of the ghetto. So I realized I don't have to have that pressure because they're going to be successful regardless of what they do."

When Beyoncé was fifteen Columbia offered Destiny's Child a record contract and, almost concurrently, Matthew and Tina reconciled. Both say that one had nothing to do with the other. "It was an exciting time," Mrs. Knowles says. "It wasn't about the money, it was just that they finally got to do what they wanted to do and they were on their way."

It's Saturday night in Cannes and backstage in a small, bright room at the NRJ Music Awards, Beyoncé is waiting to go on. She says matter of factly that her wisdom teeth are bothering her, that they've been bothering her for a while now, and she wants to get them pulled, but can't afford two weeks with her face blown up. And her nose is stuffed and it won't unclog. And her back is killing her, so as showtime approaches she runs through a series of back, calf, and ankle stretches, like an athlete warming up while wearing a tight peach and gray Armani short-skirted dress, beaded Giuseppe Zanotti three-inch heels dripping with bangles, and chandelier earrings.

She takes a moment to brainstorm with her crew about her upcoming Grammy performance. "I'd love to win," she says of the Grammys, "but it's more important for me to have a good performance, an incredible performance, than to win. Because people remember the performance." They go through reference photos that she's pulled from various magazines to explain the direction she's considering. She seems to be constantly brainstorming some aspect of her career, either with an expert or alone. She says she's already thinking of video treatments for Destiny's Child. It's frustrating to her that she doesn't seem to get credit for not being a puppet. "I work really hard," she says, "I'm a perfectionist. I'll go into a studio and figure it out. If my video is wrong I'ma fix it." She says it was her idea to reedit the "Me, Myself and I" video and have it play out backward. "This is not something anybody planned for me," she says. "I had the help of my family, I don't do it all by myself, but I write my songs, I write my treatments, I help with my clothes and anybody who, every time they're seen they're right, it's not other people. You can't be that consistent without the artist being involved."

As showtime nears her intensity grows. She stares at herself in the mirror, eyes burning. She becomes restless, her foot shaking with nervous energy. She bounces around a bit to see if she'll leap out of the dress when Sasha! arrives. Her back still doesn't feel right.

At the edge of the stage, just before she goes out, she stands alone, eyes closed, head down as if in prayer. She's introduced in French, the music leaps from the speakers, and Sasha! explodes. If Beyoncé was sick and ailing, Sasha! is a tiger who attacks the crowd. They stand and applaud from their first glimpse to their last. "They were excited and that got me excited," she says afterward. She runs through half of "Baby Boy," then half of "Crazy In Love," singing and dancing full out, then struts offstage with a smile. The dancers look dour, upset that they missed a few moves, but Beyoncé is beaming and invigorated. Now that she's performed there's a new spirit inside of her. "It's funny," she says. "Whatever hurts, when you get onstage it don't hurt no more."

The Next Queen of Soul

{ Alicia Keys, *Rolling Stone*, 2001 }

It's two days after the start of The New World. The World Trade Center towers are rubble. Five thousand are called missing and feared dead. And Alicia Keys is on the street in lower Manhattan, shooting with photographer Mark Seliger, just a few hundred yards from Ground Zero.

Many on the street wear thin face masks, a few have bulky gas masks. The cloud of debris and smoke is visible a mile away, the smell of something burned perceptible even further. A block away from the shoot is the West Side Highway. You can see where the Towers used to be and workers sifting through the rubble and other workers riding up the empty highway, away from Ground Zero, while people stand on the sides of the road and applaud and hold signs saying, "Thank You!" A young man walks by in silence, holding a small flag high above his head, saying everything by saying nothing. When the shoot ends Alicia walks off singing the Earth, Wind & Fire classic, "Keep Your Head to the Sky."

"The last couple days I been thinkin, what's happenin to this world? What's really goin on?" she says later. Her voice is kinda deep for a chick, with a distinctly street lilt to it. She spent a lot of time on the streets of Harlem, she says, and it's turned her into a ladyish street-smart tomboy, who wears heels and lip gloss, and chews gum, slaps five hard like a guy, and has a street bop to her strut. "Couple weeks ago we was dealin with that plane shit with Aaliyah and now it's a whole nother thing. It's strange. For me, I can't take myself out of that equation. I feel like everyone who died in that building was part of me." Like so many of us, Alicia was saddened but remains resilient. "The thing that keeps goin through my head is the phoenix that rises out of the ashes. Although there's despair and confusion, that's definitely not the end of the world and it's not gonna stop us. It's gonna make us stronger."

The photo shoot was originally scheduled for the day of the attack. In the middle of that day she called and said she needed the shoot's concept changed. She had to do something relevant. "To see Chambers Street and the Brooklyn Bridge lookin like some old spot you might see in Kuwait on TV just puts things in perspective for me. Some people live with war every day and we just these small-ass little children who always been protected for one reason or another. The things that people hold in high esteem is fuckin stupid. That's the reason why I wanted this shoot to mean something. I couldn't go in there and just put on some clothes. I couldn't possibly do a fuckin photo shoot after what just happened. I would feel like the person I despise. The physical is such an important part of today's society and that's sickening, sickening, sickening, and it makes it more sickening when something like this goes on."

And yet, like most African-Americans, her relationship with America is complex. The country that once enslaved her, that constitutionally considered her three-fifths of a human, that kept her from the schools and drinking fountains and voting booths just a generation ago, now demands patriotism. That can be a hard shift. "All day I been seein everyone rockin flags in they hats and on the street and I'm torn," she says. "I look at that flag and I'm not able to completely go there for some reason. I see lies in that flag. I can't suddenly be all patriotic. But this is about human life beyond any country or flag. That's why it makes me feel so strange. Because I'm so torn and there's so many layers involved."

Immediately after the shoot a car takes Alicia and her crew to the police checkpoint at 14th street. Another car takes her uptown and then to D.C., where a tour bus is waiting to take her and her band to Atlanta for a show Friday night in Chastain Park. She's opening for Maxwell, even though after six weeks in the marketplace the twenty-year-old's debut *Songs in A Minor* is number one on the charts and has been purchased three million times. *A Minor* unleashes Neo-Soul's newest princess, a Black woman impacted equally by hiphop, soul, Prince, and classical. A singer-songwriter with the nubian beauty, sex appeal, and diva presence of Aaliyah and Janet and Toni Braxton, with a street edge. "When every-body moved up to Dolce & Gabbana," says Jeff Robinson, Alicia's long-time manager, "and drivin Bentleys and I'm fabulous and the five-thousand-dollar shit, they forgot about all the kids on the street that can't afford that. Left them without any kind of role model. I knew if we did it right Alicia Keys could fill that gap. She was around the way, but she was beautiful, but she was not fabulous. She wasn't tryin to be iced out, but ghetto hot."

It's an eighteen-hour ride from New York to Atlanta. Cruising through the country, surrounded by friends, it's easy to switch from CNN to *Shaft* and lose yourself—"Is it Sunday?" she asks on Friday morning—and for a moment, forget that the country is at war, while telling a long story. Even though she's young, the story of Alicia Keys's triumph is a long story, far from an overnight success, the result of the patience—a word rarely heard in the record business—to allow an ob-viously talented girl to develop into an artist who could musically speak for herself. The journey took shape when she was thirteen, seven years ago, but began long before with a little girl who loved music above all else.

"I've had a deep love for music since I was four," she says, laying on the bed in the back of the bus barreling through North Carolina. It's well past three a.m. and she's sporting a purple scarf and matching purple oversize sunglasses by Gucci so decadent Prince might rock 'em, and corn braids punctuated by Stevie Wonder–ish beads of blue and black that clink when she moves her head, and maroon Nike running pants, the left leg rolled up Harlem style, and size six and a half white-on-white Adidas shelltoes, barely laced, the tongues kicking up the way Run-DMC used to do. "Music came before everything, everything, everything," she says. "It just meant more than anything ever meant. I would risk everything for it. I'd mess around and get kicked out of school for it or kicked out my momma's house for it. There was nothin that was more important to me." Her friends became musical groups, her piano was a constant companion, her feelings were expressed through songs even before she knew how to write them. "My grandfather died when I was thirteen and I was so upset because they had to call 911 like seven times before the ambulance ever came. He was dyin and no one was there to help him. That made me write one of my earlier fragmented songs, 'I'm All Alone.' "

Alicia grew up with her white mother, Terry, an actress who'll soon be appearing in a production of Neil Simon's *Jake's Women* in Philadelphia, after Craig, her Black father, split. "I do know who my father is," she says. "He didn't live with me, he didn't raise me, I don't call him Dad. But I'm funny about talking about it because people like to interpret it like the lost Black-man father and I hate to support that stereotype. I hate it. I almost feel as if I would prefer not to tell the truth about the matter than to give people that stereotype." Right now, the most her father can do for her is let her hang out with her little brother, Cole. He's eleven. "That's the relationship that I want to cultivate. That's my heart."

If you ask, Alicia will tell you she's of mixed race, but in her heart she feels she's Black. "It's a little bit strange, but not really. It may sound like an oxymoron. But my mother is not 100 percent white. I mean inside. She was always around a lot of different types of people, so I was around a lot of different types of people. Her closest friends were never white. They were African-American, Hispanic, Dominican. So I never felt I had to choose. From the beginning I felt enough of both to be comfortable with both. I never felt that identity crisis. I felt I could be a part of any group. If the bus happen to stop in an all Asian neighborhood, I'll be ai-ight."

Back in the day Terry and Alicia lived on 42nd Street and Tenth Avenue in Manhattan, a neighborhood then called Hell's Kitchen. "All the people that didn't fit in went to 42nd Street," Alicia says. "Runaways, loonies, ho's, pimps, everyone who was an outcast was right there." But Alicia found herself constantly running up to Harlem, attracted by the style, the energy, the flavor. "Harlem raised me in a lot of ways," she says. "Harlem taught me how to think fast, how to play the game, how to not get stuckup in a Chinese store, taught me leadership, how to get out of bad situations when you need to, how to hold my own." Harlem is why she carries herself in a way that demands you take her seriously.

Walking through the projects one day a brother calls out, "Yo, shorty," and another quickly corrects him, "That's not a shorty! That's an excuse-me-miss!" (While we're up close and personal, the girl's got an innie belly button so deep it's like there's a hole in the middle of her stomach, and a kittenish nose; she prays at least three or four times a day, keeps a journal, looks good without makeup, loves to sleep—"sleepin, I think, is a form of meditation," she says—loves to swim, loves to read about the Black Panthers—she's currently reading *Assata*, the autobiography of Panther Assata Shakur—was high-school valedictorian, and earned a full scholarship to Columbia University; and if she seems thin on TV it's a miracle because she's thick. I'm talkin serious thighs and a juicy nubian onion. And she has a boyfriend. "I'm seein a man," she says, blushing. "A person I've known for a long time." He, like her, is cool, streetwise, and high yellow, with musical ability and a deep love of hiphop. "We been rockin for a long time and it's cool. I know he cares about my heart. Not about anything else. Not about what I'm doin, not about TV, not about how I look. It's all about my heart.")

Harlem introduced Alicia to Marvin Gaye and Biggie Smalls. "*What's Goin On* and *Ready to Die* was that whole realism, talkin about what was really goin on right in your face, the dark side of life. Biggie and Marvin told me, Write what you know. You don't have to make it up, it's right there. Then I wanted to discover every type of music like that—Donny Hathaway, Curtis Mayfield, Nina Simone, Miles Davis, Jimi Hendrix, Rakim, Prince—everyone who had that thing. That true emotion. For real. Not for fun, not for money, for real. That's what I listened to, that's what I lived, that's what I fell in love with."

At the same time, she was determined to play the piano well—"I definitely remember havin a 'Fallin' type of relationship with the piano"—and studied classical from age six to eighteen. "There's classical music that's, I call it, for the queen. Very light and airy. Never liked that stuff. All classical music is good for fingering and speed and building your skills, but for my heart, hated that shit. I gravitated toward Chopin. I love Chopin. His preludes! He has these songs that are so deep and have so much passion you say, What was he possibly thinking? What was he feeling? Chopin is my dawg."

At thirteen she met a manager named Jeff Robinson. Robinson is a gruff and tubby man who wears expensive sunglasses on a face that makes Biggie look pretty. The product of a rough Bronx project, Robinson is tough and smart with a loyalty to Alicia unheard of in the record business—he worked with her for seven years before the real money began coming because he believed in her and in the power of slowly grooming musicians, better known as artist development. "There's no artist development anymore to develop these kids and teach 'em the rights and the wrongs of this business," he says. "We just throw 'em out there and hope they get a hit on the radio, then have 'em run around the country for two years, but when the second album don't work out, you never hear from 'em again. This [working with Alicia] has been a building, constant talkin to, counseling sessions, bonding, communicating, the real meaning of artist development. She's not gonna break down in a couple years. She's here for the long haul." His loyalty is a profound reason for her success. Alicia says, "Jeff held tight to the plan when it woulda been easy to be like, We gotta get this paper, this shit's takin too long, so you need to go ahead and do this song and let's go." In retrospect, investing in Alicia seems as easy a call as investing in Microsoft, but it wasn't always that way. "It's always been Jeff," Alicia says. "It was Jeff in the P.A.L. [Police Athletic League] on 134th street. It was Jeff when I was puttin together my demos. It was Jeff when I didn't know how to produce nothin and I was just tryin to figure it out and I'd be in the bed, under the covers tryin to hide because I was depressed that shit was not goin right. It was always Jeff. It wasn't nobody else."

Robinson always knew Alicia would win. Over and over he says, "She's not a blip on the radar screen! She's not a guest star! She's not an opening act! She's," he says, while pointing at his shoulders with his thumbs for extra emphasis, "*the whole fuckin show!* Oh, it's true. It's damn true."

Robinson's brother had been giving Alicia singing lessons at the Police Athletic League in Harlem. "My brother kept telling me to come down," Robinson says. "I kept delayin like nah, nah, but finally I came down. I heard her singin and I said, OK, she got soul. Then she sat down at the piano and started playin a Mary J. song and then the Beethoven stuff and I said, Yo this is some next-level stuff here. This girl could be major. Then when I started talkin to her she was thinkin thoughts like an adult. The problems of the world and philosophy and the future. And she had a star vibe to her. I told her, If you come with me you'll never have a cause to regret. You'll make millions."

Within a month he set up a showcase for major label executives. After a short lifetime of studying all sorts of sounds and doing recitals and talent shows and choirs and small-time singing groups, she was ready. Robinson says, "I knew, the way Alicia personality work, she cute, she could sing and play, and she's got star appeal. Once she's put in front of an audience it's over. It's a wrap. So I let her do her thing on the piano, no band, no background singers, just her and a piano doin what she do best. She played the piano and talked on the mic and won everybody over." The ensuing bidding war was won by Columbia Records. Industry figures with ties to the label say she may have received as much as $400,000. Alicia and Robinson both say only that she hasn't had to worry about money since she was thirteen. "Money hasn't really been an issue," she said. "My life has been blessed to be set up like that since I was young."

Cash, and Robinson, gave her the freedom to slowly pursue the sound she heard in her head. "Her main thing," says L. Green, Alicia's backup singer and friend, "was to do music from her heart and not worry about what labels say is what's hot and what'll sell. She was concerned about what made her feel good as an artist." But finding her sound was tough. Robinson and Columbia sent a slew of high-priced producers to work with her, but years went by without anything fruitful. "The producers would be like, just go in the booth and sing and that got her frustrated," Robinson says. "They'd be like, Yo I worked with this one and that one, I know how records should go. You a new jack. Just get behind the mic and sing how you sing. I'd come in the studio and she'd be all upset, eyes all red, about to cry, ready to fight. I'd be like, alright, session's over. We out."

"That was hell," Alicia says. "It was terrible, horrible. Some of the worst experiences I've had. They were like, why don't we just go hang out and shit. Have dinner and shit. Come back to my place and shit. Very disrespectful. And the music coming out was very disappointing. You have this desire to have something good and you have thoughts and ideas but when you finish the music, it's shit and it keeps on goin like that. You start wondering what's goin on? When is this gonna turn into somethin good?"

The tide changed when Alicia took the weight of writing and producing on herself. "We had to learn to back off and let her do her own thing and trust her," Robinson says. "At the time it was like, We gonna let this little sixteen-year-old girl produce tracks? That's insane. But over time people had confidence in her." Alicia says, "I knew the only way it would sound like anything I would be remotely proud of is if I did it."

She began sitting in with producers and engineers and asking questions, trying to learn how to create music. "I already knew my way around the keyboard so that was an advantage. And the rest was watching people work on other artists and watching how they layer things and oh, that's why it sounds bigger and oh, you put three and four instruments doing the same line just to make it thick. Then all I had to do was figure out why a Babyface song sound like a song and mine sound like an idea."

At seventeen she got her own apartment on 137th Street between Fifth Avenue and Lenox—Harlem, of course. "It was necessary for my sanity," she says. "I needed the space. I needed to have my own thoughts, to do my own thing. I was goin through a lot with my mother, myself, figuring out shit." Urged on by her friend and writing partner Kerry Brothers, who's now copresident of her production company, Krucial Keys, she put a recording studio in the apartment. Now she could tinker and explore and really learn how to write, engineer, and produce music. One day she found herself living on her own and struggling through creating an album and going to the Professional Performing Arts School and it seemed too much to handle. "I'm on my own and tryin to be all grown and still tryin to figure it out and not really knowin what the hell I'm doin and I was all confused and all over the place and losin my mind. And I remember goin to my mother's house, because that was where my only real piano was, and I wrote a song that was really a conversation with God. The verses was all things I was feelin at the moment and the chorus was actually Him or Her answering me. I came back to Harlem and started to work on it, startin with the piano and building up with all the little things I was learning and it became "Troubles." Finally, I knew how to structure my feelings into something that made sense, something that can translate to people. I knew how to get it sounding like what I wanted to hear it sounding like. That was a changing point for me. Instead of feelin like, What the hell am I supposed to do, my confidence was up, way up. That's when the album started comin together."

Toward the end of her creative process she came up with her signature record, "Fallin." *Songs in A Minor* is a strong album on which Alicia shows the songwriting, producing, and performing prowess to indicate that her career could be long and storied. But greater albums have been released to less media fanfare and commercial acceptance by Neo-Soul divas like Jill Scott, Erykah Badu, Angie Stone, and Macy Gray. The difference is "Fallin." Not since D'Angelo's "Untitled" has R&B heard a single that comes close to the power soul ballad with the gospel edge that combines writing of Prince-ish complexity about the simultaneous joy and pain of love with soul piano of depth and subtlety and soul singing worthy of the classic soul giants. The song began in her Harlem home studio and was completed in Electric Lady Studios, made legendary by Jimi Hendrix (and where D'Angelo recorded "Untitled"). "'Fallin' started when I thought it'd be so ill for someone really young to sing a crazy deep song that you'd be like, How does that person know what that feels like? Like how Michael Jackson used to do when he was younger. It came from the relationship I was in, the different dynamics we were goin through at the time, me bein the independent person that I am and really feelin somethin so strong that it made me just sometimes hate him."

But the story of "Fallin," and Alicia, cannot be understood without considering the video, a daring clip in which Alicia travels to visit her man in prison. The video set Alicia apart from other beautiful but image-conservative soul singers who seem afraid to muddy their public face as a more thought-provoking diva. Robinson says, "We thought,

What would be a different kinda video on a subject that effects the streets that hasn't been talked about? A message, but we ain't preachin to you. Something thought-provoking." Rare among videos, it actually deepened the meaning of the song by giving an interesting reason why she struggles loving him while raising the provocative point that the incarcerated still deserve love and that people may make mistakes in one part of their life, but still have people who care about them nonetheless. "You can't say, I all of a sudden don't love this person," she says. "They deserve just as much love when they're in as you was givin them when they were out, if you really love them.

"I read an article in *F.E.D.S. Magazine* that just tripped me out about this woman named Santra Rucker and basically it was a wrong-place, wrong-time type shit and the first thing she was ever charged with, but she was guilty by association and sentenced to 390 years—thirteen consecutive life sentences. And according to her she wasn't involved in it, she just knew this cat. I mean, how many times have you been in a situation with your peoples, and they do whatever they do, but those are your peoples and y'all hang out or whatever, and you ignorant to the fact that you could fuck around and be in jail for 390 years and didn't even have nothin to do with it. So that made a huge impact on me. I wrote to her. I still speak to her. So when it was time to do the video I thought of that."

Actually, the initial concept was for Alicia to be behind bars. "The first video was supposed to be me locked up for not telling on my man," she says. "How deep would your love for someone be that you would do that? That you go through that and although you may hate it and you may hate the person, you love him."

Why didn't that happen? "Well, people get a little nervous with things that are different," Alicia says. "And that was really different. My first video, the first thing anybody ever saw of me. But I personally still think it woulda been bonkers. It woulda been fire."

The album was nearly complete and the video mapped out when Columbia's management changed, and creative differences arose with the new people. "They wanted to go back to the traditional sing-over-this-loop type thing," Robinson says. "After years of workin we wasn't tryin to hear that. Alicia looked at me with tears in her eyes, like, What we gonna do?"

A call was placed, a deal was struck, and her new boss became Clive Davis, the man who discovered Bruce Springsteen, Patty Smith, and Whitney Houston, gave Puffy his label deal, and relaunched Carlos Santana. Perhaps the greatest record man of the past quarter century. "I knew Clive had the golden touch," Robinson says. Clive Davis has an office overlooking Central Park and FAO Schwartz lined with pictures of himself alongside the galaxy of stars he's helped build and a Congressional Record of Honor behind his desk. At sixty-eight he's a warm teddy bear of a man who you might like to have as a grandfather. When he saw Alicia he kissed her softly on the cheek and told her how much she would enjoy her upcoming trip to Paris. He was wearing a thin, button-down grandpa sweater over a tie and large, hip, gold-tinted sunglasses. Certainly, Davis knew that the beautiful young songbird would cause a commercial commotion. "Did I know she was going to sell a million records?" he says. "Of course not! I knew she was unique, I knew she was special, I knew she was a self-contained artist. But did I know with Janis Joplin? Did I know with Springsteen? Did I know with Whitney Houston? When you sign them you don't know, but you feel this is something special and unique, so waiting for artistry to flower and giving them the space to do it is the thing. Then, when the album is done, you take nothing for granted."

Generally, new artists are introduced via the radio and MTV, but Davis knew, as Robinson had known years before, that Alicia could be successful performing by herself in front of small groups of influential people. "Few new artists can be showcased this way and blow people away," he said. "But she can cause a hurricane onstage. So we showcased her for tastemakers. Her maturity and electricity allowed her to do it for herself." At one of these showcases a scout for *The Tonight Show* fell in love and decided to air her immediately. Then Davis personally took the "Fallin" video to MTV, a rare step for him. "When it finished playing half the women had tears down their faces." Finally, he wrote a letter to his friend Oprah Winfrey. "I said, 'What you've done for books is well known. In music you play established artists. How about new women in music? Why don't you put on Jill Scott, India Arie, and Alicia Keys, my artist without an album.' I'd never written to her before. I got a call the next day."

Alicia did *The Tonight Show*, *Oprah*, and heavy rotation on MTV before her album was released. The first week the album was available, her label, J Records, shipped 240,000 copies, somewhat large for a new album. But by the second week, word of mouth and television exposure was so deafening that record stores demanded another 450,000 copies. She was on her way. "Alicia," Davis says, "was her own goodwill ambassador."

It's about two in the afternoon when the bus pulls into Atlanta and back into reality. At the mall across the street there's a row of flags from around the world, all of them at half-mast. A nearby sign says, "United We Stand." A truck drives by covered in American flags with "They Must Pay" written on the back window. As Alicia moves from the bus into the hotel, fifty members of the hotel staff are in a large circle, holding hands, bowing heads, praying silently. "I'm feelin that," she says softly. A few hours later, at the concert, she finishes her set alone onstage with Donny Hathaway's "Someday We'll All Be Free," then walks off as the crowd stands to applaud. Back in the dressing room, with Robinson, Green, and Brothers, there's no cheers, no exalting, no noise at all. Just a long period of stillness and quiet. A group exhale.

Lauryn in Love

{ Lauryn Hill, *Rolling Stone*, 1999 }

America is at war. The radio of a black Chevy Suburban inching down Broadway in midtown Manhattan drones: Day Two and the air strikes on Iraq continue tonight and for the days ahead. President Clinton—the blade of the impeachment guillotine hovering above his neck—says it's what we have to do.

Lauryn Hill swivels in her seat, careful of her long, cream-white, queenly dress, her crisp blue and white man's dress shirt, her eye-popping turquoise-and-white ankle-length mohair coat. She places a delicate, loving hand on the very broad shoulder of Rohan Marley, her ever-present boyfriend and the father of her two children ("I'm damn near married," she says). Her face is bent with concern. "This war thing makes me uneasy," she says with quiet denunciation. "It happened so sudden. There was no buildup."

"Is a sign of revelay-tion," says the Jamaican-born Ro, his voice husky and thick with patois.

"Well," I say, "they say they didn't want to attack during Ramadan." "Oh," she says, "but attacking the day before is OK?" She shakes her head. "The media have made people so accepting of war. They're so cynical, they'll believe something stupid. I was in Rwanda and we went to the places where the genocide happened—yards full of bones and skulls, and it seemed like props. My friend said, 'Lauryn, I thought I'd be more upset than I am.' He was completely desensitized. He was more upset about not being upset." She goes quiet, letting the thought hang in midair. "Ro's theory," she adds, "is that all of Hollywood is meant to desensitize us."

A moment later, Lauryn says, "Bono said my album is one of the most important of the year." She is incredulous, but calm and respectful. No one else in the car is surprised. "He wants me to do Lalibala, Ethiopia, on the eve of the new century." Ethiopia is the Rastafarian holy land.

"Iz a spiritual ting," Ro says. "Ya go out there for the people. Nah fah self."

"If I'm not performing, I'll be in church."

"Lalibala iz the church." The conversation flows on, touching on war and the media and modern America, Lauryn consistently siding with the unempowered with an earnestness and a conviction rarely heard outside of vintage Black Panthers footage.

"The small-business man who made America individual is gone," she says. "There used to be flea markets by my house where you could buy all sorts of little things. Now it's all Home Depots."

This is the Lauryn Hill who doesn't just want to make music—she wants to change the world. "We're in this war," she says. "Well, there's always a constant spiritual war, but there's a battle for the souls of Black folk, and just folks in general, and the music has a lot to do with it."

Lauryn has fought this war for eleven years, first with the Fugees and now with her self-produced debut solo album, *The Miseducation of Lauryn Hill*, a talking book that tells the history of soul, R&B, reggae, and hiphop. Its instant success has put her in the vanguard of the modern hiphop-soul movement. "Black music right now is like this whole *Star Wars* battle," says Ahmir Thompson (aka ?uestlove), drummer for the Philadelphia hiphop band the Roots. "There are very few people who are on the side of art and are goin up against the Death Star. D'Angelo is Luke Skywalker. Prince, Stevie, James, Marvin, and George are our Yoda and Obi-Wan Kenobi. And, most definitely, Lauryn is Princess Leia."

Lauryn believes she's already having an impact.

"Music is about to change," she says. "I think now people feel a little more comfortable playing with the parameters. Writing more intensely. I think we [D'Angelo and herself] have helped to make people less afraid. There are a lot of young people who will be given more leeway. People can't really hear potential. There's a lot of people who need to hear a ready-made, instant-meal, TV dinner–type thing—where you just put it in the microphone—the microwave, as opposed to potential."

We arrive at the Hill home, a three-story brick house in an upper-middle-class neighborhood of South Orange, New Jersey, five minutes down the road from the house where Lauryn grew up. Lauryn lives here with her parents; she bought the place for them "when I got a little money." It's roomy enough for Lauryn, her mom and dad, her children—year-and-a-half-old Zion and three-month-old Selah—and her man, Rohan, as well as a driveway long enough to fit Lauryn's green Land Rover Defender, Rohan's red Range Rover, and Mom's Range, too. It's a house of such grand size and tasteful decoration that the Huxtables, Bill Cosby's TV family, might have lived here. There are cream walls and a huge ornate mirror in the front room, and all sorts of comfy chairs and couches everywhere. In the bathroom, an exquisite Asian-style dragon's mouth is a faucet, and dragon tails are knobs.

There are a few plaques celebrating the millions of "Killing Me Softly" singles sold in the U.K. and Australia, but where are the two Grammys Lauryn won with the Fugees in 1997 for *The Score*? Where are the plaques commemorating the three million people who have purchased *The Miseducation of Lauryn Hill* (recently nominated for eight Grammys, with Lauryn getting another two nominations for her work on Aretha Franklin's "A Rose Is a Rose")? Or the eighteen million who have paid for *The Score*?

"I have about thirty plaques that stay in one closet," Lauryn says. "And if you saw where the Grammys were, you'd be like, 'This is a travesty!' But I can't look at that stuff all the time, because I don't ever wanna become complacent like that. This is not a museum, and I'm not in any rush to impress anybody. I don't feel like my money or my success defines me. I've always been very happy just bein me."

It's two days before Christmas and the Hill home is in full festive swing, with white candles and red poinsettias and a Christmas tree with blinking lights, a porcelain black Mary and Joseph at its base and a little black angel on top. Around ten-thirty p.m., Lauryn's holiday party starts bubbling. Her band members and managers and assistants and dread technician stroll in, and the dining room is filled with turkey, spaghetti and meatballs, vegetable lasagna, barbecued wings, rice, stuffing, biscuits and gravy. Everyone gathers hands, forming a large circle as Lauryn slides into the room, the jangling of silver wrist bangles preceding her. There's chipped silver polish on her toenails, and a red Abercrombie and Fitch long-sleeved top and green army pants over her new-mama chest and long legs. She is the color of dark chocolate, about five-foot-four and thin, but a collection of perfectly placed African curves proves she's not underfed.

She blesses the food, then praises her people: "I've surrounded myself with people who believe in what I do, because I can't do what I do alone. I'm a regular person. I'm not a corporation. I need a babysitter sometimes." She turns to her man, standing a few feet away. "And I have to thank Ro, who has the patience of a clam—a clam takes one hundred years to make a pearl. I love you very much. I know it's rough, but we here."

Lauryn met Rohan more than two years ago, after a Fugees concert. He has become the love of her life. He is yellow skinned, with a long, sharp nose, natty shoulder-length dreads, and a long, wily goatee, the unmistakable scion of Bob Marley. Ro exudes peace and humility and is deeply spiritual—"I be in constant prayer," he says. He also was a standout football player for the University of Miami and the Ottawa Rough Riders of the Canadian Football League, a linebacker known for making explosive hits. He seems perfect for Lauryn, who is described by friends as "spiritual, with an underlying soft-spoken militancy."

"Ro came in my life," Lauryn will say a few days later, "in the exact time that I wasn't looking for anyone and also the exact time that I needed someone very badly. Everything that happened in my life up to the point of me meeting him kinda showed me why he was the right one. He's kinda like the most sincere person that I have ever met, with the most sincere heart. He's real funny, because on the exterior he's like stone, but on the inside he's so sweet. He wears his heart on his sleeve in this relationship, and that's where I put my heart, so we're cool. It's really deep to be in a relationship when both people are working equally hard. That's some really, really interesting stuff. I could really get used to that. He actually may be working a little harder than I am, cuz my schedule is nuts. To be involved with an entertainer, you have to have the patience of Job. But he's dope in a very nonobvious, unpretentious way. It's his heart. His heart is sooo pure. Our meeting just confirmed to me that there is God."

Once the food is blessed, Lauryn runs upstairs with her dread technician. The musicians sit down to dinner and later take over the living room. A plaintive guitar picks out the melody of Bob Marley's "Redemption Song." Assorted finger snaps and boot stomps mark time as everyone sings. "Emancipate yourself from mental slav'ry! None but ourselves can free our minds!" Papa Hill videotapes the scene as the crowd grows, and the singers move through Marley classics—"Natural Mystic," then "I Shot the Sheriff," then "Trenchtown Rock"—the voices thinning in the verses, rising for the choruses. Everyone sings except Ro, who sits beside the guitarist, eyes closed as if in prayer, head nodding in a happy trance until the zenith of "No Woman, No Cry," when the entire room sings, "Everting gon be alright! Everting gon be alright!" Ro jumps up into the room's center, eyes squeezed shut, dancing, no, moving with the rhythm as if to summon Rasta spirits. Lauryn comes back downstairs and stands quietly at the edge of the room. "This," she says, "is a very Kingston-Hallmark holiday party."

Lauryn grew up in a working-class section of South Orange, the second child and only daughter of Mal, a computer programmer, and Valerie, a high-school English teacher. Before they met—she was coming from a school dance, he was running from a neighborhood lunatic—Valerie would spend every cent of her allowance on 45s. "I amassed a nice little pile stacks and stacks of Motown, Philly International, Stax, Marvin, Stevie, Aretha, Donny Hathaway, Gladys Knight that whole thing," she says. After her daughter was born, Valerie boxed the collection and stuffed it in a corner of the basement. "One day little Lauryn found 'em," she says. "They all came upstairs. And thus began a journey. She started to play that music and loved it. One o'clock in the morning, you'd go in her room and you'd see her fast asleep with the earphones on. The 60s soul that I'd collected just seeped into her veins."

By age eight, Lauryn was an expert on the history of soul music.

"I'd be the kid at family barbecues in the middle of Newark listenin to the oldies station with the old folks," she remembers. "They'd go, 'Oh, that's Blue Magic!' And I'd go, 'No, it's the Chi-Lites.'" The Hill home was already music-drenched: Mr. Hill sang at weddings, Mrs. Hill studied piano, and Lauryn's brother, Melaney, played guitar, sax, and drums. But Lauryn was born with musical aptitude—"Her violin teacher kept telling us, 'I don't believe how musical she is,'" Valerie says—and with rare presence. "She just had this effect on people who listened to her."

By her teens, Lauryn was determined to sing for her supper. "At thirteen, she sang Smokey Robinson's 'Who's Lovin You' on *Showtime at the Apollo*," says Valerie. "When the day came, we marshaled the forces, rented a big van, took a bunch of kids from her school for moral support and went off to the Apollo. But when she started to sing, she was terrified, so she stood far away from the mic and the fans started booing. My brother-in-law screamed out, 'Get close to the mic!' and she grabbed the mic and sang that song with a vengeance, like, 'How dare you boo me.' She sang her heart out. At the end of the song, they were clapping and screaming for her.

"When we got home, she felt she had let herself down, and she started crying. I said, 'Lauryn, they're gonna clap for you one day and maybe not the next, but you gotta take it all. This is part of the business that you say you want to be in. Now, if every time they don't scream and holler you're gonna cry, then perhaps this isn't for you.' And she looked at me like I had taken leave of my senses. To her, the mere suggestion that this wasn't for her was crazy."

Around the time of her Apollo performance, Lauryn began hanging with a friend from junior high named Prakazrel "Pras" Michel and his cousin Wyclef Jean. In the following five years, Lauryn did various local plays and a stint on *As the World Turns*, and had a large part in the Whoopi Goldberg vehicle *Sister Act 2*, all the while spending hours in Wyclef's basement studio, jumping from writing lyrics to doing Spanish homework and history papers until early in the morning. In time, the three became known as the Fugees. She was eighteen when the group's 1993 debut album, *Blunted on Reality*, flopped. But three years later, with *The Score*, she established herself as an introspective, spiritual-minded Lennon to Wyclef's fun-loving, pop-melody spewing McCartney. The two were widely said to be a couple.

But success was corrosive. Lauryn and many who know her well say that the past two years of her life have been sad ones, that her current happiness arrived only recently. "There was a point where I had decided that I wasn't gonna pray anymore," Lauryn says. "And the reason why I stopped praying was because there were some things in my life that I knew weren't good for me. But I had decided that I needed those things." She seems to be referring to her much speculated-about relationship with Wyclef. "I knew that if I prayed, God would take them from me. So I was afraid. I was devastatingly terrified of prayer. And the moment I did pray, lo and behold, he removed all the negativity. Quicker than a snap. In the same speed, he loosened my tongue and a creative voice just came and wrote. It was really, really heavy."

She sat down to "write songs that lyrically move me and have the integrity of reggae and the knock of hiphop and the instrumentation of classic soul." Then she worked with her engineer on getting "a sound that's raw. I like the rawness of you being able to hear the scratch in the vocals. I don't ever want that taken away. I don't like to use compressors and take away my textures, because I was raised on music that was recorded before technology advanced to the place where it could be smooth. I wanna hear that thickness of sound. You can't get that from a computer, because a computer's too perfect. But that human element, that's what makes the hair on the back of my neck stand up. I love that."

The songs that became *The Miseducation of Lauryn Hill* revealed her to have Joni Mitchell's intense singer-songwriter integrity, Bob Marley's revolutionary spirit, and young Chaka Khan's all-natural, everywoman sensuality. They also purged her soul. "What's in that record, to me, is a movement from a darker space and a return to a brighter space," she says, "because that's exactly what happened to me. I was speakin to a girl I grew up with the other day and she said somethin real funny. There was a period of time when I wasn't as happy as I am now, and we were talkin about that period in my life, and she talked about when I was a kid. I was real crazy and always like [sings], 'Let's put on a show!' I was that kid. Always singing and dancing—everything I did was dramatic. I was wild.

"My friend said to me, 'Lauryn, when I see you right now, you remind me so much of the you when you were a little girl.' I took that to mean that when I was a kid, I was this sort of bright and shining kid who had a real pure heart and pure spirit—and, hopefully, I've returned to that place."

It's about three-fifteen a.m., and in the dimly lighted sound booth of Chung King Studios, in lower Manhattan, Lauryn is seated sideways on a wooden stool, in dark jeans and a gray zip-up sweatshirt, a beige knit cap containing her dreads. Behind her, a herd of empty mic stands rests like a flock of black and silver flamingos. At her feet sit a half-finished Nantucket Nectars lemonade and two lyrics-coated legal pads. Lauryn is working on a rhyme for a new Curtis Mayfield song from the upcoming Mod Squad movie soundtrack, produced by Atlanta's Organized Noize, who have worked with Goodie Mob and OutKast. She comes up with "There ain't no excuses/ cuz in every situation man chooses/ His own plate/ His own fate/ His own date at redemption/ And only fools and babies get exemption/ In the hereafter school/ See, we all stay for detention/ And, uh, did I mention/ It's either ascension or descension/ No third dimension/ So pay attention."

She listens to the beat, searching for the right spot to enter ("As the keyboard comes in?"), then prepares to rhyme. "It's a very strange poem," she tells her engineer. "Hopefully, you'll get it. L-Boogie does poetry." She rhymes over the exquisite track, powered by a soft conga line and a world-weary acoustic guitar, in a style that's slightly more Last Poets talk-rapping than MC flowing. The engineer assures her the take is perfect, but she's unhappy. She tries again and again. It's not working. She calls me over and stops to talk music for a few moments. She assures the engineer she'll just be a moment. She won't. As soon as the tape recorder is rolling, before a question is even asked, she begins. She speaks in paragraphs, flowing from topic to topic, practically interviewing herself, talking quickly and with the sharp articulation of an English teacher, in a deep, throaty voice without pauses, never mincing words or biting her tongue, always coming with a deep self-confidence powered by moral certainty.

3:52 a.m. "I feel beautiful not because of my features, really," Lauryn says. "It has nothing to do with my face. I feel beautiful because of my heart. I think I have a very loving, kind spirit. I think it's the God in me that makes me beautiful. It doesn't really have anything to do with my physical features. That's not the emphasis here. Right now I feel beautiful because God is in me, and when people are happy with themselves, they're happy, period. Sometimes they use other things to mask what's goin on inside, but I feel beautiful inside. That's what I really try to maintain. If there was an 'inside pomade,' I'd buy some. Grease my insides, slick 'em down . . ."

4:19 a.m. She's still talking: "It's just so deep to me to have children, plural, because I remember being on punishment. I remember vividly, very recently, bein on punishment. But my children are beautiful. We call them hiphop-reggae, because they're half Ro and half me, split down the middle. Right now, Zion is practicing for the terrible twos. He's like, 'I'm a get this right.' He does this thing where he falls back and you just gotta let him lay on the ground. He'll literally throw himself on the ground. He is so dramatic. I know I'm getting paid back for all the drama that I ever gave.

"From the moment my daughter was born, I could tell she was a girl. She just had a feminine quality about her. It was so cute. She squealed and she cried like a lady. I was like, 'Wow.' The second child is much easier. With Selah I'm like [pantomimes tossing her in the air]. With Zion I was like [pretends to hold him delicately]. Meanwhile, in the nursery they throw these children around like footballs.

"I don't want them to feel like they miss Mommy. So I challenge myself to make sure I'm with them as much as possible, but when you're a perfectionist at music and you spend all those hours on your craft, it makes it hard. Raising children is a twenty-four-hour job, and makin music is a twenty-four-hour job, so I have to really be careful

how I do things. But I'm up for the challenge. I think God gave me these
children so young because I have the energy to deal with it. And I need
a lot of energy. I am a walking vending machine. That's what I am in my
house. I know my place. My children look at me like, 'Lunch.'"

She stops a moment. "Did you see my G-Shock?" It's a black
watch given to her by Sony Japan. "It's a special-edition L-Boogie
G-Shock." Push a button and it lights up, as any G-Shock would, but you
see her face as seen on the cover of *Miseducation*.

4:57 a.m. She's beginning to get personal: "When I was a kid, I had two
gifts. I knew all the old records. I could do the Rock [dance inspired by
Michael Jackson's "Rock With You"]. And then I have this other gift: If
you ask me any two colors, I could tell you what NFL team they belong
to."

"Gold and black?"

Without hesitation, she says, "The Saints . . . Pittsburgh Steelers,
as well . . . Damn, you went for a hard one right away."

"Blue and green?"

"Seahawks. I don't watch football, though. Keep testin me. This is
for real."

"Red, white, and blue?"

Immediately: "Bills, Giants, Patriots. Should I explain to you how
I got this gift? This is how I know that trauma is very deep and kids who
are traumatized remember all types of shit. I used to be terrified of the
dark and every scary thing that could possibly get you in the dark, and
when it was dark, I went into my brother's room and slept in the bed
with him. He had football curtains and sheets. And I'd be so scared that
I'd stare at those curtains and sheets and stay awake, making sure nothin
attacked us until my eyes got so heavy I had to pass out. But from this I
have remembered the colors of every single team in the NFL. It's crazy.
Oh, and I could do the Smurf, too."

Is "Lost Ones" about Wyclef? Is "I Used to Love Him"? Is "Ex-
Factor"? Is Wyclef's "To All the Girls" about Lauryn? At 5:03 a.m. she
gets into her brother bandmates. "The album," Lauryn says, "is not
about me bein upset about a love lost. It's not even really about bein up-

set about bein stabbed in the back." But the fact is this: Lauryn and Clef were once very close and, right now, are not.

"To be honest with you, I haven't spoken with Clef in a long time," she says in a low, quiet voice, measuring each word. "A couple months now. I think, in our own sweet time, we're gonna get into a room and talk to each other about all of our issues and make some music. But that can't happen too prematurely or I think it would damage things. We all sincerely loved each other. And we still do. But in any relationship there's ups and downs. People grow up, they grow apart. And just like a relationship, if things are based on the right things, they'll come back together, and if they're not, then they won't. I have a huge amount of love for them, but I needed to learn some things about myself. I've found my voice. I've found my sound, the sound which is distinctly me. I needed to become the woman that I'm becoming, and it was necessary for me to make this record. But I think, at the same time, this record may have revealed some insecurities in other people. And I think it made it a little difficult. I don't think that everybody was necessarily that happy that I decided to do a solo project. I think that they thought the worst as opposed to the best.

"But I know that (a) time reveals truth. And (b) time heals wounds. So I'm not in any rush to rip any Band-Aids off. Actually, maybe I am. Maybe I do wanna rip the Band-Aid. I think this album definitely ripped the Band-Aid off, because it helped the wound to breathe as opposed to fester. But I'd rather let the healing process take its own natural time than rush into a situation." Do you miss them? "Yeah, I do. I definitely do. We were a crazy bunch. We used to do some wild things. Not bad wild things—we had a lot of fun. But the funny thing about liberation is that once you get it, anything other feels awkward."

She pauses. "I just can't do anything if I'm not inspired," she says. "I always sorta wait for the inspiration to come, and if the spirit doesn't drive me to do it, then I won't do it. Cuz I definitely know that what I'm doin is sorta bigger than me. It's somethin that I've been assigned."

D'Angelo Is Holding Your Hand

{ *Rolling Stone*, 2000 }

D'Angelo is holding your hand. His thick, muscular fingers are interlocked with yours. You can feel the baby oil that he rubs on his skin before each show. You can feel the pressure of his vise squeeze. You can feel his rings cutting into your skin. It hurts. It hurts good, though.

"Dear heavenly Father," someone is saying to the silent room, "please give us the ability to touch this crowd." All thirty-six members of D'Angelo's touring band and crew are stuffed into his dressing room, hands linked, heads bowed in a large prayer circle. "And when our ability fails, Lord. Please. Take over." The room answers with a loud "mm-hmm."

Prayer ends, and the entire group collapses into a giant moving hug, all yelling at once in a joyous din—"*Soultronic force! My re-deeeeem-er!*" It seems they're gearing up for some high-energy smash-mouth football. Or a musical mission.

As the scrum disperses, D'Angelo turns to you and slaps you five. And nearly breaks your hand. D, as they call him, gives pounds with injurious intent—stiff-handed smacks that make a firecracker *pop* and then meld into a tight clamp, a finger snap, two fist bumps and another clamp, or some such combination. The more he likes you, the more he uses the strength in his bulky shoulders and arms for some hand-cracking friendly force, an immediate, tactile, visceral way of saying, "You're family." "It's just a camaraderie between the family, between all the soldiers," he says of the pound thing later. "I'm lookin at this like an army of musicians and free spirits and music. It's very much like a war."

D turns from you and gives a pound to every soldier in the room, some of them quick, hard slap-grip-snaps, many of them long, choreographed affairs with fourteen or fifteen stages. Backstage, or in the hotel, or just about anywhere, you can hear him coming because of the firecracker slaps and loud-ass finger snaps as he moves down the hall dapping up everyone he loves.

The band members leave to find their places onstage, the room clears, and D is left alone, his Shaft-like black leather coat stretching past his knees, his cornrows tight and clean, every last wisp whipped into place, his skin brown like chocolate Häagen-Dazs. He is shortish, maybe five feet six, but his shoulders and biceps are thick and glistening from the baby oil and defined to a hair's breadth of perfection, the protruding veins of a weight lifter evident in his forearms. His lips are big pillows, the top one a bit larger with a thick line running down its middle. They stay moist. His lashes are long, the eyes deep-set, large and intense, staring piercingly into you.

With three bodyguards around him, he smooths from the dressing room down the stairs, not rushing, moving with the muscular grace and power of a panther, strutting his macho-pimp stride, shoulders swaggering, exuding the masculinity and bravado of a champion prizefighter ready for combat. He reaches the curtain shielding the stage and stands still as a soldier, feet spread wide, head bent, his hard breathing betraying a touch of nerves. He is motionless for a full four minutes until the lights go dim and the standing-room-only crowd at L.A.'s House of Blues on Sunset Boulevard begins to scream, a mostly female scream, and the drums, bass, and keys slide into the groove of "Playa, Playa." At seven after ten, the curtain opens and D'Angelo cools his way out to the place he was born to be: center stage.

Two days later, on an afternoon in New Orleans, in the ultrahip W hotel, room number 1725: This is the room of ?uestlove, drummer for the Philadelphia hiphop band the Roots and D's copilot for *Voodoo*, D'Angelo's five-years-in-the-making second album. Large and cuddly, charismatic and exuberantly Afro'd, ?uest is a real-life version of *South Park*'s Chef. He slouches on one edge of the bed, his best pal D on the other edge in a black *Tonight Show* T-shirt, black sweats, and black Nike Air

Flightposites, with a black do-rag tight over his head. They are watching a black-and-white videotape of James Brown performing in 1964. This is what they call a treat—something that gives knowledge of the Yoda figures. Mostly videotapes of shows, but also albums and books. A Yoda figure is one of the masters they revere: James, Prince, Stevie Wonder, George Clinton, Marvin Gaye, Fela Kuti, Al Green, Joni Mitchell, Sly, Jimi. One day, ?uest-love asked D, "What would your life be like if you hadn't seen that George Clinton tape?" D replied, "Totally different."

In their pursuit of knowledge about the Yodas, the two have acquired hundreds of treats. "We got bootleg-concert connects like fiends got drug-dealer connects," ?uest says. "During *Voodoo*, there was at least thirteen people providing us with stuff." "They're the ultimate collectors," says D's manager, Dominique Trenier. "Anytime I see them, they got at least thirty tapes on them. I could say, 'I'm bored. You got some old *Soul Trains* I haven't seen?' 'They'll be like,' 'Yeah. You see the one where Michael Jackson fell?'" They study the treats the way Mike Tyson studied tapes of legendary fighters, enraptured by genius, hungry to learn.

The knowledge is inspiration and ammunition for the war that D considers modern music. The war is over the future of music. *Voodoo* is an ambitious record that seeks nothing less than to unstick Black music from commercial considerations and leave it free to seek its muse. It is an album of loose, long, dirty grooves, finger snaps, falsetto serenades, gruff mumbles and bottom-dwelling bass. It is soul music for the age of hiphop, which is to say it swaggers even when it is tender. In the video for the single "Untitled (How Does It Feel)," D appears to be naked, the camera licking him down. The video would be equally at home in a museum piece on Black males and on the triple-X rack, and it provides a striking visual analogy for the music itself: raw, intimate, naked, intensely Black. Like Sly Stone's *There's a Riot Goin On* or Marvin Gaye's *Here My Dear*, *Voodoo* is purposefully difficult music. It does not bother often with melodies, and some of those it does bother with seem to come directly from old Prince records. But it is also the complex and rewarding work of a multi-instrumentalist struggling, by his own admission, to find his own voice through intensive study of Prince, Hendrix, P-Funk and, this afternoon, James Brown.

The James Brown treat we're watching is from *The T.A.M.I. Show*, a concert film featuring Marvin, the Beach Boys, and the Rolling Stones. James had been slated to go on last, but, ?uestlove explains, "the Stones management wanted them to go on after James. So he decided to make them pay by killing it, so they couldn't go on after him. This is his moment of Zen."

?uestlove and D watch silently as James dances hard and fast, his ankles on the verge of breaking, his feet a blur, his singing wafting up from the bottom of his soul—"*Are you ready for the Night Train?!*" James dances toward the mic, stops sharp, and somehow, at the exact same second, the band stops. ?uestlove rewinds over and over, amazed at the band's tightness.

"Even the light guy is on point!" ?uestlove says. "It's luck."

"It's not," D says, sucking on a Newport. "They're lookin at him, they know his every move." His speaking voice is a deep, lazy sound syruping from the back of his throat, a bass-y, Virginia-accented near-mumble.

While making *Voodoo*, the two pored over one treat or another every day—"If I wasn't bringin treats every week," ?uest says, "you'd probably have had *Voodoo* in '98." What started as the follow-up to D'Angelo's 1995 platinum debut, *Brown Sugar* (written and recorded entirely by D'Angelo in his mother's house in Richmond, Virginia), became five years of study at Soul University, complete with classes, pranks, gossip, and equal amounts of discipline and laziness. "You know how some students are afraid to leave school?" ?uestlove says. "There was a comfort in knowing you go to the studio and walk into a whole new world. The engineers come in and talk about what Foxy did this week or how someone wrote graffiti on the bathroom. Or me and Rahzel would call D pretending to be Chico DeBarge talkin shit—it was like school. That's why it took four years. There was no loose women—I wish. No orgies, no drug madness, no trouble with the law. I mean, he got into a scuffle with somebody, but that didn't hold things up."

"It was definitely school, man," D says. "I ain't never went to college, so this was my equivalent. It was a return to what we love about music. After *Brown Sugar*, I lost my enthusiasm to do all this. I coulda done without goin to 7-Eleven at three o'clock to get a pack of cigarettes and find yourself swarmed, signin autographs. I had to reiterate why I was doin that in the first place, and the reason was the love for the music. I was gettin jaded, lookin at what go on in the business. But, I had to say, even if I didn't do this, I'd still be fuckin with the music. So I'm cursed, and I'm gon' be cursed till the day I die. So this is what I'm gon' do."

Each day at Electric Lady, the studio on Eighth Street in lower Manhattan built by Jimi Hendrix, began around four in the afternoon, when D'Angelo, ?uestlove, and all those who worked for years to develop the album would gather. A crucial influence was Jay Dee, from the group Slum Village. "He's the zenith of hiphop to us," ?uestlove says. Jay Dee helped to bring out the album's dirty sound and encouraged the false starts and the nonquantized sound of the record. ("Quantized" is D-bonics for being in perfect rhythm, while "to slum," ?uest explains, "is the art of totally dragging the feel while being totally quantized. So, musically drunk and sober at the same time. Also called 'to Jay that shit.'")

From four until seven in the evening, the crew would watch the treat of the day and eat. Then they'd turn on the recorder and begin playing an album or an entire catalog by one of the Yodas—the dominant influence of '96 was Prince, in '97 Jimi and Rev. Al, '98 Gaye and George Clinton, '99 James and Nigerian star Fela Kuti. They'd jam and wait to see what the groove inspired. One night they played Prince's *Parade* until they flowed into a new groove that became "Africa."

At one a.m. they'd break for dinner at the extremely untrendy, very dive-y Waverly diner on Sixth Avenue. "One of the marvels of life," says ?uestlove, "was how this ma-fucker could eat all these eggs and twelve pounds of turkey bacon and be fit for 'Untitled.' Money was definitely overweight by '96, so they got him a drill sergeant [physical trainer Mark Jenkins]. This guy didn't take no shit. I cannot see D running in Central Park, but he did. If it was rainin, extra parka, your ass was runnin. Push-ups, weight room, sparring every day for three hours. He wouldn't take no shit." (Jenkins, who's trained Mary J. Blige and Johnnie Cochran, hits the road with D to help him through three to four workouts a week.)

The gang would return from the Waverly around two a.m., watch the treat of the day one more time and work on the new song until around four-thirty or five. Then D would drive people home in his black Range Rover 4.6. At this pace, they created 120 hours of original music that the public has yet to hear.

"But the biggest influence on the record," ?uestlove says, "was someone who never came to the studio: Prince. Way after *Voodoo* was finished, D and I sat down and listened to it, and we both admitted that this was our audition tape for Prince. I think this album was made to show him that we're capable of collaborating with him. And I don't know if it's some bold-ass shit to say we know what he needs, but we wanna work with him."

"I really, seriously wanna coproduce his next joint," D says. "Like, me and Ahmir [?uestlove] wouldn't even have to use our names. We'd just be on some pseudonym shit. That's what he meant by audition. Just, like, we wanna do his next shit."

Back in L.A., two hours into the show, and the roof is on fire. We've gone from smooth soul to rock funk to Pentecostal church, the grooves shifting without a moment's pause in a breathtaking musical assault. Five years ago, during the *Brown Sugar* tour, D was a shy twenty-one-year-old Virginia country boy who hid behind his keyboard onstage. Now he's confident and worldly, a father of two—a three-year-old son, Michael D'Angelo Archer II, and a five-month-old daughter, Imani Michael Michelle—as well as a soul-music historian. No wonder he's alive onstage now, dancing, touching the audience, slamming his microphone down, lying on the ground at the lip of the stage to sing "One Mo' Gin" while girls grab his legs, his stomach, his crotch. He's the musical counterpart to Vince Carter and Randy Moss: a young icon, abundantly gifted, eye-poppingly spectacular, embarking on a Hall of Fame career.

He returns for the first encore in a tight black tank top, yelling, "I got the baddest band in the world! The Soultronics!" And he's right. The thirteen-piece Soultronics, a group he pieced together from the worlds of jazz, soul, and the church, are light-years ahead of your average backup band. On keyboards is the renowned producer James Poyser, who co-piloted *The Miseducation of Lauryn Hill*. Bassist Pino Palladino left B.B. King's side to be here (he's also played with the Staple Singers, Phil Collins, Elton John, and Eric Clapton) and is, ?uestlove says, "one of three bassists left that can begin to emulate James Jamerson, bass god from the legendary Motown house band." Trumpeters Roy Hargrove and Russell Gunn are young jazz stars who've played with Wynton Marsalis. Trombonist Ku-umba Frank "Roots" Lacy played with Art Blakey and holds a degree in physics. ?uestlove himself is a recent Grammy winner with the Roots. Even the backup singers have impressive résumés: Anthony Hamilton has a record deal with indie label Soulife Recordings, and Shelby Johnson was on her fourth callback for *Rent* when she opted to travel with D.

"A lot of my fellow vocalists were scared of this gig," Johnson says, "because singing his stuff is so complex. But he brings you up to another level and makes you better as a musician if you're willing to work. Bein down with D has made me a better me."

The Soultronics begin each show in all black, but beyond that one requirement, each looks completely distinct. One man is in a deacon's robe, another in a long cape with a knit ski cap that says FBI. There's a feather boa, a few badass leather coats, and ?uestlove's mighty Afro. There's a P-Funkish freaky flair to the Soultronics' look.

"In the beginning we kept asking, 'What should we wear?'" Johnson says. "And D kept saying, 'Just be you.' It's rare you have an artist who's secure enough to let you be the rare motherfucker you can be. And if I'm up there feelin like I wanna feel, wearin my shit and my shoes, then he's gonna get the best out of me."

One day in Richmond, Virginia, ten-year-old Luther Archer came home to find his little brother playing the piano. "Mike was three—and it was not banging," Luther says with awe. "It was a full-fledged song, with melody and bass line. Shortly thereafter, he started playing for my father's church. My father had a Hammond organ, and he had to slide down to reach the pedals, but he did that very well."

"This is really the only thing I ever could see myself doin," Michael D'Angelo Archer says. "I knew when I was three. My brothers knew. They geared me for that. I always knew this is what I was supposed to be, what I was gonna do."

There are family stories of his early promise: of the kindergarten talent show he won so convincingly that they wouldn't let him participate in school talent shows after that, and the time seven-year-old Mike taught ninth-grader Luther how to play Prince's "Do Me, Baby," and the time Luther and middle brother Rodney took the little one to the mall, stopped in an organ store, and let him sit down at the keys. Within minutes he'd stopped traffic in the place.

"My mother had a little room set off for him where he had all his equipment, and he was in there every day for hours," says Luther, who cowrote "Africa," "The Root," and "Send It On." "There wasn't a day for sixteen or seventeen years that he didn't touch the music."

"I played everywhere I could," D says of his childhood. His father is a Baptist preacher, and he began playing music in his father's church, then went to live with his mother and played in his grandfather's church in Powhatan, in the Virginia countryside. "That's the real stomp-down, Pentecostal, holiness church," he says. "Shoutin, speakin in tongues and just fire. That's where I really grew. That's where I really was playin."

D and two cousins started a group and began tearing up local talent shows as Three of a Kind. Talent show after show they played covers off the radio and won or placed high. Luther and Rodney were local high school football heroes, on TV and in the newspaper every week, and Mike played a little, too, but no one in the family would come to his games: " 'Cause they knew it was about music for me."

Luther did support his little brother's love of Prince. Their father is a preacher, as are an uncle and a grandfather, so they couldn't just bop into the house with *Lovesexy* in hand, but the boys found ways to sneak the music in. "My love for Prince was definitely influenced by my older brother," D says. "We always had every new album the first day, and we would dissect that shit and study it, and after we listened to it, we'd have a discussion about it. We always did that."

"We used to get in my car," Luther says, "and we'd ride around the city with nothing to do and listen to Prince tapes. It was a red Ford Probe with a nice system in it. We'd hang out and listen to the music real loud."

Mike was sixteen when he got a slot on *Amateur Night at the Apollo*. He sang "Feel the Fire" by Peabo Bryson, but the audience could see his fear before the song started: "They booed before I even came onstage." He placed fourth.

The next year he went back to the Apollo. "I did 'Rub You the Right Way' by Johnny Gill, and I came out dancin, doin splits and shit. I had mad energy. I wasn't intimidated.

"When they said I won, I went off," he continues. "I'd been doin talent shows forever, and that was, like, the talent show. I went off, my family went off, my brother was runnin down the aisle, my cousins were jumpin up and down. We got back on the bus and went right back to Richmond. Everybody went to sleep; I stayed up the whole time. I was smoking cigarettes. That's when I started. I was sneakin cigarettes, and I had the window cracked, and I was lookin out the window just thinkin about everything. I got a check for $500, bought a four-track and started writing. I wanted to make an album." He went into his little music room, and wrote and recorded most of the songs that would make up *Brown Sugar*. Two years later he had a record deal.

At five past midnight in L.A., the crowd begins screaming in unison: "Take! It! Off! Take! It! Off!" D resists, but around quarter past, the tight black tank top comes off and he's onstage in nothing but his very low-slung black leather pants and his boots. No drawers, no boxers, no briefs, no belt. He's singing "Untitled" on the lip of delicious obscenity, giving you more than a sliver of his ass crack, his bare hips, his waist, his pubic bush, and the deep grooves separating his torso from his thighs, grooves that have come to be known as the D'Angelo Knuckles. A solid wall of soprano screams rises up. It's the most electric moment of the show, but D is not happy.

"It feels good, actually, when I do it," D says later. "But I don't want it to turn into a thing where that's what it's all about. I don't want it to turn things away from the music and what we doin up there." He says that once or twice women had thrown dollar bills and embarrassed him. He says that he was a chubby kid in middle school who lost thirty-five pounds in ninth grade, a kid who got chubby again during the Brown Sugar tour. He's worked hard over the past four years to transform his body and has made a video that incited audiences to demand nudity, but the artist in him takes little joy in showing off his body, and he struggles with the meanings of being a musician and an entertainer.

"He does it 'cause women want it," ?uestlove says, "but he really doesn't wanna do it. We do all this preparation to give a balanced show, and he goes out and gets treated like women get treated every day—like a piece of meat." D concurs. "Sometimes, you know, I feel uncomfortable. To be onstage and tryin to do your music and people goin, 'Take it off! Take it off!' 'Cause I'm not no stripper. I'm up there doin somethin I strongly believe in."

It's almost twelve-thirty. The band keeps on carving out the rock-tight groove, and at center stage the struggle between artist and entertainer—for D, it is like good and evil—reaches an apex: It is almost impossible to look at him, nearly naked, and not somehow think about that. The band keeps on carving. And D keeps on dancing, a single silver button the only thing keeping him from nudity, the most nahstay tease since Prince stripped to his Dirty Mind bikini.

Kurt Is My Copilot

{ Dale Earnhardt, Jr., *Rolling Stone*, 2000 }

{ *Da Capo Best Music Writing 2001* }

Dale Earnhardt, Jr., is pretty good at telling a story. He's telling one now about the thing that changed his life.

"Up until I was fourteen or fifteen, I was real short, and I was kind of an Opie," Junior begins. He's twenty-five now. "I wore Wranglers and cowboy hats and fished and raced around on boats and listened to country music. Then one day changed it all." He's telling this while standing behind the bar in the nightclub he built in the basement of his Mooresville, North Carolina, home. The basement club is dimly lit with purple neon and has tall black stools, mirrored walls, a cooler large enough for eleven cases of Bud, and a framed poster of Kurt Cobain.

"I was a junior in high school, and I went to a buddy's house, and this song came on MTV," he says. "We was gittin ready to go do some shit, and he's like, 'Man, dude, this song is kickass! Let's just sit here and listen to it 'fore we leave.' And I sit down, and, man, when it was over with I was just fuckin blown away. It was 'Teen Spirit,' by Nirvana. It fit my emotions. I was tired of listenin to my parents, I was tired of livin at home, I didn't know what I was gonna do, I didn't have any direction. The fact that Kurt Cobain could sit there and scream into that mic like that give you a sense of relief. And the guitar riffs, and the way Dave Grohl played the drums? It was awesome." Dale was, that moment, pulled from the good-ol'-boy path and rebaptized by rock & roll.

He went out and bought Nirvana's *Nevermind*. "I couldn't really get anybody else to dig Nirvana like I dug it," he remembers, "and I never heard nobody else listenin to it in the high school parking lot. When I was listenin to Nirvana, I felt like I was doin somethin wrong. But I didn't care. I'd just sit there and turn it up."

Nirvana led to Pearl Jam, which led to Smash Mouth, Tupac, Third Eye Blind, JT Money, Moby, Mystikal, Matthew Good Band, Busta Rhymes, and Primus. ("That was my first moshing experience. That was awesome.") According to Carlos Santana, "Sound immediately re-arranges the molecular structure of the listener." Junior is a prime case study.

"When I was twelve or thirteen, Dad's races came on the country station," Junior says. Dad is Dale Earnhardt, Sr., widely considered to be one of the three best drivers in the history of stock-car racing. "And I 'member sittin there playin with Matchbox cars on the floor. I had the perfect little bedroom with the perfect toys and the perfect friend up the road who always played every day I wanted to play and played all day till I couldn't play anymore, and I thought everybody fished, everybody listened to country, and everybody lived in a cool house on a lake, and it was sunny all the time.

"Then I got my driver's license and I was able to buy music and listen to it on my own, and you hear the words and you think, 'Man, I never thought about that.' I never really was rebellious against my parents. I never really thought the government was fucked up. I never really paid much attention to the schools suckin. Up until I was sixteen, I thought every cop up and down the road was just happy and glee, and now you hear these songs and you're like, 'Is that the case? Is that what's goin on?' You don't learn from anywhere else."

Junior followed Dad into big-time stock-car racing, and now, in a sport filled with good ol' boys, he's known as the rock & roll driver. That's him in the red number 8 Budweiser Chevrolet Monte Carlo in the NASCAR Winston Cup Series, facing off against heavyweights like Jeff Gordon, Dale Jarrett, Tony Stewart, and Dale Sr. In seven starts since February, Junior is ranked first among rookies and eighteenth overall. On April 2nd, he won his first big race, the DirecTV 500. He has now won more than $600,000 this season, but the numbers don't show that Junior is also a fan favorite. People see in him a kid from the MTV generation invading one of America's most stubborn subcultures. A kid like you, maybe, who on Monday, Tuesday, and Wednesday does little or nothing—fixes up the house, plays paintball and Sega NFL2K with the guys, surfs the Net, hangs with best friend T-Dawg (his mom still calls him Terrell), and watches videos on MTV, BET, and MuchMusic, a Canadian channel. A kid who gets to the racetrack and thinks, "Can't wait to get home so I can fuck off some more."

(Apparently, fuckin off actually helps him on race days. "The thing about drivin race cars is mental," he says. "How long can you concentrate? How long can you focus? And if you don't focus good and you cain't be in deep thought for a long time, then you're not gonna be very good at it. The things I do every day prepare me for that. When you're on the computer playin a game or on the PlayStation whippin your buddy's ass in Knockout Kings, you gotta be on top of it.")

When not fuckin off, Junior is raisin hell, as in gettin in one of his cars and peelin the tires, every gear wide-ass open (read: goin real fast). He's got a Corvette he won that he almost never drives. He's got a Chevy Impala with a global-positioning system, a VCR and TV screens in the front and back. He's got a hulking red four-door Chevy pickup truck with a monster stereo system, and, if you lift the back seats, on top of where the bass amps are hidden, there is this skull-and-crossbones design that Skippy from Freeman's Car Stereo etched in there without Junior even askin, and the darn thing lights up when you push a button on a keypad, but no one knows that, 'cause Junior ain't one to show off. And then there's the breathtaker: a mint-condition midnight-blue 1969 Camaro with an exposed grille on the hood and an oversize finger-thin steering wheel and a gearshift shaped like a bridge and a top-of-the-line Alpine stereo. Junior bought this piece of art for a mere $12,000.

Junior eases into the piece of art and floats down the road to get some pizza from Pie in the Sky. "When I got this," he says, "I took it out and thought, 'This thing has no fire.'" He added a new transmission, a new aluminum-head Corvette engine and a 2,500-rpm stall converter that allows you to shift and keeps the piece of art from changing gears until it reaches 2,500 rpm. Now the thing runs pretty awesome.

"It's real stiff and hard and doesn't have the handlin package like a new car," Junior says, cruising at a leisurely forty miles an hour on the thin, desolate Carolina road. "So you gotta really know what you're doin, have your hands on the wheel at all times and stuff." The piece of art is loud, the engine rumbles and gurgles and practically drowns out the stereo, but the ride is cool, and he turns *Dr. Dre 2001* up way loud and it still sounds crisp. "I like Dr. Dre," Junior says. "He's got a good attitude. I saw him on that VH1 deal, that *Behind the Music*, and that really gives you an idea of who he was. I mean, he enjoys success. I mean, that's kinda the way I've tried to be. There's a lot of money comin in, and there's a lot of talk about how good the future is gonna be and how much is gonna happen, and I'm excited about it, but I don't wanna be molded or changed. I wanna be able to go back to $16,000 a year and be OK. I wanna be able to still realize the value of a dollar bill. And I think that's what Dr. Dre's done. He's still maintained his coolness and not turned into a big jerk."

Junior pulls back on the shifter and says, "Check this out." The engine seems to constrict slowly, tightening like a coil, roaring and snarling as if it is angry at us, and then, after three slow seconds of build, the engine growling louder all the time, it reaches 2,500 rpm and there's a loud *pop!* like a gun, and we slingshot off, leaping in a millisecond from forty mph to eighty—like light speed in the *Millennium Falcon* or something— and suddenly we're flying down the backstretch, zipping past cows and tractors and horses and go-carts as the malevolent funk of Dr. Dre booms out the window: *Nowadays, everybodywannatalk, liketheygot sumpinotosay, but nuttincomesout whentheymovetheirlips, justabunchagibberish andmotherfuckersack liketheyforgotaboutDre*. . . . It sounds so alien in this Waltons-ish country town, like music from another planet. And Junior is cool with both.

Vegas two days later, a Friday, is cloudless blue sky, heavy wind, a lot of sun. Out at the Motor Speedway, it's qualifying day for Sunday's race, the CarsDirect.Com 400. The fifty-five guys vying for the forty-three spots in the race go out one at a time, tearing around the track as fast as they can. Today's top twenty-five finishers are guaranteed spots in the race, their starting positions based on their qualifying speeds.

The hours before qualifying are for practice. Crews work on their cars, send the driver out for a lap or two around the track so he can judge what adjustments are needed, and then tinker some more. Junior has spent years working on cars, so he's really good at feeling what they're doing and at communicating to his crew what will make the car go faster. After laps, the guys—Favio, B, Brendan, Keith, Jeff and Tony Jr.—jump all over the car, soldering, clipping, pouring, cramming like in the minutes before a final exam, wrenching, wiping, welding, tweaking the $250,000 beast, $50,000 engine and $6,000 transmission, turning the engine into "a time bomb," as Steve Crisp, Junior's manager, calls it. "All loose and sloppy and about to all fall to hell."

Whereas Sunday is about being consistently fast for four straight hours, qualifying is one lap of brute strength and balls-out sheer speed—so the qualifying engine isn't made to last. For example, to improve the aerodynamics, they tape over the car's every hole and crack. But this makes the engine very hot—hence, a time bomb. Another example: Just before Junior gets in the car, there'll be a little portable heater linked up to the oil tank to get the oil up around 200 degrees. "The hotter the oil, the thinner it is and the faster you can go," Crisp says. "It's like runnin with Vaseline 'tween your cheeks. If you're lubed up, you can really haul ass."

At eleven a.m., after four practice laps, Junior is the eighth-fastest qualifier. At a quarter past noon, after fifteen laps, he has fallen to sixteenth place, but he isn't worried. The tires haven't been changed all morning, and at high speeds tires wear down very fast, making them crown, which means your contact with the ground lessens and you can't grab the track—try to turn at 140 miles an hour on crowned tires and you'll think you're on ice. At one o'clock, the crew finally throws on stickers (new tires), and Junior bears around the big oval like there's a killer on his tail, finishing practice with the day's fastest lap, faster than the next guy by more than three-tenths of a second, a monster lead in this business.

When at last it's time for the qualifying lap, Favio and the guys wheel the Chevy out to the track. Soon after, Junior joins them. As he walks down pit road, the Allman Brothers' "Midnight Rider" is booming on the track's loudspeakers, and 20,000 fans are in the stands cheering, and Junior, with his impeccable military-school posture, the red and black race suit snug on his long, slender body, the blazing sun gleaming off the silver on his racing shoes, the black wraparound shades and the stubble and the chiseled chin and the movie-star cheekbones, shit, Junior looks like got-damn Steve McQueen.

He slides into the doorless beast, straps on his crimson skull-and-cross-bones helmet, pulls on his black gloves and goggles, then screws on the steering wheel, which sits about a foot and a half from his face, so close that he can't slide in or out of the beast without unscrewing it, so close that he can drive using his forearm muscles instead of his back and shoulder muscles. There is only one seat (roll bars are where the passenger seat would be), and that seat is form-fitted to Junior's body like shrink-to-fit jeans. There are gauges for water, oil, and fuel, and a tachometer to register rpms, but no speedometer, because it doesn't matter how fast you're going, just that you're going faster than everyone else. There is a thin rearview mirror about two feet wide, and a clear tube Junior can suck on to get water, and on Sunday there will also be a black tube stuck down into his suit to blow cool air, because the car's interior gets up around 100 degrees, and sometimes, during the summer, 130. One more thing: All the teams paste decals of headlights and brake lights onto their cars to heighten the illusion that they're driving the same sort of car that Bob has out in the driveway.

Ironically, stock-car racing is the most popular form of racing in America because it seems to be the most pedestrian. Back in the 60s, guys bought regular Chevelles or Dodge Chargers, yanked out the passenger seats, threw in some roll bars and went racing. Nowadays the cars are constructed by the race teams themselves—I actually saw someone bending and molding a big piece of sheet metal into a door—and they're nothing like any car you can buy from Chevy. But Junior's "Chevy" shows up on TV, shaped like the car Bob owns, with headlights and brake lights—which doesn't even make sense, because why would a race car need headlights? They drive during the day!—and Bob says to himself, "Hey, that car's just like mine," or, even better, "Hey, that's like the Chevy down at the dealership. Think I'll go get me one." You think Bob doesn't think like that? One of the oldest sayings in racing is: Win on Sunday, sell on Monday.

Early this morning, all the drivers pulled numbers to determine the order of qualifying. Junior drew a two. When his turn comes, he flicks the lever to start the engine, and the beast cackles loudly, then begins to ripple and roar as if it were a lion growling through clenched teeth, or a gigantic, demented bowl of Rice Krispies snap-crackle-popping in a fury. A NASCAR official drops his arm, and Junior steps on the gas and flies off like a low-slung comet, sounding like the humming of a six-foot-long hornet an inch from your ear, and when the lap is over and the speed is flashed on the board—172.216 mph, a new track record—the crowd thunders. He has bested the old record—correction, demolished it—by more than two miles an hour.

He parks, and his team runs over to celebrate. "When ya drove into the corner," says a breathless Favio, "ya went all the way wide open! We didn't think you was gonna lift! The whole pit road just sit and looked at ya, amazed!" (Translation: "It seemed as though you took that first corner without braking—an impossibility! We thought you'd never get off the gas! You the man, baby!")

Junior jumps out of the car, ecstatic. "It doesn't matter if we git the pole [position]," he says, beaming like a kid getting good presents at Christmas. "That was awesome!"

But when ESPN and local TV rush over to get a comment, he mutes his excitement: "The car handled real good. I don't know if it'll stand up as far as the pole goes, but it'll be up there somewhere toward the front. My expectations at the first of the week were to come in here and make the top twenty-five, and that hasn't changed."

After the cameras disappear, Junior says, "I don't wanna sit here and go, 'Whoo-hoo!' and then get beat, and have everyone go, 'What an asshole.'"

And sure enough, his track record lasts about six minutes. Ricky Rudd tops him by three-tenths of a second.

Junior looks down the track and sees his father walking onto pit road for his qualifying run. "There's Dad," he says. "Let's go talk to him. A hundred bucks says my daddy give me shit for gittin beat. He don't say, 'Nice goin.' He'll say, 'Why'd you get beat?'"

Junior jogs down the track and catches his old man. Before Junior can say a word, Dad ribs him in a barbed but loving tone, "What happened? Why ain't ya first? What'd ya do wrong?"

"I don't know," Junior says with a laugh. Photographers snap wildly behind them.

"What should I do?" Dad says as another car flies by. "What were ya doin'?"

Junior says, "Run deep, brake hard, turn left." It was about the most smartass thing he could say without being rude.

"Run deep, brake hard?" Dad laughs. Terry Labonte, another top driver, is walking by. Dad grabs Labonte's arm and says, "Listen to him," then turns back to Junior. "How ya get 'round there, now?"

"Run deep, brake hard, turn left."

The veterans laugh. "He don't even know how he did it!" Dad says. There is a pause. Then Dad pats Junior on the shoulder, silently saying, "Good job."

A little later, Junior is back in his trailer, watching other cars qualify on ESPN2. No one beats Ricky Rudd, and only one other driver, Scott Pruett, beats Junior. At the press conference for the top three qualifiers, a reporter asks about Junior's relationship with his father.

"Well," Junior says, "durin practice and qualifyin it was 'Dad, car owner.'" Junior actually races for Dale Earnhardt Inc., in a car owned by Dad, although the car Dad races doesn't actually belong to him, because he's still loyal to Richard Childress, the man who put him in a race car long before he could buy one himself. "He's all, 'How's it goin? We need to get faster. We need to do this, we need to do that,'" Junior says. "Then when the race starts, it's diff'rent. Last week at Rockingham, we were goin into turn three. I was on the inside of Jeff Gordon and got loose [lost control] goin into the corner, and I slammed into him. About a straightaway and a half later, Dad went by shakin his finger out the window at me. I guess that was where the father was goin, 'You'd better watch it. You'd better straighten up.'"

After the press conference, Junior was asked, if you were leading on the last lap and Dad was right behind you, would Dad use one of his legendary tricks to spin you out and take the checkered flag for himself? Junior didn't pause to think: "He would do what it took to win."

In the 1940s, in North Carolina, South Carolina, Georgia, Tennessee, and Virginia, there were some good ol' boys fresh from the war with a little money, a little training in how to service military planes and jeeps, and a talent for brewing moonshine. They made their outlaw liquor in hidden stills in the woods and got it to the dance halls, speakeasies, and bootleggers in cars big enough to carry one hundred gallons of the stuff— maybe seven hundred pounds—and still fast enough to outrun the cops: Ford or Pontiac sedans with killer engines and real suspensions—liquor cars. Racing's first superstar, Junior Johnson, was a moonshiner. He always said he was never caught with moonshine in his car. He could always outrun the boys, always until they got the in-car radio.

Sometimes some good ol' boys would get together and brag about who had the fastest liquor car, and if the braggin was too loud, they'd pick a Sunday, head to some deserted field, plow out an oval, and race. Thus was born American stock-car racing, now the country's most popular spectator sport—bigger than football or baseball or basketball, bigger even than professional wrestling. On any of thirty-six weekends a year, as many as 150,000 people or more show up to watch NASCAR at the tracks, and many millions more watch on TV. "In the South," says Crisp, a natural comedian, "ya see stock cars everywhere—from the time you're a little kid to the time you're put in the grave, you're gonna be around a stock-car track. Hell, ya can't sling a dead cat 'thout hittin a shop."

In the late 40s, the National Association for Stock Car Auto Racing was founded. It presided over a sport where the track and the stands and everything in between were filled with good ol' boys. Crisp describes the average fan: "He hunts, his dad taught him to hunt, and his dad taught him to hunt. He drinks Jack Daniel's and Maker's Mark. He listens to Hank Williams. He loves his huntin dog and his pickup truck, and he married his high school sweetheart, and he lives in the town he grew up in, or a stone's throw away. He puts God first and then his family, then his truck."

Dale Earnhardt, Jr., has a pickup truck, loves dogs, and maintains a certain down-homeness about him, but Junior ain't no good ol' boy. For example, he hates to hunt. He's got a story about that too: "My dad's always been a deer hunter. He loves that shit. He took me a coupla times. I went out there and sat on a tree stand all freakin day. And it's great to sit there and think about shit and reflect back on what's been happenin with ya, but, really, it's just a waste of a day. Just pissin it away.

"After a while, a deer walked out there, and I shot the hell out of it. You shoot him right in the chest, and it's s'posed to go right into his heart. When I saw it, I thought, 'Dad's gonna like this.' And then I'm like, 'Man, I don't like it.' The only excitement I got out of it was seein him bein excited, but didn't enjoy sittin there all day, and I didn't enjoy havin to drag it over to the truck and pickin it up and throwin it in there and then sit there watchin him skin it and gut it—and that pissed away all night, so there went a day and a night! So the next time I went in a deer stand, I'm like, 'I ain't shootin shit, 'cause I got shit to do tonight.' So then I'm like, 'What am I doin up here?' I got down and never went back."

Stock-car racing is still dominated by good ol' boys, though Junior is part of a class of new blood, some of whom aren't from the South—Matt Kenseth from Wisconsin, Tony Stewart from Indiana—and some Southerners who aren't good ol' boys, a titanic shift in the cultural direction of NASCAR. Imagine the NBA beginning to be dominated by white guys.

"There's a lot of drivers within this age group that are diff'rent," Junior says. "It's just the way things are goin, and NASCAR's not immune to it. Even the image is something more modern. Just look at the TV coverage. Ten years ago, when they'd go to break, it'd be some fiddle banjo-pickin music. And now it's this jammin rock music. Somebody somewhere said, 'Hey, let's change it.' "

But things change slowly. It's not easy to refuse all the cultural stimuli around you in favor of another drummer's beat. Sure, Junior hates to hunt, but there, mounted on the wall of his living room, are the head and neck of a deer.

On Friday night, the Speedway is quiet and empty, and around ten Junior heads out for a walk around the track and another story. "I'd just started drivin my late-model car," he says. The late-model series is the lowest rung of organized stock-car racing. "We had this shitbox of a car, and we was racin at this track with all the big dawgs." The Speedway's rock-concert bright lights are on. The only sound, besides our feet on the concrete, is the muffled snarl of dirt-track racing half a mile away.

"My crew chief was an old-timer everyone knew, named Gary Hargett, and he ordered a brand-new car for me from Rick Townsend, the most popular car builder. And we were so excited. So we git to the track, and Gary's like, 'Man, we ordered that car, when you think you're gonna git on it?' Rick's like, 'Well, we're behind. It's gonna be a couple months 'fore we even start on it. You guys should get it midway through the season.' And then he says, 'By the way, where's your driver at?' And I was standing a little ways away, and Gary's like, 'He's over there.' And Rick says, 'Boy don't look like much. Looks like he barely know how to get out of the rain.'

"So we started the race 'bout midpack and beat our way up through there, and two laps to go I came up on Rick's house car runnin second. And I drilled him straight in the ass, man! Right in the fuckin ass, and turned him sideways and went past him and finished second in the race. They don't do that here, but that's how we do back home. After the race, Rick come up to Gary and said, 'That was pretty awesome. We'll start on your shit Monday.' And Rick's been a good friend ever since. But I always remembered what Rick said, and everywhere I go, when I walk into a room with people I don't know, I assume they look at me and say, 'He don't look like much.' That's kept me real humble and small-time."

Junior was born in Concord, North Carolina, an hour's drive from his house in Mooresville. His parents separated when he was two or three, and he and his older sister, Kelly, were raised by their mother in a small mill house until Junior, at six, awoke to a fire in the kitchen. Everyone ran out, the house burned down, and nothing was ever the same. Mom handed over custody of her kids to Sr. and moved to Norfolk, Virginia. "She didn't have the means to git us another house or take care of us," Junior says, "She said, 'Man, your dad's doin good and he can put ya in school, so this is the best thing for ya.' I was just like, 'Are my toys here?' " She still lives in Norfolk, works as a loader for UPS. Ju-

nior has seen her once or twice a year since he was six, but she calls often. "She puts forth a lot of effort in our relationship," he says and talks
happily of her plan to retire and move back to the Charlotte area within
the next year. "She's awesome."

When Junior arrived at his dad's, racing was a very small sport.
"The tracks they raced at were shitholes," Junior says. "If you got
50,000 fans there you were lucky." Dad was away a lot of the time, so
Junior was raised by his stepmom, Teresa. "When he and Rick were
growin up," Dale Sr. says, "I was workin and racin and goin all the time."

But Dad, it seems, was a distant provider. "We'd go upstairs and sit
down on the couch," Junior says, "and he'd be sittin there watchin TV in
the recliner, and you ask him a question and he wouldn't hear you. You
rarely even get a response. He was so in his racin thing, you could
hardly sometimes have a conversation with him, 'cause his mind was on
what he was thinkin about." It's been suggested by people who know
them that Junior became a driver to get his father's attention. Both deny
it. But there seems to be a kernel of truth to it.

Dad grew up at the track, watching his father, Ralph, a champion
stock-car driver in the 50s. Dale drove his black number 3 Chevy to a
record-tying seven Winston Cup season championships. Called the Man
in Black and the Intimidator, he's the consummate winner with a ques-
tionable reputation, like the Bill Laimbeer Detroit "Bad Boy" Pistons or
the Lyle Alzado Oakland Raiders. But winning wins company, so he's
also one of the most revered drivers in the history of the sport.

He took his winnings to Mooresville and built a giant palace of a
racing shrine, perhaps the greatest ever constructed by NASCAR money,
lovingly called the Garage Mahal. There are security guards in cowboy
boots and red button-down shirts that say DALE EARNHARDT INC., surrounded by corporate offices for DEI's 160 employees, all of Dad's trophies, old winning cars preserved for public view and big glass display
cases for the tuxedos he wore to the Winston Cup banquets during his
championship seasons and the gowns worn by his wife and the cute
pink polka-dot toddler's dress sported by their daughter Taylor and pictures of Ralph Earnhardt and all the commercials Dad and Junior have
made and a gift shop with all sorts of souvenirs—spoons, toy bears,

pins, watches, shirts, robes, beer steins, shot glasses, tiny model cars (all of which earned Junior around $2 million last year), and, this just in, a Dale Earnhardt Monopoly set. The game pieces include a car, a checkered flag, and a helmet. Earnhardt's face is on the money. He's the first individual to have a Monopoly set made around him. The shop's best-selling item, the clerks say, is a decal you can affix to your car to give the impression you bought it at the old man's dealership.

As all of this was being built, Junior was at Mitchell Community College in Statesville, North Carolina, getting a degree in automotives, and then at his father's dealership working as a grease monkey for $180 a week. "I got to where I could do an oil change in eight minutes," he says. "I was really proud of that."

Then one Saturday night in Myrtle Beach, South Carolina, he raced his late-model car: "It was $1,000 to win and 100 to 150 fans, but it didn't matter. It was kickass, man! It was like buildin a freakin remote-control car and goin to where everybody else went to play with it. I learned everything—how to save your tires, pace yourself, not wreck your car, communicate with your team, motivate 'em to work—you got volunteer guys, and you gotta be able to get 'em to work or they're gonna go to the track and drink up the sodas. And that's just people skills."

In time, he moved up to the Busch Series—which is like the supercharged minors to the Winston Cup's majors—was season champ in '98 and '99, and graduated to the Winston Cup. "But growin up as a kid, I didn't try to drive race cars, so I know inside that it's not a live-or-die thing. I'm a little more three-dimensional than, 'Oh, drivin's kick-ass.' Drivin is fun, but that's not the ultimate high. Right now, I'd rather be home. I'd much more enjoy kickin it on my couch."

At ten o'clock Sunday morning, Junior is in his trailer with Crisp and his trailer driver, Shane, eating Corn Pops, listening to Pink Floyd's *The Wall*, arguing about racing movies. The race is just over an hour away, and there is about as much tension in the air as there is in your house before you drive to the 7-Eleven for milk.

"*The Last American Hero* is real red-neck-y," Crisp says of the film many consider the best ever made on racing.

"But it's the only racin movie that's about racin," Junior says. "I didn't like *Le Mans*," he said of the Steve McQueen classic. "They were just raisin hell and racin cars. There's no dialogue. It's just racin and sittin. It didn't have a plot."

"*Heart Like a Wheel* is uncool," Shane says of the Bonnie Bedelia film, "'cause they had it like she's gittin her ass beat by her boyfriend."

"What about *Days of Thunder?*" someone asks about the Tom Cruise movie. All at once everyone says, "Sucked!"

"*Grand Prix* kicks ass," Crisp says.

"Here's *Le Mans*," Junior says. "A bunch of people sittin aroun' for five minutes. Then, all of a sudden, snap, they're racin, then, snap, they're all sittin around. No dialogue whatsoever. It's like someone actually followed the guy around, filmin him."

"Yeah," Shane says. "It was realistic."

"Yeah, it was real," Junior says, "but it didn't have a plot and shit like *Grand Prix*. Who was the guy in *Grand Prix*?"

"James Garner," everyone says.

"I like that guy," Junior says.

"The girl liked him in *Grand Prix*," Shane says.

"'Member? And her husband got in a wreck and she turned out to be a bee-atch!" Crisp says as though he were Snoop Dogg. The room crumbles in hysterics. "She was a big *beeee-atch!* A biznitch!"

There is no prerace ritual, no discussion of strategy, no prayer, no psyching. It seems strange. Junior is moments away from the event that defined his week, and, more, is about to spend four hours risking his life, and he seems largely unconcerned. You don't do anything special before you go out to race?

Junior looks puzzled, as if the idea of doing something special had never occurred to him.

"I think ya do a lot of soul-searching," Shane says. "I don't think you notice it, but you usually walk around in a daze."

"One thing I do," Junior says, "is, when I walk out the trailer door, I don't wait up for people."

"His mind is already there," Shane says.

"I go at my pace. Real fast."

"Almost to the point where if ya didn't know him, you'd think he was rude," Crisp says.

"It would wear me out to psych myself up all mornin," Junior says. "I pray to God before the race. I don't pray to win. I say, 'When it's over, can I go the next five days till the next race with a content, satisfied attitude so I can live comfortably and not be all down on myself on a bad finish all week?' 'Cause if I finish bad, I'm depressed as hell for the next week."

That's it? C'mon! You could die today!

With childlike innocence, Junior says, "Ya think?"

Everyone laughs.

"Nah, man. It's safe as hell in there. All that paddin in there, how I'm buckled in there, all the bars and things? Dude, man, that car is bulletproof."

But no one is shooting at you. Seriously, man, this is worse than boxing. You must know that.

"Yeah, sometimes guys get cocked just right. That's the way it is. There's things in there your head can hit, and if it hits it just right you could be permanently injured. But guys normally walk away."

Suddenly he turns to Crisp. "You know what I wanna do? When they do driver introductions? I wanna say somethin into the mic like, 'I gotta say hi to my friend Chester McGroovy. Get well soon!'"

Then Junior says, "Last week we were drivin up to the racetrack, and there were all these people campin outside, thousands of people, and I'm like, 'That's what the fuck I'd like to be doin.' That's fun! Just raisin hell at the racetrack with your buddies, drinkin beer, campin out, watchin the race. No pressure, man. I mean, you don't get no money, but, shit, you're havin a good time. It'd be fun. And I'll never get to do that."

He pauses. "When I turn seventy, that's what I'm gonna do. Go campin and park outside the track and sit there and drink beer and just raise hell and aggravate all the fuckin rednecks with all this rock & roll music."

6. Get Up, Get Out, and Get Involved

Jay-Z Has Got Guts

{ *Rolling Stone*, 2001 }

It's minutes to midnight in Manhattan and we're up by Central Park, at the Trump International, in a fifth-floor suite done in shades of beige. Jay-Z and eight friends are sitting around a table in the living room playing Guts, their favorite card game. Jay's sixth album, *The Blueprint*, booms from the stereo. His companions are streetwise young men and execs from Def Jam, his record label. Everyone is cracking jokes, laughing, trying not to show fear, as crisp hundreds fly around the room in the high-stakes poker game that's all about balls.

Jay is in a white T-shirt, baggy Rocawear blue jeans, and new blue shelltoes, the laces running through every other hole. The thirty-one-year-old is tall and lanky, with large, round lips; long, curled lashes; and a cool that's unshakable. A close friend said he's "comfortable in his own skin." Jay seems to take everything in stride.

Guts is deceptively simple. Each player is dealt three cards, face-down. You examine your hand—aces are high, pairs preferred—then decide whether to stay in the game. Everyone who stays in turns over his cards. The best hand wins the pot. Each of the losers replenishes it. At midnight the pot is $2,060; by two a.m. it will be $4,000.

Guts is all about poker faces, reading people, and having the co-jones to not care about losing thousands of dollars in a few seconds. All night long, the wall of hundreds in front of Jay remains three to four inches tall, about $30,000—and he seems unafraid of losing. You might be, too, if you were worth "north of $50 million," as Lyor Cohen, the president of Island Def Jam Music Group and one of tonight's players, estimates. But friends say Jay has always been fearless; that fearlessness

234 Never Drank the Kool-Aid

itself is the reason he's worth north of $50 million. Other men's piles rise and fall wildly. In two hours I went from winning $2,000 to owing $4,000 to profiting $3,000—but Jay's stacks are consistent because he's less focused on cards than on character, keeping you from predicting him and reading you perfectly.

"That's me in life," Jay says later. "I really have a feel for people. I can read people. I know people." In the next hand, Jay's got good cards, but Cohen calls "Guts." "What?!" Jay says. "I know Lyor doesn't like risk. He doesn't cross the street if it doesn't say Walk." Jay drops out. He takes the joint that's going around: "This gone really give me a cool face." He takes a pull. Lyor wins the hand. By dropping out, Jay saves $2,800.

All night long, *The Blueprint* plays on repeat. Jay's 1996 debut, *Reasonable Doubt*, was a classic, art for art's sake: the street stories of a man unaffected by the business of hiphop, out to prove he was the number-one MC. *In My Lifetime,Volume II*, his second classic, from 1998, was filled with bright, pop-y hits and hard-core street anthems, and showed his knack for delivering the sounds people wanted to hear. Now, with *The Blueprint*, his third classic, he's just playing for the love of the game, with nothing to prove. The album mixes his trademark conversation-chill flows with samples of 70s bluesy soul, disco, and hard rock—the sounds of his youth, the blueprint of his musical education. "These aren't the exact records I grew up on," he says, "but it has that feel. And it made me vibe; it brought back memories. I felt comfortable recording."

For *The Blueprint*, he wrote and recorded nine songs in an inspired two-day stretch. "The songs just started happenin, comin out of nowhere," he says. "I was in a zone." Jay's recording process itself is a bit miraculous. He picks a track, turns it up loud in the studio, then sits off to the side mumbling to himself. In minutes he's got rhymes and hooks with astounding economy and filled with his trademark double entendres. Instantly memorized. No pen, no paper. Sometimes, he says, there are four or five songs in his head at one time. Rapper Beanie Sigel has learned to do this from being around Jay, and says it's made him a better MC. "It make your flow so wicked," Sigel says. "Without the pen and paper, your flow be so ridiculous." Adds Jay, "What I have is a gift from

God. It can't be explained." This is what he means when he calls himself the God MC and Jay-Hovah.

After six albums filled with the chilly world-weariness of an O.G., rhymes complex enough to lend Shakespearean gravitas to the scene, and his monumental self-assuredness, Jay-Z is one of the best MCs of all time and certainly the best alive and working. As Ahmir Thompson, drummer for the Roots, says, "Rakim is the Father, Biggie's the Son, and Jay-Z's the Holy Ghost."

Jay-Z himself brushes off the issue of who's the best MC. "I can't get into that argument," he says, "because the people at the top of the game are no longer here with us. Big and Pac didn't really get a chance to grow as artists. We never got to see where it woulda went. But I always felt that's what I was comin to do, to be the best. I wasn't comin in the game to be nothin less."

At the Trump, as the night goes on, Jay munches a Caesar salad, smokes a cigar, and lets slip a few details from his recent life. "He has nearly the same lifestyle as a billionaire," says Cohen, "except he doesn't have a wing of a museum named after him." Jay rides in chauffeured cars and flies in private planes and helicopters. One recent weekend, he zipped from the recording studio to the boxing gym, then from the U.S. Open final between Serena and Venus Williams to the Felix Trinidad fight to a meeting about his work on the director's cut of the film *Scarface*. He's executive producing the soundtrack, supervising the music, and doing the score for the 2002 release.

Another weekend, he flew to Chicago to spend time with Michael Jordan. "We just really sat down and kicked it like gentlemen," he says. "I was like, 'Dawg, I'ma ask you everythin. I'm comin right at you.' He was like, 'Man, you could ask me anything.'" When he returned to Manhattan, he went to the studio to rhyme on Michael Jackson's "You Rock My World" remix. "I was talkin to him on the phone, and he was talkin about 'Hard Knock Life,' and he was like, 'You was just so in pocket on that record, landin right on the beat. Incredible.' I'm like, 'Thanks.' But I'm lookin at the phone like, 'What? Stop playin, man!'" Jay says. "Mike was a superhero when I was a kid. Him wanting to work with me, period, was bananas!"

Then there was a summer weekend at his place in East Hampton, Long Island. Every forty-five minutes, his chef, Cynthia, emerged from the kitchen with something new—French waffles with blueberries, jumbo fried shrimp, barbecue wings, banana daiquiris, homemade thick-crust pizza, candy salad, figs, mojitos, lobster with special sauce. "You gotta hide from her," Jay says. "She'll feed you nonstop." Manicurists and masseuses dropped by. Supermodels Carmen Kass, Leilani, and Noemi are regular guests. So was Aaliyah. Two weeks before her death in a plane crash in the Bahamas, she and her boyfriend, Roc-A-Fella Records president Damon Dash, visited Jay in the Hamptons. "He is the sweetest person," she said. "I have so much fun when I'm with him." Her voice was soft and delicate, her eyes hidden under a large hat. "I admire him because he's an amazing talent, and on top of that he's a beautiful person. He's really good people."

The day she died, Dash paged Jay 911. "We don't call each other 911, so I knew it was serious," Jay says. "I didn't really wanna call back for a second. I'm goin over all kinda things in my mind, tryin to pinpoint what could be wrong. Finally, I said, Fuck it, and I called him and he told me, and I just went over to be with him, cuz I knew he was gonna go through it."

In October, Jay-Z, surprisingly, pleaded guilty to misdemeanor assault in the third degree for the 1999 stabbing of record executive Lance "Un" Rivera. Jay had long planned to plead not guilty. His attorney, Murray Richman, said the district attorney's office was pursuing the case only because it had lost the Puffy trial. "It's a bullshit charge," Richman said before the trial. "I examined Un in a deposition where he said he wasn't sure Jay was even close by. He said, 'Jay was not that close, but I recognized Jay, so I said it was Jay. I was down on the floor. I didn't even see who came in close to me.' How bullshit is that?" The DA's office declined comment.

Jay was nervous about going to trial. "Where I grew up, I seen a lot of people get wronged," he said a few weeks before the trial. "No matter how much you believe in the truth, that's always in the back of your mind." Richman, always combative, was looking forward to fighting the charge. "They made us an offer," he said. "No jail and five years' probation. But he's not guilty!"

At the last minute, much to Richman's chagrin, Jay changed his plea and received three years' probation. Afterward, Richman was seething. "Everybody's a tough guy," is all he would say.

What does that mean? "You figure it out."

After September 11th, Jay donated money to the victims' families and the fire department but was torn over whether he should donate to the police department, which he said has continually followed him through the city, looking for a reason to arrest him. "I'm conflicted through all this," he said. "I feel sorry for everybody. I got empathy, compassion, I'm really sick. Same time, this is still a land that's not really for my people, and I can't just forget that. I wanna say that during this so no one else forgets." He ended up donating to the police department as well.

Back at the Trump, it's a little past three and I've got a pair of nines. That's a good hand. The pot is $2,500. Four men drop out, then Jay calls "Guts." It's just me and him. I stare Jay in the eye. I know I'm gonna win. He gives me an ice-grill—a steely poker face with a cold glint in his eye—not intimidating but unflinching. A lot of money is on the table.

"If I beat you, I'm gonna put it in the article," I say.

"But will you put it in if you lose?"

He looks confident, but I know that when he's unnerved, he just doesn't let you know. "Guts," I say.

I flip my cards. He looks at them nonchalantly, says, "Hmm," and scoops up the pile of cash. I reach for his cards: two jacks, known in this room as two Jiggas. Across the table, he's carefully stacking his money, not gloating at all, as though he knew he'd win all along.

As Jay shuffles the cards, "Momma Loves Me" comes on. It's a hiphop ballad in which he shares impressions of his life from childhood to the present, starting at the beginning: "Momma love me/Pop left me."

Mom and Pop are Gloria and Adnes Carter—Lou-Lou and AJ. "My pops did anything from cabdriver to truck driver to working at the phone company. My mom works in investments for the city." Jay grew up in Brooklyn's Marcy Projects with his older brother, Eric, and his older sisters, Annie and Mickey. "One day when I was four years old," he says, "I rode this ten-speed. It was really high, but I put my foot through the top bar, so I'm ridin the bike kinda weird, like sideways, and the whole block is like, 'Oh, God!' They couldn't believe this little boy ridin that big bike like that. That was my first feelin of bein famous right there. And I liked it. Felt good."

His parents had a giant record collection, with their names taped onto every single album. "These people shared everything," he says, "but not those records. It was like, 'This is my son and your son. This is my house and your house. But this is my record.' That's just to show you how much they loved their music."

Every day there was music, especially Saturday, when his mom would open the windows and Pine-Sol the house down while blasting her favorite funk and soul. Eventually it started to pour out from him. "After a while, I just started tryin to write rhymes. I used to be at the table every day for hours. I had this green notebook with no lines in it, and I used to write all crooked. I wrote every damn day. Then I started running around in the streets, and that's how not writing came about. I was comin up with these ideas, and I'd write 'em on a paper bag, and I had all these paper bags in my pocket, and I hate a lot of things in my pocket, so I started memorizing and holding it."

In the sixth grade, a test showed he was reading at a twelfth-grade level. "I was crazy happy about that," he says. "When the test scores came back, that was the first moment I realized I was smart. I always liked to read. I still do." He recently read the spiritual tomes *The Celestine Prophecies*, *The Prophet*, and *Conversations with God*.

When Jay was about eleven, his dad left the house, and it devastated him. "I look just like the guy," he says. "You wanna walk like him, talk like him. That's your superman right there. And then there's no more contact with him. The scorn, the resentment, all the feelings from that—as you see, I'm a grown-ass man and it's still there with me." AJ took his records with him, but Jay's musical education continued. "I think my mom had better records," he says.

His mom is one of Jay's best friends, someone he can talk to about anything, at any time: "If I get an idea, a flashback, I'll call her. Three in the mornin: 'You remember when I was four years old, and I learned how to ride a bike, and . . .' She'll get right into the conversation."

The relationship goes both ways. "I'm like my mom's husband," he says. "I'm a very good friend to her." He says he pulls the ends together for his family, like a father would. "I'm really the dude in the family," he says. "And I wanna be that. I take care of everybody, and they love me and respect me for that. But they don't kiss my ass or treat me any different because of it. That's the beauty of it."

Suddenly, from out of the Trump stereo comes "Takeover," a grinding hiphop-rock anthem, on which he disses both Nas and Mobb Deep rapper Prodigy: "Went from Nasty Nas to Esco's trash/Had a spark when ya started but now you're just garbage."

"I ain't really hit Nas that hard," Jay says, with comic understatement. "I gave him a break. He lucky." Damon Dash says it's rare for anyone in their crew to tease Jay because his comebacks are too harsh. They call him "Jay-Jugular." After "Takeover," we all understand.

Jay says Nas has been throwing darts at him on mix tapes for years. They spoke on the phone once, and Jay thought things were cool between them. Then he heard Nas dissing him on the radio in L.A. Prodigy, Jay says, called him a bitch in *The Source*. They ran into each other at Puffy's restaurant, Justin's, and squashed it, but Prodigy kept going at Jay on mix tapes.

"Everybody wants to be respected," he says. "Even if we're not friends, we gotta respect each other. And I felt I was bein disrespected by them, so I had to show them. And I really waited it out because I didn't want people to think I was a bully. Because I have the ear of a lot more people than them. You have to be very careful with that power. It wasn't a bully move. It was, 'Keep goin. Keep goin. Keep goin. OK, now you gotta respect me.' I'm sure they respect me right now." Nas and Prodigy declined comment.

"Takeover" is one of the illest battle records in hiphop history, but now you can't hear a battle record without fearing the worst. This is hiphop. Someone could get killed. "I definitely think pride's on the line," Jay says, "but I'm not dealin with emotion. I'm not upset. My feelings was not hurt. With me, it's all music. If you ever hear anything happen with me, it was purely 170 percent self-defense, because to me it's records. Once it's on records, it's a joke to me. You can't really be mad, you can't really wanna do something to me, or you wouldn't put it on a record for the whole world to hear."

At five minutes to five, the Guts game is finally winding down. But some people can never get enough. Kevin Liles, the president of Def Jam, a Buddha-shaped man brimming with ego in an orange Phat Farm shirt, challenges Jay to a single hand for $10,000. Someone suggests they do it for a million. Jay says no. "Ten thousand dollars ain't gon make a nigga sick," he says. "A million'll make a nigga sick."

The room assembles around the table. Jay sits back in his chair. He's calm. Liles flips over Jay's first card. A queen. Liles gets a two. Jay yells a little bit. His next card is a king. He bangs the table. It's getting hot. Liles gets a three. Jay's ahead, but it's still anyone's game. The next card, to Jay, is . . . a queen. He wins. The table flips over, the room goes nuts, a riot ensues. Jay stands on his chair yelling like he's nailed a three-pointer to win the game, smacking five hard with everyone in the room. "I bodied him!" Jay yells. It's the most emotion he's shown all night.

Jay struts out the room at a quarter past five with his money in his hand, fingers stretching to hold onto his five-inch stack. He says he made $30,000 tonight. Whether hustling or rhyming or playing Guts for big cheddar, where others lose their head, Jay-Z keeps his. "We introduced the game to Will Smith and them in Aspen," he says, stepping from the elevator, struggling to stuff the money in his pockets. "Now they do Guts tournaments. They can't stop. This game'll claim your life."

Do You Like My Jesus Piece?

{ Kanye West, *Rolling Stone*, 2004 }

Kanye West is in his bedroom, getting dressed. This often takes a while, sometimes up to sixty minutes (as a child he dreamed of becoming a fashion designer), which gives a reporter time to look around his apartment while he gets ready. He's got a luxury loft in Hoboken, New Jersey, on the twelfth and top floor of a newish building, with a spectacular view of the Hudson River and Manhattan. It's sparsely decorated because he's been traveling a lot thanks to the success of his freshman album, *The College Dropout*, which debuted at number two and has already been bought by more than a million people. The album confirms his place as one of the great modern hiphop producers as well as a witty, funny, neo-backpack rapper. "Kanye works for the same reason this [Andre 3000's *The Love Below*] works," says Jay-Z. "There's too much music out there with no feeling and everybody soundin the same. People'll give it up for creativity." The apartment has affordable Ikea solutions, like Japanese paper lanterns, beside the spoils of new money, like a pricey buffalo-leather couch with kangaroo-fur pillows because West's bank account is swelling each day, thanks also to extracurricular projects like producing Alicia Keys's chart-topper "You Don't Know My Name." According to industry insiders, he gets seventy-five to one hundred thousand dollars per track. And on the wall in the main living room there's a larger-than-life poster of West himself, evidence of a certain arrogance he's long had. "When he was in kindergarten," his mother says, "the teacher said to me, Kanye certainly doesn't have any problem with

242 Never Drank the Kool-Aid

self-esteem, does he?" But the poster is coming down soon because he's very consciously trying to downshift into greater humility. "I put me on the wall because I was the only person that had me on the wall at that time," West says later. "And now that a lot of people have me on their wall I don't really need to do that anymore."

West has made money because of the soulfulness of his music, which is often built on speeding up old soul samples, as well as the integrity of his rhymes. So many hiphop heroes are invincible alpha men like Jay-Z and 50 Cent, but West, twenty-six, comes from the De La Soul family tree as a rapper unafraid to be intellectual, playful, and vulnerable. "In hiphop we been waiting for some music that's pure and honest and a person that people can relate to and connect with," says Common, a longtime friend. "He shows his human side."

West's lyrics are brimming with thoughts about the Black experience, the world of college, and life itself. On "School Spirit" he rhymes, "Back to school and I hate it there, I hate it there/ Everything I want I gotta wait a year, I wait a year/ This nigga graduated at the top of our class/ I went to Cheesecake, he was a motherfuckin waiter there." He's also quite free with his shortcomings. On "All Falls Down" he says, "I got a couple past due bills/ I won't get specific/ I got a problem with spending before I get it/ We all self-conscious, I'm just the first to admit it."

Though West is a better rhyme writer than a rhyme sayer, Common is a fan. "His delivery is clear and catchy and he got content," Common says. "So, to me, he's an A-level MC. I can't tell you the last time I listened to someone's album and knew the words and put they shit on and was singing to it." "My niche is that I'm the funny version of Dead Prez," West says. "I'm the rap version of Dave Chappelle. I'm not sayin I'm nearly as talented as Chappelle when it comes to political and social commentary, but like him I'm laughing to keep from crying."

Recently, on a hiphop Web site, Chuck D questioned why West was getting props for speeding up old soul samples. West doesn't contend that it's a complex thing he's doing. "It's so simple," he says. "It's just speeding the records up so there'll be a tempo we can rap to. It's a natural process. If I speed Chaka Khan up to 83 rpm [which he does on "Through the Wire"], I'll be able to rap on it, but it'll sound chipmunky. I do my best to fight against the chipmunky shit." He finally emerges from the bedroom in a Ralph Lauren sweater with a huge teddy bear on it; Paper, Denim, and Cloth jeans; and New Balance sneakers. Ralph Lauren is his second favorite brand, and you know who his favorite is because of his brown Louis Vuitton buffalo-leather jacket, the Vuitton card holder in his pocket, and the classic Vuitton monogram duffel by his side at all times. But the center of today's outfit is the Jesus piece West picked up yesterday from Jacob the Jeweler, perhaps the top custom-jewelry man in hiphop. About the size of a grown man's palm, it has a cluster of clear diamonds for the crown of thorns, a river of yellow and light brown diamonds making up Jesus's blond hair, aquamarines for his blue eyes, and little rubies for the tears of blood on his face. It's an ornate rendering, a twenty-five-thousand-dollar piece, and he's very proud of it. "This is so fabulous it could be in *The Robb Report*," he says.

It doesn't bother you to sport a blond-haired, blue-eyed Jesus?

"Only thing that bothers me is how other people are going to react to it," he says.

But don't you believe Jesus was Black?

"Yes, I believe Jesus was Black. When I saw it I said, I don't particularly want to wear this as far as what I represent, even though I love it, but I do think it's a beautiful piece of artwork." But an hour later he's back at Jacob's.

Jacob Arabo has a small office at the corner of 47th Street and Sixth Avenue in Manhattan with a wall of photos of him and everyone in hiphop who's made a little money. He's got the classy, ready-to-bend-over-backward air of a luxury-goods salesman.

"I wanted to know if you could pop out these blue eyes," West says.

"Sure," Jacob says reassuringly. "Change the eyes to what color?"

"Do you have brownish-orange diamonds?"

Jacob yells out to his assistant, "Go in the safe and bring me all the colored stones!"

"I actually love the way it looks with the blue eyes," West says, "but I'll get too much flak for it. I can't explain that blue-eyed shit. I need to do another one. A Black one. Because I have socially conscious lyrics and I'ma get flak. This really is the blond-haired, blue-eyed Jesus."

Jacob pops out the blue stones, but West discovers that no other colored stone looks good. So even though the blue eyes bother him politically, they go back in. Can he live with a blue-eyed Christ on his chest? Can he handle the inevitable flak?

"I gotta get my explanation together," he says as he leaves Jacob's. Twenty minutes later he's got his defense. "I'll say it's the one off my grandmother's wall!" he says. It's a eureka moment. "It's Grandma's Jesus!" Huh?

West was born in Atlanta, the only child of Donda West, a professor of English at Chicago State University for the past twenty-four years, and Ray West, a pastoral counselor who holds two master's degrees. The couple divorced when Kanye was just three, and Dr. West moved to Chicago with her son. Kanye grew up in a single-parent, single-child home and became extremely close with his mother. Even nowadays, West sometimes has the air of a guy who was treated like a prince at home, who could do no wrong. "I've always worshipped the ground he walked on," Dr. West says. "People could say I spoiled Kanye. I don't think so. He was very much indulged." (He spent summers with his father and is less close with him. Kanye calls their relationship strained, though Ray West disagrees with that. "There's never a phone call we don't end with 'I love you,' " his father says.)

Dr. West is Kanye's biggest fan. She bought fifteen copies of *The College Dropout* and accepted no freebies. She listens to it constantly and can repeat his rhymes and deconstruct his songs. "I'm a fan of 50 Cents, Ludacris, Eminem," she says. "I even like Chingy. But I really haven't been as impressed by their lyrics as I am by Kanye's. Everything you listen to by Kanye is gonna have something in it that's heavy. I mean, Kanye has a way of putting a unique twist to things. [On "Through the Wire"] he doesn't say, Thank God I ain't too cool for the safety belt. He says, Thank God I ain't too cool for the safe belt. So he's gonna put his little Kanye twist to everything and I just think it's so brilliant."

"With me bein so close to my mother is part of why I put so

much thought into my lyrics," Kanye says. "I don't have any raps on there that I can't say in front of my mother." He was a kid who lived in his own head, sometimes made his own toys, and always had tremendous presence. "My son displayed his charisma even in day care," his father says. "From his earliest age my son would be focused on what he was focused on and you'd find other kids gathering around him to be focused on what he's focused on."

West began rhyming in the third grade. Asked why he started, he says simply, "Run-DMC." A few years later he got the itch to design video games. "Being an only child, whenever I want to do something I try to do all aspects," he says. "For a video game you need a design program and characters and movement and animation and background and music. So my mother's helping me get all these programs for all these different parts that you need for this game. And I remember the day, back in seventh grade, getting the sound program and goin home and startin to play with it and getting hooked onto it." He became obsessed with sounds. "I never had to worry about where's Kanye," Dr. West says, "because he was sitting right there in front of that keyboard. He stayed at home a lot on the keyboard making beats."

At fourteen West met the man he calls his stepfather, Willie Scott. "He taught me just like Boyz 'N Tha Hood," West says. "I'd come home and there'd be trash in the yard, and he'd say, Pick up that trash. And I'd be like, Why? I ain't put it there. He'd say, It's your house. You have to take care of it. That's the reason why I'm here today."

In high school West took honors classes, dominated school talent shows, made beats that he sold for fifty to two hundred dollars, and became an acclaimed visual artist. His drawing and painting won him a one-semester scholarship to the American Academy of Art in Chicago. But he already knew he was going to make it in hiphop and was harboring doubts about whether he needed college. "I didn't believe in school," he says, "but I didn't have anything better than that." When he was asked to take out a loan to pay for a second semester, he balked. "I was like, if this is not my dream then why would you take out a loan for something you don't want?" he says. "That's like getting somebody to loan you some money for a car that you're not really into."

His mother was the head of the English department at Chicago State, so he went there at a steep discount but remained disenchanted with the entire exercise. "One of my courses in college was piano," he says. "I actually went to college to learn how to play piano. Talk about wastin some money." After a semester and a half at Chicago State, once again, he dropped out. "I put my hand over my heart like Fred Sanford when he said he was dropping out!" Dr. West says. "It was very hard. First thing I said was 'Kanye, no, you can't drop out. I've saved money for you to go to Morehouse.' But he had the right words to convince me that it was the right thing for him to do. He said, 'Mom, all my life I've had the professor in the house.' What could I say to that? That melted me down." Three years later he was still living with his mother when an A&R man at Roc-A-Fella Records named Hiphop took a liking to West's sound, and he began making his way into Jay-Z's inner circle.

It's minutes to midnight. In the parking lot of little Kean University in Union, New Jersey, amidst affordable Hondas and Volkswagens, there's a hulking tour bus devoted to West and there's a Maybach, which is, right now, the ultimate hiphop ride. The superluxury vehicle costs $350,000, and only six hundred were sold last year. The miracle whip is owned by Jay-Z, but chances are his chauffeur is the only one who's driven it.

West signed with Roc-A-Fella in 2002 and developed a close relationship with his boss. "I still look up to Jay like a father figure," West says. "You know how Jewish families show their sons how to make money and keep the wealth going in the family? Jay's like my Jewish father." That doesn't mean he speaks to Jay all the time. "It's just like the relationship I had with my father where I'd go months without talking," West says. "I wanna stand on my own, but I want your support, too." Jay agreed that there's something of a father-son bond between them. "We talk about a lot of things," he says. "About how shit will go, what shit he gonna step in, and what to look out for."

West hops out of his tour bus, zips over to one of the Maybachs, and climbs into the front seat. Jay's lounging in the back, in a blue Rocawear jacket, crisp Rocawear jeans, and sneakers so white he's probably never worn them before. Beside him is a sexy woman in a short skirt and fabulous Pucci boots. There's an assortment of Dentyne packs in the console and *The Love Below* on the sound system. Jay-Z has this air of confidence so towering that if you've got even a speck of insecurity, it'll come out. Surely West knows this, but he's got a new toy that he's excited about. He takes the Jesus piece from around his neck and hands it to Jay for inspection. At first Jay's impressed with the exquisite craftsmanship. Then a reporter says, "Don't it look funny to you that Mr. Jesus Walks's Jesus is white?" And with that Jay's whole mood changes, his eyebrows lower, and skepticism comes over his face. "That is a little different," Jay says, no longer impressed. "Nah," West argues. "That's Grandma's Jesus!" It's his first time testing the excuse. Jay's unmoved. "You gotta darken that face up, man."

"And get rid of them blue eyes," the sexy woman chimes in. "He's a little too blond-hair, blue-eyes. Or tuck him in."

"We tried to get rid of the blue eyes," West says, on the defensive. He knew this would happen. "The blue eyes look best."

"Yeah," Jay says, knowing he's got West cornered. "That's what they make you think." Then he blurts out a laugh at the young rapper's expense. West tries to explain further, but Jay's heard enough. "Yo man, we got a friend of ours party to go to," he says. "What time you get onstage? Kick them niggas off or something." They all say it's tough love at the Roc.

Ten minutes later West hits the stage, still wearing his troublemaking Jesus piece, for what'll surely be this little college's concert of the year. Most of the few hundred students in the crowd know all the words to West's songs, which is a bit ironic. *The College Dropout's* songs and skits poke fun at the imperative to attend college to a bitter effect, as if the message were, You're a fool for staying in school. ("I do think [the skits] are a little harsh myself," West says.) But West's rhymes play up his intelligence while mocking the world of books. Jay-Z won't let him off the hook for wearing a white Jesus, but with his fans West can have it both ways. Long past midnight the Kean U. crowd raps right along with West's smart anticollege rhymes: "Ain't no tuition for havin no ambition," he says on "We Don't Care." "And ain't no loans for sittin yo' ass at home." There'll be no hitting the books tonight.

You Can Call Him Prince

{ *Icon Magazine*, 1998 }

I'm deep inside Paisley Park. Past the front hallways where walls are painted sky blue with real-looking clouds and the ceiling is night-navy with stars and cosmos. Past walls filled with platinum and gold album plaques—some commemorating sales in Sweden, Germany, Japan, Portugal, Australia. Past the doves that live there. I'm in the back, in the rehearsal room, where, on one end there's a stage, and on the other end, amid some plush couches and sound-mixing boards, there's a basketball hoop. It's a little bit too high.

I'm playing two-on-two. My teammate? Guess who. He's pretty good. He jitterbugs around the court, a sleek little lightning bug in red and white high-tops, so fast he'll leave a defender stranded and looking stupid if a defender ain't careful. So I've got the ball at the top of the key and I'm dribbling and I see he's in good position under the basket. I flick a quick pass toward him. The ball is floating through the defense safely, then I realize he doesn't know it's coming. Instinctively, I call out to him. The man I've known, sort of, for fifteen or twenty years. The man who, like Sinatra for another generation, made our official love-making music. I call out, "Prince!"

But he's not Prince anymore! What happens if you call him Prince now? No doubt, he'll storm out of the room and banish you from the Paisley Palace! Titanic faux pas! But before the second part of the word slips out, before I can say more than "Pr—" I catch myself, put my hands over my dirty mouth, and watch the ball fly out of bounds, thankful I caught myself before . . . Then, he smirks and says happily, and to no one in particular, "He didn't know what to call me." Laughing with my quandary, forgiving my mistake, and being, just, cool. *He didn't know what to call me.*

Two weeks before that I flew to Paisley Park to interview The Artist. Paisley is a large, modern-looking building located in a field just outside of Minneapolis, in tiny Chanhassen. From the outside, the large white tiled walls make it look kinda like a Mercedes dealership without windows. Inside, the decade-old Paisley, which houses recording studios, a large rehearsal stage, and offices, has a quiet manicness to it, like a music lover's *Alice in Wonderland*. Oversize comfy chairs of all colors sit amid pillars topped with gold disks. Underneath there's thick blue carpeting dotted with zodiac symbols. On one wall is painted a flock of golden doves seeming to tumble from the sky. Beside each door is painted a label of what's inside: Storage or Studio A or Copier/Fax or Elevation, for the elevator. Open one door and there's a museumlike corridor of photos of each Prince era, from a '78 afroed shot to a huge portait of him holding his wife of two years, Mayte Garcia-Nelson. Behind another door there's a rehearsal room and, in the corner, a box of vinyl records. Peering into it feels like peeking into a section of his head—Al Jarreau, Sam Cooke, the Horace Silver Quintet, Nancy Wilson, the Watts 103rd Street Band, Eddie Kendricks, Dave Brubeck, The Band, Jimi's Isle of Wight, and lots of Nat King Cole. From behind one locked door serious live funk grooves spill out, then, suddenly, stop. Out back a child's jungle gym sits quiet. I sneak into studio B. No one's there. This, the engineers say, is where he recorded his latest album, *New Power Soul* and does most of his current work. After a foyer with cream walls dotted with blue neon stars, there, on the floor, are boxes of studio tape reels of unreleased songs "Don't Talk 2 Strangers," "Journey 2 the Center of Your Heart," and "This Crazy Life of Mine." Inside the studio's control room is a small black-and-white painting of Miles Davis during the 80s. It stands in front of a sepia photograph of a light-skinned man. Could be his father.

As you can see, I had a few hours to snoop. I was fourth in a line of five journalists who flew into Paisley to interview The Artist. Because The Artist is, or once was, a megastar, it seems only right to momentarily turn our cameras on the other cameras capturing him. The other four journalists were from relatively small news outlets—the Philadelphia *Daily News*, some British magazine—with the exception of *Newsweek*. In '96, when he released his three-disc set, *Emancipation*, he appeared on *The Today show* and *Oprah*, and gave interviews to *Time*, *Rolling Stone*, and *The New York Times*. But a string of underappreciated records since then has apparently shored up much of that mainstream interest. Where was *Rolling Stone*? *Vibe*? Prince demanded they give him a cover for an interview and so far, they've both said no. "People go on the covers of magazines for a variety of reasons," said Joe Levy, the music editor of *Rolling Stone*. "One is the artistic impact they're having artistically. Another is the impact they're having culturally. A third, sometimes, the impact they're having commercially. Right now those factors are not conjoining together to make it inevitable, or a given that we would put Prince on the cover."

Danyel Smith, the editor in chief of *Vibe*, explained Levy's point further. "I think it's a struggle for many R&B artists as they get older for them to be real true pop stars because pop is kept alive by very young kids most of the time and I think a lot of very young kids are into things other than Prince right now. That doesn't mean he's not legendary and exciting. Especially to those of us who grew up with him.

"When 1999 and *Purple Rain* were hot," Smith continued, "the people who were buying his records were the same age that he was then, which was sixteen to twenty-four years old. Those are the kind of people who make pop stars. The people who buy Prince's records now, some of them are between sixteen and twenty-four but most of them are between twenty-four and thirty-two, or thirty-two and thirty-eight. Those are the kind of people who are loyal music buyers, but not the people that mostly contribute to number-one pop, number-one R&B, platinum singles, double platinum singles. Which is not to say he doesn't still have all the greatness that he ever had. Even with Michael Jordan. Yes, he sank that last basket, but he's no longer the player he was at twenty-five. That's just what it comes down to. He's a bit older and so are his fans." It's become cliché to point out that Prince—like Michael Jordan and Mike Tyson and Michael Jackson and Janet Jackson—is not as great or as famous as he used to be. But, then again, clichés are true. It's telling that recently, when celebrity comedian Chris Rock interviewed The Artist, it wasn't broadcast on MTV, the king of the music channels, but VH1, the smaller network, tailored for the more mature audience. The Artist seems to be heading further and further away from the cutting edge and closer toward a sort of R&B Legends tour. Unlike, say, Al Green and Sly Stone, who sadly flamed out Bobby Fischer–style, or Stevie Wonder, who has dipped into a sort of quiet retirement, the R&B Legends circuit was pioneered by men like James Brown, until recently, and George Clinton, still, who continued to release little-noted albums and tour in the nation's smaller, more intimate venues for years after their prime, their value less recognized by the teenage hordes who horde Hanson albums and *Titanic* tickets, but still beloved by a certain legion of never-say-die lovers. The Artist may now matter less to lots, but Prince still matters lots to a few.

After a few hours of snooping I was finally ushered into a white conference room dominated by a giant glass table to meet The Artist. He sported a maroon velour Prince suit (a sexually alluring top-and-matching-pant outfit you can't buy in stores), gripped a gold cane, and wore a sly, Cheshire-cat smile. I noticed that base makeup covered his face and that his frame was so wispy a strong man could probably snap him like firewood, but I never once thought he was short. Later, realizing that, I remembered the legendary dancer Rudolph Nureyev had once said, "Onstage I can be as tall as I want."

Before I could ask a question, The Artist began speaking in a deep, warm, masculine voice. "We've been talking about how freedom has affected our people," he said. "It's so liberating to work on music with no dogma at all. It's so freeing to record without a clock ticking, without knowing you owe someone royalty money." He was referring to his recent split from Warner Bros., his record label of eight years. In 1993 he began having friction with the label when they began pushing him to release music less often because he was selling less. In '93 he began writing "slave" on his face, and announced Prince was dead, then changed his name to an unpronounceable symbol in order to get off the label, and to distance himself from his past material and past life. Funkmaster George Clinton, a friend of The Artist, said, "People didn't really realize that when he said Prince was dead he really meant that."

He escaped from his Warner contract and struck a distribution deal with EMI that gave him tremendous autonomy. But in '96 EMI went out of business, and Prince now records only for NPG Records, which he owns, distributing records himself, many through Web sites and 1-800 numbers. With selling albums more incumbent on him, he suddenly became less press-shy than ever. Record-label freedom is his current obsession. A young recording artist said, "The last time I saw him, his first words to me were, 'Did you get off the label yet?' Not, 'Hi, how ya doin?' But, 'Did you get off the label?' " And that freedom, along with marriage, has led to major changes in The Artist. Once a moody recluse when not onstage who was considered weirder than even Michael Jackson, he has become at peace with himself. A former girlfriend of his who wished to remain anonymous said, "When I first met him he was quite miserable. Now he doesn't have any negativity surrounding him. Now he's totally happy and totally comfortable in his skin. When you actually look at his face, you can tell that a weight has been lifted off his skin."

But that freedom has also led to albums that are underpromoted and too long. The man who wowed the world in nine songs on *Purple Rain* this year released the four-disc *Crystal Ball* and, in 1996, the three-disc *Emancipation*. Both sold respectably—*Crystal Ball* moved more than 250,000 units at fifty dollars each, and *Emancipation* crossed just over 500,000 cash registers. The royalty structure he'd won from EMI, then distributing his records, made them two of his most profitable. But despite some great moments on both records, both suffered from a lack of editing. And, like his latest release, *New Power Soul*, all lack the complex thematic unity that characterized his greatest works. Prince's greatest works, said hiphop drummer Ahmir, from the Roots, were constructed with the same dramatic structure as Shakespearean plays—with rising action, comic relief, climax, and denouement. But, it seems, no longer. Does he know? In an interview on VH1, The Artist told Chris Rock, "I pick up some reviews of my work from time to time and you'll hear a lotta talk about Will he ever match the success of such and such, but I'm not on that road . . . It's [my] journey. It's not for somebody who doesn't play music to say that's not as good as."

The Artist continued talking to me. "For me to create an album, tour all over night after night, and get less than the $140 million it grosses is ridiculous."

"How much would you get?"

"I'd get at most $7 million."

"Still," I said, "how could you call yourself slave in light of the history of that word among our people?"

"Imagine yourself sitting in a room with the biggest of the big in the recording industry and you have 'slave' written on your face. That changes the entire conversation. You know what they think of us. They say it makes it real hard to talk to you with that on your face. Why? And it got real quiet. They don't wanna get into all that. Adding that language into the conversation worked perfectly. It changed the dynamic of the conversation."

He dodged a follow-up question about a multimillionaire music maker likening himself to a dawn-to-dusk cottonpicker. Meanwhile, I furiously scribbled notes. Years ago he banned tape recorders from his print interviews (though not video recorders from his television interviews). He speaks quickly, often using parables and sentences so cryptic they could work in a David Lynch film. An old girlfriend said, "Sometimes he says things that make you feel like you haven't gotten an answer. He leaves you to have to think about every word he says, which is kind of irritating." My quotes, then, are close approximations—sometimes more his intent than his exact words, other times, when I was lucky, the actual words were captured but, upon reading them back I couldn't understand what he meant. If you read a quote and don't get it, that's the point: I don't either.

As we went on talking he remained friendly and verbose, though somehow, interview-resistant. After half an hour I realized he'd given up very little of his substance—except on the issue of money and record-label freedom. I pushed harder.

"Why are you being so open now?" In his first years Prince

courted the press, even befriending certain journalists and writing about them, though vaguely, in his classic "All the Critics Love U in New York" from 1999. But during his height he became a Katherine Hepburn–esque recluse, refusing all interviews for years, then summoning one select journalist to speak with him every couple of years—though demanding they be unable to tape record the interview or even take notes. For years the few journalists who spoke with him spent lots of time running to the bathroom every few minutes to write down whatever they could remember. So for him to simply consent to a major magazine interview is itself a huge shift. For there to be a line of journalists waiting to speak with a superstar is normal. But for Prince? It seems downright strange.

"As the millenium approaches we all must look inward and check the fiber and speak the truth. I had a boss and I didn't like it. No more than you like it. I feel free now that there's no daddy around to spank me. It's time for us to stand up for what we believe in."

"Is there a difference between Prince and The Artist?"

"Only that Prince owns nothing. None of those songs."

"So you're happier now. Did the old music come from a place of pain?"

"I won't speculate on where the music came from. I look back in awe and reverence. It's made me become courageous."

"Courageous around music?"

"Regarding everything."

"Do you realize you've changed a generation with your music?"

He became defensive. "I don't think about that. Why would I? There's no gain in that. Being in control of someone's thoughts? You'll second-guess your writing."

"So," feeling stifled, recalling photos of Mayte and him at Lakers games, I said, "you like basketball?"

He seemed to loosen up a bit. "Yeah."

"What's your team?"

"Bulls," he said, like, *of course.*

"Still? You think they're comin back?"

With an *oh-please* air, he said, "Jordan's gonna be player-coach.

That's why Phil Jackson left. Scottie's gonna get paid, Rodman's gonna get paid. It's gonna be rock 'n' roll time next year. The Bulls are gonna be like the Beatles. He's Superman. He don't have to do that much to whup them people."

We shared a laugh but a moment later, somehow, we were back to money. He expressed admiration for the music of Erykah Badu, De La Soul, A Tribe Called Quest, and D'Angelo, then said, "D'Angelo's really gotta search his heart deeply on being part of the problem or the solution. What's his whole consciousness? He's got to own his masters," he said, referring to master tapes that confer true ownership of a song, which are generally owned by the record label and not the artist. "Black Americans are walking away and getting nothin! How can you not own your masters and try to uplift the community? Let's all of us be part of the solution. Or we gonna get our problems solved for us. The situation in Africa is testament to that. Twenty-one million with AIDS! Don't that spook you? We got to solve our problems or they'll be solved for us. And a man can't solve your problems for you. You and your faith will solve 'em for you."

He told me another journalist had asked him, "Do you ever get tired of being so flamboyant all the time? Don't you ever wanna wear a T-shirt and jeans?" at which point he reared his head back, eyes wide, in mock indignation, as if to say, *How ridiculous! Don't you know who I am?* Full of macho bravado, he thrust the cuff of his maroon Prince suit out toward me and said, "Feel that!! If you could wear that every day, wouldn't you?!"

I felt the cuff. It wasn't a rare and special feeling. It felt man-made. "What is it?" I asked.

Immediately his entire demeanor switched. He went, in a heart-beat, from larger than life to hushed and humble. It was an emotional stop on a dime.

"Oh, I don't know," he said quietly, dismissively, feigning igno-rance of the fabric of his fabulous garment. "If you have money you should act the same. It's currency. It's supposed to move like a current. You ain't supposed to horde it. You get sick otherwise."

I walked out feeling as though he'd never truly shared himself. As though I'd been given the day's propaganda, along with a few tasty side bites, and sent on my way. And today's propaganda—that insistent business talk—had made me feel as though I'd spoken to Curt Flood, an average baseball player known only for sacrifing his career in the 60s to force the introduction of free agency, when I'd planned to meet Willie Mays. I felt I'd attended a well-choreographed, slightly improvised one-man show. I felt I understood what actress Kirstie Alley said, in the role of frustrated interviewer, on his 1992 so-called Symbol album, "Just once will you talk to me, not at me, not around me, not through me?" I flew home feeling used.

By Prince's design, much of his early life remains an unpenetrable mystery. An associate said, "The background story depends on who you're talking to. It's never very clear. Minneapolis is a tight-knit community and people aren't really willing to talk about him." Indeed, in researching almost anything about Prince's pre- and nonpublic life it's nearly impossible to get a straight answer about almost anything. Just about everyone who comes in contact with The Artist must sign a confidentiality agreement—girlfriends, employees, journalists, anyone—and people tend to take them seriously. Many who knew Prince declined to give interviews because of those confidentiality agreements. Others refused to speak about him because they so closely guard their relationship with him. They either fear being cut off, or want to protect him, but, the point is, most of those who know Prince won't tell.

We do know this: he was born Prince Rogers Nelson on June 7, 1958, the son of pianist and Honeywell factory worker John L. Nelson and Mattie Shaw (or possibly Mattie Baker), a singer in her husband's band and later, a social worker. Both are Seventh Day Adventists, as is one of Prince's later guardians, Fred Anderson—the strict faith encourages vegetarianism and abstinence from tobacco, alcohol, and all drugs. (The Artist is a vegan and has always maintained that he has never smoked, drank, or done drugs.) Contrary to lingering rumors, both are Black. Prince grew up first in North Minneapolis, in a middle-class multiracial oasis in the Wonder Bread–white Twin Cities.

When Prince was seven the two divorced. His mother (who nicknamed him "Skipper") soon remarried and Prince began spending lots of time playing the piano his father had left behind and listening to Minneapolis radio, the latter leaving an imprint on his sound. "In New York, or D.C., or Chicago, or Atlanta you had great Black radio that was 24-7," said Alan Leeds. "If you got tired of one station there was another one up the dial. He didn't have that in Minneapolis. So he was forced to listen to pop radio and absorb pop records as much as Black music. So as he grew up, with every James Brown record he heard there was a Beatles record or a Rolling Stones record. And all of that mixed together so that you hear all of these things in his music." But when his mother's new husband tired of him, Prince bounced to an aunt's home, then his father's, then a friend's, all the time struggling to find a place where he was wanted.

The family trouble and ensuing struggle to find somewhere he belonged led to a deep interest in music. During his teens Prince taught himself to play fourteen instruments and led a band first called Grand Central and later Champagne that often played at Minneapolis's First Avenue—many times before Prince was legally old enough to get into the club. In high school he voraciously studied the business of music and wowed his music-class classmates—including future super producers Jimmy Jam and Terry Lewis—with his ability to play so many instruments so well. Still, late in his high-school career he became a total introvert and loner, opting to have his picture omitted from the school yearbooks in his junior and senior year. (But further investigation becomes difficult—details become sketchy, stories begin to conflict. Some sources say Prince was a D student who cared not at all for school. Others call him a good student.) But while he became a loner, he became ever more obsessed with becoming a star. "He sat down as a youngster and designed himself to be a rock star. Not a musician, but a rock star," said Alan Leeds, who served as Prince's tour manager and the vice president of Paisley Park Records from 1983 to 1992. "There was an acceptance and power and security that he envisioned could come from massive appeal. He was ostracized, he was the shortest kid in school, he was an excellent basketball player but nobody took him seriously because he was too short, his older brother got all the girls because he was taller. He was constantly in the shadow of everybody and everything. So, OK, here's how I can get back at the world. Here's how I can get the girls and be the number-one guy and get the attention that I never get."

Music poured out of him. "His every waking moment," said Leeds, "there was music or lyrics flowing to a piece of paper. If he doesn't have anything to do he'll go to the studio. He wakes up in the morning with a melody or a lyric and he can't wait to get to the studio to turn the tape on. You just wondered how any one brain could process as much music came out of him. All of it wasn't good. But enough of it was."

In 1976, shortly after graduating from Minneapolis's Central High School, he charmed recording-studio owner Chris Moon into allowing him to have a set of keys to his Minneapolis studio, and Prince ended up teaching himself everything about studio technology. Moon hyped Prince to a local manager as a Stevie Wonder–level talent, and Prince soon had a legal representative: Owen Husney. Husney financed Prince's demo tape—on which Prince wrote and played every note of some very lewd funk—then flew him out to L.A. and booked studio time. One day, while Prince was recording and rehearsing, Husney quietly brought in some executives from a record company to watch the young phenom. Shortly after, he became a corporate cousin of Bugs Bunny when he signed a record contract with Warner Bros. In April 1978 the nineteen-year-old released the first of his twenty-eight albums, entitled For You. Prince unveiled a new album nearly every year, each one surprisingly different than the one before. Harvard professor Cornel West said, "Like Coltrane, he's continually journeying and searching. One hundred years from now they'll play all the albums and it'll be hard for them to realize one person wrote all that."

Prince's audience built slowly, but steadily, until more than thirteen million people bought 1984's Purple Rain. Suddenly, it seemed, the whole world had one eye on Prince. Artists old and young took note. Seventies funk legend George Clinton told me that he's been influenced by "his way of doin pop music and makin it a blues music." Nineties soul legend D'Angelo told me, "Listening to him taught me to not really give a fuck lyrically. He taught me that when all of the music is coming from you that's the best way. He taught me everything, really. I can't stress that enough."

Prince came to be dominated by music. "He lives and breathes music," said Alan Leeds. "His friendships are not normal. He doesn't have normal relationships. It's not like he's got guys that he hangs out with on Friday night. He's not one for small talk or casual conversation. If he's on a tour bus he may have some conversation that's relatively casual, but nine times out of ten even that will be something related to the show or the album or something. Almost everything in the ten years I was with him, save some very specifically allocated leisure time, almost everything else was somehow about music or the show. He's so strictly defined by his career that there really hasn't been a normal life away from that. I sense that with Mayte and the marriage he's trying to find something like that now. Certainly the Prince that I know is not a guy who just picks up the phone and say, Hey, how ya doin? He's a very distant personality."

"He has no control over his life," an associate explained. "The music is channeled through him. When the music tells him to play, he does. When the music tells him to sleep, he does. He considers it a blessing and a curse."

Alan Leeds recalled occasionally seeing a jovial, glib, outspoken side of Prince. Every once in a while, Leeds said, he'd cancel the almost-constant rehearsals in favor of a cookout and some hoops. "Once," Leeds remembered, "we were rehearsing for a tour and suddenly there was the first warm day of the year and when everybody showed up for rehearsal we found out that Prince and his assistant had bought ten baseball gloves, a couple softballs, a couple bats, and we went to the local school field and played softball all day.

"But," Leeds continued, "in the midst of that, he's constantly talking about the last record he did and the tour we're gonna do and what should we do tomorrow in rehearsal. That function never ends. You're at a club somewhere, when he suddenly says, Hey, you got a notepad? And he starts dictating orders of what we're gonna do the next day in rehearsal."

After the explosion of *Purple Rain* the high-school outcast was, as he'd long dreamed, one of the biggest stars in the world. An international icon, he toured the world putting on concerts that were explosions of funk and sex and soul and Baptist church–like ecstasy—and then, after the concerts, he'd pop up, unannounced, at some tiny local club and do another two hours for free. It only exponentialized the thrill of seeing him perform. He was awarded his own vanity label, called Paisley Park, which, as an imprint of Warner Bros., released his albums. He opened up nightclubs in Minneapolis and Los Angeles, called Glam Slam, where he often strolled in, unannounced, to jam. He made four movies—the stunning, semiautobiographical *Purple Rain* in 1984 (the title song netted him an Oscar for Best Song); in 1986, the forgettable *Under the Cherry Moon*, costarring Kristin Scott Thomas (from *The English Patient* and *Four Weddings and a Funeral*); in 1987, the *Sign of the Times* concert film, widely considered one of the most brilliant concert films ever; and in 1990, the silly *Graffiti Bridge*. He became a modern Casanova, dating a legendary string of gorgeous women, some of whom he would make famous, at least for a moment—Vanity, Apollonia, Sheila E, Carmen Electra, Cat, Nona Gaye—some of them already famous—actress Kim Basinger, singer Sheena Easton, model Troy Beyer, actress Vanessa Marcil. How much of the sexual legend was overblown? "Like most things it's exaggerated," said Alan Leeds. "But he's got a very impressive scorecard."

History will record that at the very top of the 80s solo-megastar mountaintop, Prince's sole company was Michael Jackson. In his comprehensive history of Black music, *The Death of Rhythm & Blues*, Nelson George called the two the most important artists of the 80s, as well as the era's "finest music historians, consistently using techniques that echoed the past as the base for their superstardom." In a 1984 *Village Voice* essay called "Stagolee Versus the Proper Negro," Greg Tate opined, "Although Michael may have kicked the door in [for Black rock 'n' roll to come in], Prince done stormed the castle and come back handing the brothers and sisters the keys to the rock-and-roll kingdom (or, to paraphrase Bill Murray in *Ghostbusters*, he came, he saw, he kicked ass.)" (For the record, in our interview, The Artist refused to consider Jackson his main competition, saying he wasn't "worried" about people as famous as he, but other guitar killers. "I'm just a guitar player," he said. "I look out for the Johnny Langs tearing up the guitar. I don't stress nobody else." [Lang is a teenage blues phenom from Minneapolis].)

Still, Prince was unhappy. "The person I met," said Leeds who joined Prince shortly before *Purple Rain*, "was suspicious and paranoid of people and life in general and sarcastic and cynical and clearly troubled by his personal demons. And of course the more we learned about his background—his mother basically walked away from him, and his father struggled to raise him and threw in the towel, and the kinds of rejection he suffered as a youngster—that certainly don't add up to a very secure, well-rounded individual."

In our interview The Artist said, "People think I must miss the old days. No way. One time I was doing the Seventy-fifth *Purple Rain* show, doing the same thing over and over. For the same kids who go to Spice Girls shows. And I just lost it. I said, I can't do it! They were putting the guitar on me and it hit me in the eye and cut me and blood started going down my shirt. And I said I have to go onstage, but I knew I had to get away from all that. I couldn't play the game."

After *Purple Rain* he continued making great music—journalist Anthony DeCurtis said, "Between '82 [1999] and '87 [*Sign of the Times*] he was in the zone. It was that moment when the zeitgeist flows through you and as it moves through you you're shaping where it goes once it passes you. He was channeling, man."

Sign of the Times was a towering zenith. After two quirky, but brilliant records—1985's *Around the World in a Day*, 1986's *Parade*—*Sign* was a critical watershed that remains the favorite Prince album for many musicians and nonmusicians. "His best album to me is *Sign of the Times*," said Ahmir. "That's his look-ma-no-hands record. No one but him would put that coda at the end of 'U Got the Look.' No one but him would use the method called varispeed which, thus, you get the Camille sounding voice. Basically it's just him singing with the tape slowed down. That's some sick shit. No one but him would omit the hi hat in 'It.' No one but him would put backward drums on 'Starfish and Coffee.' No one but him would write a song like 'Starfish and Coffee'! And put that shit six on his record! Artists today put all their eccentric shit way towards the end cuz

they're all worried about makin sure the first six songs are absolute
bangers. Meanwhile, he covers the whole spectrum of music in the first
four songs. He covered Santana, James Brown, Curtis Mayfield—just as
far as styles—Joni Mitchell, Pink Floyd, all within the first five songs. No
one does epic shit like he does. I consider that an unbelievable record."

But in retrospect, *Sign of the Times* was Prince's last climax, so far. It
did not sell incredibly and, despite the brilliance of 1988's *Lovesexy*, and
near-scintillating moments on 1992's so-called *Symbol* album, he would
never again sell superstar truckloads or unveil genius albums—'91's *Diamonds and Pearls*, a critical disappointment, moved more than two million albums, but then his subsequent seven albums moved a combined
three million—some, like 1996's *Chaos and Disorder*, moving a mere hundred thousand. Part of the problem, as with all superstars over time, is
not simply that Prince has changed—at forty years old it's certainly
much more difficult for him, or anyone, to interpret and create the
zeitgeist, and thus make great pop music, than it would be for a talented twenty-nine-year-old, as he was when he created *Sign of the Times*.
Just as the thirty-five-year-old Michael Jordan of today isn't as great as
twenty-nine-year-old MJ. But in The Artist's case, we, his audience, have
changed, too.

"When he came out," said journalist Nelson George, "he was the
most controversial artist of the time, dealing with incest and raw sexuality and sexual ambiguity and racial ambiguity. All that worked for him.
And then a new movement came in called hiphop. Once the Rakim,
Run-DMC, Big Daddy Kane era came in the whole level of masculinity
was different. There was no room for ambiguity. There was definitely a
cultural backlash, among men. A lot of people suddenly said, Prince?
He's a sissy." However, George added, not all Prince fans changed with
the times: "Of all the artists I know, I don't know anyone who's had so
many unabashed women fans who love him to death."

Warner Bros. believed Prince's sales were slipping after *Sign of the
Times*, because he was oversaturating the marketplace—between 1978
and 1992 Prince released thirteen albums, two of them double sets,
while Bruce Springsteen, known for his hard work, released only eight.
For years Warner had given him unusual latitude. "He was less a slave

than any Black artist I know of!" says Nelson George. "There's no other Black artist you can look at during his era who had more artistic freedom than Prince. They really let him have control of his career in ways that Black artists never have. They let him pick the singles. With the *Sign of the Times* album, 'Housequake' was never a single. It was the biggest record in the country at one point, but never a single. 'Adore' [many people's favorite Prince ballad] was never a single. They put out 'If I was Your Girlfriend' as a single, which was a great record, but it wasn't an obvious direct commercial single. And those are his calls."

George continued, "As the stories go, Prince could do anything he wanted to and Mo [Ostin, then the president of Warner Bros.] would cosign it. Prince would go in his office and literally get on top of his desk and dance and sing for him and make Mo spend money. They never pigeonholed him as a Black artist, at least internally. They put out two-sided singles and double albums and gave him mad tour support. They supported him as an artist to the highest level for most of his career. But the freedom they gave him at Warner, he became a victim of it. They'd spoiled him so long and indulged him so long that when they started trying to rein him in they couldn't."

In '92 Warner signed Prince to a new record contract, reportedly worth one hundred million dollars, and thus, announced as one of the richest in record business history. He received a reported thirty million dollars in cash up-front and a ten-million-dollar advance per album, but only if the previous one made over five million dollars.

The size of the deal made Warner more interested in slowing Prince's release schedule, so that they could have more time for their promotion and marketing, and they pressured him to slow his release schedule. But to Prince, the problem was how Warner was promoting the records. And besides, impeding his creative process was completely unacceptable. The situation would only get worse. "He's on some hard-core militant shit now," said Ahmir. "Like, you got to control your shit and let no one else control your shit for you. I was like, Yo man, what brought this on? He was like, I've been through hell and back and I've been through hell and back again."

Prince made some major changes. In 1993 it was announced he

was changing his name to an unpronounceable symbol (he was soon called The Artist Formerly Known as Prince and, eventually, The Artist). In our interview he said, "I changed my name to get out of the contract. [Once he'd changed the name and began to be known as the symbol] they said, We don't want any more Prince albums. I said, That's the name on the contract. They said, That's not the name people know you by now. I said, You didn't sign him."

In '94 Warner struck back, dropping its distribution deal with his vanity label Paisley Park, and afraid he would never record again, releasing a pair of albums against his will: the long-underground *Black Album* and *Come*, a collection of outtakes. At the time The Artist told a journalist, "You don't know how much it hurts not owning your own material. When a record company goes ahead and does something with a song you wrote . . . it can make you angry for a week." The disagreement deepened when Warner consented to allow The Artist to release a single, "The Most Beautiful Girl in the World" on another label, the tiny Bellmark, and it was an international success. Proving to The Artist, at least, that his decreasing record sales were not his fault. At the time, Bob Merlis, the senior vice president of Warner Bros., told *The New York Times*, "He wanted to release more albums than his contract called for. . . . Eventually we agreed that his vision and ours didn't coincide." Warner agreed to end the contract, though it retained ownership of his voluminous and lucrative back material.

He signed a deal with EMI for them to distribute the records he put out on his label, NPG. He would finance his own albums and videos and release them as his own whim. EMI, which allowed The Artist to retain ownership of his master recordings, got a small cut for employing its own distribution system. At the time The Artist told journalists they were like "hired hands, like calling a florist to deliver flowers to my wife."

On Valentine's Day 1996, he married Mayte. She grew up around the world, a military brat stationed longest in Germany, who, as a very young girl, belly danced on *That's Incredible*. In her teens she became a prima ballerina with the Wiesbaden Ballet in Germany. At a show in Germany he caught sight of her and said to a friend, "That's my wife."

She was sixteen. Now twenty-four, and taller than her husband, she has
an angelic smile and a shapely, unforgettable dancer's body; two overly
friendly Yorkshire terriers, Mia and Mary, who scamper around Paisley at
will; a hot-pink BMW 750il; a five-carat wedding ring; and a sweet, just
slightly Spanish accented voice not unlike Jennifer Lopez's. Described as
an "iron fist in a velvet glove," she choreographs for the NPG Dance
Company, in which dancers move to Prince's music in ways based on
classical, modern, and hiphop style, and directed the video for her husband's latest single, "The One," and will make others. "Their marriage is
the best thing that could've happened to him," said a former girlfriend,
who said that her background as a mover is part of his attraction to her.
"That woman obviously is for him. All that has transpired in the last
four years, in making him more human and willing to be open, is because of her." In our interview, The Artist, asked how he knew Mayte
was the one, said, "God tells you who's the one. If you don't have a relationship with God you're in trouble. That gives you something to put
everything in line." Then asked if he enjoyed being married, said, "I'm
not afraid of the rain anymore because my wife built me a garden. Now
the lightning and thunder put energy in the vegetables and give me energy to talk to you."

In 1996 Mayte became pregnant. Prince sampled the baby's heartbeat for a song on his album *Emancipation* and transformed Paisley Park
into the eye-popping wonderland it is now. In our interview he said,
"There was no color in this building before I got married. It was all
white with gray carpet. For fifteen years I was just in the studio every
day, on a grind, not even thinkin about it." But though he spoke of the
changes in Paisley, it was made clear to journalists that they were not to
ask about the sad event that had inspired the changes. According to published reports, in October of 1996, Mayte gave birth to a boy with Pfeif-
fer's Syndrome, a skull deformity. After seven days on life support, he
passed. The Artist has said that "Comeback," a short, lonely, beautiful
ballad from his oft-sublime acoustic album *The Truth*, the fourth disc of
the *Crystal Ball* set, is about the child: "Spirits come and spirits go/ Some
stick around for the after show/ I don't have to say I miss you/ Cuz I
think you already know." The refrain is, "If you ever lose someone dear

to you/ Never say the words they're gone/ They'll come back." There are plans to build a children's hospital on the land across the street from Paisley, where vacant shacks stand now. "It's part of his commitment," a friend said, "to get his own money and spend it the way he wants."

Needing more quotes and more substance, I e-mail The Artist twelve questions, mostly about music. Then, at the last moment I tack on one more—Will you play one-on-one basketball with me?—and zap the queries into cyberspace.

Two days later answers float back. On music he's a little more open, shunning any specific discussion of his past songs except to express an awe toward his own oeuvre, as though it was created by someone else. He writes "Ultimately, spiritual evolution is the axis on which inspiration and creativity spin . . . there r so many songs that I've written and recorded, sometimes it is hard 4 ME 2 believe it comes from one source!" And, intriguingly, "All of my musicality comes from GOD . . . the blessing/curse ensued when I kept sneaking back in2 the talent line dressed as another person . . . I got away with it several times be4 they caught me!!"

Then, at the bottom, in response to my hoop question he wrote "Anytime, brother . . . :)." Anytime? He didn't mean it. I'd get to Paisley and there'd be some excuse. Could I risk not trying? History awaited. I stuff my basketball in my overnight bag and leap on the next flight to Minneapolis.

For three hours the *Icon* photographer sets up in a Paisley Park side room, adjusting the lights, prepping the film. Then, suddenly, a white BMW Z roars up to Paisley and in strolls Prince. Not That Artist who's offered us this awkward parody of a name that seems designed to militate against familiarity, but a real person—Prince. Journalist Anthony DeCurtis said, "The name thing has become a punch line. I mean, can you imagine an artist who's sold tens of millions of records suddenly confronting his audience with the problem of *how to say his name?* That's deep." Anyway, word is that friends and family still call him Prince. According to Ahmir, "He lets Black people call him Prince."

So Prince, in a long, flowing, buttoned-up basketball-colored top

that stretches down to his knees and cream heels, sits down in front of
the camera and, for twenty minutes, lets the wall down a bit, keeping us
in stitches with his dry, quick-witted humor. Outside of interview mode
he shows off more of the changed man, the Glasnost Artist, a freer, more
relaxed man, prepared to really chill.

Already wearing one Prince ear-cuff earring in each ear, he con-
templates adding a hoop to his right lobe. He holds it up to his ear and
asks in a deep voice, "Earring or no?"

"Yes!" the female assistant says. "Wear it."

"Who buys the magazine?" he asks.

"Men," he's told.

Right on beat he drops the earring to the ground. "Women always
get me in trouble," he teases. In a womanly voice he adds, "Oooh, you
look so nice in that."

A Paisley employee runs in. Prince says to him, "Ask them to clear
out in the back to play basketball."

A moment later, flipping through *Vanity Fair* with Chris Rock on
the cover, he comes to a story about Ronald and Nancy Reagan.

"Think Reagan has alzheimer's?" he asks.

"Yeah." Who doesn't?

He gives me a sly look as if to say, *don't believe* it. I'd heard he was a
conspiracy theorist. I laugh and begin writing.

"Don't write that," he says playfully. "I already got enough trouble.
I'll have the Secret Service at my door." He adopts a mock federal agent
voice. "You say somethin about Reagan??"

We all crack up. When the laughs subside I ask, "Why would they
lie about that?"

He says, "To keep him from answering questions."

The shoot concludes and the photo team and I are led into the rehearsal room in the back. When we arrive he's changed out of the
basketball-colored top and into a tight, almost sheer, long-sleeved black
top and tight black pants. But then he tucks his gold symbol necklace
into his top, slips off his cream-colored heels, and laces up some old,
but not tattered, red and white Nike Air Force high-tops. And the one-
time Central High sixth man—he played guard—is ready to ball. Alan

Leeds told me, "He's not a person who finds it easy to share, whether it's his thoughts or his time or his energy. If it isn't within the context of a specific purpose he doesn't enjoy or solicit sharing life. Everything has an agenda." But now he seems willing to share. He seems spontaneous and playful. Maybe that's the agenda. (Don't put it past him, suggested someone who knows The Artist, to decide now, at this low point in his career, with a men's magazine watching, let me play basketball with a writer for the first time.) Or maybe he just feels comfortable.

He picks up the ball and makes a face understood in international shit-talking parlance to mean I'ma kick yo ass and starts knifing around the court, moving quick, dribbling fast, sliding under my arm to snatch rebounds I thought for sure I had. He moves like a player and plays like one of those darting little guys you got to keep your eye on every second. Blink and he's somewhere you'd never expect. Lose control of your dribble for a heartbeat and he's relieved you of the ball. With his energy and discipline it's a rapid game, but never manic or out of control. Still, we're both rusty so most shots just miss, clunking off the side of the rim, and after a little while there's not much of a score. Finally, I score on a drive that feels too easy. As the ball drops in I look back at him. "I don't foul guests," he says. Then, on the next play I drive again and the joker bumps my arm tough, fouling me.

He and I team up against the photographer (Prince had told him not to take pictures of the game) and Morris Hayes, his six-foot-four blond afroed keyboardist. Prince takes the point, a natural leader, sets picks and makes smart passes, showing a discipline street players almost never grasp. Then, he takes it boldly to the hole, twisting through the air in between both opponents, sometimes a bit too aggressive, but exhibiting the confidence of a man who's taken on the world by himself and won. And sometimes, in those too-bold drives to the hoop, he scores. The game teeters back and forth, one team gaining point-game then the other, until at 13–12, our lead, I pass to him on the baseline and, full of poise, he coolly throws up a jumper and . . . it swishes in. We win.

He plops down on a nearby couch and blurts, "Now I can put my pimp clothes back on." Everyone laughs. "That's a joke!" he says teasing himself. "An old self resurfacing."

He and I, alone now, walk back toward the front of Paisley Park. After a moment of quiet he's talking music. "There's nobody worth seeing anymore. Sinbad's bringing the Ohio Players back but really there's no one."

"If you could get Sly Stone out here, that'd be something," I offer.

"If he's still with us. I keep getting conflicting reports."

We fall quiet. I feel I'm walking with a buddy. I have two million questions, but I hold back. Now I know that's not how to play the game.

He breaks the lull. "Rhonda plays tennis." Rhonda plays bass in his band. I love tennis. "I was too small to play"—he points back toward the basketball court—"in high school. I like tennis better than that."

Then I say to him, "I thought you were gonna play in heels." I'd heard he sometimes did.

"Oh, no," he says. Then, "Can't play guitar in tennis shoes."

"Why?"

"Sacrilegious."

"I've heard that you do play ball in heels."

With a confident smirk he says, "A *jealous* man told you that story."

Wynton Marsalis Wants to Kick Your Ass

{ *Icon Magazine*, 1999 }

On a bright, slightly breezy midweek afternoon on Manhattan's Upper West Side not long ago, two men, both Black and of similar height, build, and athletic ability—one of them Wynton Learson Marsalis, the other a writer—raced down a not-so-crowded street toward a basketball court, eager to settle a year-old challenge.

"This ass-whippin is gonna be painful," Marsalis said with relish in his city-paced but twang-flavored voice. "Nothing can save you from the ignominious fate of my foot being shoved," he paused, ". . . and with *feeling* . . . into the crack of yo ass." Then he raised his eyebrows and fixed the writer with an impish gaze that said, *I'ma have fun beatin you.*

The verbal jabs continued as they strolled onto the well-kept courts of the Amsterdam Homes, which could be called Marsalis's home court.

"Yo," the writer told Marsalis, remembering their ten-year age difference, "if nothing, my youth will carry me against yo old ass."

"Hey man. I can't jump, I'm slow, I'm a streak shooter, and I cannot go to the right. But," Marsalis added calmly, "no amount of hustle can make up for your lack of technique."

Stepping onto the court in rimless glasses, a neat navy *Late Show with David Letterman* T-shirt, loose but not-quite-baggy navy sweatpants, and black Adidas, he was fully Skayne now, and eagerly strutted toward one free hoop, black and netless. The game began.

They played carefully at first, feeling each other out. The score stayed close and intense until the writer hit a baseline jumper over Marsalis to take a 7–6 lead. Then, a crucial error was made.

Holding the ball at the top of the key, planning a drive, the writer taunted Marsalis. "There's a national audience watching," the writer teased. Marsalis didn't respond. "Hundreds of thousands will know the final score," the writer ribbed. Marsalis remained stoic. The writer dribbled to his right, shot, missed. Marsalis grabbed the rebound and took control of the game. He shot well from the outside, then muscled inside, then diligently followed up his shots for offensive rebounds. 6–7 turned, quickly into 9–7, then point-game, then suddenly, it was over: 12–7 Marsalis.

As they walked back to Marsalis's apartment neither man said much, until Marsalis tilted his head so to see over his glasses, smiled wide with his mouth tight, and fixed the writer with a look that said, *Losing is part of life, son. Take your whipping like a man.* Then, together, they laughed.

Marsalis's approach to basketball is no mere errant riff, it's a blueprint for his approach to jazz and nearly everything he takes seriously in life. He practices seriously and consistently, concentrating on mastering his craft; he strives to know himself, warts and all; and he always maintains a blues-based attitude, which means, in part, accepting loss and tragedy and moving forward.

Following those principles Marsalis, in the last fifteen years, released more than thirty albums, won eight Grammys, and earlier this spring, became the first jazzman to win the Pulitzer Prize. Yet some still question the strength of his playing.

Where, say, Miles Davis, though often technically unremarkable, revolutionized jazz through mountainous intellect and style, even Marsalis's staunchest critics agree that he is a trumpet virtuoso. But, they ask, to what end? Maurice André, widely considered the world's greatest classical trumpeter, called Marsalis, "potentially the greatest trumpeter of all time." But longtime jazz writer Nat Hentoff felt, "There's nothing he can't play, but I don't think he has a voice. I tell you, this guy can do anything on a horn. He can growl and go up high and all that, but I don't hear much soul."

Marsalis grew up first in the small town of Kenner, Louisiana, and later in New Orleans, in what would become the first family of contemporary jazz. Father Ellis, sixty-three, is a pianist and the director of jazz studies at New Orleans University, and mother Dolores doesn't play, but has said, "It was very important for me that they have some aesthetic thing they could express themselves through." Of their sons, four are jazz musicians: firstborn Branford, thirty-seven, a saxophonist who's played with Sting and led the band for *The Tonight Show with Jay Leno*; second son Wynton; fourth child Delfeayo, thirty-two, a producer and trombonist; and the baby, Jason, twenty, a drummer. Third-born Ellis III, thirty-three, works in Baltimore as a computer analyst, and fifth son Mboya, twenty-six, is autistic and lives with his parents.

Supported chiefly by Ellis's piano work, which Wynton has said brought in about thirteen thousand dollars a year, the family, Wynton recalled, was, "extremely lower middle class. Basically poor. But not impoverished. We weren't on food stamps." But for growing musicians there were a wealth of resources. For one, there was New Orleans, the birthplace of jazz, and a seemingly ancient city where seriously soulful music seems to be always floating through the air. "New Orleans is the most African of all the American cities," Branford said. "Living in New Orleans, where music is just fertile and in the culture, is something else."

Mother Marsalis made a mark by engaging her sons intellectually. "At dinner," Branford recalled, "we'd talk about what was goin on in the newspapers, Africa, Vietnam, everything. That had a large bearing on the musicians we are."

And Ellis led by example. "My daddy," Delfeayo said, "was goin on gigs where there'd be two and three people in the audience. That amount of seriousness and that level of responsibility made an impression. We said, 'It must be somethin about this music.'"

At nine Marsalis got serious about playing basketball. "Wynton would go out," Branford recalled, "and shoot fifty free throws a day.

Every day he shot. In the rain, whatever. And when he shot those fifty free throws he was focused on his form, his technique, everything."

Three years later Marsalis heard John Coltrane's "Cousin Mary" and decided he wanted to play trumpet. He attacked the instrument with the same diligence he'd used on basketball. He wrote a schedule: practice before school from six-thirty to seven, after lunch from twelve-thirty to one, at school from two-thirty to three, and after school from six to six-thirty. He followed it for years. "At first I was just thoroughly sad," Marsalis said. "But I knew if you just keep doin it and concentrate and you will get better."

Marsalis studied funk, jazz, and classical and soon was able to dive into all the music New Orleans had to offer. "I loved being in New Orleans," he said, "because I could play with the symphony, a jazz quartet, a funk band, a New Orleans parade. In most other cities I'd never have had all those chances."

At fifteen he entered the New Orleans Center for Creative Arts, but learned more playing with Branford in a funk band called The Creators. "We'd see each other's eyes," Branford said, "and know what the other's thinking. So we were playing some shit technically that was unbelievable. We were the only band in the city that could play those Earth, Wind & Fire horn parts. That closeness was developed on the football field, not in the band. See, what we were to each other is far greater than tootin on a fuckin piece of pipe. That's the shit that made us the musicians that we are."

At seventeen Marsalis won a scholarship to the Julliard School in Manhattan and moved up north but left midway through his sophomore year. By his departure he'd met three men who would have a profound effect on his horn and his mind: Art Blakey, Stanley Crouch, and Albert Murray.

Jazz has a long tradition of mentoring. Most great players spent their early days as sidemen in the bands of geniuses: Louis Armstrong had an apprenticeship in King Oliver's band, Miles Davis was brought along by Charlie Parker and Dizzy Gillespie, and Davis helped John Coltrane blossom. However, by the early 80s, musicians who could and would mentor were in short supply. One of the few was Art Blakey. Often called the greatest jazz drummer of all time, from 1954 until his passing in 1990 Blakey headed a band called Art Blakey and the Jazz Messengers that helped mold numerous talented players—among them saxophonists Jackie McLean and Wayne Shorter, trumpeters Lee Morgan and Freddie Hubbard, and pianist Keith Jarrett—into giants.

Olu Dara is a trumpeter who played with Blakey in the mid-70s, and with Marsalis in the 80s. "Art Blakey didn't say much," Dara recalled. "He just instructed through the way his drums sounded. Man, he had such a commanding sound and effect on you that if you were not a good musician, if you stayed there long enough you'd become a good instrumentalist." At eighteen, Marsalis had decided he needed to be in Blakey's band, so he started going to Blakey's gigs and begging the drummer to let him in band. With growing talent and reputation and Blakey's ability to see promise, it didn't take long—"He took me, sad as I was," Marsalis said—and Marsalis soon found himself reaching a new level of horn playing. But he remained largely unaware of the history of jazz.

That history, difficult to encapsulate in a book, impossible to summarize in a paragraph, begins early in this century in New Orleans, with men like Jelly Roll Morton, Buddy Bolden, and King Oliver. In the 30s, the swing era, Louis Armstrong became the music's first international superstar, with Duke Ellington not far behind. By the 40s, the world center of jazz was New York, where Charlie "Bird" Parker, Dizzy Gillespie, and Thelonious Monk were architecting a strain of jazz called bebop while a young trumpeter named Miles Davis was hanging around. During the 50s and 60s a new crop of players, including saxophonists John Coltrane and Ornette Coleman, began driving the music in directions that were new, deeply spiritual, and often aggressively avant-garde. In the 70s, following the lead of Davis, fusion ruled.

About the same time he began playing with Blakey, former jazz drummer and influential jazz critic Stanley Crouch heard Marsalis in a jazz club one night and started talking to him after the set. The two hit it off immediately and became fast friends. Crouch invited Marsalis home for dinner and began teaching him jazz history.

"When I first met him," Crouch recalled, "he seemed to be interested only in Coltrane and Miles Davis and Wayne Shorter. And once he started really listening to Louis Armstrong and Thelonious Monk and Duke Ellington, then his perspective broadened. He realized that one of the things that distinguishes music is the thoroughness of design. All art, finally, is about design, and as a player and a composer Wynton's work reflects that a great deal."

In time Crouch introduced Marsalis to Albert Murray, a novelist, essayist, and polymath who got Marsalis reading novelists Andre Malraux and Thomas Mann as well as the *Odyssey*, the *Iliad*, and Murray's own classic jazz treatise, *Stomping the Blues*. The knowledge gave Marsalis, "a richer take on life," Murray said. "It means that his intellectual chords are gonna be thicker and richer. See, art is an ongoing dialogue with the form. So the more you know about how those before you said it and did it, the more prepared you are to find a way to say something about what impinges upon you."

In 1982 the twenty-one-year-old Marsalis signed to Columbia Records for twenty-five thousand dollars and released a jazz album called *Wynton Marsalis*. "It wasn't really that good," according to Marsalis. "It started selling because it was different from everything else that was out. But I was trying to play and was serious about it. The one thing I knew was I wanted to play and that's what's on that album. And that's all that's on it. Somebody *wanting* to play."

The following year Marsalis recorded a classical album of Haydn, Hummel, and Leopold Mozart trumpet concertos. In 1984 Marsalis performed both jazz and classical music on the Grammy telecast, then won Grammys for Best Jazz Soloist and Best Classical Soloist With Orchestra, becoming the only person in Grammy history to win in both categories in the same year. International fame was cemented. "I think the reason he became so famous," said Ted Panken, who writes about jazz and broadcasts on WKCR, "was his ability to satisfy so many camps. He played classical music with such mastery it gave a high-art validation to everything else he did and made him socially acceptable to white high culture and Black bourgeoisie. He became someone whose record you might commonly have in your record collection without necessarily having a sense of who he was."

Marsalis began recording constantly and touring incessantly—
between one hundred and two hundred nights a year and soon began
earning in the mid to high six figures annually. (Recently he said, "I
make way more money than I ever thought I would make. Way more.")
He also started collecting numerous awards: Down Beat's Jazz Musician of
the Year, the Netherlands Edison Award, and France's Grand Prix du
Disque, but, friends say, he was unimpressed. "For someone who's done
so much," Crouch said, "he's extremely unimpressed with himself. He's
got more of a Joe Frazier conception, rather than Muhammad Ali. Joe
Frazier wasn't out here talkin about I'm the greatest. Joe Frazier was
more involved in putting his foot in your ass."

He also began working with Lincoln Center, the home of New
York City Ballet, the New York Philharmonic Orchestra, and other fine
arts institutions to establish jazz as part of their cultural landscape. Since
1959 various groups had tried to get Lincoln Center to accept jazz, but
Marsalis was able to change their minds. "He stood in front of our
board," said Rob Gibson, executive director of jazz at Lincoln Center,
"and said, 'I play jazz and I play classical music and I love playin both of
'em. But playing jazz is much harder.' Their vibe had been, basically,
fuck jazz. But that put something on their minds." In 1987 Marsalis became the artistic director of Lincoln Center's classical jazz festival. Nine
years later, Jazz at Lincoln Center became the first new full constituent in
twenty-five years.

By the mid-80s, Marsalis had begun his formal relationship with
Lincoln Center. Fame, kudos, money, and power had arrived quickly. But
they brought along their own problems. "Being rich can destroy you,"
Murray said. "The real problem with Wynton is success. The temptation
of being a millionaire, don't you see what that means? If everything you
touch is gonna turn to gold and be successful, then are you really gonna
be a great musician or are you gonna bullshit? Contending with those
temptations is hard."

Marsalis began using his clout to help jazz and, in his eyes, society
at large. "What he has," said Marcus Roberts, a pianist who has often
played with Marsalis and is now a close friend, "is an earned aristocratic
position. That's when you see yourself as the king, and you do the work,

and then, you take that position and put yourself at the *service* of a regular person. So that's what makes him a special cat. He's not looking to be handed something. He's takin the stuff he's getting and he's puttin it back to the people by turning people on to the grandeur of what jazz music can bring to you."

As far back as his days in Kenner, Louisiana, Marsalis was able to deal with racism and other life pressures, he said, because of jazz. "You don't really know how to process information when you're young so a lot of times you turn to anger. I was lucky to have jazz music cuz that's an art form I can have a constant dialogue with and it will constantly heal me and inform me and give me a greater understanding because I'm dealin with the mind of Coltrane or Monk or Duke Ellington and strivin for a higher level. But if you don't have that, let's say you just listen to the radio every day, man, that stuff—no one is tryin to really heal with that, they tryin to make some money."

Feeling most of modern popular music and culture akin to slavery or "some general sickness that's imposed on the people," he set out to introduce a younger generation to jazz. Marsalis began working feverishly to demystify jazz, explaining its language and traditions, often talking directly to younger audiences, by speaking constantly in high schools and grade schools, holding young people's concerts at Lincoln Center, and in 1995 filming a series of shows for PBS called *Marsalis on Music,* and releasing a companion book. "He's a great communicator," said Ted Panken. "I've listened to him talk about Monk and Jelly Roll Morton to eight- and ten-year-olds and he can speak to them without condescension, make some extremely cogent musical points, and let them have a good time."

He also worked with young players, actively following their musical education, giving advice over the phone, and inviting them to his house for lessons. A teenager need not know Marsalis or have any particular credential in order to get his attention. Backstage at Lincoln Center, after the premiere of his most recent epic, *Blood on the Fields,* in a small reception area crowded with well-wishers, a reed-thin teenage ragamuffin of a boy with thick glasses pushed through a crowd of admirers and up to Marsalis. He looked away while he shook Marsalis's hand, then revealed that he too was a trumpeter. Marsalis began peppering him with questions about playing the horn, then asked, "You bring your trumpet?" The boy hadn't. Marsalis pulled out his own horn, a specially made Monette worth somewhere in the mid five figures. It is gold-plated brass with numerous designs carved into it: stars, a tree, a bull with a "2" by the legs, a tambourine with wings, branches, a trumpeter, a piano, notes, chestnuts, and on one of the valves, the words "Prof. Marsalis."

The boy began blowing through the horn and Marsalis stopped him. He began speaking to the wispy blond boy with a patience and sweetness reminiscent of Mean Joe Greene's famous Coca-Cola commercial. "Try to get the biggest sound with the least volume on one note and hold it for sixty seconds," he said. The boy nodded quickly. "It's very hard. It takes a lot of concentration. And it's very boring. But if you do it every morning for three years you'll be the best trumpet player. It'll take you a year to get it, but you'll get it."

The boy tried a few times, but failed to go longer than twenty seconds on one note. Marsalis coached him until about fifteen minutes passed, then said good-bye. The boy, elated and shaking, turned to go, and as he walked out of the room, Marsalis called out encouragingly, "Next time, bring your horn."

In the jazz world Marsalis is famous and powerful, but that hardly halts debates about his playing. Critic Gary Giddins said, "I don't think he's a particularly significant jazz trumpeter anymore. His sound has gotten colder and more mannered, somewhat showy and empty."

Jazz critic and essayist Greg Tate, considering Marsalis within the history of jazz, said, "He's a bad motherfucker, but it's like bein a bad figurine maker in the face of the Sphinx. You can be bad, but these other guys made a two-hundred-foot-tall stone figurine out the side of a mountain and we still ain't figured out how they did it."

It can be difficult to find players who will criticize Marsalis. "There are so many major musicians," Giddins said, "who abhor his playing and they wouldn't dare say it because he has the power to get them work. There's the sense that this guy is gonna be around for a long time and he's running the biggest cultural shopping mall around and people don't want to be enemies."

Drummer Max Roach, who is, like Art Blakey, often called the best jazz drummer ever, said diplomatically, if a bit cryptically, "If I nail Wynton to the cross in any kind of way, or if you nail him to the cross, we really nailin ourselves to the cross. Just say, he's a bad motherfucker."

Supporters say those who question Marsalis's playing haven't really listened. "I had an argument with a friend who said, I hate Wynton," said Peter Watrous. "I said, 'Name me one of his records,' and he couldn't. Wynton is so big people feel free to pass judgment without knowing his music. But really, it doesn't matter what anyone says. It's moot now. He's entered the Madonna league. You can say she can't sing, it doesn't matter. Regardless of the bitching and moaning he has entered history and shaped the future."

Marsalis himself is nonplussed by critics because he is his own harshest critic. Once, in an interview with Crouch published in *Down Beat*, Marsalis said, "Were I to play the level of horn I aspire to, I don't think I would be giving interviews: I would be making all my statements from the bandstand. But at this point, words allow me more precision and clarity." That was ten years ago. He's still doing interviews and still struggling to get the clarity of a human voice through his horn.

"I need to have a more vocal style," he said recently. "I wanna play more ideas and more human things. It's like you might think somethin and a sound might come into your voice and you don't know that I can tell that you're thinkin that and then you start to suspect that I can tell and you start tryin to change your voice. You know what I mean? To be able to do that on your horn. I can't even describe it in words. I can hear it in my mind. That's what I would like."

Marsalis is tough on himself because, he said, "the accuracy of your assessment of yourself, a lot of times, will determine your success. You can't be too hard on yourself and you can't be too easy. You have to be accurate."

One night after a performance at Lincoln Center, Marsalis walked into an empty home. The tastefully decorated twenty-ninth-floor apartment, a horn's throw from Lincoln Center, has a spectacular view of the river and the west side of Manhattan. The outer rooms are filled with images of Armstrong and Ellington and art by Romare Bearden; the bedroom is decorated with photos of Art Blakey and of unmarried Marsalis's sons Wynton, Jr., nine, Simeon, seven, and Jasper, one, as well as several large detailed drawings of trains. Moving through the living room, Marsalis passed a table on which sat Ellington's autobiography *Music Is My Mistress*, open to page 286. Marsalis glanced at the page and said with a laugh, "Duke's a trip, ain't he?"

On page 286 Ellington, who is, in the opinion of nearly all jazz aficianados, including Marsalis, the greatest composer in the history of jazz, discussed his brush with the Pulitzer Prize committee. In 1965 the music committee recommended Ellington for a special Pulitzer, but the full committee rejected the suggestion. In *Mistress* Ellington related his elegant first reaction: "Fate is being very kind to me; Fate doesn't want me to be too famous too young." He was then sixty-six years young. The Ellington snub highlights the Pulitzer committee's longtime antijazz bias—Max Roach said, "Miles, Dizzy, Roy Eldridge, Duke Ellington, they all deserved Pulitzers. Gimmie a break." It questions the value of Marsalis's Pulitzer for *Blood on the Fields*. It questions whether the award says less about Marsalis's skill as a composer and more about the growing respect for jazz as a fine art form, and if the committee is even able to evaluate jazz. (Thirty-two years later Ellington still hasn't been offered a Pulitzer.) However, Marsalis's ability to accept the prize's tainted history and laugh confirms his blues-based attitude toward life, his ability to accept life's ironies, and move forward. "In life you got to be grateful for what come your way," he said. "Even the fucked-up shit. Even that, man."

Marsalis walked into the kitchen, loosened the tie of his tuxedo and microwaved a cup of tea. The show had been long and challenging, but Marsalis was filled with energy and he toyed with the idea of running downtown and sitting in with another musician. A writer asked about artistic excellence and Marsalis began talking about one of his favorite subjects: shedding, or woodshedding, jazz slang for practicing.

"One thing about excellence," he began, "it's an exclusive club.

And it's only those who really want to pay dues to the shit. My daddy told me when I was a boy, 'The only way you can be different from other people is to do some shit they don't wanna do.' "

"Like what?"

"Get up at six in the morning and shed for an hour. Then go work. Then stay up all night dealing with your horn. Do that every day for six or seven years. Don't miss no days. That's some shit that they don't want to do. See, everybody wanna hangout, get some girls, get high, be considered to be a nice guy, have they ass kissed, make some money. But guys don't wanna have to shed. None of us wanna do it. I don't wanna do it."

"You still don't want to do it?"

"Fuck no, I don't wanna do it. Well, now I wanna do it more."

"More than when you were a boy."

"When I was a boy I didn't want to do it. Thirteen, fourteen, fifteen, sixteen, all them years when I was just sheddin my ass off every day I didn't feel like doin it. At all. But I really realized that if you practice you could get better. By the time I was eighteen, nineteen, I was different from a lot of people who played my instrument in general, because I did that work. And that's what the difference was about—the work."

The doorbell rang. It was just after one a.m. Marsalis went to the door and found a saxophonist and a trombonist from his band with girlfriends on one arm and instruments on the other. After a little talk everyone went into the living room, Marsalis sat at his grand piano, and they started playing. Soon a few more people came in and then a few more players. By three the place was crammed with musicians playing a whole lot of saxophone and trumpet and trombone over the rhythms of the three men on congos, led by Marsalis, swinging on the piano with his mouth closed tight, his eyelids low, his head bouncing along with the three or four impeccably dressed couples cutting the rug, and forty or so others leaning on the wall tapping their toes, or in the kitchen sipping hot New Orleans–style gumbo, or on the couches sitting back as seriously soulful music floated through the air.

A short time before Marsalis had been awarded the Pulitzer Prize for *Blood on the Fields*, his piece about slavery and survival, and when the music stopped, he stood up from the piano, his crisp white shirt open, and spoke.

"Awards and shit . . ." he said and shook his head disdainfully.

Someone in the back called out, "Man, just accept the damn award, man!"

"*Swing* and *play*, goddamn!" he said loudly, mostly, it seemed, to himself. "That's all we're dealing with: *swinging*!"

Snifters were passed out, the musicians were poured a bit of cognac, and one by one, they stood and toasted Marsalis. After the last player finished, Stanley Crouch cleared his throat. "On the plantation in 1850, when everybody said, 'You can't get away,' there were a few people who said, 'I'm leaving. I'm getting out of this.' That's what we doin now. There's a plantation in every era and there's a few people who say, 'I'm not stayin.' That's what everybody in this room is about: *I'm not stayin*. And believe me, when it's over, they gon know we were here." With that, everyone raised a glass and cheered.

A short time later, as a new crop of musicians grooved in the living room for a new group of dancing couples, Marsalis stood in the kitchen with a cup of tea and pondered his next move. "I really don't know what I'm gonna do," he said. "I'm gonna do something, though. I gotta do something to express all this gratitude. Man, you start sittin around, then the ideas stop comin to you. When you're workin the spirit understands that you are serious and that you are preparing yourself to receive that information. Stay in the state of preparedness. Coltrane said that. You got to stay in the state of preparedness all the time."

Just Jen

{ Jennifer Capriati, unpublished, 2002 }

For years women's tennis seemed like the greatest sports show on earth, with all the on-court fireworks, dazzling iconography, and backstage drama that P. T. Barnum himself would insist upon. We had the brilliance of Hingis, the power of Davenport, the rapid ascendence of Venus and Serena, the blondness of Kournikova, and a stew of manic, self-embarassing fathers, catfights, rivalries, short skirts—an international soap opera dancing around one of the greatest periods in the history of women's tennis. In the late 90s the women's tour surged past the men's in popularity and drama, strong-arming the Association of Tennis Professionals into considering a new alliance with the Women's Tennis Association and forcing the U.S. Open to put the women's final on prime-time television.

Now, those days seem long ago. In 2002 the sisters clogged the finals of the French, Wimbledon, and the U.S. Open, and suddenly it seemed that beyond their breathtaking play the tour was veering toward boring. "The dominance of the Williams sisters is not a problem for women's tennis, not yet," says S. L. Price, who covers tennis for *Sports Illustrated*. "But this year it will begin to be. There's no doubt that tennis, men's and women's, is most interesting when there's at least three intriguing stars capable of winning at a time. People have gotten tired of the Williams story. It's not hot anymore. Selling the tour this year will be a problem for the first time in a long time. People will take a fresh look at the tour and see that it's full of holes."

The world's number-three player, Jennifer Capriati, has lost to the Williamses ten consecutive times, making her an alarmingly distant number three. As little as two years ago no one outside the Capriati family thought she could break the top twenty. But now she's the only player in the world with strength and speed equal to them, the only player who seems unintimidated by them, and the only player most close observers believe can shove at least one of them off of the top of the hill. "Jennifer has what it takes if she doesn't grow discouraged by the losses," says Mary Carillo, commentator and former player. "She's like Agassi trying to beat Pete. Sampras, like the sisters, has all the natural God-kissed talent and great desire. Players like Andre and Jennifer, very talented in their own ways, have to be incredibly fit mentally, physically, and emotionally to take on that big a challenge."

Thus, in 2003, the player the game most needs to succeed is Jennifer Capriati. "The pro game will move on in positive ways without any one or two of these characters," says Pam Shriver, the great player who's now a Hall of Famer. "But, is it a more balanced, fun tour if Capriati's playing well and beating the Williams sisters every once in a while? Sure." For Capriati to fail to break up another year of all-sisters finals could mean the entire women's tour would suffer. "Capriati is under tremendous pressure," says Bud Collins, the legendary tennis writer. "She appears to be the only one able to counter Venus and Serena, but they're rising and she's not."

Capriati hears the critics saying the game is losing steam and feels the direct reflection on her. "I don't want people saying the game is boring!" she says defiantly. "I'm part of this game. You're talking about me! You don't understand what we put in, how hard we work. Maybe there's that extra pressure to win and not have them [the Williamses] win everything because otherwise everyone will think it's boring and women's tennis is going down . . . That's a lot of pressure for one person to hold."

She stops a moment. "I'm happy that Lindsay's back [from knee surgery]. Martina. I want these girls to get their shit together just to make it more exciting. I'm tired of hearing everyone saying it's boring." But who in the world can stop that talk but her?

Jennifer Capriati is the Drew Barrymore of tennis. A child star who grew up in public, took a sabbatical while her generation was still in high school, did drugs, got in trouble (not necessarily the same thing), returned to tennis but struggled, but stuck with it, and eventually reached prominence. In 1990, at thirteen years and eleven months old, Capriati became a professional tennis player, the latest in a long line of phenomenally good and frighteningly young girls, expected to be the best of them ever. She finished her first pro tournament in the finals and finished her first full year on tour ranked eighth in the world. From the outside it seemed her spot in the Hall of Fame was reserved. But the canker was already in the rose. "Everything kinda turned out like a fairy tale for a while," says Denise Capriati, her mother. "But it didn't take long before you realized that it was gonna be grueling. It's cutthroat, the jealousy, the sharks. Nobody really warns you about that part of it." Capriati will be twenty-seven years old on March 29. She has won three Grand Slam titles and will almost certainly end up in the Tennis Hall of Fame, but the thirteen years since her debut have unfolded like great Greek drama, or, to be culturally consistent, epic Italian opera.

Capriati lives in Tampa, Florida, on the Saddlebrook Resort, a lush, sprawling gated community and vacation resort with golf courses, tennis courts, restaurants, a spa, and streets like Lady Bug Lane. She lives in a modest-size, one-level ranch-style home along with her father, Stefano, a tanned, stout, former movie stuntman and pro soccer player who lived in Italy until his twenties. Her mother, a former stewardess, lives in West Palm Beach. They divorced in 1995. In front of Capriati's house is a green Range Rover, a silver Mercedes sedan, a white golf cart, and a red Ferrari. "I don't drive it," she says of the Ferrari, a gift from Fila. "I just enjoy looking at it."

You would expect after years of celebrity, years in which Capriati often bristled at her portrayal in the media, that she would become a private, guarded person. Word around the tennis-writer campfire is that Capriati is terrified of journalists. But when a journalist asked to see her home she walked away to ask her father and he—famously protective and still hurt by post–U.S. Open stories saying she was finished—exploded in a rage, yelling at her in his thick Italian accent that journalists are not to be trusted. She held her ground and after a moment he relented.

Over the past decade and a half her life has been filled with the chaos of corporate attention, the mountain-peak highs of youthful success, and the gutter lows of a child struggling to be a child while celebrity makes that all but impossible. So, it's no surprise her bedroom is all about serenity. There's a bright white bedspread, fresh white tulips in a vase in the corner, and a large, flat-screen television on the wall across from the bed positioned perfectly for watching under the covers. In her plush but minimalist room, the hi-tech flat television is less postmodern than delicate. "It's one of my few splurges," she says. To the left of the television is one of the fluffy kangaroo dolls that represent the Australian Open. Directly above the television, alone on its own little shelf, is her trophy for winning the 2001 Australian Open, her first Grand Slam title, the day that announced her comeback was complete. "Of course, this one means the most," she says. (The trophy is maybe a foot and a half tall, about a quarter of the size of the trophy she smooched for the cameras. If you've ever won any amateur tennis trophy your trophy is probably taller than the take-home prize from a Grand Slam.)

Capriati says she won that Australian (and the one after it) because the Australian is her favorite tournament of the year, not the other way around. In this way, her tennis has always flowered or floundered based on her emotions. "You gotta be feeling happy off the court to do well on the court," she says. "It all ties in together. Some people say they can totally separate what's going on personally from what's going on on the court. I have a hard time doing that. Usually what's bothering me outside the court I'll be taking out on the court. If I'm having boyfriend troubles, whatever."

Later, in her Mercedes, as she cruised slowly through Saddlebrook, she shuffled through the CDs in her system. She found Tupac, Outkast, Jay-Z Unplugged, and then, from the speakers poured Enrique Iglesias and his song "Hero." Capriati cringed. "I like that song," she said, sheepishly. "He has a pretty good voice." He also has a video for the song in which he canoodles with his girlfriend, at press time, Anna Kournikova. According to all sources, Kournikova resentment runs high in the WTA locker room.

"Some players like to think they're celebs," she said later. "They like the limelight."

You mean Anna?

"I'm not sayin any names."

When you saw the Enrique video did you throw up?

"Yeah."

She had dinner at a sports-bar sort of restaurant a mile from her home. She was in a Fila jacket, loose blue jeans, and Fila flip-flops, with her reddish-brown hair hanging long and a touch of makeup on her face. She had a filet mignon, a heaping salad, a club soda, and a big bowl of berries. (Dinner for her is often some sort of meat with a vegetable. Breakfast is commonly eggs and oatmeal, with a Cobb salad for lunch and a protein shake or energy bar as a snack. She eats little processed food, no sugar products, no sugars, preferring whole foods and natural proteins.) There were nine football games on nine TVs throughout the room, but Capriati asked the waitress to change the channel on a nearby set to the Emmys.

Have you ever watched the Emmys before?

"No," she says. "I never cared about it before. It's all about TV, right?"

When Capriati was in the crib her father gave her a racket. At three she began hitting balls. "[Her father] definitely had it in his mind that he wanted to groom her to be a tennis player," said Denise Capriati. (Stefano politely refused an interview request.) When she was five Stefano went to Jimmy Evert, the legendary coach and father of Chris Evert, and asked him to coach her. Evert snubbed the child, calling himself too busy. Then he hit a few balls with her and suddenly found the time. She was just happy to be on the court. "When I was in the juniors I was never aware of all those things people were saying," she says. "You're gonna be the next Chris Evert. I was just a happy-go-lucky kid."

Little Jen Capriati was a Girl Scout (she was in Brownies), played with dolls, played soccer, loved school, and practiced her tennis every day. When she was six she played her first tournament. "She was so tiny she didn't know how to keep score," Denise Capriati recalled. "After the match she said to the umpire, 'Who won?' He said, 'You did.' And she smiled and it was really cute. And then she played the second match and it was a real long match, the same day, to the number-one seed, and when it was over and she said to the umpire, 'Who won?' The other girl did. And she cried. It was very cute." Just seven years later, in March of 1990, she played her first professional tournament.

"By the time she was ten or eleven everyone had heard about this kid," Pam Shriver said. "When she made her debut it was incredible. It was a regular tour event and it had the media presence of a major. That began the start of her feeling a great deal of pressure. Nobody was ever in Capriati's shoes. The level of attention she got at twelve, thirteen, fourteen years of age was unique. Sponsors, agents, media, tour—it was coming from all angles."

In 1991, at fourteen, she had a wonderful year, beating Seles, Gabriella Sabatini, and, in the quarterfinals of Wimbledon, Martina Navratilova. She finished the year ranked number six. She got millions for endorsing a truckload of stuff including Rolex and Oil of Olay. No one would've believed that would be her best ranking until 2001. "At first she enjoyed the whole thing—the playing and the winning and the attention," said Mary Carillo. "By the second year she was a professional prodigy, which changes everything. She was a kid living as a grownup. I don't think that's what she'd signed up for, and it broke her down."

Denise Capriati often felt she and her family had gotten more than they'd bargained for. "Once you're in it it's really hard to go back," she said. "You want to slow down, but you have commitments and people coming at you left and right and money in your face that's very hard to turn down and it's very hard to maintain the balance of it all. I wanted her to stop because maybe I felt in my heart, I noticed that she wasn't as happy as she used to be. She wasn't enjoying it. She was changing. The desire wasn't there. The spark was gone."

In 1993, at sixteen, in the midst of a rough year on the court, Capriati lost in the first round of the U.S. Open, and quit tennis. The years from eighteen to twenty she calls "That Bad Time." "She was just tryin to find out what she really wanted in her own way," Denise Capriati says. "She was doing her own thing and just struggling, trying to figure out life, and who she was, and what she really wanted to do, and if she had a passion or a spark left to do it." According to her mother, Capriati had lost part of her childhood. "[She] wasn't able to live a normal life and lost whatever it is within, the spark, the spirit of being a child. And no one should lose that. But it happened and it's very hard to get that back." She moved away from her parents, got a nose ring, took SAT prep classes, was cited for stealing a cheap ring at an outdoor mall and again a few months later for possessing a bag of marijuana. She considered suicide. She did time in court-ordered drug rehab. Some think the pressure of being the teenage family breadwinner overwhelmed her. Many think, ultimately, she just wanted to be a child. "Jennifer may be more normal than we give her credit for," Pam Shriver said. But most teenagers aren't famous. Where Capriati had leveraged fame to sign multimillion-dollar endorsement deals before she turned pro, now, when she tried to be a regular teenager and test limits, fame taxed her deeply, putting her mug shot on the evening news nationwide. "People don't know the real truth of why things happened," Capriati said. "Maybe someday I will tell the story of my life or whatever, if it helps someone, if it helps people in a good way. You know, about whatever happened that time . . . I didn't love myself and I didn't feel loved by anyone else . . . How can you have confidence if you aren't even comfortable in your own skin?"

During her three years away from the game she didn't consider herself retired. "I never really saw myself as being out. I thought of it as taking a break. It's not like I ever thought I'd never want to play tennis again, that was it, career's over. I just wanted a break. It ended up being kinda a long break, but I think deep down I knew I was gonna come back."

The thing that pushed her back was her reputation's nosedive. "I was just a has-been. I hated that word 'has-been' and I said, 'Oh my God, this is gonna bother me for the rest of my life having to hear that. Burnout. What a waste.' That motivated me. I used all the negative comments to fuel me. They just made me angry and maybe if they didn't say all that maybe I wouldn't be here right now. Keep saying I can't do something, keep saying there's a gap, because it's gonna motivate me and fuel me to go out and change that and prove them wrong."

She rejoined the tour in 1997, but remained unhappy. "I was still a mess inside," Capriati says. While the big five struggled for supremacy, Capriati just struggled, ranked sixty-sixth in 1997 and 101st in 1998. "I didn't like myself," Capriati said. "I thought everything was my fault and I was such a bad person and that's why my life all went to shit and that's why that all happened and I screwed up, I was a loser, blah, blah, blah. And for a long time I couldn't look at myself. I was just constantly living in this disappointment. Are you gonna be a disappointment? Are you not gonna be a disappointment? You just can't take it personally. I'm a loser so, yeah, I'm a loser. That's ridiculous. It's just a game, just as simple as that."

She began working with a trainer, sweating in the gym and in the pool and on the track, losing weight and gaining muscle. Davenport famously said, "She walked into the locker room and it was like, uh, Jennifer, is that you?" She began dating Xavier Malisse, a hot-looking, low-ranked player from Belgium. And she began to see herself with new eyes. "Slowly, I started to say it's not just about me playing tennis. That's not why my family loves me. That bad time when I wasn't playing, my family was still there, my friends were still there. It doesn't matter to them if I play tennis or not. They love me for who I am."

That realization, and her new body, and leaving Malisse in late 2000, freed Capriati to play the best tennis of her life. She shocked the world winning the Australian in January 2001, and the French a few months later. That year she was the only woman to reach the semifinals of all four Grand Slams. On October 15 she became number one in the world.

The Emmys roll on, handing out awards just for TV, and her bias toward one actor becomes clear. "Matthew's always on, always funny," she blurts out. "Not just like Chandler, but . . ." Once she gets started she brings Friends star Matthew Perry up quite a bit. He was her guest at numerous tournaments last year. If he's not her boyfriend, he's a good friend who's on her mind quite a bit. "Matthew approves," she says of her Amex commercial in which she stuffs an orange under her tennis dress like it's a tennis ball. "He kept saying, gimme the script, I'll make it more funny. I was like, um, maybe the next one."

The tennis grapevine says they're dating, her flushed cheeks while she talks about him says they're dating, but she won't admit to being more than (sorry) friends. "There really is nothing to say," she says. "I swear. Who knows. Maybe someday, there could be, or potential, I don't know. Just, right now, we're just friends more than anything. Just getting to know each other on that level and things get complicated if you get romantically . . ." For now she's taking it slow. "I wish I hadn't had all these bad relationships. That's made me a little, like, put my guard up. You know, your self-esteem says, what's wrong with you? Why am I having these really bad relationships? Why can't I find a nice guy? If there are a million guys who'd like to go out with me where are they?"

At ten o'clock on Monday morning, as millions are reporting for work, Capriati gets in her silver Mercedes, drives ten miles an hour for about five minutes, pulls up to Court 10-L, does a light jog, and begins hitting tennis balls. Most days, when she's in training mode, she hits for two hours in the morning, eats, naps, hits for two hours in the afternoon, then does sixty to ninety minutes with her trainer. This morning she takes the court across from two men at once. Jimmy Brown is one of her coaches. He was in the world's top one hundred for nine years and retired ten years ago. Ricardo Gonzalez is a hungry, nationally ranked eighteen-and-under. They are among the best male players in the world not currently on the tour. They are clay pigeons for Capriati.

Her shots fly like low-slung comets. She meets each ball waist high, sends it over the net by a few inches, and still, it lands deep every time. She doesn't use a lot of topspin, so her shots don't make much of a parabola, they're more like line drives. "Everyone that I hit with says, Man, your balls are so hard to return. I'm like, Why? They say, Your balls, they don't come up. They just, like, skid near the ground. They get really low. They don't sit up at all. And it's like oh, OK. I wish I could hit against myself to see."

She finds her ability a little miraculous. "You just hit it and it just goes where you want it to go," she says. "Sometimes it doesn't, but most of the time it does. And you know it's gonna go there. Sometimes I don't know how I do it. Like, OK, thanks God." Brown has a more scientific explanation. "She has perfect timing. The body and racket work together seamlessly so she can get her hips into her shots. And she's strong. But small guys can get power from great timing. Thing is, she's always attacking the ball. You can tell a player to do that, but if they don't have great hand-eye coordination, can't do it. With Jen there's no wasted motion."

"She's one of the greatest ball strikers ever," says Pam Shriver. "She's just got an incredible gift to pound the ball with control. I love watching her play."

At noon, finished toying with Brown and Gonzalez, she lets me get on the court.

Her shots are indeed low, hovering somewhere around your knees, making you feel you need not a racket but a shovel to dig them out of the ground. Her on-court rhythm is incredibly fast: she's so quick and efficient to the ball that no matter where you hit it, a second after you follow through it's coming back at you, as if she were a ball machine gone wacky. There's no time to think about where you might hit it. You just react as you would in a fistfight. After you make contact with a few of her shots, and it feels like someone's pushing against the face of your racket as you swing through, then you realize your right forearm is sore and swelling. The whole incident takes on the feel of intense aerobics mixed with a back-alley mugging and you're just deflecting and defending and, eventually, after eight or nine minutes, your arm starts to throb and your lungs start to shriek and each new shot racing at you is like a punch to the chest and you feel her inner bully.

In 2003 the tennis world will be watching to see if that bully comes out. We want to know: Is there a moat separating the Williamses from the world or separating the Williamses and Capriati from the world? Capriati's supporters are quick to point out that all of Capriati's six recent losses to Serena have been extremely close matches and many times she led late in the third set. After a tough loss in L.A. at the end of the 2002 season Denise Capriati said, "Jen had her. She did everything but win. But Serena's balls kept falling over, and she came up with a couple big serves, and . . ."

Brown thinks that the consistently close losses means the only difference between them is mental. "She had Serena the last three times they played," he said. "I don't think she has to do anything different. She just has to believe it, and one win can do that."

Capriati thinks she does need to make changes to surmount the sisters, may need a new coach. She recently hired a new trainer and, in November, had laser surgery on her eyes to improve her vision. "Next year she'll be seeing a lot better," Denise Capriati said. "For sure it'll make a difference on the court." Capriati admits the sisters are a challenge, but she refuses to submit, or even to admit that they are currently dominating the tour. "Steffi dominated," she said. "Martina Navratilova dominated. I don't think they've quite established that they're dominating yet. And, besides," she said defiantly, "nobody dominates me. I'm not gonna be dominated by anybody." Many are watching for signs of Capriati becoming discouraged. Her mother says her resolve is only deepening. "She's determined to make that streak change," Denise Capriati said. "[After she lost in L.A.] she said, 'This is the last time I'm losing to her.' She just made up her mind and said, 'I'm not losin to her anymore.' "

7. Microphone Fiend

"Crack Is Responsible for Hiphop"

{ Ahmir Thompson, aka ?uestlove,

The Believer, 2003 }

If hiphop were like high school (and on too many days it is just like high school), it would be a wild public high school with ice detectors: if you're not wearing any you can't get in. Like most high schools, the most popular kids would be the toughest kids and the richest kids, the ones who go to class bling-blinging or don't go at all. But every high school has its nerd element, the kids looking to actually learn something, the kids so unashamed to be smart they sneak into the library on weekends. The Roots are not nerds. Ever since De La Soul Is Dead, hiphop's so-called alternative groups (which means they're not exalting the world and the values of the ghetto) have been making it clear that just cuz they're smart doesn't mean you can kick their ass. But the Roots have carried on the legacy of De La Soul and A Tribe Called Quest by making hiphop that's artful, unconcerned with alpha-male machismo, and unafraid to show its intellectual side. They are so important to the overall well-being of hiphop, if they did not exist we would have to invent them.

The Roots began in 1987, as a quartet called the Square Roots. For three years the art school students played on street corners in Philadelphia to build their skills. In six years they've released six albums, two of which are classics—their major-label debut *Do You Want More?!!!??!* and their latest, *Phrenology*. Their leader, in front of and behind the camera, has always been Ahmir Thompson, aka ?uestlove or Questo, the widely loved, big-afroed musical dynamo who owns every episode of *Soul Train* and thousands of videos of the legends of soul in performance (these are the people he calls the Yodas). He's worked on some of the greatest albums in modern music, including D'Angelo's landmark *Voodoo* and Erykah Badu's *Mama's Gun*.

Our interview took place on a Tuesday, between eleven-thirty a.m. and two p.m., in his room at the Paramount Hotel in Manhattan. He wore a yellow Muhammad Ali T-shirt and a red, black, and green wristband. His tall, thin sister sat nearby. As we spoke his various phones rang repeatedly: his tour manager asking when he'd be done and ready for the next appointment, the hotel asking what time he'd be checking out. At least four times he told the hotel he'd be down in five minutes while rolling his eyes, then went on with the interview.

I. "It's blasphemy to say this, but crack is responsible for hiphop."

So you have a theory that Black people make better music when Republicans are in office. Explain the theory and how it's playing out now, in the midst of this regime, I mean, administration.

My theory is that nine times out of ten, if there's a depression, more a social depression than anything, it brings out the best art in Black people. The best example is Reagan and Bush gave us the best years of hiphop. I think had Carter and then Mondale won, or if Jesse were president from '84 to '88, hiphop wouldn't have been the same. Hiphop wouldn't have existed. I think you would have more Black Tom Waits. Marsalis would be goin double platinum. There would be more Black Joni Mitchells. [Gets impish grin.] The Roots would sell ten million.

You think that if the Democrats are running America in the 80s, instead of Reagan and Bush, then hiphop is not invented.

Probably, but it would depend on who was replacing them. I don't know if Gary Hart really had a special place in Black people's hearts.

But hiphop was already being built as early as 1972 and some even say '69.

As a result of Nixon. But you have to understand, it's not just him being there, but what was allowed to go on. I really doubt that if Jesse Jackson had become president in 1984 he would've let the crack epidemic flood in, Niagara Falls–esque, in the ghettoes. It's such blasphemy to say this but crack is responsible for the hiphop movement. It's a direct result. The politically correct way of saying it is that Reagan's neglect of the inner city is responsible for hiphop. Hiphop is created thanks to the conditions that crack set: easy money but a lot of work, the violence involved, the stories it produced—crack helped birth hiphop. Now, I'm part conspiracy theorist because you can't develop something that dangerous and it not be planned. I don't think crack happened by accident.

Don't be PC. Spit it out. You're saying the government pushed crack on us, those of us in the inner cities in New York, L.A., Detroit, D.C., etc.

Yes. And as a result created the lifestyle in which the wordsmiths and the turntablists and the great African tradition created hiphop.

But when you say crack is partly responsible for hiphop, what exactly are you talking about? More money in the community in the pockets of young dealers? A higher level of determination in certain people because of the climate on the street? Great stories to tell?

First of all, there's upstart money. Eazy-E wouldn't have developed Ruthless Records if it weren't for the crack game. So Dr. Dre would've just been a Prince clone. One of the greatest works of art, *It Takes a Nation of Millions to Hold Us Back* [by Public Enemy], would've never got made. Half the narratives of hiphop would've been erased, the street cred, the danger, so hiphop would've been more of a jazz thing with virtuoso rhyming and it could've easily faded away.

Crack makes the world of the street that much more tenuous and fast and dangerous and filled with money.

Crack offered a lot of money to the inner-city youth who didn't go to college. Which enabled them to become businessmen. It also turned us into marksmen. It also turned us comatose. Let's not forget that people actually used the shit!

But the ones who actually used it, are they really the ones who're impacting hiphop? Isn't it really the dealers and the friends of the dealers?

I know about maybe five people in the entertainment industry who did their peak work as a result of crack usage.

Are you serious?

Melle Mel will admit it. Melle Mel made "White Lines" high.

He used coke while making the record?

No, no I'm talkin about crack.

He did crack while doing "White Lines"? Do you mean, during that period in his life, or that night in the studio?

He said, "The most ironic thing about doin 'White Lines' is I was doin this antidrug message, but was snortin the shit as I was doin it. That was the most ironic thing about doin 'White Lines.'" He said he was makin the quintessential antidrug song while drowning in his own shit.

Wow.

I've seen two people in my life actually do crack. One was just a passerby on the street in San Francisco. The other was in the studio. Like, It's time for a break. Some of us say, Oh I gotta eat. This guy says, I gotta get my mojo on.

Before you do the song, he's beaming up.

He said, quote, I gotta get my mojo on, and excused himself from the room. I happened to go in the hallway and it was the foulest stench I ever smelled. I was like, What the fuck is that smell? People were like, Oh, he's smokin rocks. It's somethin you see on TV, but never in your real life.

Was he able to be a productive member of the session after that?

I'll put it this way. His whole career is based on that.

Wait. Here's a yes or no question. Was it Flavor-Flav?

No.

Was it ex-Root Malik B?

No. Wow, I forgot about Malik. Shit, my best song came from crack! ["Water," on Phrenology, the new album.] [He laughs.] Anyway, the guy was highly productive and I would dare to say that it still fuels this person to be a creative entity. To this very day.

Does Black art need social strife in a way that white art does not?

Well, Black music is often used as a survival tool. It's not an expression of art for many people. It's not, Yo man, I can sing. It's, I need help, I need to survive, I need to make money. If I can't do this my life is over. So Black art needs extremes. We can't be halfway crooks. The social conditions have to be so drastic that it brings the creativity out of us.

So, following your theory, the reason why much of Black music got a little stale during the 90s, all obsessed with bling-bling, is because of Clinton.

I mean, the Clinton days were a collective sigh of relief, but what were we celebrating? Remember when Chris Rock said, We're celebrating OJ's victory, but where's my OJ prize? What did we win? That's how I feel with Clinton becoming president. We were like, Whew. One of our own finally made it. We really thought he was Black. My vision of Clinton is him in Kentucky Fried Chicken, soppin his bread, eatin his greens. I was like, we are finally in the White House.

Toni Morrison wrote that he was the first Black president. In The New Yorker. Toni Morrison.

And we all believed that.

I remember talking to politically connected D.C. Black folk and them breaking down all the ways you could see he was truly part Black. And their biggest piece of evidence was, you never saw his birth father. The second biggest piece of evidence was Chelsea's hair. They all said it was too curly for her to be all white.

When Clinton came in there was a false sense of relief that Black people probably hadn't felt since Kennedy. When Kennedy was president there was some iota of hope. Black people felt, with this guy we have some sort of chance at dignity.

At what point in history does the theory begin? Nixon presided over the most incredible soul music of the late 60s and early 70s. Carter led to disco.

Well, I would start back in the Great Depression.

That's interesting because the Depression and the Harlem Renaissance happen around the same time.

No matter how far back in time people wanna go it works. Start with King Oliver or Ma Rainey or Louis Armstrong. The worse the social conditions, the better the Black music. I'm not sayin strictly, a Republican has to be in office. Social depression, financial depression, and an overall hopelessness brings the best of art. Gospel starts in slavery. The blues start around the depression. Jazz starts in the post-Depression period. At the beginning of the civil rights movement you had doo-wop, rock 'n roll, and soul. The glue that held that together was a spiritual bond. That's what's missing from today. That's what made hiphop great in the 80s. Now, with Bush in office and the war and Al Qaeda and everything goin on we should be seeing the best music. But . . .

II. "Are we gonna hate the house nigger because he gets air-conditioning? He's still a slave."

How do you feel about hiphop today?

Does it speak volumes that I listen to the White Stripes more than I listen to anything in hiphop? The only album I'm listening to from start to finish right now is *Elephant*. I'm at this rubicon in my life where I'm trying to figure out, am I rebelling to rebel or am I honestly choosing this? Am I searching for something new or am I dried out with hiphop? I don't know. But I'll listen to anything and I'll listen to it a lot whether I like it or not. I have this ritual of buying *Straight Out the Jungle* [the Jungle Brothers' classic debut] a billion times, acting like it's the first time again.

What?

I buy records only to lose them, on purpose maybe, in hopes that I'll wake up and go, oh, lemme go record shopping again.

So you'll have that first-time-getting-it feeling again and again.

There's no classic hiphop record that I've not bought ten times just for that feeling. When I opened up *Apocalypse '91* [Public Enemy's final great album] and I heard "Lost at Birth," the first song, and that siren goin off, that was the last great adrenaline moment in my youth. I opened it up and didn't know what to expect. I just put on my headphones, they happened to be on ten, and when that sound came through I was like oh shit! One day I walked past Tower and I said, I know I have the shit at home, the shit's on my iPod, my iPod's at the hotel, but I gotta hear it now.

So [incredulous] you went into Tower and bought it?

My logic was, to me buyin a record's like voting for president. I helped you get up one on the Soundscan, so maybe Chuck will get a two million plaque by 2014 when I buy my five hundredth copy. That's pretty much how I operate.

Why do you listen to things you don't like?

I don't believe in good music and bad music anymore. I'm through with that phase of my life. Sometimes I just wanna feel good, so I put on a good record. But mostly I'm more of a businessman than a music fan, so I'm listening to music in terms of, is this effective or not effective? In other words, I can get Ashanti's new album and say, OK this is effective. I see how this is infectious. I see why this works. I mean, are we gonna hate the house nigger because he gets air-conditioning? He's still a slave. Yeah, I get mosquito bites, but he didn't ask to come here, either. The thing is, we, the Roots, have mastered the groove element. We've mastered virtuoso lyricism. We've mastered the art element. But we haven't mastered the pop craftsmanship of writing songs. You like Prince because he wrote great songs. And what that leads to is, I walk past a couple. Guy stops in his tracks, girl keeps on walking. Guy looks back. He says, ?uestlove? I turn around. He says, Ohmigod! The girl keeps on walking. He's like, baby wait! It's ?uestlove from the Roots. She's like, who?

So, you're respected, but you want to be loved instead.

Damn. You really hit it. I was trying to figure out what one sentence could sum up all these feelings and that's it.

III. The Fro.

So let's talk about your hair. Your hair is iconic and I have basically the same style, so what's your hair-care regimen?

Really, nothing. It's absolute neglect. I think I stroked this hair maybe ten times when I woke up, washed it, maybe. If something important is coming up, I'll braid it the night before so I can take it out and make it look full. This hair is a result of laziness and not really wantin to sit in a barber's chair for two hours. It's so not a statement. Now it's a marketing angle. There've been moments when I was ready to get rid of it, but now I'm stuck.

I use the Kiehl's leave-in conditioner. I won't leave the house without it. I love that shit so much I'd do a commercial. I can't believe you don't have some product you rely on.

I don't. I'm supposed to put it in braids every night and then take it out in the morning, but I don't. I've not cut this hair since my prom night, June 2, 1989.

You haven't had a haircut in fourteen years? You lie.

1989 was the last time I had hair of shortish, Malcolm Jamal-Warner, proportions.

Shouldn't your hair be much longer?

Exactly. If I did what I'm supposed to do—oil it every night, braid it up every night, take it out—it would be the size of a lion. It's actually bigger than this. It does take effort to make it look unkept.

Believe me, I know.

What I do is I spend five seconds in the shower so it can shrink and then just let it go. I'll shape it however I want it to be designed and then go on with my day.

IV. "Had D'Angelo known the repercussions of 'Untitled,' I don't think he would've done it."

So, who are the Yodas?

Back in '97 D'Angelo and I were sorta living through *Star Wars* episodes. But the thing is I'm probably the only man alive who has not seen *Star Wars*.

Shocking.

I went to see it when I was six and I fell asleep. When it got rereleased in '97 I went again and fell asleep.

Do you normally fall asleep in the movies?

Ever since *Rain Man* I've realized that if I sit still for more than two hours I'll fall asleep. Anyway, I never saw *Star Wars*. So one day D says, [his voice gets deep and growly, a solid impression of D'Angelo. He pantomimes pulling on an imaginary joint twice, three times.] Yeah, nigga. The way I see it [pulls on the joint again] the radio stations and the media is like the Death Star and I'ma be Luke Skywalker. It was this whole revolution that was going to save music. Q-Tip was gonna be Harrison Ford. Lauryn [Hill] was gonna be Princess Leia. Erykah [Badu] was Queen Amidala. I said, Who am I gonna be? D said, You're gonna be Chewbacca. I said OK. I accepted the role of Chewbacca without knowing who the hell Chewbacca was. But I knew that Yoda was the wise figure. I said, Who's gonna be Yoda? He said, We gotta divide Yoda up into different people and they'll just be collectively known as Yoda. So, it was Jimi [Hendrix], Marvin [Gaye], James Brown, [Bob] Marley, George [Clinton], Stevie [Wonder], Al [Green], Aretha [Franklin], Miles [Davis], and Nina [Simone]. We had a token white entry. Who was it? Oh, Joni [Mitchell]. The youngest one of all the Yodas is Prince. They are the elements that we refer to when we talk about Yoda.

Who's out here now that'll be a Yoda for your kids thirty years from now?

D'Angelo. Quiet as it's kept, the reason why I worked on *Voodoo* was because I wanted to be a part of something that could possibly be on that level. [He played on most of the songs and was musical director for D'Angelo's tour.] One day my kids could say, 'Wow. My Dad was a part of that.' My involvement was never monetary. I didn't get the rest of my check.

Are you still owed money from "Voodoo"?

Stop playing.

How much are you owed?

Stop playin! You know I can't go there.

Four figures? Five figures?

If creating music were a political party, then we were sort of being socialists. But it should be that way. Here's a funny sidenote. John Mayer is incredibly underrated. Ohmigod. Severely. His whole Abercrombie and Fitch, nice guy, moms love him, that's whatever. He wants to do his *Voodoo* so bad it hurts. I just finished workin with him and the songs we were doin were John Mayeresque, but it was the stuff we were doin in between. I mean, it was like *Voodoo* all over again. We worked on his song for an hour and then we worked on five other songs that were just crazy awesome. Then my manager calls and says, How's it going? I say, Man I ain't had this much fun since *Voodoo*. Man, we did this one song and then we created like five other songs. He said, Whoa, whoa. How many songs you work on? I'm, casually, like, Maybe six. The next day all the jamming stopped. His manager was like, do the song you're supposed to do. All this extracurricular jamming you're doing is costing us money. See, the way you're supposed to do business is, if you add a chord or something significant you might be a songwriter or if you do whatever you might be a producer. We blurred those lines during *Voodoo*. It was just, let's get it done. We'll deal with the business later.

So you're a writer and producer on "Voodoo," but you were neither paid like that nor credited as a producer.

I was paid for my work on *Voodoo*.

You were paid as a worker, a session drummer. Not as a writer and producer.

I wasn't.

How much are you owed?

I can't tell you, Touré. But my point was that, I saw him as the chosen one . . .

A lot of people thought that.

I still think it. Even though we're not cool, I still think it.

Was there a fight?

It's just me becoming a new person and one of the roles of the old me was my role as enabler. But I can't control my world and then go do maintenance on his world.

Makin music with D'Angelo is more than going to the studio and jamming?

It's so much more than that. It's a whole lifestyle.

Because he's genius? Because he's troubled?

He's all of that, but more than that he's amazingly insecure. I mean, everyone's insecure, but he's insecure to the level where I felt as though I had to lose myself and play cheerleader. Some nights on tour he'd look in the mirror and say, I don't look like the video ["Untitled," which featured nothing but a chiseled, naked D'Angelo from the waist up]. It was totally in his mind, on some Kate Moss shit. So, he'd say, lemme do two hundred more stomach crunches. He'd literally hold the show up for half an hour just to do crunches. We would hold the show for an hour and a half if he didn't feel mentally prepared or physically prepared. Some shows got cancelled because he didn't feel physically prepared, but it was such a delusion.

It was the trap women often fall into, thinking they're fat when they're not.

Yes. In the world of karma it was sweet poetic justice for any woman that's ever been sexually harassed, that's ever had to work twice as hard just to prove she could work like a man. Literally. When we started this *Voodoo* project we were like, Man, we're gonna give a gift to the world, and not on a pretentious level. We're gonna create something that's totally our world and we're gonna bring people to our world and they're gonna love it and it's gonna be art. But the first night of the *Voodoo* tour the take-it-off chants started not ten minutes into the show. This is a three-hour show. And he had mastered all the tricks from the Yodas. The Al Green Yoda tricks of him giving a wink to the drummer and all the music stops and Al Green goin away from the mic and singing to the audience without the microphone. We planned every trick out. But the girls are like, Take it off! Take it off! That put too much pressure on him.

To be the sex god.

Yep. And by night four he was angry and resentful. He was like, Is this what you want? Is this what you want?

He was being viewed as a sexual being and not as a genius.

They didn't care about the art, they didn't care for the fact that Jeff Lee Johnson was doing the note for note "Crosstown Traffic" solo in . . .

They wanted to see the abs, the bod.

They wanted "Untitled." He hated every moment of that. So in order to motivate him past night four became problematic. He'd say, Well, [frustrated] let's do "Untitled" earlier. We'd say, No, you gotta end with "Untitled." Then it became just compromise. How can we stop the bleeding so that we can at least get the show out the way before the take it off chants come? But no night was unscathed. Three weeks into it, it became unbearable. Absolutely unbearable. So as a result the cheerleading starts. If we need him to get out of his disappointment, depression thing you might have to start at four o'clock in the afternoon, like, What's up, man [with exaggerated happiness]! Yo, let's go record shopping! Like, let's con him into being happy all day! We go record shopping, then it's like, Let's go to Roscoe's! Oh, that's right, you can't eat, so you go exercise. Alright, Mark [the physical trainer], you're it. Mark comes, trains him. I come back. Yo, man! I got this new Prince joint! We watch Prince. We get amped. Rewind it a couple times. All right, you ready? I'ma get dressed and in fifteen minutes we'll get in the car, go to the venue. Some nights that would work. Other nights he'd just be psychosomatic. Like, Yo man, I can't do it. I'm like, What? He's like, I can't do it. I'm like, just go out there. They love you! He's like, They don't love me, man. That's the respect-and-love thing. He wants the respect. I want the love.

Everyone wants what they don't have.

He was like, they don't understand. They don't get it. They just want me to take off my clothes. So every night for eight months it was how to solve this Rubik's cube in one minute before the bomb detonates. Every night. And sometimes I failed.

And the show did not go on.

The show didn't go on.

How many shows did you cancel?

Maybe three weeks' worth. We threw away at least two weeks of Japan.

That's unbelievable. What's going on with him now? Is he retired?

He's recording. I heard he's got like four songs done. I know him, he'll stop at song twelve. But what he wants is to get fat. He doesn't want his braider braiding every nook and cranny of his hair. He doesn't wanna have to have ripples in his stomach. He doesn't want the pressure of being "Untitled" the video.

So we'll never get that kind of unbridled sexuality from him again.

I don't know.

Do you think "Untitled" was a mistake? Because I remember when he was shooting that and he did not want to make that video. They had to coax him into doing it and maybe he was right to not want that if it created expectations that he wasn't emotionally prepared to shoulder.

Had he known what the repercussions of "Untitled" would've been, I don't think he would've done it.

V. "When I saw De La Soul I said, that's me."

It's very easy for a hiphop historian to say, Oh yeah, the Roots are a post–Native Tongues band and they follow in the line of groups like De La Soul. But how does that work for you? Is there an actual connection for you or are we making that up?

The same way a white kid would look at Eminem and say, Hey, that's me, I saw De La Soul and was like, Yeah, that's me. I saw it with the Jungle Brothers at first, but De La pushed it over the top. They were full of inside jokes, full of inside cultural references that only I got. They had Led Zeppelin samples . . .

They weren't afraid to be suburban, weren't afraid to be polyglot, weren't afraid to be intellectual . . .

They wore it like a badge of honor. They were my entry into hiphop. I worked at Sam Goody when *Three Feet High and Rising* came out and my first act of theft at that store was taking the promo cassette. I took that cassette and made a lifestyle with it. With *Nation of Millions* I heard my father's record collection inside the record. I said, How can I utilize that so I can make that work for me? Then De La totally introduced me to the lifestyle that I could relate to. They validated me.

They allowed you to feel comfortable being yourself, being nonghetto, nonthuggish, nonanti-intellectual.

Exactly. I welcome people calling us post–Native Tongues. I wanna be a Native Tongue! We were very much like De La Soul in our theory and our lifestyle and the way we dressed and the way that we just wanted to be different for different's sake and then came into our own and found our own nitch.

VI. "*Phrenology* easily cost two million to make."

If you were the commissioner of hiphop, what would you institute as new rules?

My life's goal is to find a happy medium for sampling to be not only legal but for the right parties to benefit from it. There has to be sampling laws. The survival of hiphop is based on that. Just make it legal and have an actual scaled rate for it. I mean, Pete Rock is wasting some of the best years of his life right now because he's being handicapped because he can't sample. It's way too expensive. The reason why Jay-Z was able to make The Blueprint [filled with great soul samples] is because the motherfucker's got a two-million-dollar recording budget. He could pay for samples like that.

Do you have that kind of budget?

Well, each Roots album has cost a million dollars plus, which is unheard of. Each album has cost between one to three million. *Phrenology* easily cost two million to make.

What adds up to two million?

Mostly studio time. I use the best studios. The type of mics I use are expensive. If you want the shit from 1940 that Louis Armstrong played on that's still in great working condition that might cost you three hundred dollars a day. Engineers aren't cheap. Bob Power [perhaps the most legendary hiphop engineer] charges five thousand dollars just to have a conversation. Things add up. It's damn near five figures a day for every day at the studio.

What do you think The Blueprint cost with all those samples?

Wow. Well, it really depends what people are charging for samples. The reason George Clinton gets used a lot is cuz his charge is cheap.

What's cheap?

You can nibble off of George for a flat rate of maybe five thousand dollars. He'll actually go above and beyond the call of duty and send you the master tape. I'd never do that, but he goes above and beyond the call of duty so you keep coming back. He's like a smart crack dealer. Why do you think his sound was so prevalent? George allowed people to sample him. He's smart with his. Prince doesn't let anyone touch his stuff because the way his deal is with Warner's, they would get the lion's share of the money. He even goes so far as to tell people, "Don't cover my shit because I'm not getting the money."

VII. "They don't have turntables in Cuba, but they have hiphop."

Everyone in hiphop has a list of their top five MCs of all time. What's your list?

Five is Posdnous [from De La]. The most untrumpeted hero of lyricism. Four is KRS-One. Three is Biggie. Two is Melle Mel.

Wow, you went way back with him.

Well, you have to. Everyone is derivative of Melle Mel. Number one is Rakim. He's the Christopher Columbus. There are people more complex than he was, but him being first, he has to have it.

Is there any female MC that you'd fuck?

I'm totally in love with Foxy Brown.

You claim your life as an enabler is over, but tell me, whose life are you saving in your spare time?

Right now in Cuba it's 1981 in terms of hiphop. They're just getting started. They don't even have turntables in Cuba, but they have hiphop. I'm gonna do to Cuba what Dizzy Gillespie did to Cuba. Totally reinvent the arc. I'm gonna buy Cuba its first set of turntables. I've always wanted to find a place where they have little concept of hiphop. If you go there and reinvent the wheel you'll be the shit.

8. Strange Fruit

Condoleezza Rice Is a
House Negro

{ *Suede* magazine, 2005 }

Perhaps it's time to reconsider the House Slave. In the Black consciousness the House Slave, or House Nigger, has always been the big traitor,
one who shows greater loyalty to white people and their institutions
than to the Black community and our institutions. To be called a
house nigger remains one of Black America's deepest Black-on-Black
insults, a nasty pejorative worse than "oreo," worse even than "Uncle
Tom" (though in many ways they're synonymous). It's a remnant of slavery, when slaves who worked in the house were perceived to have it easier, butlering, nannying, and cooking for Massa indoors rather than
struggling through backbreaking labor under the hot sun out in the
fields with the Field Slaves. It's also a remnant of the thinking of Malcolm
X, who convinced us that Field Slaves were authentic Blacks while House
Slaves were an embarrassment to the race.

But maybe House Slaves had a good idea. The House Slave's loyalty
wasn't truly to Massa (or in the modern version to, let's say, the White
House) but to him or herself. During slavery the House Slave's physical
proximity to whites offered an opportunity, albeit slight, to find a path
up from the very bottom of society. Who can blame someone for trying
to better their life? Some house slaves learned to read and write either by
looking over Massa's shoulder for years or by being taught by Massa or
some member of his family, almost always in secrecy, for it was against
the law to teach slaves to read and write. Those lessons often proved critical to personal and social ascension. Frederick Douglass began learning

318 Never Drank the Kool-Aid

how to read and write when he was a young House Slave and it propelled him to become one of the greatest abolitionists of his era.

When I see Condoleezza Rice I see a hi-tech House Slave. (It came as no surprise to me to discover her great-grandmother Julia, a Rice family hero, was a House Slave emancipated by the Civil War.) Sure, Rice is making lots of money working with the most powerful man in the world and directing thousands of people as secretary of state, the first Black woman to hold the position. But there's something in the way she happily toils closely with a president who's deeply disliked and rightly distrusted by the vast majority of Black Americans. Something in how she never speaks for herself, but always for the president, calmly articulating his simplistic and often tautological rationale for his crazy international policies as if he's her marionette, unlike her predecessor, Colin Powell, who was clearly his own man. Powell, alone in the president's inner circle, preached the need for caution in using the American military, but no one expects Rice to provide a countervailing voice to the war-loving hawks Dick Cheney, Don Rumsfeld, and Paul Wolfowitz. I see something disquieting even in the way she walks dutifully through the Rose Garden beside Dubya, her posture so prim and stiff she appears trapped in the midst of an ongoing panic attack, while Dubya's body language blares relaxed macho cool. Unlike Clarence Thomas, Rice is not hated in the Black community, but unlike Powell, she inspires little or no sense of pride.

Black Americans have historically chosen one of two responses to white supremacy: either boldly confront it or try to ignore it. Attack it or accept it and move on. We have great respect for confronters because they validate the idea that past crimes against the race continue to hold us back and must be rectified or at least answered for. The ignorers make us uneasy. They seem to say that the rest of us are dumb for clinging to the past. Their professional successes send the tacit message that the confronters have made much ado about nothing, that racism is over, and if the confronters would stop complaining then they too could get ahead. Rice's parents chose the path of ignorer for her when she was a child. She grew up in Birmingham, Alabama, in the 60s when it was widely known as the most racist city in America. In 1963, when she was just eight years old a bomb exploded in Birmingham's 16th Street Baptist Church, killing four schoolgirls. Rice was in a church not far away and heard the bomb go off. One of the girls was a schoolmate. And yet, she has said, the Rice family's strategy was to ignore racism. "My parents were very strategic," she has told interviewers while recalling childhood classes in figure skating, concert piano, flute, violin, French, ballet, and etiquette. "I was going to be so well prepared and I was going to do all of these things that were revered in white society so well that I would be armored somehow from racism." It seems Reverend John and Angelina decided early on that Rice would take to heart the strange "advice" offered by the dying grandfather in Ralph Ellison's *Invisible Man*: "Live with your head in the lion's mouth. I want you to overcome em with yeses, undermine em with grins, agree em to death and destruction. Let em swoller you till they vomit or bust wide open."

Rice's parents inspired her to become a lifelong overachiever. She graduated from high school at fifteen, then graduated cum laude from the University of Denver at nineteen, earned her master's in government and international studies from Notre Dame a year later, and her Ph.D. in international studies at just twenty-five. She taught at Stanford for years, winning awards for her teaching, and at forty became the school's youngest provost ever. In her six years as provost the tenure rate for female professors dropped and the number of Black professors declined. A Stanford colleague has said Rice "set a tone of open season on minorities and women." When a professor introduced a resolution to make affirmative action an explicit part of the tenure process, Rice vehemently opposed it and vowed to squash it "as long as I am at Stanford."

At the university she met Brent Scowcroft, who became national security advisor in the first Bush administration and made her director of Soviet affairs at the National Security Council. In time Poppa Bush introduced her to his son, then the governor of Texas, and when Dubya became president he gave Rice the job Scowcroft had once occupied.

Rice enjoys such a close relationship with the president—in the first term her office was closer to his and she spoke to him more frequently than any other advisor—that she has often been called the president's political wife. That discussion was egged on by a bizarre gaffe she once made at a Washington power dinner where several *New York*

Times journalists and editors heard her say, "As I was telling my husb—" then stop and say: "As I was telling President Bush . . ." What an interesting Freudian slip.

But I know of no modern wife who shows their husband the kind of dutiful deference that Rice displays. After Bush's disastrous first debate with John Kerry, the president refused to believe he'd come across as irritated until tough-as-nails communications director Karen Hughes forcefully convinced him of it. Hughes has a reputation for telling the president what he doesn't want to hear. That's a modern wife: the one person in the room who will tell you that your shit stinks. Rice strikes me more as Dubya's political daughter, one of those dying-to-please daddy's girls so devoted she'd jump off a bridge if he asked nicely.

(Speaking of wives, fifty-year-old Rice has never been one, leading many in and out of Washington to wonder aloud if she's gay, but many intensely careerist, overachieving straight women find themselves sacrificing personal dreams for professional goals. Rice's unauthorized biographer, Antonia Felix, confirms that Rice has indeed had boyfriends, including more than one NFL player—football is a passion of hers—and was once engaged.)

In the past months several women have suggested to me that Rice could one day be a viable candidate for president. We'd be silly to dismiss the lifelong overachiever right away: she's a darling of the right wing, has the loyalty of the most powerful political family in the country, and seems to have no compunction about selling out Black people to get ahead. She won't leave red staters wondering whether they're voting for a president or a Black president. But she's never held elective office; never even run for elective office; no cabinet member has ever run for the presidency; her personality is as stale as a day-old cracker (what's the antonym for charisma?); and plus there's no evidence the presidency is something she covets. She's said repeatedly that her dream job is to become the commissioner of the NFL. But whether or not she succeeds Bush or NFL commish Paul Tagliabue, if her great-grandmother Julia can see Rice now she must be beaming with pride. She's done extremely well for herself living with her head inside the lion's mouth for all these years. I just wonder how lonely it is in there.

Show Me the Money

{ Michael Jordan, *The Village Voice*, 1999 }

It's like a death in the family. I mean, MJ is gone. For a decade and a half he's lived in a section of the collective consciousness marked Ubiquitous, alongside Sinatra and Picasso and Brando. Unleashing Baryshnikovian dunks, slicing through Nike commercials with his American prince manner, and winning, always winning. The cult of Jordan got its first spark from his undeniable artistry, but grew to mythic and hypnotizing proportions because rooting for Jordan paid such handsome dividends. Fandom is filled with heartbreak—crushing defeats, sudden trades, mortality clipping the wings of yesterday's invincibles. To sit on the sideline is to embrace helplessness. Your hero battles, you do nothing. Hollywood guarantees everything will end up okay. In sports you know only that your guy will lose—if not today, then some soon tomorrow. Jordan cut through that. He won so often it was ridiculous. From the first time we noticed him, as a UNC freshman, beating Patrick Ewing's Georgetown with a last-second shot, to the final time we saw him, getting out on top, a triumph over mortality itself.

Yes, he never made it hard to root for him. Never made us accept him along with his controversial opposition to some war or his strong public stance on something like apartheid. Never demanded we enjoy anything more than his style and his shoes. He's bigger than basketball, so measure him against men like Joe Louis and Jackie Robinson and Muhammad Ali, men bigger than their sports, men with an impact so nuclear they changed society. Louis, heavyweight champion while Hitler was mulling over squashing Europe, opened a world of pride for Black Americans. Robinson and Ali moved mountains in society so large that the reverberations can be heard almost daily. They were senators representing the world of sports and they are inseparable from the political history of their generation. Jordan is a man of rare dignity and an even rarer pursuit of excellence, but his political impact has been zero. Certainly, the opportunities of Louis and Robinson have evaporated with time, and the self-sacrificing example of Ali seems an impossible standard. But Jordan has the fame, charisma, and grace of a Mandela. Any cause he might have championed—from something as morally simple as supporting the candidacy of fellow North Carolinian Harvey Gantt, who lost two close Senate races against Satan's cousin, Jesse Helms, to any stand against any sort of American injustice—would have been taken seriously because it was endorsed by Jordan. Yet as careful as he has been at vacuuming every possible penny into his pocket—did he really have to do ads for Rayovac? Ballpark Franks? Long-distance ads costarring Tweety Bird?—he has been equally diligent about leaving every bit of political potential on the table. Couldn't the world's greatest endorser have sold us something besides shoes?

Pulitzer Prize winner David Halberstam records much of what Jordan did do, as well as the doings of many of the major figures of his life in *Playing for Keeps*, his four-hundred-plus-page look inside Jordan's life from the JV basketball squad he dominated after being cut by the varsity ("the entire varsity began to come early so they could watch him play") to those last seconds in Utah last summer when the Jazz decided not to double-team him and, suddenly, Jazz defender Bryon Russell was the loneliest man in the world, out there isolated one-on-one with Michael Jeffrey Jordan. It's an epic, detailed vision of the landscape that shaped and was shaped by Jordan, though strictly about basketball—the game and the business—with scant information on Jordan's life away from the court (on his days off, Halberstam uncovers, he takes the kids to school, and he runs a lot of boring errands). In the absence of an interview with MJ, Halberstam relies on the words of Jordan's friends and associates to fill in the tiny crevices of the big story you already know. He also looks inside the locker rooms of the Bird Celtics, the Isiah Pistons, and the Magic Lakers, as well as the offices of Nike, the NBA, and ESPN to fill out his trip inside the practice sessions where Jordan schooled Pippen into greatness, the weight room where Jordan worked to extend his career, the Bulls team bus where Jordan took on Bulls GM Jerry Krause with his sharp tongue (dissing Krause in front of his teammates, extending the world of "the school yard, where some boys are popular, and some seem to be born to be targets"). Halberstam, in this book, is more of a reporter than a historian—he's especially verbose on the byzantine dispute between Jordan and Krause that eventually broke up the mighty Bulls dynasty, and he's light on Jordan's place in history. Sports fans who love behind-the-scenes maneuvering get their fill, as do those who live for well-recounted tales of great games, such as the greatest pickup game ever played, during a 1992 Dream Team practice. Once Charles Barkley began talking trash to Jordan and:

> The game became raw and physical, all territorial and all ego. Michael Jordan more than anyone else set the tone. He simply took over the game, driving to the basket every time he got the ball, rebounding, stepping in the passing lanes for steals, hounding [Magic] Johnson on defense, screaming at everyone, opponents and teammates alike, pushing himself. There was one stretch where he made twelve points in a row, though some witnesses claimed that it was actually sixteen. When a call went against his team, Johnson yelled out, "What is this, Chicago Stadium? Are you going to get all the calls here, too?"
>
> "I'll tell you what it is," Jordan shouted back. "It's the nineties, not the eighties."
>
> The play on both sides was frenzied . . . a level of ferocity almost unmatched in basketball history. . . . It was, [coach Mike Kryzyewski] thought, like being in a house and hearing a terrible hurricane outside, then opening the door and seeing that the storm was even more powerful than envisioned.
>
> [After Jordan's team won 36–30, a journalist asked,] "You just have to win every time, don't you?"
>
> Michael smiled that wonderful, radiant smile. "I try to make a habit out of it."

Near the end, Halberstam makes excuses for Jordan's apoliticality, his silent unwillingness to confront society, suggesting, "He was clearly not very good at it. Some people had a natural feel for it, grievance was in their souls, while others did not." But also because of "a fear that he might taint his value as a commercial spokesman."

It is so difficult to be a capitalist with a cause. But I cannot accept that there is no grievance in Jordan's soul. Can his intelligence and legendary warrior spirit be limited only to hoop contests and golf? Is his burn to compete against the Knicks greater than his burn to compete against real enemies like racism? We will know the full answer eventually, as his prime selling years dwindle and his tongue, once so visible, loosens, maybe enough to let us know what he's thinking in between backdoor cuts and back-end profits. But for now we just know that he has grabbed more than $250 million in nonsalary income in this decade, generated $10 billion for the economy, and wasted so much more. The premier shoe salesman of all time, he is a fitting member of the show-me-the-money era. That is no compliment. He was bigger than basketball, but, in the end, our beloved was just a ballplayer.

The Five-Mic Personality, or Why I Hate Mary J. Blige

{ *Vibe*, 1998 }

1. You can tell a five-mic album—that rare, flawless LP that senses the direction of the wind of the zeitgeist and distills it into sixty or so minutes of recorded bliss—cuz you hear it boombapping throughout the community, seeping from Land Cruisers and lips, rooftops and headphones. Smoke a little and the birds seem to be singing along and the trash cans doing the bankhead bounce to that ubiquitous beat. Rarer still than the five-mic album, though, is that rarest of cultural diamonds, the five-mic *persona*. That artist who doesn't just talk about the dreams and fears of the generation, who embodies them. Who steps onstage and immediately reminds you of people you've known or dated or shared family dinner with. Who reminds you of yourself. Who says things—with their voice, their clothes, their attitude—that you've felt but been unable to say, or afraid to say. Who is you writ large. Who doesn't keep it real. *Is* real.

They are our cultural senators, elected to the American Zeitgeist Parliament, to tell our stories and spread our gospel by the way they sing, move, dress, live. They may or may not make five-mic music, but you vote for them—buy the records, call the radio station, see the concert, wear the T-shirt, sing the songs, give up the love—because they are your true representative. You probably can't name your congressman in Washington, but if you're a badass recklessly rebellious modern James Dean you know the name Tupac. If you're an ambitiously sweet and sweetly ambitious fast-maturing teenage girl you know the name Brandy. If you're struggling to keep your soul in a drug-encrusted universe you know the name Biggie. If you're a sensitive, street poet-prince, you know the name Nas. If you're a Juneteenth-celebrating, boho, head wrap rocker with dreams of visiting Africa, or plans to go back, you vote for Erykah Badu. And if you're a chronically underloved working single mom with a wack baby's fava, who still walk the ave with the head-held-high pride of a street queen, oh yeah, every day you vote for Mary J. Blige.

In an interview for his autobiography, KRS-One told me:

"Back when my hiphop career was starting the relationship between the artist and the audience was completely different. Back then it wasn't the record that rocked, it was the artist. You bought the artist. You were like, I wish I was you! You got a record? I'll buy that! You got a T-shirt? I'll buy that! You got a cookie? I'll buy that!! It's your lifestyle that people loved and bought into: the music was secondary. When Michael Jackson was on top he didn't have to prove himself to the audience— the audience had to prove themselves to Michael Jackson by buying his shit!"

Today that's truer than ever.

2.   Remember Arrested Development? What happened? When we in Atlanta first heard them we were in love. They crystallized a euphorically Afrocentric mood that many of us were feeling. But, we wondered aloud, would they be embraced by Joe Iowa, or, more importantly, Kareem Detroit? Of course, AD had it on lock in '92. Platinum sales, Grammy, *Saturday Night Live* performance, picture on the cover of *The Wall Street Journal*. They were that Afrocentric fresh breath of air that hiphop had been waiting for. Or so it seemed. After one great album and one good *MTV Unplugged* record, we'd had enough of Speech the preach.

Two summers ago someone slipped me an advance tape of music from this new girl from around the corner in Fort Greene, Brooklyn, via Dallas. At that point in Fort Greene there was a movement goin on. A youngish community of Black artists and intellectuals were building a world where sistas in head wraps from Black-owned Moshood could go online at Alice Walker's daughter's Internet cafe and chat live with the Motherland. It was euphorically Africa-centric, but with a strong urban Nueva York flavor. The songs on the tape and the mature, reflective timbre of her voice—warm, but weathered, like Langston Hughes's rivers, she sounded like someone who'd been here before—she captured our Fort Greene boho mood. But, we wondered, what would Kareem Detroit think?

> The last thing I said to Erykah when we finished her album was, Don't you wanna sell any units? You got a chance: you sing. Stop tryin to be so artsy. I thought the marketplace wasn't ready. I said, It's brilliant, but it's not gonna do anything. This is basically the Roots with a songstress in front. I always do little focus groups with the kids on my block and with Erykah I didn't even bother. I couldn't imagine Shaquana next door likin it. Erykah just said, Watch. You'll see.
>
> —?uestlove, the Roots

Kareem and Shaquana loved it. Gave Erykah platinum sales, Grammy, *Saturday Night Live* performance, picture on the cover of *Vibe*. Maybe they were looking for messages. Maybe they wanted a woman who wouldn't be foxy and sell her body and soul to sell records. A woman as regally earthy as that of Maya Angelou's "Phenomenal Woman" and Nikki Giovanni's "Ego Trippin." Who came with a little Southern hospitality, a little contemporary Garveyism, a little urban worldliness, a little otherworldly spirituality. Erykah had, as my pretend aunt says, "a crude gracefulness about her. Her movements are graceful, but her connection with the audience can be crude." Still, maybe, with her respect for the earth and respect for the body and respect for the babies, maybe Erykah was loved because she—strong, proud, culturally aware, universal, spiritual, original yet ancient, with the moral authority of a runaway slave, a truly five-mic sistuh—Erykah represented the best potential in all of us.

Kareem and Shaquana loved it. Loved it even when they, and Fort Greene, started noticing the hint of artifice peeking from behind her curtain of naturalness. She seems culturally centered, but what's with the tricknowledgical rhetoric? She comes off deeply mature, but what's with her childish incense fetish? Then, in one swipe, she changed everything. She said, "I'm gettin tiiiirred of yo shit . . ." and told the story of triflin-ass Tyrone. She was cursing, she was gettin her house in order, she was tearing away the seriousness, she was winking at us, she was, finally, human. She took herself down a notch, stopped, at least for a day, taking herself so seriously, stopped being the untouchable Afro queen, became a regular struggling woman. Arrested Development? Not anymore.

3.   Dear Mary,

I still hate you. It's been like five years since we last saw each other and I still think that shit was fucked up. I know you were young—you'd just put out My Life—and you weren't really feeling journalists. But we were just taking a limo ride out to the Schlobohm projects where you grew up and talking over a few things so I could write a little article for The New York Times and you just started wilding. I asked you something like, 'Is it harder to sing over hiphop beats instead of classic melodies?' and you flipped on me. You were like, "You're so fuckin stupid," and you cursed me out in a limo filled with people. You told me not to talk to you for the rest of the day and for an hour we rode back to Manhattan in tense silence. Not before or since that long day have I ever felt so small. Never have I gone to interview a star—someone I respected and fought to be able to write about—and walked away so embarrassed I wanted to fucking cry.

I went home and put your records behind the shelf. It was a long time before you made it back into my speakers. I think around the time I started talking to Keisha. She kinda reminded me of you from the first. A lot of sistas kinda recall you, but if you didn't have that voice, you might be Keisha. She was a career secretary with an attitude and little chance for advancement and two beautiful kids from two trifin niggas. A good-hearted woman kinda beat down by life. A woman with baggage—a complete matching set from Louis Vuitton—too savvy to not let you know it, too mature to drop 'em in your lap right away. Kinda like you.

One of the first nights she stayed over she whispered, "Boo, go put on that Mary CD." Have you ever made love to *My Life*? You might be the only one in the Hiphop Nation who hasn't. Girl, that was a deep night. In '66 Amiri Baraka wrote, "If you play James Brown (say, 'Money Won't Change You . . .') in a bank, the total environment is changed . . . An energy is released in the bank, a summoning of images that take the bank, and everybody in it, on a trip. That is, they visit another place. A place where Black People live." That night me and Keisha took a trip to a place inside the Black woman's heart, where you, a pre-slipper Cinderella, sang out for the prince's love as an elusive, all-powerful cure-all. With the sweet vulnerability in your voice and the honesty and pain in your lyrics—your music constantly reminds how fragile a woman is, how much you've got to appreciate finding a good one and establishing a true connection and real love with her, and how rare it is to be happy.

After Keisha left I began to think about the day you and I met. How maybe you reacted to what you saw in me, the prep-school kid from *The New York Times*, coming from that establishment that always judged you and you wanted to break my neck before it could judge you again. Or maybe I misread you—I asked about singing over beats instead of classic melodies because I was thinking hiphop soul was a musical innovation of Puff's—taking that mix-tape blend flavor to the masses. But maybe I was wrong—maybe hiphop was in your blood and even if Sean Combs had never become an Uptown A&R man you would still have been a hiphop soul queen because hiphop is where you came from and what you are. There's nothing else you could sing. In your own way you were saying, "It ain't harder to sing over beats. It's me."

Then I was able to forgive you. And I fell in love with your music, again. So what *Share My World* is slicker and less heart-on-your-sleeve autobiographical? It's not a five-mic triumph like *My Life*, but you're a

330 Never Drank the Kool-Aid

five–twenty-four karat–mics persona. You're common among human beings—a troubled woman who hurts, who bleeds, who cries—but a singular artist able to transmit the pain, blood, and tears to an audience through uncommon performance integrity. That's why, now, I love you. But I still ain't speaking to you.

9. Somehow, There's Love in the Hiphop Nation

I Live in the Hiphop Nation

{ *The New York Times*, 1999 }

I live in a country no mapmaker will ever respect. A place with its own language, culture, and history. It is as much a nation as Italy or Zambia. A place my countrymen call the Hiphop Nation, purposefully invoking all of the jingoistic pride that nationalists throughout history have leaned on. Our path to nationhood has been paved by a handful of fathers: Muhammad Ali with his ceaseless bravado, Bob Marley with his truth-telling rebel music, Huey Newton with his bodacious political style, James Brown with his obsession with funk.

We are a nation with no precise date of origin, no physical land, no single chief. But if you live in the Hiphop Nation—if you are not merely a fan of the music, but a daily imbiber of the culture, if you sprinkle your conversation with phrases like "off the meter" (for something that's great) or "got me open" (for something that gives an explosive positive emotional release), if you know why Dutch Masters make better blunts than Phillies (they're thinner), if you know at a glance why Allen Iverson is hiphop and Grant Hill is not, if you feel the murders of Tupac Shakur and the Notorious B.I.G. in the 1997–98 civil war were assassinations and no other word fits—if you can say yes to all of that (and some doesn't count) then you know the Hiphop Nation is a place as real as America on a pre-Columbus atlas. It's there even though the rest of you ain't been there yet.

The Nation exists in any place where hiphop music is being played, or hiphop attitude is being exuded. Once I went shopping for a

Macintosh. The salesman, a wiry twentysomething white boy rattled on about Macs, then, looking at the rapper, or as we call them, MC on my T-shirt, said, "You like Nas? Did you hear him rhyme last night on the Stretch and Bobbito show?" Inside, I felt as if my jaw dropped. He had invoked a legendary hiphop radio show broadcast once a week on college radio at two in the morning. It was as though we were secret agents and he had uttered the code phrase that revealed him to be my contact. We stood for an hour talking MCs and DJs, beats and flows, turning that staid computer store into an outpost of the Hiphop Nation.

The Nation's pioneers were a multiracial bunch—white boys were among the early elite aerosol artists (aka graffiti artists) and Latinos were integral to the shaping of DJing, MCing, b-boying (breakdancing), and general hiphop style. Today's Nation makes brothers of men Black, brown, yellow, and white. But this world was built to worship urban Black maleness: the way we speak, walk, dance, dress, think. We are revered by others, but the leadership of this world is and will remain Black. As it should.

We are a nation with our own gods and devils, traditions and laws (one of them is to not share them with outsiders) but there never has been and never will be a president of the Hiphop Nation. Like Black America, we're close-knit, yet still too fractious for one leader. Instead, a powerful senate charts our future. That senate is made up of our leading MCs; their every album and single is a bill or referendum proposing linguistic, musical, and topical directions for the culture. Is Compton a cool spot? Can Edie Brickell, an embodiment of American female whiteness, be the source for a sample? Is a thick countrified Southern accent something we want to hear? Is police brutality still a rallying point? Like a politician with polls and focus groups, an MC must carefully calibrate his musical message because once his music is released the people vote with their dollars in the store and their butts in the club, ignoring certain MCs and returning them to private life, while anointing others, granting them more time on our giant national microphone.

Unlike rhythm and blues, hiphop has a strong memoiristic impulse, meaning our senator-MCs speak of themselves, their neighborhoods, the people around them, playing autobiographer, reporter, and oral historian. Telling the stories as they actually happened is what is meant by the catchphrase "keep it real." Outsiders laugh when the hallowed phrase is seemingly made hollow by obvious self-mythologizing—materialistic boasts that would be beyond even the Donald, or tales of crimes that would be envied by a Gotti. But this bragging is merely people speaking of the people they dream of being, which, of course, is a reflection of the people they are.

How do you get into this senate? The answer is a complex equation involving both rhyming technique and force of personality. To be a great MC you must have a hypnotizing flow—that is, a cadence and delivery that gets inside the drum and bass patterns and creates its own rhythm line. You must have a magnetic voice—it can be deliciously nasal like Q-Tip's, or delicate and singsongy like Snoop Doggy Dogg's, or deep-toned like that of Rakim, who sounds as commanding as Moses—but it must be a compelling sound. And you must say rhymes with writerly details, up-to-the-minute or self-created slang, bold punch lines, witty metaphors, and original political or sociological insights.

But, again like a politician, to be a great MC you must seem like an extension of the masses and, simultaneously, an extraordinary individual. There must be a certain down-homeness about you, a way of carrying yourself that replicates the way people in your home base feel about life. You must be the embodiment of your audience.

At the same time, you must seem greater than your audience. You must come across as supercool—based on toughness or sex appeal or intellect or bravado—that inspires your listeners to say, I'd like to be you.

In the first decade and a half since the first hiphop record was released in '79, hiphop was a national conversation about urban poverty and police brutality, the proliferation of guns and the importance of safe sex, as well as the joy of a good party, in which the only speakers were Black men.

In recent years that conversation has opened. Hiphop has become more democratic, cracking the monopoly that Black men from New York and L.A. have long held over the Hiphop Nation senate.

Traditionally, hiphop has been hypermodern, disdaining the surreal for gritty images of urban life. But Missy Elliot and her producer,

Timbaland, have constructed a postmodern aesthetic that manifests, on her latest album, *Da Real World*, in references to the sci-fi film *The Matrix* and videos in which Missy dresses as if she were in a scene from *Blade Runner*. Her music also has a futuristic feel, from Timbaland's spare, propulsive beats filled with quirky sounds that evoke science fiction to Missy's experiments with singing and rhyming, as well as using onomatopoeias in her rhymes. They have become part of the Nation's sonic vanguard, as well as door-openers for a new genre: hiphop sci-fi.

Groups from the South Coast like GooDie Mob, Eightball and MJG, and Outkast have brought new perspectives. (The Hiphop Nation reconfigures American geography with a Saul Steinberg–like eye, maximizing cities where most of the important hiphop has come from, microscoping other places: we speak of the East Coast and mean, largely, the five boroughs, Long Island, Westchester, New Jersey, and Philadelphia; by West Coast we mean Los Angeles, Compton, Long Beach, Vallejo, and Oakland; the region comprising Atlanta, New Orleans, Virginia, Miami, and Memphis is called the South Coast.)

Outkast is a pair of Atlanta MCs, Big Boi and Dre (or Antwan Patton and Andre Benjamin), who are not new to many in the Hiphop Nation—*Aquemini* is their third album—but, with their latest album's success and months of touring as the lead-in to Lauryn Hill, they are new to power within hiphop. Their hiphop mixes the cerebrality of New York and the George Clinton–drenched funk favored out West with a particularly Southern musicality, soulfulness, twang-drenched rhymes, and Baptist church–like euphoric joy.

But the most polarizing and revolutionary new entry to the hiphop senate is Eminem (born Marshall Mathers). There have been white MCs before him, but none have been as complex: either they were clearly talentless (like Vanilla Ice) or they worshipped Blackness (like MC Serch of 3rd Bass). Eminem is something new. The fervancy of fans Black and white marveling at his skill and laughing at his jokes have kept him in office, despite the hordes offended by his whiny white-boy shock-jock shtick. He is an original voice in the national conversation that is hiphop because he speaks of the dysfunctionality of his white-trash world—his absentee father, his drugged-out mom, his daughter's hateful mother, his own morally bankrupt conscience. With Eminem the discussion turns to problems in the white community, or at least—because he is from a Black neighborhood in Detroit—the problems of whites in the Black community. On a recent song (called "Busa Rhyme" from Missy's new album *Da Real World*) Eminem rhymes darkly: "I'm homicidal/ and suicidal/ with no friends/ holdin a gun with no handle/ just a barrel at both ends." Finally, someone has arrived to represent the Dylan Klebolds and Eric Harrises of America.

A rash of overprotectiveness within our nation keeps many from enjoying the hiphop of a sneering white MC, but why shouldn't we welcome a frank discussion of white maladies into our home when millions of white people allow our MCs into their homes to talk about our disorders every day?

The Hiphop Nation senate is swelling to include white boys, women, and Southerners, but don't expect that senate to become a true melting pot anytime soon. As long as upper-class white men stay in charge of the United States Senate, urban Black men will remain our leading speakers. Our history is long enough to grant us the maturity to open our world, but this America is still white enough that we know how much we need a Blackened oasis.

It all began with a few parties. Jams in New York City parks thrown by DJs like Kool Herc, Grandmaster Flash, and Afrika Bambaataa. To your eyes it would've appeared to be a rapper in a public park, a DJ behind him, his cables plugged into the street lamp, the police not far away, waiting for just the right moment to shut it all down. But to us those parks were the center of a universe. The cops—or rather, five-oh (from *Hawaii 5-0*)—were Satan. The music—James Brown, Sly Stone, Funkadelic, and anything with a stone-cold bass-and-drum rhythm you could rhyme over—the music breathed meaning and substance and soul into your body. It gave life. It was God.

From behind the turntables in his roped-off pulpit in the park, the DJ gave a rousing sermon sonically praising God's glory. Then up stepped the High Priest, the conduit between God and you—the MC. How crucial was he? In 1979, in its seminal song "Rapper's Delight," the Sugar Hill Gang explained that even Superman was useless if he couldn't flow: "He may be able to fly all through the night/ But can he rock a party til the early light?"

A few years later, in the early 80s a trickle of cassettes began appearing in urban mom-and-pop record stores like Skippy White's on Blue Hill Avenue in Mattapan Square in Boston. As a twelve-year-old I would walk there from my father's office. Every other month or so a new hiphop tape would arrive, direct from New York City: Run-DMC . . . MC Shan . . . The Fat Boys. A kid on an allowance could own all the hiphop albums ever made. For all the force of the music, the culture was so small and precious you held it in your hands as delicately as a wounded bird.

In the mid 80s hiphop won the nation's attention and was immediately branded a fad that would soon die, like disco. Hiphoppers closed ranks, constructed a wall, and instituted a siege mentality. We became like Jews, a tribe that knew how close extinction was and responded to every attack and affront, no matter how small, as if it were a potential death blow. Where Jews battle anti-Semitic attitudes and actions, we fought fans who are not orthodox and music not purely concerned with art. Where Jews hold holidays that celebrate specific legends, ancestors, and miracles, hiphoppers spoke of the old school with a holy reverence and urged new jacks to know their history. Our Zionism was the Hiphop Nation.

By the late 80s and early 90s mainstreaming had arrived, bringing powerful gifts, as the devil always does. Now our music was broadcast on prime-time MTV and our political views, via Chuck D and KRS-One, were heard on CNN and Nightline. Hiphop, like jazz and rock 'n' roll before it, had become the defining force of a generation. It was not going to die. The siege mentality subsided.

The guards at the gate were retired. The fan base grew and the music diversified, which caused the fan base to grow larger still and the music to diversify further. But we continue to live in America and suffer the daily assaults of racism. And our sanity continues to rely on having a place where the heroes look like us and play by our rules. As long as being a Black man is a cross to bear and not a benediction, you can find me and my comrades locked inside one of those mass therapy sessions called a party inside that tricoastal support group called the Hiphop Nation.

Love Your Niggas

{ *The Village Voice*, 1996 }

It's because we're so thirsty, musicwise, that we were so easily distracted. Sure, Tribe's album is great, as are De La's and Nas's, but where is this summer's undeniable classic? The "One More Chance"? The "Flava in Ya Ear"? The "G Thang"? (Ubiquity does not connote classic, "Killing Me Softly" fans.) Except for a few warm spells, this summer may be as cold musically as last winter was meteorologically: Our heavyweight title holders—Snoop, Dre, Biggie, and Wu-Tang—are basically on vacation, and of the two most-talked-about men in hiphop (Puff and Big), only one can rhyme and only one can produce to save his life. So when *One Nut Network*, a hiphop fanzine, published a profile of an anonymous MC called "Confessions of a Gay Rapper," of course we got distracted. Of course it became our hiphop "War of the Worlds."

"I learned the hard way," the artist said, "that niggas don't think that I can be hard and true to my craft if I'm putting a dick in my mouth . . .

"Yo, that shit is like crack. One good whiff and your ass is whipped! You see, only another brother can satisfy your need. . . . Only a man can satisfy another man." Who could it be? We jumped to our cellulars and found suddenly everyone knew someone who knew someone who knew some MC who liked to suck dick. Suddenly everyone had gaydar.

In time, conventional wisdom declared *One Nut*'s piece fiction. That's probably right: It was written under a pseudonym, with the intent of luring us into a guessing game rather than shielding a real person or demanding attention to the serious issues. No doubt, there are

MCs who represent both Myrtle Ave. and Christopher Street. But we needn't creep through hiphop's nooks and crannies to find its homosexuality and homosociality. They're out in the open, because hiphop is a very public celebration of intense Black male to Black male love.

> Male Christians stand up in church every given Sunday and claim to love a God who became a man, and talk about, "I love Him so!"—just incredible erotic language to express their devotion to Jesus, the God who was a man. It's the same way in hiphop culture. The profession of male love is so deep and the bond is so profound it forges this deeply erotic communion that gives the lie to their own homophobic passion. There's a deep homoerotic element.
>
> —Michael Eric Dyson, Professor of Communications Studies,
> The University of North Carolina, Chapel Hill

> Love your niggas that you rollin with. Love them.
>
> —Raekwon, Wu-Tang Clan, in *Ego Trip* magazine

Hiphop has always been some boy shit. Boys talking to boys about things they have done, or will do, with, or to, other boys. Black women have slid in by submitting completely to masculine desires or muffling their femininity. Or found themselves only slightly more accepted than white men. Even when the audience or subject is ostensibly female, the real audience and subject is the brothers. At base, pussy getting and pussy wrecking are no different than check getting and mic wrecking: playing fields for a boy and his dawgs.

And in a country where, historically, the center of *so much* has been the Black penis—whether motivated by violent fear, or curious longing, or proprietary desire, or some reaction to one or more of those, or some reaction to that reaction—Black masculinity remains equally threatening and threatened, powerful and fragile. So it's the Black male's

effort to keep up with his legendary dick, and the resulting caricatur-
ishly exaggerated manhood that emerged to quash even a hint of waf-
fling, that are the source of the homophobia grafted onto hiphop.

But, as in so many homosexual political fantasies, the homophobia is a mask for gayness. In hiphop, we need barely scratch the surface
to find the influence of queer culture: "Rapper's Delight" and the Village
People-esque regalia of Grandmaster Flash and the Furious Five recall
the sound and vibe of the exuberantly gay disco era. Bald-headed,
Black-clad, slam-dancing, cartoonishly ultramasculine Onyx borrow the
idioms of hardcore S&M, as do the Wu-Tang Clan, who feature thinly
veiled homoerotic torture scenarios on their debut album, in which
Raekwon and Method Man jokingly threaten each other's tongues,
asses, penises, and testes: "I'll lay your nuts on a fuckin dresser . . . and
bang them shits with a spiked fuckin bat. . . . I'll hang you by your
fuckin dick off a fuckin 12-story building. . . ."

Gangsta rappers en masse have much in common with drag
queens: "They're two different kinds of drag," notes Kendall Thomas,
Columbia School of Law professor and self-described Black gay intellectual activist. "The very elaborate sartorial style, the stylization of the
body, the sort of self-conscious deployment of sexuality as an instrument for the assertion of subjectivity, the very self-conscious represen-
tations of the male body—there are uncanny resemblances between the
gangsta and the diva." And then there's egotistical diva supreme Lil' Kim
from Junior M.A.F.I.A., neck and neck with Foxy Brown for female MC
of the year. In "Get Money," Kim sounds like a dominatrix, tauntingly,
seductively rhyming, "Get me open while I'm comin/Down your
throat and/Ya wanna be my main squeeze, nigga/Don't ya?/Ya wanna
lick between my knees, nigga/Don't ya?" She invokes the type of female
icons male homosexuals have showered with obsessive love: Mae West,
Eartha Kitt, Grace Jones. These are observations that any unsentimental,
nuanced look at our culture would turn up. Observations that, save for
the taboo, would be very, very cliché.

Perhaps the primary reason behind hiphop's homosexual influences
and, more importantly, its intense homosociality—the culture's boy's-club-
house or locker-room quality—is the massive fatherlessness, de facto and

de jure, of the hiphop generation. The billion-dollar industry of crack and the lure of Mafia dreams had a hand in forming our generation, but why were those boys running the streets all night? Why were they looking to Michael Corleone (from *The Godfather*) and Tony Montana (*Scarface*) and Goldie (*The Mack*) and Priest (*Superfly*) for the path to manhood in the first place? Because their families ran low on Y chromosomes. The lack, in a childhood home, of any significant older males at all has led many rappers, as adults, to place tremendous value on their relationships with men. "A lot of us in Wu-Tang ain't really had older brothers," Raekwon said in an interview, seemingly taking it for granted that they wouldn't have had fathers. "So now, when you got nine brothers around you, it's like the brothers that I never had, the older ones that when I need somebody to talk to and shit. Can't always go to Mom duke and talk to her. You need a man's point of view. . . . We learned to be the father of each other."

When Raekwon and his love-fathers convene, like the assemblages of nearly all hiphop crews from the Death Row inmates to Mobb Deep's niggas on the 41st Street side of things to the GangStarr Foundation to Erick Sermon's Def Squad, it is often an exclusively male gathering in the studio. By and large, women, who account for a minority of artists and a minuscule number of producers and engineers (if any at all), are completely barred from the studio by cultural convention. In her essay "Black Texts/Black Contexts," New York University professor Tricia Rose admits that "Even male rap producers with either very strong feminist friends or some sort of feminist ideology themselves have found that the men just don't feel comfortable if there are women interns around in the studio. They can't say all the things they would normally say because they might offend these women. And even when these women say, 'It doesn't matter. You can say whatever you want to me, I want to learn this stuff,' eventually the male creative process is challenged."

This mix of gender exclusivity and cultural innovation directly evokes ancient Greece. "Women played no part in Athenian high culture," Camille Paglia writes in *Sexual Personae*. "They could not vote, attend the theater, or walk in the Stoa talking philosophy." The Stoa is the great hall where Athenian philosophers lectured. And, of course, the studio, where rappers and their crew, their personal senate, convene to talk their philosophy, is hiphop's Stoa. The parallels between hiphop and Athens continue; Paglia goes on to say: "The male orientation of classical Athens was inseparable from its genius. Athens became great not despite but because of its misogyny. Male homosexuality played a similar catalytic role in Renaissance Florence and Elizabethan London. At such moments male bonding enjoys an amorous intensity of self-assurance, a transient conviction of victory over mothers and nature."

These hiphop senates often address issues of survival, planning not only how to express themselves musically but also how to improve themselves economically, and how to protect themselves physically. In 1993, Snoop said of L.A. gangs: "Niggas will do anything for you, do time for you, take a bullet for you, kill somebody for you. You can find that kind of love on the streets." That conflation of male-to-male love and combat recalls nothing so much as ancient Greece's homosexual fighting armies. In a 385 B.C. speech, Plato opined:

If there were . . . an army . . . made up of lovers and their loves . . . when fighting at each other's side, although a mere handful, they would overcome the world. For what lover would not choose rather to be seen by all mankind than by his beloved, either when abandoning his post or throwing away his arms? He would be ready to die a thousand deaths rather than endure this. Or who would desert his beloved or fail him in the hour of danger? The veriest coward would become an inspired hero, equal to the bravest, at such a time; Love would inspire him.

Within a decade Plato's vision was realized: In about 378 B.C. the general Gorgidas put together the Sacred Band of Thebes, a force of one hundred fifty pairs of lovers. Behind them, Thebes remained the most powerful state in Greece for forty years. Asked what he could accomplish with a crew that loved him and would do anything for him, Raekwon replied, "We could run the world, man. We could rule the world."

In the music there's a strand of Black unity which requires brothers to love brothers. The question there, however, is what is the nature of that love? And there, I think, hiphop gets confused. Because the extant models of love between men are inflected, unavoidably inflected, by a homoerotic component.

—Professor Thomas

In the straight mind, the gay man is defined primarily by his sexuality, by what he will and won't do with his dick. But, as with any human, the most important and powerful part of the gay body is not below the waist. Politically and romantically, the most critical organ is the heart, which gay men choose over and again, in the face of all sorts of societal rejection and oppression, to open for a deep, intense, self-assuring love with another male.

It is that sort of love, completely selfless, not necessarily sexual, between Black men that has brought on all of our culture's epic successes. Its wane—the moment when male-to-male love leaves the center of hiphop social organizations and they lose their small family quality to become small business collectives—will directly precede our final failures. Black unity is still paralyzed by the misunderstanding that unity equals uncritical acceptance, but at their best, hiphop crews, those informal boy's clubs, demonstrate true functional unity. In those moments hiphop is a national, daily Million Man March, not in what is said on records, but in the work of groups of men talking, battling, rescuing, engaging, hugging, feeding, loving, uplifting, fathering.

Black men loving Black men is the revolutionary act.

—Marlon Riggs

Love your niggas that you rollin with. Love them.

—Raekwon

Are Gay Rappers Too Real for Hiphop?

{ Caushun, *The New York Times*, 2003 }

It's Friday night in Bed-Stuy, Brooklyn, and Caushun is chilling on the third floor of his parents' brownstone. He is totally street: baggy jeans, wrist bands, fresh black Timberlands, a diamond stud in his left ear, and a baseball cap (worn to the back, at an angle) with his name spray-painted across the bill in graffiti bubble letters. Caushun is a rapper, and he's getting ready to rhyme for us, but right now he's flipping through *Vogue*. He did Kimora Lee Simmons's hair for her photo shoot, and he wants to see how it turned out.

Caushun can get fierce with some hair. "I'm nasty with mine," he said.

He calls himself "the weave king," an extensions specialist. He's done hairdos for J. Lo and Sarah Michelle Gellar, and he's the stereotype of the celebrity hairdresser. He's a b-boy with a poodle named Wesley and an apartment with ornate pillows with silk flowers on them and beautiful vases filled with giant lilies. Caushun is a twenty-five-year-old openly gay rapper from the same neighborhood of Biggie Smalls, with flippy wrists, a gay twang, and a flow that is liquid and cool and ready for the big time. He wants to be hiphop's homosexual Jackie Robinson.

Hiphop is now as large a cultural stage as baseball was in the 50s, yet the mainstream is just as closed to gay rappers as the major leagues were to Black men before Robinson. And, as with Robinson, for Caushun to break through could have a profound impact on how gay people are perceived throughout America.

"He's going to open up discussion about one of the last acceptable prejudices," said his manager, Ivan Matias. "With homosexuals having so much influence over hiphop from behind the scenes, it's time that they had a voice." He was referring to the gay executives, managers, stylists, and magazine editors in the music business.

Caushun said simply: "Look, I'm keepin it real. Don't let me find out that I'm keepin it too real for hiphop. Should that be the name of my album? *Too Real for Hiphop?*"

Caushun recently signed with Baby Phat Records, and his debut album, *Shock and Awe*, will come out at the end of June before Gay Pride Day. His self-confidence is so strong that he doesn't believe his being gay will keep him from selling a million records and having a video played on MTV twenty times a week—in other words, from becoming a star.

The hiphop impresario Russell Simmons, whose wife, Kimora Lee, is the owner and chief executive of Baby Phat, knows it will be hard to make Caushun a star, but he's hopeful.

"Rap music is one of the most homophobic musics we know," Mr. Simmons said. "But he's dope and he's unique because of his perspective on the world. I can't imagine that people aren't going to buy it. You think women and gay men won't buy it? It's a huge possibility."

Caushun says there were labels that wanted to turn him into a house-music artist or into the RuPaul of hiphop, but he said no. He wants to be mainstream: "You got Jay-Z talking about girls, girls, girls. Nelly, take your clothes off. They put their sexuality out front. What's the big deal if I put mine up front and come out open?"

He learned to rhyme just hanging around his neighborhood. He says he would sit up in his parents house with his boys, smoking weed, and someone would start to rhyme, it was no big deal. "I rhyme about everything," he said. "I just rhyme from a gay perspective. And it's not like it's a flamboyant gay perspective. It's the next-door neighbor. We saying the same thing. I just might put a little gay terminology in there."

He plucked a few grapes from a bowl on a table, walked over to his iMac, and put on a beat. The beat's just OK and the hook is kind of corny, but Caushun is witty, and he surely can flow.

What is recognized as the first hiphop record by an openly gay person was "Hip-Hop Don't Stop" by Man Parish, recorded in 1986. According to industry figures and Web sites devoted to the subject, there are now at least forty to fifty openly gay rappers worldwide. Most don't use homosexuality in the campy, cartoonish way Caushun does. The Deep Dickollective is a loose assemblage of Black men based in San Francisco. Two regular members are Juba Kalamka, who rhymes as Pointfivefag, and Tim'm West, a widely respected rapper. Mr. West, who is HIV-positive, is also an AIDS activist and a schoolteacher.

Their 2002 debut album, *BourgieBohoPostPomoAfroHomo*, deals with homosexuality less sensually than politically. In one rhyme Mr. West notes that the struggle going on inside his body is far more frightening than the street violence so often discussed in hiphop. "I got T's and disease fightin for possession of me. How am I gonna be scared of Glocks you pops, G?," he rhymes in "Rhyters Retreat."

The collective uses live instruments and plays with forms the way the experimental rappers the Roots do. Its rappers, or MCs, rhyme with the intellectual revolutionary pose of Chuck D and the erudition of Cornel West. They feel that just being homosexual in hiphop is a revolutionary act.

"We're just trying to shatter that whole notion that a real MC has to be straight," Tim'm West said. The collective's most recent album, *Them Niggas DoneWent and Said*, was released on April 19.

The collective and Caushun are part of an openly gay hiphop world that is as varied as its straight counterpart. A rapper named Semaj from Brooklyn, who calls himself "a thug who happens to be homosexual," wants to appeal to the same people who love Jay-Z. Tori Fixx from Minneapolis calls himself a cross between the mellow rapper Q-Tip and Prince. Mr. Fixx released an album called *The Mochasutra*. Miss Money, a rapper, singer, and producer from Houston, has been called the gay Missy Elliot. MaaSen, from Sweden, rhymes in a high-energy style reminiscent of the Irish-American rap group House of Pain. Katey Red is a transvestite from New Orleans. There are others in England, Switzerland, and France.

Many say the best openly gay MC is a short white lesbian named

Cyryus (pronounced Serious). In 1998 she released an album called *The Lyricist*, which recalls the moody, brooding, lyric-focused feel of the rap group Black Moon. On a song called "Y Us?" she rhymes about a lesbian friend who's pretending to be straight. "You doin ya own thing/ a portrait of success/ congratulations!/You've been nominated best supporting actress!/ I certainly hope the enemy is impressed/ now I carry the struggle on my shoulders cuz I've inherited your stress."

But Cyryus hasn't been able to test her talent because just being gay in America is challenging enough.

"When I met her in 1996 she was like, 'I got a record, I'm pushing it,'" said Dutchboy, a rapper in the group Rainbow Flava and a central figure in gay hiphop. "She was playing all these shows at all these pride events. Then she had some family problems and had to go live with her mom for a while. Then she was like, I'm joining the army. She lasted about a year before she got thrown out on some don't ask, don't tell. Last I knew she was bouncing around the South." No one I spoke to knew how to find her.

Many in gay hiphop feel it's inevitable that a gay rapper will gain mainstream success. They point to the once unthinkable success of a white rapper like Eminem. "It'll be like D-Day," Dutchboy said. "A lot of people will go down trying and then someone will make it off the beach."

The record business isn't so sure. Executives from major hiphop labels, who spoke on condition of anonymity, said there was little chance of an openly gay rapper succeeding in the ultrahomophobic world of hiphop. "A manager plays a record for us," one executive said, "and it's incredible, then the manager says, 'Oh by the way, he's gay.' Everything stops. I really think we would probably tell him don't talk about it. Don't rock the boat."

Mr. Simmons says there is a chance, if a gay artist can find the right niche. "The hiphop hard-core kid may think it's funny, may buy a single," Mr. Simmons said, "but he's not likely to buy an album because you're not speaking to a lifestyle that they're aspiring to. All these rappers are talking about a lifestyle that people relate to or aspire to. I don't think the average straight hiphop consumer is going to buy it, but there's a lot of gay consumers buying rap records."

Of course, it would be tough for a gay rapper to get the discussion off of his sexuality and onto his rhymes. The cultural critic Michael Eric Dyson, who is a professor of African-American studies and religious studies at the University of Pennsylvania, said, "Your flow would have to be so ridiculous that Biggie would be envious!"

Hiphop has long ignored gay rappers and straight hiphop stars who visit gay clubs, some of whom use homophobic language in their rhymes. "I haven't had sex with any famous rappers, but I know about some," Dutchboy said with a hint of mischief. "It also gets complicated when you say what do you really mean by gay? There are a lot of artists that the grapevine suggests have sex with guys on tour. Does that make you gay? People have written books about it."

Mr. Kalamka said that before he came out he was unable to freestyle because he was afraid of what he might say. Now he can. Hanifah Walidah, a San Francisco rapper, agreed that coming out gave her new strength. "I look at old videotapes of me performing when I was in the closet," Ms. Walidah said, "and I could see through my body language that my body was tight, that I was holding something in, I wasn't giving all that I had to give. Sometimes I look at these MCs who I know are gay and they're off the hook and I'm like, Damn, wonder what they'll be like when they come out? How dope will they be when they're truly free?"

Asked whether or not the Hiphop Nation is ready for a gay MC, Tim'm West said: "The question is irrelevant. The openly gay MC is here. Will you or will you not respond to it? If you don't, I'm still going to keep making rhymes. I'm not interested in whether or not America is ready for me. I'm here."

Hiphop Familigia

{ Junior M.A.F.I.A. and the Wu-Tang Clan,

The Village Voice, 1995 }

> Slaves responded to these assaults on their familial relations by restructuring their social institutions into new forms, at times based on their African heritage, to establish distinctly Afro-American relationships that often preserved their families in the face of the most adverse conditions.
>
> —John Hope Franklin and Alfred Moss, *From Slavery to Freedom*

> If you one of them niggas that's just all about money, there gotta be love first. Love your niggas that you rollin with. Love them. Cause it's hard to see who care. So when you do get a chance to absorb some real live niggas around you that's on some money shit and know how to go about business and got love, it's gonna make your trip mo' better . . . It's all about having a family.
>
> —Raekwon the Chef, *Ego Trip Magazine*

Son, you don't even know how real hiphop is keepin it. Check the technique: like most Black people, MCs have only two paths to success. One is being born exceedingly gifted: with boundless athletic ability, off-the-hook physical beauty, or a creamy singing voice. The hiphop counterparts are the butter-voiced MCs who could've been singers: Big Daddy Kane, Q-Tip, Method Man, Snoop, Rakim. The only other route to the top is to outthink, outwork, and outdo the competition like all the hustlers from 125th to Hollywood. In hiphop: KRS-One, Chuck D, Raekwon, Ice Cube.

'Course, white folks have a third path to the top: de facto affirmative action, otherwise known as white privilege (represented by the self-parodying, quirkily talented Beastie Boys, and Vanilla Ice). This is the door that prompted Arthur Ashe to remark that Blacks will never be truly equal with whites until we can be mediocre and get by. This is the reason why, after sealing the lunch box and before meeting the first-grade school bus, Black mothers like mine pulled their babies close and told them, "You have to be twice as good as those little white kids."

Mom, of course, was right. But as I grew up I also discovered that there are a small handful of Black kids who, thanks to the extreme success of their parents, grow up with a sort of privilege that is otherwise only available to whites. Enter Junior M.A.F.I.A., the JFK, Jr. of hiphop. Junior M.A.F.I.A.—Masters At Finding Intelligent Attitudes—are nine homies of Biggie Smalls from around the way in Brooklyn. And right now, they couldn't be better connected.

Biggie helped Junior M.A.F.I.A. get their deal and rhymed on their lead single, "Player's Anthem." The group is clear about their debt. In the liner notes of their debut album, Conspiracy, Little Kim, who kicks the bulk of the rhymes and nearly all of the good ones, writes, "To B.I.G. Poppa—My mentor and friend. You've paved the way for me. Without you I wouldn't exist in this rap game. Forever your lieutenant, Love ya!" Like few groups before it, Junior M.A.F.I.A. is generally insignificant musically, but very significant culturally.

In the late 80s and very early 90s, when a rap album was, for many, part of campaigning for a shadow senatorship, hiphop was punctuated by nationalism, Afrocentrism and, occasionally, Pan-Africanism. But in the mid-90s, the industry grew and the intense regionalism that had bubbled under took its place, then seemed to morph into an ideology that could best be called "Blockism."

Blockism is the idea that your neighborhood block is the center of the world, and the most important audience to impress. It's also the directive that if you get off the block your peeps come with you. Blockism is a manifestation of our African communal nature and our African-

American sense of rootlessness; the power of numbers, the scarcity of jobs, and probably the idea that the less often you have to step up to the mic, the more likely you'll always have dope lyrics. And it's led to the familylike structure behind the three biggest entities in hiphop today: the Wu-Tang Clan, Death Row, and Biggie Smalls/the Junior M.A.F.I.A. Clique.

Unlike loosely organized tribes of groups like the Native Tongues or the Hit Squad, collectives like Wu-Tang, Death Row, and Junior M.A.F.I.A. are hiphop families: large groups of almost exclusively men, many of whom grew up together, some of whom are related by blood, that, through the direction of a single leader, work together to make a series of hiphop albums united by a thematic and sonic manifesto. When a collective bands together to make an album it can often be larger in aesthetic and emotional scope than most hiphop albums in the same way that a jazz septet makes music that isn't necessarily better but is qualitatively different than that of a trio. The albums are marked by rituals, clearly defined mores, and idiosyncratic language that makes the listening experience something like entering a foreign country, or someone else's home.

The first true hiphop family was Public Enemy. PE's pseudo-militaristic structure, and the Black Panther–esque titles that punctuated it, only added to the group's aura and surely, future members of Wu-Tang, Death Row, and Junior M.A.F.I.A. grew up paying attention. Wu-Tang and Death Row, especially, differ from PE's model only in character, not structure: instead of military motifs, they borrow from crime families like the mafia (hence "the Wu-Gambinos,") and the gangs (hence the Dogg Pound hand signs). What all three share, in keeping with African-American tradition, is a matriarchal family structure. However, the role of matriarch is occupied by men because again, in classic African-American family tradition, family roles are adaptable. (That Black men organize themselves into largely femaleless families speaks to sexism—which PE wore on its shoulder through its first two albums and Death Row celebrated at the end of The Chronic—but also a hunger to experience maleness, which took an extreme turn with the unforgettable repressed homosexual torture skit on Wu-Tang's debut.)

The matriarchs are the lead producers—Hank Shocklee in PE, the RZA in Wu-Tang, Dr. Dre at Death Row—who run the family's de facto home, the studio, and keep the family nourished with butter tracks. They are never the most-celebrated cog of the organization. And most significantly, like a real mother, they almost never leave the family. While the rappers of Wu-Tang and Death Row rhyme on various singles with other artists, the matriarchs refuse to be producers for hire like Puffy, Jermaine Dupri. (Dre's long, long-awaited collaboration with Ice Cube, *Helter Skelter,* will not be an exception: as a founding member of N.W.A, Cube is, without a doubt, an uncle of Death Row.) This stability is crucial: as in real life, many families can withstand the father leaving, but they will have a hard time regrouping if the mother leaves, which is a large part of PE's demise.

The fathers are the ones who first take the group's message and image and sell it to the public. They play the ambassador to the outside world: Chuck, Snoop, Method Man. And of course, what would an extended Black family be without elders—the eccentric and deceptively wise Flavor-Flav, Ol Dirty Bastard, the D.O.C.; outcasts and runaways: Professor Griff in PE; RBX and Warren G. in Death Row; and children—the artists who follow the family's initial album, whose road to success is eased by the presence of the parents: Raekwon, the Dogg Pound. (PE, unfortunately, never had kids, but they're from a different era. This moment, the era of the remix and off-album single, where artists saturate the market, seems to represent a sort of sexual revolution making PE's time seem puritan by comparison.)

Junior M.A.F.I.A., essentially the children of mother *and* father Biggie, is too young to have experienced the type of family drama that is legend with Death Row and Wu-Tang. What they do share with the others, though, is the essential element behind every African-American family: the desire to create a structure that will protect its members as they move about this strange land.

Whitepeople believed that whatever the mannners, under every dark skin was a jungle. Swift unnavigable waters, swinging screaming baboons, sleeping snakes, red gums ready for their sweet white blood . . . But it wasn't the jungle Black brought with them to this place from the other (livable) place. It was the jungle whitefolks planted in them. And it grew. It spread. In, through and after life, it spread, until it invaded the whites who had made it. Touched them every one. Changed and altered them. Made them bloody, silly, worse than even they wanted to be, so scared were they of the jungle they had made. The screaming baboon lived under their own white skin; the red gums were their own.

—Toni Morrison, *Beloved*

The block: an indigenously Black space that the outside world views as uncivilized. Those who live there know better. It is the birth-place of much of Black culture and a place that is slowly, constantly, being crushed, the way a barrel of grapes is crushed by a slowly twisting press, by America.

The music industry: an insanely capitalist, white-invented and -run structure (Juice? Keep it real: Aren't Andre, Russell, and Puff well-paid, high-powered overseers for Al Teller, the head of MCA; Alain Levy, the king of PolyGram; and Clive Davis, the top master at Arista?). In the industry, Blacks are placed into legally binding relationships where they usually work very hard and get the short end of the financial stick and spend much of their time making and performing music that protests their condition (no other form of music or group of musicians criticize the music industry with the persistence and fervor of hiphop). Families, hiphop families, are usually split up. And unless you leave the industry you'll probably never get off your plantation.

The block: Africa. The industry: America.

Blockism, then, is a more pragmatic nationalism and the hiphop family a comfort zone for strangers in a strange land. A mobile home to make your trip—through the industry, across the Atlantic, from the cradle to the grave—a little mo' better.

No Drinks in '96!

{ Funkmaster Flex, *The New Yorker,* 1996 }

Not since Adam was rib to rib with Eve has the battling been so heated. Sightings are pouring in from clubs across the city: homeboys, eyes slitted, leaning against the bar at a forty-five-degree angle, gripping the neck of an ostentatiously shaped bottle of champagne and boldly eschewing the time-honored ritual of buying drinks for the admirably evolved ladies around them. "You know you ain't gettin no drink," some have been reported to bark. Sistas have responded by threatening to quit merging with interested young men. A stalemate has been reached. Negotiations, to put it lightly, are tense. It looks as though a long, hot, drinkless and/or sexless summer lies ahead.

The controversy dates back a few months to the night when Funkmaster Flex (not his real name), the top radio and club hiphop DJ working today, began using his late-night radio show on WQHT-FM, 97.1, aka Hot 97, as a bully pulpit, urging men to quit buying drinks for women. "Dinner and a movie is cool," Flex says. "Then you're gettin to know somebody. But in a club, she's gonna talk to you while you're buyin drinks. The drinks stop, and she'll be like, 'Alright, I'm gonna just walk around for a minute and I'll be right back.' Naw, you walk around all you want, cuz you're gonna walk around thirsty. You want a drink? Have a drink of water."

Flex, who is dark-skinned with a goatee, a sweet round face, and an infectious smile, pauses from mixing records in his small booth at Hot 97, and recalls the start of the skirmish. "I was spinnin at a club, just watchin what goes on at the bar. I'd never paid attention to it before." In the background a woman's voice sings plaintively, "Money is the sweet-est hang-o-ver . . . I don' wanna get over."

"I saw one guy with a bottle of Moët," Flex says. "He was kind of chillin by himself. These girls came around him, geesed—that's old school for when you get jerked—his Moët and bounced"—left him—"and he didn't even catch the whole thing. By the time the bottle was empty, no one was around. I said, 'Yo, his Moët got geesed.' So, I said, 'You know what, I'm gonna shout that out.' "

The self-proclaimed national spokesman for the ad-hoc "No Drinks In '96" committee is Busta Rhymes, a larger-than-life rapper with the hyped-up energy of an overactive little brother and the charisma of the most popular kid in class. "Traditionally, man, things got to change, man!!" Busta preach-rasped excitedly. "Comin up we got a lot of new shorties"—women—"in this hiphop thing, comin up with old-school expectations and all these traditional, backwards way of frame of thinking!!! We got to think differently!! Women can buy drinks, too! Claim they independent, claim they so self-sufficient, represent that, then!!! REPRESENT!!!! Ya know what I'm sayin?!!"

Busta downshifted a bit. "I still got friends that I see and I'm like, 'Yo let's get a drink.' But I can't see no woman comin up off the dance floor, hot and sweaty, and because homey probably look a little intrigu-ing at the moment, gettin a drink. Can't happen!! She will see a six-pack of *empty, drippin Heineken bottles!!!* Word up!!"

Enter Angie Martinez, also a popular DJ at Hot 97, and a breath-takingly cute mamacita with a perfect ponytail and the voice of the world's coolest little sister. Angie ain't havin it. "Granted, guys shouldn't *have* to buy drinks," Martinez says coolly, "but girls don't go around ha-rassing guys at the club. We have to deal with all the nonsense. So they should pay, in some way, for the nonsense."

Though Flex and Busta claim some success, Martinez maintains that the guys are full of it. "It's not working," she says flatly. "They're not gonna be successful at all. Not at all. Flex would be changing the whole mating ritual. He may be powerful, but not that powerful. Boys will be boys." Then, she said a bit conspiratorially, "You'll see Busta at the clubs buyin girls drinks, and on the low, so will Flex." She also took a moment to thank Flex for, "always comin through on Ladies Night"—her Friday night show—"with a bottle of Cristal."

Both men sternly denied the allegations and vowed to press on. But how long? "It depends on how the ladies handle themselves this year," Flex decreed pensively. "Some girls have been like, 'Well, can I buy you a drink to show you everyone isn't like that?' But I also got girls that come up to me and say this is my fourth drink, you ain't stoppin it. Sometimes little cups fly up into the booth. I just tell 'em, I'll make it worse. If you wanna come to an agreement, a medium, fine. But I think this is a war I'm gonna ride out." To be continued . . .

10. Boys Will Be Boys

Trainspotting

{ *The New Yorker*, 1996 }

Cope is a heavyset, twenty-eight-year-old Bronx-born Puerto Rican father of two who is nearing the end of an illustrious fifteen-year career as a graffiti writer. He writes his name—"writes" is the preferred verb to describe spray-painting graffiti, or graf, on a public surface—in color-filled letters that blend and slope in a way that suggests live animation. Sabe, a protégé of sorts, is a wiry, eighteen-year-old Bronx-born Dominican whose height of about five feet two inches includes the large Black curls that lounge atop his head like an Afro crown. He became a graf-world celebrity in a mere three years, because in place of his name he often writes a six-foot-tall demonic face that appears to be laughing at the viewer. Since 1977, when the Transit Authority introduced the buff (essentially a giant chemical car wash that removes paint), many of New York's graf writers have given up using subway cars as their canvases and have turned to walls and storefront gates. Still, a handful continue to write on trains—a discipline that combines the skills of a visual artist and a second-story burglar.

On a Sunday morning, at two-thirty a.m., Cope and Sabe arrive at the Bedford Park Boulevard station, on the No. 4 line, next to a train yard filled with parked No. 4 and D trains. They split up to scope the train yard for cops, transit workers, or anyone else who might interfere. They are particularly wary of the vandal squad, an N.Y.P.D. division set up to combat graf. Sabe likes to play cat and mouse with the squad. "I talk to them on the phone," he says. "I tell them, 'This is Sabe. Have you seen my trains lately?'" He goes on, "In graffiti, what everybody's really out for is fame. And one part of fame is when a writer gets caught, he is questioned. They say, 'Do you know Sabe? You get less time if you turn him in.' "

For some time, Cope and Sabe stand outside a fence in front of the station looking for cops and rival graf artists. The yard looks empty, so Cope reaches into Sabe's black duffelbag and pulls out a pair of large red fence cutters. He calmly walks over to the fence and begins to cut a square—quietly, efficiently—about three feet by three feet. As he moves back to the bag, two bells announce that a train is coming into the station. The train deposits and collects passengers, then lumbers on, and Cope pries back the fence with his hands to enlarge the hole. Sabe squeezes through. Cope follows, cutting his left hand on the jagged wire. He doesn't seem to notice the gashes or the trail of red dots he leaves behind.

Following a winding, well-trod dirt path through a stand of trees, Cope and Sabe make their way to the back of the yard, where the trains are parked for the night. Then Sabe opens his bag and pulls out six cans of Krylon spray paint in white, off-white, yellow, black, and two shades of blue. Before Cope begins to write, he puts a surgeon's mask over his mouth and nose and notices he's bleeding. He licks the blood off his fingers and follows Sabe to a No. 4 train. Both write in short controlled blasts of paint: off-white outlined in black for Cope; white dotted with light-blue spots and outlined in dark blue for Sabe.

During one of Cope's blood-licking breaks, a D train begins rumbling into the yard on the tracks next to the train that Cope and Sabe are writing on. For a moment, its headlamps flash directly on them.

"Oh, shit!" Cope says.

They dart to the rear of the subway car, pull open the door, and climb on board. They creep to the front car, weaving between poles, ducking under windows. Cope asks nervous questions. "Yo, did that conductor see us? Is he gonna go phone it to the vandal squad? How come you didn't see him? Do you think he saw us?"

They find seats next to the conductor's booth—out of any possible line of vision—and catch their breath. Sabe looks around and announces it's "time to play locksmith," and goes to the door of the conductor's booth. "If we get raided, we can hide in here," he says.

After twenty minutes during which neither of them makes a sound, Cope grows confident that they weren't spotted, mainly because there hasn't been any sign of the vandal squad. When the D train pulls out of the station, he and Sabe go outside to complete their pieces. Both add a yellow background. Then they step back. Later that morning the paint will be discovered and washed off, so Cope pulls out a camera and records their night's work for posterity.

Night Moves

{ *The New Yorker*, 1995 }

How do you know when the party's over? One recent evening, the downtown club Nell's was clogged with young Black men and women dressed, coiffed, and dancing in the most cutting-edge styles. After considerable quantities of Moët had been drunk, blunts smoked, phone numbers exchanged, and deals—some legal, some perhaps not so legal—closed, the DJ launched a string of singles by the hottest rapper in hiphop, The Notorious B.I.G. At that moment, everyone knew that the party was just getting started.

In minutes, the room was bouncing with B.I.G.'s "Who Shot Ya"— a slow, pulsing song with a delicately malevolent quality that seems to capture sonically the air of living on the edge of danger which some young Black men work hard to project and others are saddled with. Moments into the song, a group of male dancers decided to prove their manhood with pullups on a water pipe running across the dance floor's ceiling. The party's end seemed close.

As one young man strained to complete his fifth pullup, a pipe broke. Soon water began raining into the room. The pullup men rejoiced, dancing in the downpour as though it were a fire hydrant on a scorching summer day. And, though the crowd cringed away, only a third actually left the room.

At first, the remaining crowd danced tenuously, torn between their attraction to the groove and their impulse to get out of the rain. But as it became obvious that the rain wouldn't soon stop, the DJ faded into "One More Chance," which is B.I.G.'s syrupy smooth ode to his immense ability to mack—that is, get women—and a current monster hit.

Suddenly, no one was dancing tenuously anymore, and, though it was raining on the dance floor, everyone seemed comfortable dancing amid the chaos. Someone yelled, "Rain, motherfucker! Rain!"

But after the second chorus of "One More Chance" the DJ stopped spinning, and people began filtering out of the club. The party was, finally, over.

Bling-bling Makes the Dictionary!

{ unpublished, 2004 }

Brothers and sisters raise a glass! It's time for a celebration. Your friend and mine, the great slang word "bling-bling" has been voted into the Oxford English Dictionary! For slang like him to be immortalized in the dictionary is as good as making it into the Word Hall of Fame. I haven't been this proud since "ain't" got the call.

Say what you will about the concept of bling-bling, but linguistically, he's invaluable. He conveys what it once took numerous words to express. He filled a void in the language. Ain't that what we always tell the young slang when they first slink into the language with big ambitions? If ya want have a long life, ya can't just be a synonym for some word already in the dictionary. Ya gotta fill a void in the language.

I remember the day "bling-bling" first came into this crazy party we call American English. He was just a little onomatopoeia. Nothing but a clever colloquialism from New Orleans. A single syllable said twice that put into words the gleam of a diamond. No one thought "bling-bling" had a chance to make it far in the language. But these kids today love their diamonds and Black people have always loved slang with repetition in it. Remember "somethin-somethin" and "keep on keepin on"? Well, "bling-bling" got into a few rap songs and suddenly people everywhere wanted to use him in all kinds of sentences. He was fun to say, looked good on a page, and he had charisma. You couldn't hate the word any more than you could hate nonconflict diamonds.

But then he grew up and matured linguistically. He moved from representing diamonds to the larger sense of being conspicuously consumptuous, of trumpeting your financial success, of wearing your bank account. Those were the years before the dot-com bubble burst and the timing was perfect for "bling-bling." He capitalized on how well he fit into the zeitgeist.

Nowadays, every once in a while, you hear someone speak of a bling-bling generation. I'm not sure he's a large enough word to define his times, but do you know what an honor it is for a word to be considered worthy of defining a generation, even if by just a few people? That's a special moment. There were days we feared "bling-bling" was close to becoming a cliché, and maybe he did become one, but now he's a superstar.

I'm sure "bling-bling" will want to share this triumph with the whole family, all the great Black slang words for money that came before him. His grandfathers, "bread" and "dough." His uncles, "duckets," "lucci," and "dead presidents." And his famous older brothers, "ghetto fabulous" and the "Benjamins." See, this victory isn't just about "bling-bling." It's about the entire hiphop community coming together and talking about themselves and their money with so much passion that they gave birth to language. And with "bling-bling" they done made some slang so bad the white folks had to put it in the dictionary! Amen.

Some have said that the era of bling-bling is over and the usage of him will decrease in the future because of the still-slumping economy and the anti-SUV movement, which is an attack on the showy consumerism that's behind bling-bling. But I say nonsense! We're Americans. We supersize everything from french fries to SUVs. Bling-bling is as American as microwave apple pie, a baseball labor strike, and a Hummer that's twice as big and runs half as well as its Japanese counterpart. As Martin Amis wrote in his novel *Money*, I am pussy-whipped by money, but then so is the United States. The Brit had it right. In America you work like a Puritan in hopes of spending like a Puffy. And in the bling-bling generation, if you've got money, you never leave home without wearing it.

An Invitation to Carnal Russian Roulette, or Memoirs of a Sexual Desperado

{ *The Bastard on the Couch: 27 Men Try Real Hard to Explain Their Feelings about Love, Loss, Fatherhood, and Freedom, 2003* }

It is perhaps the greatest game ever created. It blends seduction, deception, danger, and electric illicit sex. It demands a gambler's heart and a cat burglar's cool. The Game can be expensive emotionally as well as financially, and if the other member of the threesome catches you, physically. People have played carnal Russian roulette for thousands of years and many have been killed because of it. I am not necessarily proud of my behavior, but this is no cautionary tale. Consider it a recommendation. The Game is among the great, rare pleasures in life. Imagine the cactus with milk so sweet it's worth the needles.

I've heard of bank robbers who continued their career after becoming filthy rich because the thrill of stealing was a greater pleasure than even the money. Those sensitive artists are my brothers. They'll understand me if no one else does. You see, the Game is not about love on any level. It's about trying to touch fire without getting burned. It's about embracing your inner bad guy and being a slave to your id. It's about gambling with life and love. I once saw a Hitchcock tale about a gambler who'd bet you that you couldn't light a lighter ten consecutive times. That's a boring proposition until you hear the wager: if you succeed you get his beautiful Cadillac. If you fail he gets to cut off your pinky. Now that's excitement. If big risk can supercharge the most boring little contest, imagine what it can do to sex.

I've always found the word "cheating" to be a simplistic, flaccid, and overall pathetic choice of words to describe the complex missions I've completed. Besides, they say all's fair in love and war. Is it cheating because I combined love and war? Why don't you decide. Sit a while and listen to the memoirs of a twisted young man who believed the only good sex was forbidden sex. A man who could enjoy sex only when served with a side dish of danger. Names have not been changed to protect the innocent because no one in this sordid tale is innocent. We have lied, deceived, and committed sexual theft [translation: cheated]. Of course, the lying and deceit came mostly at my urging. I was a carnal cat burglar, a sexual desperado, one of those little devils willing to risk life and limb for forbidden fruit. Sure, I made a mess of my life, but I had fun. What happened exactly? As Humbert Humbert said at the outset of his sordid tale, look at this tangle of thorns.

The trouble began long ago. I once thought it started with the trauma I experienced after a bizarre threeway involving a restaurateur, a waitress, and a handgun, but, no, it starts much, much earlier that that. You see, as a child I had a bad habit. I liked to steal. As early as age seven I was developing sticky fingers and a flexible moral compass. I did it for the adrenaline, the outfoxing, the conquering of fear, and the excitement of getting over. There is no rush quite like opening a wallet you've liberated.

But all that came to an end one horrid afternoon when Dad caught me in a little crime and punished me cruelly. (That was not when my conversion came.) That evening we went to Grandma's house and he trumpeted the story to her, casting himself as the self-righteous sheriff collaring a jailbird in training. Such vulgar fiction. Grandma pulled me aside and exposed me to the cold truth. "It's not bad that you did it," that wise sage said. "It's bad that you got caught." That old angel, a professor of moral relativism, showed me the light.

Many years later the second of the three moments that transformed me from an ordinary citizen into one who hungered for the Game arrived in the form of a brief, wordless invitation from a player. It was the beginning of a summer during my college days. I was hired to do menial tasks at a hip and romantic little restaurant on the Eastern Seaboard. As the youngest member of the staff I was apparently seen as something of a tasty morsel, for no less than three members of the staff moved in to have a bite of me.

The first made her move within the first week of my employment there. We went for a drink after work and before I knew it her tongue was down my throat and her wedding ring was in her pocket. It lasted just a moment—then she ran—but her danger-charged kiss was more electric than anything I'd ever felt. Still, I was not ready. There was one last incident that completed my transformation into a monster. The bizarre threeway. It took place at the end of the summer.

Long before I arrived at that little shop of sexual horrors it'd been widely rumored among the staff that a particular sexy waitress was dating the owner, but despite plenty of circumstantial evidence, both of them denied the relationship. This threw a strange shroud over the story, for there was no reason for them to lie. I had not yet discovered the Game, but was attracted to the supposedly single waitress all summer long. At the end of the summer, since they both refused to admit to a relationship, I made a play for her. And thus one night during my last week there, I found her and me alone in the restaurant after closing, with her tongue down my throat. Then the owner walked in on us. Without a word from anyone he put his gun on the table, took off her dress, and initiated a threeway in which he never acknowledged me. It was as if we were having independent encounters with her at the same time: even when we were both touching her he never even grazed my soft fingertips as he manhandled her. It was a moment injected with danger on so many levels, a moment so bizarre that while it was happening I wondered if I would one day discuss it in front of a jury. But hours later, after I caught my emotional breath, I realized I'd stumbled onto another level.

That night left me so scarred I needed all my sex to have some sort of danger and I began playing the Game. My sexual war games are, of course, threesomes. The third member isn't consenting and usually isn't fully aware of the threesome in which he or she is participating. But it's that other person, the one who's getting screwed without getting sex, who we can thank for the sense of risk that gives the Game its supercharge.

In the following years I had a few brief conquests (I once lured a lesbian away from her girlfriend and twice had actual threesomes) but was unable to play the Game robustly until I met, let's call her Debbie (because that's her name). Debbie was a beautiful modern dancer who didn't know she wanted to play, but even though she'd been living with her boyfriend for three years, she neglected to mention him until forty-five minutes into our first date. She spoke of him in passing and with a minimum of feeling, as if he were a small chore she had to do later that evening but didn't know why. Clearly, this was a difficult moment in their relationship. A greater man would've walked away, respectful of the challenge of making any relationship work. But I'm not that type of guy.

Over the next two weeks, as we went to dinners and out dancing and to the movies, she told me repeatedly that she wasn't going to sleep with me. She told me every day. But in those days she was staying in New York where her dance company was rehearsing. The boyfriend (and she) lived in another city. She was borrowing a gorgeous apartment on Riverside Drive from some Columbia professor on leave (off in Italy playing the Game, no doubt). It was a cavernous place, a romantic fantasy with majestic views and a giant bed with four engraved mahogany posts, the sort of apartment only Hollywood would envision as a plausible place for two young, Black, largely penniless artists to find themselves alone and horny late one morning. We ripped each other apart in a lust frenzy. But if that wasn't enough, either fate or the great director in the sky cued the phone to cry out for attention just a moment after we finished. It was her freshly cuckolded boyfriend. She spoke to him briefly while wearing nothing and struggling to hide her labored breathing. As the light from the window pointed out a small dimple on her ass that I hadn't noticed during our strenuous workout she told him, "I love you." I could tell he knew something was awry, but didn't know what. I loved it.

For the next year Debbie lied and deceived while I aided and abetted and her boyfriend played the perfect foil, chasing after us in the shadows, quick enough to smell the smoke but too slow to find the fire. It was dramatic and messy and occasionally called for the cloak-and-dagger work of a cold-war spy. (He almost caught us together once, unwittingly of course.) Every time we had sex she said it was the last time. Every moment together was stolen, and thus, precious. (So twisted.)

After a year of our ongoing fiasco Debbie left him for me, and we began seeing each other on more conventional terms. This went bad quickly. It wasn't nearly as much fun without the Game. But she was beautiful, and I didn't want to leave her. Then one night a friend of mine introduced me to Keisha and mentioned that it didn't matter to her that I had a girlfriend.

Keisha was a sexy little buppie with big tits from upper-crust Connecticut who rebelled against her privileged upbringing through deviant sex. She loved the Game. Thus began a new threesome. It seemed like the right thing to do because at that point the entire country was talking about a presidential intern named Monica Lewinsky.

Now, I understand that the intrusion of that name into this tale is overtly self-mocking and caricaturish. If this were fiction, this subplot would be too easy, too pat, too hokey. But in some way, knowing that the president of the United States was still one of us, one of that band of crazies who just love the Game, made me feel I should be playing, if for no other reason than to support my leader. Keisha was more than happy to second my motion, sharing my vitriol toward the evil Ken Starr and showing up for our trysts with her hair bobbed and peeking out from under a beret, a blatant copy of Monica's famous look, an appropriately twisted little joke.

For months there was lying and deceit and a shadowy threeway transfixing Keisha and Debbie and me. But this time the stakes were higher. I hadn't cared about Debbie's boyfriend's feelings, and I wasn't scared of him. I enjoyed stealing from him. But in the new threeway I was gambling with Debbie's feelings. This level of danger made things with Keisha not electric but explosive. But if Debbie ever found out what I was doing, it'd break her heart. I couldn't have that. So I dumped Debbie and started seeing Keisha exclusively. That was stupid. Any good West Coast rapper will tell you, Ya can't turn a ho into a housewife.

I really tried to leave the Game alone then. For the first year of my relationship with Keisha I stayed away. But for some reason Keisha never trusted me. A lack of evidence only fed her suspicion, made her think she wasn't looking hard enough. Eventually it didn't make any sense not to play because she was already acting like a bitter, jealous cuckold. So I had brief flings with Debbie, a couple of tenderonis in L.A., and the babysitter for the baby downstairs, a low-level model from Eastern Europe. Through it all Keisha played the perfect foil, chasing after me and my cuties with the competence of Inspector Clouseau.

One day around this time an old, old girlfriend of mine had twins, and I went to visit them. When she started to breast-feed in front of me, her boyfriend flew into a jealous rage and threw me out of their house. I couldn't be too mad. It was a bit like being accused of a crime you didn't do, when you've committed that same crime on other occasions. I guess I'd acquired the look of a criminal.

Three years ago I retired undefeated. Never once was I caught by any of them. I don't think I've ever been the third member of a threesome, but you can never be sure. Alas, all that's behind me now. I leave this as a testament for those who will play in the future. Hopefully my story will reach some young people at the beginning of their romantic careers and let them know there is another path. There is an electricity that comes from illicit, ill-begotten, stolen sex that is unlike any other feeling. The Game is a roller coaster everyone should know once.

How does my current flame keep me happy? Let's just say that covert public sex has quite a high degree of danger. But more, I've found that being able to share my danger with a single rare angel can be even more intense than the chaos of the Game. The bottom line is she's the best thing that's ever happened to me. It's cool to go to Vegas and get into a little trouble, blow your funny money, and have the time of your life, but the guy at the craps table gambling with his rent money is an idiot. I might be crazy, but I'm not stupid.

11. Who Do You Think You Are?

What's Inside You, Brother?

{ *The Best American Essays 1996* }

You ache with the need to convince yourself
that you do exist in the real world,
that you're a part of all the sound and anguish,
and you strike out with your fists,
you curse and you swear
to make them recognize you.

—from *Invisible Man*, Ralph Ellison

From outside the circle of Spandexed actresses jumping rope, their ponytails bouncing politely, Body & Soul appears to be a boxing gym rated G. But push through the circle, past the portly, middle-age lawyers slugging through leg lunges and past the dumpy jewelry designers wearing rouge, giggling as they slap at the speed bag. Keep pushing into the heart of the circle, toward the sound of taut leather pap-papping against bone, toward the odor of violence, and as often as not, you'll find two men sparring, their fists stuffed into blue or red or black Everlast gloves, T-shirts matted down by hot perspiration, heavy breaths shushed through mouthpieces, moving quick and staccato and with tangible tinges of fear as they bob and weave and flick and fake, searching for a taste of another man's blood.

Sometimes Touré will be in the heart of the circle, maybe sparring with Jack, hands up, headgear tight, lungs heavy, ribs stinging after Jack backs him into a corner and slices a sharp left uppercut through Touré's elbows into the soft, very top section of his stomach. Then, for Touré time stops. He loses control of his body, feels briefly suspended in air, his thoughts seemingly hollered to him from far away. Life is never faster than in the ring, except when you're reeling from a razing punch. Then, life is never slower. Sometimes Touré will be in the heart of the circle sparring, but I don't know why: he's not very good.

I've known Touré a long, long time—you could say we grew up together. He's just over five feet ten inches and about one hundred sixty pounds. That's one inch taller and a few pounds lighter than the legendary middleweight Marvelous Marvin Hagler. Touré however, has neither long arms to throw punches from a distance, which minimizes vulnerability, nor massive strength to chop a man down with a few shots. He has the stamina to stay fresh through five and occasionally six rounds, yet after four years of boxing, he still lacks the weapons to put a boxer in real danger, and that puts him in danger. Being a lousy fighter is far different from sucking at, say, tennis. So, if he's not good, why does he continue climbing in the ring? I went to the gym to find out.

"Three men walkin down the deck of a luxury liner," says Carlos, the owner of Body & Soul. He is a yellow-skinned Black man and a chiseled Atlas who always gives his clients good boxing advice and a good laugh. "Italian guy, Jewish guy, Black guy," he begins, giggling. "Italian guy pulls out a long cigar," he says and begins walking stiff and tough like Rocky. "He whips out his lighter, lights the cigar, puts it in his pocket, and keeps walking. Jewish guy wants to be as big as him, so he takes out a slightly longer cigar, grabs out his matchbook, and strikes the match on the book. It won't light."

"Oy vay!" a Jewish woman interjects dramatically.

"So the Jewish guy strikes the match on the deck. It lights. He puts the match in the ashtray and keeps steppin. Now the Black guy . . ."

"Aww shit," you say.

". . . the Black guy want to be as big as them—you know how niggas are," he says, and everyone cracks up. "So he takes out the longest cigar and a match and goes to strike it on the matchbook. Won't light. Tries it on the deck. No dice. So finally he strikes it on the seat of his pants. The match lights! He lights the cigar, tosses the match overboard.

But when the match go overboard, the luxury liner is passing an oil slick. The match hits the oil and the boat blows up." He pauses and smiles like the Kool-Aid man. "What's the moral of the story?"

Everyone grins expectantly.

"If a nigga scratch his ass he'll set the world on fire!"

You and Carlos laugh hard, doubling over together.

Nigga scratch his ass he'll set the world on fire, you say to yourself. How ridiculous. More of the silly, Black chauvinist—negrovinist?—joking that we waste time with instead of thinking of ways to get ahead. Black is more often lit on fire by the world! How stupid to think that by doing something as crude as scratching your ass you could grab the world's attention, shake it up, maybe even Blacken it. That just by being your Black self, you could make the world ours.

As Carlos's audience for the joke disperses he pulls you close to put on your headgear the same way your parents once pulled you close to zip up your snowsuit. Your hands stuffed into large gloves in preparation for combat, you are immobilized, unable to do anything for yourself—not hold a cup of water, not scratch your ass—anything but throw punches. Carlos squeezes the thick leather pillow past your temples, down around your ears, and pulls tight the laces under your chin. The padding bites down on your forehead; your temples, your cheeks. You look into the mirror. Your head and face are buried so deeply in padding, you can't tell yourself apart from another head wrapped up in headgear. You can't recognize your face.

The buzzer rings, launching the three-minute round, and you turn to the heavy bag, a large sack of leather and padding that hangs from the ceiling like a giant kielbasa. You approach the bag as you would another fighter, working your rhythms and combinations and strength, sinking in your hooks and jabs and crosses. You begin hitting slowly, paying close attention to each stinging shot, moving in slow, sharp rhythms like an old Leadbelly guitar-and-harmonica blues, each punch slapping the bag and sounding like a dog-eared, mud-splattered, ripped-apart boot stomping the floorboards of a little Alabama juke joint where they chased away the blues with the blues, sung in a key so deep whites thought they could hear it, but Negroes knew only they could. Because slaying the blues was a never-ending gig halted only for one thing, and that was radio dispatches of a Joe Louis bout. That cured the blues in a hurry, hearing the Brown Bomber slaying one or another white boy by fighting so slowly he looked like sepia-toned stop-motion, his body stiff and slow like a cobra, hypnotizing his man, until the precise moment for the perfect punch. Then, lightning: a left-right would explode from Louis, and quick as a thunderclap his man would be sprawled on the ground below him, that's right, an Italian or a German with his spine on the canvas as thousands listened on, Louis having done what Negroes dreamed of doing but hardly dared think. Then Louis, the grandson of Booker T. Washington, the grandfather of Colin Powell, humbly retreated to his corner, his face wooden and emotionless, his aura as unthreatening as only the highest of the high yellows could manage.

So you go on hitting the bag and talking to yourself in body English, the dialect of Joe Louis, talking with a near Tommish lilt as you slink slowly around the bag, but not quite Tommish because after a few racially quiet sentences you slash a few, quick, deadly words and leave your opponent counting the sheep on the ceiling. You speak to yourself in the most necessary Black English in America, that of the humble assimilationist, and you move around the bag, trying to hypnotize your opponent, then lashing two, three rocket shots at him, and imagine yourself, like the Brown Bomber, lighting the world on fire, quietly.

The bell ring-ring-rings: The round is over. Fighters wander from their bags over toward Carlos, in the center of the room. Jack, a gruesome-looking thirty-year-old white dentist, bumps into you, feigning an accident. "Touré! I didn't even see you!" he lies with a laugh. "I can't recognize you without my jab in your face."

People crack up. During breaks the fighting doesn't stop, it just turns oral. A crude variant on the verbal fisticuffs called the dozens takes its place. But instead of attacking your poverty, or your mama, it's your boxing or your looks. The one who makes everyone laugh loudest wins. And as with the dozens, sometimes it hurts. But when it's done by your own, to strengthen you for the onslaught from without, you know that a beat down is really a build up and you just keep on. "What's the point in us fighting?" you ask, looking at Jack's flattened nose and honeycombed skin. "That face cain't get ruined no worse." More laughs. This round is a tie.

The bell comes again and you head back to the heavy bag for three minutes more of fervor. You attack the bag savagely now, punching harder with all of the strength in your arms and all the evil in your hands, making the bag suck hard and send back flat, dull beats like the cold, thick drumbeats of raw, gutbucket Southern soul, maybe Otis Redding, and now you are speaking Sonny Liston.

This is the body English of the back alley, the backroom, the back corner of the prison's back cell, where Liston, serious criminal, Mob enforcer, learned to box and became a straight-ahead, raw-and-jugged black-as-blue bruiser nigga. The grandson of Nat Turner, the grandfather of Mike Tyson. The scion and hero of every bully who ever lived. This is not the English of the street, no, too much bustling energy and zooming hustler's pace, no, this is the English of the street corner. Home of the long-faced, too-silent black-black nigguhs who work only at night, who don't read *Ebony*, who have a look that could make death turn around. Liston knocked his man out and strolled over to a neutral corner with a glower that took the whole stadium right back to some alley that ain't seen the sun in decades, off some long-forgotten street at the end of the world. You're slamming your hands into the bag, but you're in that same alley, scrapping as you're sidestepping ancient garbage and streams of green water and body parts without bodies, as a single long-broken street lamp looks on, saying nothing. Liston lit the world on fire as the most hated man on the planet, and now here you come fighting ugly, banging the bag, banging like a ram, talking that crude, foul, dirty Listonese.

"Hey, Touré!" Jack screams out from across the gym as the buzzer ending the second round begins to sound. "What's goin on inside that voodoo-do up on your head?"

The gym goes into hysterics. "Get out my face," you shoot back, "you melanin-challenged mothafucka." People double over. This round to you.

Before the third round starts, you stop moving long enough to get your heart back and your head together. This round you're going to put it all together. When the bell sounds you're a flurry of movement and flow, dancing out, then stepping in, weaving your head through the air and sliding in to land two, three, four, five quick punches and then out, dancing and bobbing, then three, four, five more quick shots to the bag on which you play a hot staccato tempo borrowed from high-pace jazz, from the sheets of sound of Coltrane. And now you're talking Muhammad Ali, the smooth-flowing, fan-dazzling rhythm poet, the melding of Louis Armstrong and Malcolm X and Michael Jackson and the zip-bam-boom, the speed, swagger, swish, rope-a-dope, jungle rumbler, Manila thriller, who turned the ring into an artist's studio, the canvas his own beautiful body.

Now, in front of the bag is a true African-American, a cool synthesis, not merely assimilating, not merely rebelling, but blending like jazz, melding what is gorgeous and grotesque about Africa and America. It's a body English that's the high-tech version of that spoken by Brer Rabbit, the Negro folktale trickster and blues-trained hero whose liquid mind and body could find a way past any so-called insurmountable force on any so-rumored impossible mission without the force even knowin he been there and gone. It's a body English filled with signifying, which means you say "bad" and mean "good" or you say "bad" and mean "bad," and either way everyone who's supposed to know always know and know without anyone having to explain because everyone who's supposed to know know about signifying even if they don't know the word.

But you know all that, so you fire through the round in constant, unstoppable motion, lighting the entire universe on glorious, ecstatic, religious-fervor fire with your Ali-isms, and of Black, and of beauty. And then, as punches rain from deep within your heart onto the bag you see that Carlos was right, a Black man can light the world on fire, wake it up, change it up, Blacken it up, by something as crude and simple and natural as scratching his ass, that is, simply by being himself.

The round ends and Jack comes rushing over. You two are about to spar a few rounds, and he is teasing you now with a half speed flurry of pantomimed jabs and hooks. Everyone looks on. "He's attacking me!" you call out in mock horror. "I sense a bias crime! Is there a lawyer in the house?" Again, laughter carries the day, but then the laughter carries

you back, back to the laughter of the playground, back to the beginning
of your fight career.

On the playground you sat alone, the only Black face as far as you could
see on the playground of that century-and-a-half-old New England prep
school. Matthew came over. He never liked you. He was brown-skinned
with curly black hair, and Mom always whispered that he had to be part
Black, but he never claimed it, never even admitted to being adopted.
He saw you sitting alone in the playground and said, "Hey, Touré, why
don't you come over and play?" You don't mean it. "If you get dirty, no
one will know!" Then he began to laugh.

You sprang at him in a frenzy, flinging tiny fists into his face, one
after another without aim or direction, punch after punch flowing
overhand and sloppy at his head and face and shoulders. Tears flying as
easily as arms, finding room on your cheeks amid the hot sweat breaking into the brisk New England cold, you didn't feel his tiny fists jolting
back at you, didn't hear the delighted screams of other children—Fight!
Fight!—didn't hear the teacher Miss Farrah running to break it up after
a few seconds that seemed like a year spent roaring at each other with
tiny fists. You weren't even certain who you were as you rolled about in
a gale of blows until you crawled inside yourself and found a serenity
inside your embattled self, a peace beneath your warring skin, because
you were fighting back, and that made you certain that you could light
the world on fire because there was a fire lit inside of you.

The Body & Soul buzzer screamed. Touré snapped back to attention as Jack came toward him, beginning their first round of sparring.
Right away, Jack stepped close and stung Touré with a left jab in his
nose, then another and another. Touré backed up and slipped a jab that
landed on Jack's nose, pushing his head back sharply, then another jab
that Jack blocked. Touré was much better fighting from the outside than
the inside. The outside is when there's a few feet between fighters. They
stand a polite distance away from each other, moving on their toes, occasionally jabbing or blocking and always looking for openings. When
the boxers are outside, relatively speaking, there's a gentlemanly calm
and leisurely pace about the fight. Inside, the fighters are just inches

away from each other and it's point-blank range for both men, and it's at once sexy and dangerous. Over and again Touré tried to get inside, and finally Jack made him pay for coming into the wrong neighborhood. Touré stepped close to Jack and tried a quick left hook. Then a hard right uppercut caught Touré in the ribs. Jack saw him coming and pulled his trigger faster.

In the locker room of Body & Soul I caught up with Touré. Since we've known each other so long I felt I could be completely honest. I was wrong.

"Why do you keep boxing?"

"I can't stop," he said without looking up.

"You mean, you won't stop."

"No. I can't. I love it."

"You get in the ring and get knocked down. Aren't you worried about . . ."

"Yo man, a punch in the face ain't but a thing."

"Are you trying to take physical punishment to absolve your middle-class-based guilt and be literally banged into the gang of proletariat Blacks who live to give and take lumps every day and . . ."

Then he lunged at me. He swung at me with force and fury and I fell hard on the ground. I saw my blood then, and for a fleeting second I felt a jolt of adrenaline. I was hot with anger and humiliation, but I was also not at all self-conscious, and still wonderfully aware, as wide open as the sky. I was in pain and ecstasy. And from somewhere deep inside I laughed loud and hard.

He stood over me and roared down, "I don't need to hear yo shit, man. I've sparred a few times. I beat myself up all the time." He paused, then spoke with a soft intensity. "See, before my moms sent me off to first grade she said, 'You have to be twice as good as those little white kids.' And that shit was real. But not here. In that ring all you got is two gloves and your head. That's a real . . . what's the word . . ."

"Meritocracy?"

"Boxocracy? Fightocracy? Whatever. I can do whatever I want and be whoever I want to be. All fighters live until the day they die. That's not a thing all men can say. But while he's alive, a fighter lives."

Then, I looked away and my mind floated back and I saw myself in college, junior year, at a party. As things broke up, a group of juniors stood talking, fifteen or so others within easy earshot. A small argument began, quickly turned hot. Then, finally, The Whisper was stated—The Whisper that had begun my freshman year when I arrived on campus and, after a decade-plus in a white prep school, didn't join the Black community but pledged a white fraternity and vacationed with white boys and dated white girls. I was branded a traitor then, a Black Judas, and The Whisper started, followed me through sophomore year, when I consciously and conspicuously turned away from my white friends to party and protest with Black students. The Whisper chased me into junior year when I moved into the Black house and became a campus political figure. And that night, at that party, as things broke up, The Whisper stepped from the shadows. "Touré, you ain't Black."

And I said nothing. I stood in the middle of a circle of my Black classmates and heard the silence screaming in my ears and saw my chance to fight back against The Whisper, and said nothing. I just turned slowly and walked away. I went to bed and promised myself to never tell the story of that night, not even to myself. I locked the memory away, closed my eyes. But the memory seeped out and kept me awake. And worse than the public humiliation was my nonanswer: I had taken the knockdown sitting down.

The memory was obsessively replayed for me again and again as I crossed the quad, ate lunch, sat bored in class, furtively took sex, sometimes adding something I should have done—a witty retort, a tough reply, a physical attack—sometimes not. And it germinated in me and festered and burned and with time turned inventively malignant, burning him anew each time, a tumor inside his personal history, throbbing, reaching out around the corners of my mind, grabbing toward my self-image, threatening my internal balance. Then, realizing the power of my conscience, my sense of regret, the fire inside me began burning hotter.

"No matter what," Touré said, looking directly at me, "I've got to fight, always fight, even in the face of sure defeat, because no one can hurt me as badly as I can."

I knew exactly what he meant. And he bent down and helped me up.

A Funky Fresh Talented Tenth

{ unpublished, 2000 }

I always loved the first day of the year at Milton. People fresh from Nantucket, a little sand still in their shoes, clutching new books and strolling to classes in ivy-covered buildings that stood over us as they'd stood over students a hundred years before. I loved being educated alongside extraordinary people, even though some were extraordinary only because they had extraordinary problems. I loved late Saturday afternoons, after all the games, and matches, and meets were over and sweat-drenched warriors ambled toward those open-stall showers and across the campus you could sense the embers of competition cooling. I loved finals, the pressure so audible the campus hummed like an electric current and for a week your mind was on its toes. I loved graduation and the boys marching in blue blazers and the girls floating in white dresses. On my graduation day the rain held off until the ceremony was nearly over. When it came time for everyone to sing, then-headmaster Pieh, shielding his face from the drizzle with his hand, announced they would conclude the ceremony without the planned singing. With benign defiance we launched right into it. And as the drizzle landed on us and our parents and our grandparents, we sang. I walked off that day confident I knew how to dance through life the Milton way, a style that serves me even now. Some of the time.

Two years before that drizzly last day, on the next to last day of sophomore year, I had a short talk with a senior we all called Keisha Mac. She was a woman with the grace of a ballet dancer and the seriousness of Angela Davis. And being a senior, she was, I was certain, unspeakably wise. On the third floor of the library, by the windows where you could see girls with their long hair pulled back giggling in the sun as it tickled their bare pink feet, I asked her, "Would you send your kids to Milton?" She looked off a moment, then said, "No." A little earthquake tremor rumbled through my mind.

"Milton teaches you to be white," she said. "That's just fine if you are, but for us? Coming here as a Black child—and as old as we think we are, we're still children—like learning to put your head in the lion's mouth so deep that you forget how to live outside it."

After twelve years as a black fly in the Milton buttermilk, I flew to Atlanta for college. I breezed in the classroom—after Milton it was easy—and struggled with my Black classmates. I pledged a white fraternity. That's when The Whisper started.

The Whisper clung quietly to my shadow through sophomore year when I began actively courting Black friends and became a Black-studies major, and junior year when I moved into the Black house. One night at the Black house, after a party, a stupid argument turned hot. And someone, finally, stated The Whisper. "Shut up, Touré," it went. "*You ain't Black.*"

It was a searing epiphany. Years later I understood the flimsyness of that so-called spear, the ease with which almost anyone at almost anytime could be stabbed with a you-ain't-Black for any number of offenses—where you live, who you love, what you think, how you walk. But still, that day there was some truth in it. There's some truth in it now. I can't simply blame Milton, it's just that I hadn't realized until it was too late that I had to unlearn some dance steps.

My truth is this: I love Milton and I hate Milton. Love and hate the way I love and hate America and my ex-girlfriend, who both blessed me and burned me, shaped me in ways I appreciate and abhor. There is nothing Milton could do to improve life for its Black students—no amount of orientation or Black-history classes or campus-wide sensitivity, though those are good steps. It's up to Milton's Black students to learn to approach Milton with equal doses of love and contempt.

Well, actually, there is something Milton could do for us. Imagine this: the admissions department institutes a manilla-folder test, demanding that all but a few students be *darker* than a manilla folder. Overnight the student body turns bronze and beige, sable and khaki, café au lait, mocha, cocoa, sandalwood, caramel—all the colors of the ebony rainbow. After completing the summer reading *Manchild in the Promised Land*, tanned students stroll in for a spirited first day of classes, the hallways filled with a joyous din as people swap new hairstyles, handshakes, and slang words picked up on vacations in Johannesburg, Nairobi, and Kingston. At the bell they sprint off to Chemistry, or Harlem Renaissance Poetry, or Algebra, or The History of Africa Pre-Christ, or European History from 1196 to 1945 (The Predatory Era). As the year moves on the fourth class presents their play, August Wilson's *The Piano Lesson*, and college counselors organize trips to Morehouse, Spelman, Howard, and Hampton. Every Sunday a Baptist preacher, backed by a forty-woman choir and a small band, delivers an exuberant sermon that rips the roof off the chapel. In class and in between students and teachers discuss, sometimes with words, sometimes with glances, how to dance through life the new Milton way, moving as a Black intelligensia grounded in Black culture, fly enough to stay late at the party, soaking in our mores and rituals, then waking up to slay 'em on Wall Street. A funky fresh talented tenth as ignant as Coltrane on a ThinkPad and so Black no one could ever put The Whisper on them. At commencement Toni Morrison dares us to vanquish the dusty and vacuous school motto *Dare to Be True*. It must've worked wonders, she says, in the days before *Catcher in the Rye* was written but who's been able to say it with a straight face since Kent State? She suggests Dare to Have Soul, or Dare to Love, or, maybe, Dare to Be Black, which is really a challenge to be yourself in a post-Milton world that will demand otherwise at nearly every turn.

Imagine that. Close your eyes and see my Milton. Maybe you'll begin to know how I felt at yours.

The Blackest Tennis Club in the World

{ *Tennis* magazine, 1999 }

Let me tell you about the last of the great dreamers. The last of this
century's Jackie Robinson revolutionaries, who dreamed out loud,
broke down doors, and opened the gates wide. There was Alvin Ailey
and Arthur Mitchell in dance, Spike Lee in film, Jean-Michel Basquiat in
painting, and in tennis, there was Mister Smith. A man with a belly as
large, round, and solid as Santa's, a wisdom as encyclopedic and a face
as ageless as Yoda's, and a fire-snorting mien as gruff as Sonny Liston's.
Like the others he knew it would take Puritan-style blue-collar hard
work to get where he wanted—"Spit in one hand and wish in the
other," he loved to say, "and see which one fills up faster." But like those
others he never looked at what is in the world and asked why, he saw
what is not in the world and asked, why not?

In the early 70s Mister Smith built four indoor courts on Blue Hill
Avenue in Dorchester, Massachusetts, chased donations, sold an hour of
court time for eight dollars to bring in as much business as possible—
hence the motto "adults pay so kids can play"—and created Sportsmen's
Tennis Club, aka Franklin Field Tennis Center: a not-for-profit tennis
mecca in the middle of the ghetto. When I tell you it was a Black club, I
don't mean just that damn near everyone in there was Black (but not
everyone—a few Irish families and an Indian one were part of The Club
family). I mean the fabric of the place was Black, the rhythm was Black,
the fucking air felt Black if you can believe that. And not white-sweater-
vest Black. Not *So-nice-to-see-you-again-General Powell* Black. The place was

ghetto. It was a place where Conway, Julius, and Bootsy could feel at home. Where there were cracks in the courts and holes in the nets and no one cared because the place had the kinetic, propulsive energy and high theater of the Mississippi juke joint, the Watts backyard BBQ, the late-night Harlem street corner. It was a place where they played tennis Blackly.

In time Mister Smith added three outdoor courts, three more indoor, and two red clay, but the upkeep quickly killed those two. And he attracted street kids from Dorchester, Roxbury, and Mattapan—Boston's little Vietnams—by charging five dollars for an entire winter of twice-a-week after-school lessons, another five dollars for the spring, and less than a hundred dollars for an entire summer of all-day camp. He was a genius at turning a beginner into a top regional player and he trained us to be little tennis assassins, programmed to win junior tournaments, possibly go on to major college tennis, and maybe, with hard, hard work, make it to the Tour. It was like a tennis program in a third-world country—threadbare in materials, heavy with the dreams of a nation.

We arrived at New England junior tournaments as if they were racialized Davis Cup ties, infused with a healthy disdain of white people. We were at war with tradition, class, privilege, expectation, and all those little white kids whose strokes seemed so crisp and coached you could hear a cash register *cha-ching* when they swung. And when we beat them we learned we didn't need the advantages they had. We learned that the white man's ice is no colder.

In that pre-Venus, pre-Zina world, African-American tennis meant Arthur Ashe and Althea Gibson. Ashe came to The Club once and gave an inspiring clinic (as did Billie Jean King), but mostly the only serious players we ever saw were each other. Until the ATA Nationals.

The ATAs were a festival of Blackness and tennis where long-distance friendships were rekindled, life lessons were learned, and Big Fun was had. Every summer The Club's elite juniors went off to San Diego or D.C. or Atlanta for an all-expense-paid week of tennis, parties, and no parents. One year the gang drove to Detroit, spending twenty hours on the road, switching radio stations every hour, screaming each time Rick James's new hit came on—"*Supafreak! . . . Supafreak! . . . She's supa freeee-kay, yow!"* In San Diego, after lights-out, Drew, Karl Junior, Patrick Perry, and Glen Lloyd snuck out, climbed the fence, and went wild on the university's football field until campus security arrived and they had to sprint and hide their way back. In New Orleans, it was rumored, one of us conspired with an old friend to ensure a good show in the finals: they would trade the first two sets, get to 5–all, then play it out. The other boy took the third 6–4 and all hell broke loose. One year Karl Junior got pushed into a pool and, even though he couldn't swim, remained too cool to call for help. We stood there and watched him struggle and splash for two full minutes. Every year the girls from Houston mesmerized. Most for their hourglass shapes, two for their knockout playing: Lori McNeil and Zina something or other. On the final night in Detroit, Drew, Karl Junior, Steve Perry, and Malcolm had a pillow fight so wild that Malcolm's brand-new trophy for winning the ten-and-unders was broken in three. He cried all twenty hours home. All of the The Club's top players scrapped all winter and spring for that moment in early summer when Mister Smith convened us on the side of court one and announced which eight or nine of us would make the long trip, stay in the cheap motel, and have the Big Fun.

But for Mister Smith, the trip was yet another motivational ploy. He'd do anything to make us better because each time one of us got better it got him one step closer to his big dream: creating a professional tennis player, or in his words, a player. He wanted just one who would make it to the Big Dance. To him we were little pawns he could push through the ranks and maybe turn into a queen who would win big, prove what a great coach he was, and bring more attention and thus money and thus power to The Club. Mister Smith dreamed of college scholarships, full or partial, for most of us. But every time he looked over his crop of juniors he was like an 1849 California prospector, carefully sifting his pan, searching for one bright glimmer of gold.

You were six or seven when yours took you to that place your brothers and sisters had been going, with the two light-green warehouselike buildings on Blue Hill Avenue. You walked inside the doors, past the front desk and Sandy the cranky receptionist, past the life-size photo of

The Club's first nine juniors, past the bathrooms that were really little clubhouses where girls made up new dances or practiced the Smurf and gossiped and boys listened to cassettes of a new rap group called Run-DMC and complained about scrub teachers. As a beginner you went to court seven, way in the back, waiting until a teacher came and unlocked a giant black chest that held all the little wooden rackets. You grabbed one, got in line, had a ball or two tossed to you, tried to make contact, then took your place at the back of the line behind twenty or so other children.

Once, while waiting in line, I asked a boy where he lived.

"I live in a project," he said.

"You can't live in a project." Of course not. A smart first-grader like me knew better than that. "A project is something you make."

Eventually, you learned enough to make it onto the intermediate courts where you had fun teachers like long, tall Paul White, who oozed charisma even as he fed balls with a Connors T-2000 and created a mystique by never, ever taking off his sweatpants, even on July's hottest days. You did the Buddy System—tossing balls to a partner to hit into the backdrop until it was your turn. And you played games like Around the World, where everyone forms a single-file line on each baseline, hits the ball, then runs to the back of the line on the far side of the court. Miss a stroke and you're out. When there were four or three kids left you had to hit a moonball just to have the time to sprint from one baseline to the other.

After a few years, and Mister Smith pointing out a few kids who learned faster than you and already moved up, you ascended to the tournament caste, playing and drilling on Court One in front of the glass window. Now you rubbed elbows with The Club's living legends. There was Patrick Perry, who had the backhand slice of life: the ball leaped off his Wilander Rossignol, crossed the net in slow motion, landed inches from the baseline, and just skipped like a perfectly thrown rock across water. There was Velina Rhodes, an Energizer bunny who made you hit twenty strokes per point. She had perfect brown skin; a smooth, deep voice; a slim, shapely figure; high, almond-shaped eyes; and was probably your first crush. There was Benny Sims, the beloved drill sergeant head pro with crisp strokes and military-starched clothes—he was so clean he could sweat and not get dirty. And there was Lars: the tall, thin, red-faced blond with a serve as fast as Roscoe Tanner's. He gave the ball a few tense bounces, tossed it an inch above his head, let it hang there for a heartbeat, then slashed his little wooden Jack Kramer Wilson through the air and did violence to that ball. His violence often landed near the baseline, but we were still impressed. He cemented his legend one year in a club tournament by hitting a backspinning backhand drop shot that crossed the net then came back to his side for an unbelievable winner. And more, he'd been telling us he could hit that shot for years.

Come summer you lived at The Club, hitting on the rickety wooden backboard, jogging on the abandoned clay courts, lunching on McDonald's or a 50-cent so-called pizza defrosted in a toaster oven, and, in every free moment, playing mini-tennis, a game of touch using just a single-service box.

There were constant trials by fire. Like a Roman emperor with Christians and lions to spare, Mister Smith looked for a matchup that intrigued him—two kids of similar ability or age, or, best of all, two who had talked smack to each other, saying, maybe, "I'll beat you a donut and a french fry!" (meaning love and one), or, "I'll beat you *double donuts!*" (love and love). The two would be snatched by their collars and thrown into a public steel-cage match (after Mister Smith, like a kid egging others on to fight, had told them things like, "He's gonna hit the ball so hard it'll make your head swim.") (Weird thing, he was always talking about making your head *swim*.) More than once I suffered through a tense set against my sister, a year younger and, during the first half of our teens, taller and stronger. Everyone watched while I played, terrified that one early misstep would give her a slight lead and multiply my fear of losing to my so-called little sister and paralyze me into further errors that would end in a defeat I would never, ever hear the end of. I never lost, but never felt like a winner. Still, after that crucible, no one could make me fear losing. (This system didn't always work: after Kyla beat her big sister Crystal in front of a crowd, the older girl quit the game.)

And there were annual trips to the pro tournament at the Longwood Cricket Club in upper-crusty Brookline. We'd mull around the courts for a while, then one of us would distract the guard while another snuck by and went into the clubhouse and the player's lounge. We were assumed to be Ashe's cousin or Yannick Noah's little brother, so no one complained as we walked through the locker room and sat in the clubhouse and watched Ion Tiriac chomp through a sandwich, or Jose-Louis Clerc towel off, or Guillermo Vilas strut, South American machismo style. These were men with an inner calm, a deep seriousness, a minisculely apertured concentration, and an unshakable confidence. Men who knew they were *baaad*. These were not normal people. Climbing Everest seemed easier than entering their club. We would not tell Mister Smith that.

Every summer morning began with all the juniors assembled on the side of Court One for yet another of Mister Smith's unscripted lectures delivered in the barking tone of a hellish lieutenant and the dramatic timing of a Baptist preacher. He waddled out, his giant belly somehow supported by two bowlegs so thin and spindly it looked like spider's legs steadying a beer keg, and invariably began, "If you wanna be a player . . ." and then meandered for up to forty-five long minutes through mental toughness, cutting-off angles, and thinking two shots ahead. He would always work in one or all of his mantras—"You're no good until you beat somebody better than you" and "A player will win with a frying pan" and "When I say jump, you don't say, 'How high?'" [you were supposed to just jump as high as you could]—and in his never-ending crusade to omit needless movement from our strokes: "K-I-S-S! Keep it simple, *stupid!*" To him the worst things we could ever do were choke or push—he hated the words so much he spat them from his mouth like dirty gum. And not a day went by that he failed to speak of poise—that quality that the great ones used to make the difficult appear easy, the final gloss needed to be a player.

There are about sixty weekday mornings in a summer and no more than four stock lectures in Mister Smith's repetoire, so even though he improvised somewhat, sprinkling in new anecdotes, pasting in patches of other lectures, your attention would float as he rumbled on, thinking *I've never seen him play . . . I wonder when we'll get to play . . . I've never even seen a photograph of him playing . . . Keisha Mac looks good in that skirt . . . I can't even imagine him playing . . . Isn't this the same lecture he gave three days ago?* Still, you had to listen because he might ask a question—"When I say jump, what do you say?"—and you feared getting it wrong. You feared Mister Smith more than your father, or the school principal, or maybe even God. God was far away. Mister Smith was up in your face, wagging his short, stubby finger, calling you a turkey when you blew an easy shot.

Even though he stayed cloaked in humble, frugal clothes—tan Member's Only jackets, cotton Izod shirts, plain polyester pants, cheap, padded shoes, all from Filene's Basement or Marshall's—Mister Smith always appeared to be draped in full general's regalia as he strutted about The Club like a European dictator, espousing his unyielding dogma on how strokes should be hit, beheading teachers who crossed him, keeping all the juniors in fear by playing shameless favorites. He would anoint one member of the tournament caste and lavish them with extraintensive teaching and attention—*Maybe*, you could hear him thinking, *she'll be the one.* But that weight was too great to bear and after a few months he lost faith in his favorite and chose another. We all stood in the corner grumbling, *Why does Courtney deserve all that?*, secretly hoping to be next.

If you were Black you probably had a father or uncle like Mister Smith, whose meanness was his way of expressing love, so some of his abuse and belligerence rolled off your back. But also, you knew that he alone was responsible for bringing The Club to Dorchester, that he alone had schemed and networked and somehow made tennis affordable for kids with food stamps. But he also made tennis available to us on a cultural level. The same way Alvin Ailey came along and breathed Black into those old white dance moves, Mister Smith breathed Black into this white game. I'll never forget how he taught us that when you hit the backhand slice approach shot, "you got to crossover step like you're *dancin*," and as he showed us he would do what seemed like a little soft shoe.

Very, very few of us would've had the opportunity to play without the door he alone opened. And to play for Mister Smith was to learn how to deal with strategy, human nature, pressure, and the white, white world. He brought this beautiful game to us. And for that we loved him.

He loved us, too, I think, but not well. Despite his genius, there were levels of this game above his head. If tennis were math, he got us to understand geometry and algebra and trigonometry, but not the advanced calculus of national junior tennis or the quantum physics of the Tour. But in his mind taking outside private lessons was the ultimate betrayal. It meant you felt the white man's ice was colder than his. In the tiny Boston tennis community it was impossible to have a long-term relationship with a coach without Mister Smith eventually hearing of it. So the better Mister Smith made you, the more you had to choose between paralyzing Club loyalty and self-destructive advancement. He was a jealous lover and it doomed him: only two of the many talented kids of my generation ever made it anywhere near the Big Dance. Those two, twin girls who took lessons at The Club and with private coaches and endured Mister Smith's griping—it may have been easier for them being white—are currently in the top seven hundred fifty in the world.

My last summer at The Club, before I went off to college, there was a men's tournament. At the last moment I entered the doubles with Charles Hardison, a dark-brown sixteen-year-old with twinkling eyes, a warm smile, and a smooth manner that let him get along with everyone in The Club, no small achievement in that cuckoo's nest. I was small for my age and he was smaller than me. He was lightning-bug quick, but a risk-taking shotmaker who either has a great day or an awful one. I expected only to play hard and have fun.

We won two matches against much older but far less well-schooled men and then, thanks to Charles's eye for the perfect sharp angles, pulled out a tough three-set semifinal as Mister Smith watched with glee. We were the longest long shots to ever make a final, a full head shorter than our opponents. We succumbed quickly, but just being there was victory enough. At the summer's end we decided we would try some local men's tournaments when I returned from my freshman year. I don't remember our good-bye. I knew for sure that I'd see him again.

The next spring, on a late Sunday night, after a long raucous weekend at Mardi Gras in New Orleans, I called my father. His voice was cold. He asked if I was sitting down. "On Friday afternoon," he said, "Charles was found dead in his mother's house."

She had come home late Thursday night and found his keys still in the front door, assumed he was in his bed, and went to sleep. The next morning she found his bed still made. He was in the basement, lying faceup. Her ex-boyfriend, whom Charles had never liked, had shot him with a silencer, while Charles's grandmother sat upstairs, unaware.

I wanted desperately to phone his father and ask for one of Charles's rackets as one last thing to remember him by. I couldn't. I quit tennis instead.

That was ten years ago. Patrick Perry took his beautiful slice to Dartmouth and has become a lawyer. Drew, inspired by years of playing the ATA sectionals on Yale's courts, went to school there, and is now a financial consultant at Merrill Lynch. Benny Sims is on the pro tour coaching Chanda Rubin. We've become a producer for Oprah, a fashion model in Paris, a doctor in Brooklyn, and a computer programmer. We've started a power-washing company, a casting agency, joined the navy, and done time. After years of trying, Lars finally gave up his dream of playing on the Tour and now drives a limo.

The cost of court time at The Club soared to eighteen dollars an hour, but chronic financial problems continued. In time a new board of directors developed, one that did not remember The Club's old days. Tired of Mister Smith's histrionics and power games and ceaseless dreams that became more and more fanciful as he grew older, they kicked him off the board. Like an old powerless dictator, he was exiled. He was almost eighty then. A year or two later his wife, Gloria, always his partner in The Club, succumbed to cancer. Mister Smith died just over a year later. I never asked how. With no Gloria, no Club, and none of his juniors to watch play on television, he must've been quite alone.

There are no Jackie Robinson dreamers anymore. Those days are over. Now most Blacks know any Antarctica that won't have us ain't worth going to. That the white man's ice ain't worth a damn.

But I think Mister Smith is still here.

After nine years away from the game I picked it up again and found him still in my muscles and my mind. Now I'm playing tournaments again. Maybe I'm still enamored with striking balls. Maybe I'm trying to see how far I can get without Mister Smith breathing down my neck. Maybe I'm looking for the respect I missed as a child. A few weeks back I pulled out three tough three-setters and found myself in the quarterfinals of a big tournament in Manhattan's Central Park. Up a break in the deciding set of a rough match I heard a voice in my head say, "Wish Mister Smith was here."

The next point I got a short ball on my backhand side and, with him in my blood, danced through it, nailed it down the line, and knocked off the weak return for a volley winner.

Then I knew he was there.

12. I Can't Take It

At Jam Master Jay's Funeral

{ unpublished, 2004 }

Last Tuesday morning, at Jason Mizell's funeral, there were hundreds of men and women in sneakers. There are very few funerals where sneakers would be tasteful, but the thirty-seven-year-old Mizell was Jam Master Jay of the legendary rap group Run-DMC, and the sneakers were Adidas shelltoes, white with black stripes. They were in extremely good taste, especially those pairs that had that just-bought crispness. In 1986, at Madison Square Garden, at the zenith of their career, Run commanded everyone in the crowd wearing shelltoes to take one off and hold it up in the air while the group performed "My Adidas," their paean to the sneakers. Thousands of shelltoes went up. The shelltoe remains cool to this day because it's relatively inexpensive and easy to clean, but also because of Run-DMC's enduring endorsement. Run-DMC remains cool, in part, because of the shelltoe. Before Run-DMC emerged in 1983, popular rap groups dressed like they were from Parliament-Funkadelic or the Village People, with tall boots, tight pants, and wraparound glasses. Mizell was the one who chose the deceptively simple sartorial approach of Run-DMC: a black fedora, a black leather blazer, a black T-shirt, a thick gold chain, black Lee jeans, and Adidas shelltoes. The genius of that was this: that was what their fans wore or (with the exception of the gold chain) what all their fans could afford. When Run-DMC appeared on the cover of *Rolling Stone*, the Johnny Carson show, *Saturday Night Live*, MTV, and Live Aid, they were lionizing the common man. Back then hiphop was the voice of the voiceless and wearing commoner's clothes on the world's stage told the nascent hiphop community that they could be themselves and be loved.

Outside the Greater Allen Cathedral of New York in Jamaica, Queens, just minutes from where Mizell lived and died, a man arrived and began handing out the small yellow tickets required for entry to the church. He was instantly mobbed by former rap stars and friends of Mizell, but the throng remained silent as he bestowed tickets, engulfed in a quiet scrum. A man in a black T-shirt with Jam Master Jay's face airbrushed on it emerged from the crowd holding two tickets. He turned to a friend and spoke of getting revenge on the man he believed to be the killer, whom he named. "Hollis don't play that shit," the man said. It seemed the cycle of violence would not end soon. A man in a suit regarded the crowd in front of the church, politely squeezing toward the entrance, and the woolly mob of media and fans behind barricades across the street, and said, "Inside, it's a normal funeral, but outside it's like a cartoon." The hush seemed to get even softer when two white horses strode up to the front of the church pulling a white box with glass walls that held Mizell's remains.

During the service Run, now a reverend, sat or stood on the stage in his clerical collar and black dress shoes, singing happily, seemingly at peace with the tragedy. In his short prayer of comfort he spoke without a note of pathos in his voice, maintaining the familiar smoothly confident tone of his rhyming voice. "Why murder?" he said. "Jason was a dramatic DJ and God knew he couldn't leave without drama, so, why not murder?" DMC spoke a few moments later, reading from loose white pages that he handed to Run as he finished each one. "Jam Master Jay was not a thug," he said, his voice breaking. "He was the personification of hiphop." Usually, when the three of them were together on a stage, Mizell was behind them, behind the turntables. This last time he was in front of them. DMC looked down at Mizell, a devoted father of three lying in his coffin, wearing a black fedora, a black leather blazer, a gold chain with a gold shelltoe, and, on his feet, white shelltoes. "Let's use Jay's passing as a symbol of a new day," he said, his voice breaking.